Field Guide to the

SPIDERS

of South Africa

Ansie Dippenaar-Schoeman

Published by Struik Nature (an imprint of Penguin
Random House South Africa (Pty) Ltd)
Reg. No. 1953/000441/07
The Estuaries No. 4, Oxbow Crescent,
Century Avenue, Century City, 7441
PO Box 1144, Cape Town, 8000 South Africa

Visit www.struiknature.co.za and join the Struik Nature
Club for updates, news, events and special offers.

First published by LAPA Publishers (Pty) Ltd in 2014
This edition first published by Struik Nature in 2023

10 9 8 7 6 5 4 3 2 1

Publisher: Pippa Parker
Managing editor: Roelien Theron
Editor: Heléne Booyens
Designers: Gillian Black, Neil Bester
Concept designer: Janice Evans
Typesetter: Deirdre Geldenhuys
Proofreader: Emsie du Plessis

Reproduction by Studio Repro
Printed and bound in China by C&C Offset
Printing Co., Ltd

MIX
Paper from
responsible sources
FSC
www.fsc.org
FSC® C018179

ACKNOWLEDGEMENTS

Many thanks to the Agricultural Research Council (ARC) for its logistical aid, the National Research
Foundation (NRF) for its incentive funding, and the South African National Biodiversity Institute
for funding and support. The University of Pretoria and the University of Venda also provided
invaluable support.

This book would not have been possible without the help of many contributors, including the
more than one hundred people who provided images. Many thanks to:

- Peter Webb †, who travelled throughout the country to collect spiders and study their behaviour.
  Some 60% of the book's photographs are his. Without him, there would be no book.
- Vida van der Walt, who photographed most of the salticids as well as several other spider
  families. Her beautiful cover photo deserves a special thanks.
- Allen Jones, who shared his photographs of Free State spiders and many beautiful webs.
- Linda Wiese, who collected and photographed a large number of Eastern Cape spiders.
- Johan van Zyl, Wynand Uys, Rudi Steenkamp, Len de Beer, Ruan Booysen, Bruce Blake and
  Andrea Sander who made all their stunning photographs available.
- Charles Haddad, who assisted with the Salticidae, Corinnidae and Trachelidae identifications.

Thanks are also due to:

- The South African National Survey of Arachnida (SANSA) team members for their collecting and
  identification efforts. Special thanks to Charles Haddad, Stefan Foord, Leon Lotz and Robin Lyle.
- The provincial conservation agencies and South African National Parks for issuing collecting
  permits and for allowing the SANSA survey teams to sample in their reserves.
- E. Oppenheimer & Son (Pty) Ltd for supporting collecting trips to their reserves.
- Everybody involved in the World Spider Catalog at the Natural History Museum of Bern for the
  valuable updated species data.
- Heléne Booyens for her dedication in overseeing the production of this book and Gillian Black
  who managed the design side of the project.

A special thanks to my family: Nico Dippenaar, my husband, for all the gum babies; Nicole and
Craig West, my children, for their support; my sister, Saar de Jager, for her daily support; and
Paris, my dachshund, who kept me company 24/7.

PREFACE

This book is a product of the South African National Survey of Arachnida (SANSA). It was initiated in 1997 to meet the requirements of the Convention on Biological Diversity, which arose from the United Nations Conference on the Environment and Development in Rio de Janeiro, Brazil. Signatories are obliged to develop a strategic plan for the conservation and sustainable use of biodiversity.

The main aims of this national project are to document and describe the arachnid fauna of South Africa; to make this biodiversity information available to science; and to address issues concerning arachnid conservation. Extensive sampling took place in a variety of locations throughout the country, and the SANSA database contains a wealth of data that are used to provide answers to ecological and taxonomic questions.

This is an exciting time in the study of spiders. DNA research has enabled a massive overhaul of spider classification. This revised edition of *Field Guide to the Spiders of South Africa* reflects these changes and remains the most comprehensive guide to South African spiders to date. Since the publication of the first guide in 2014, several new families have been described: Bemmeridae, Entypesidae, Euagridae, Ischnothelidae, Pycnothelidae, Stasimopidae, Cheiracanthiidae and Trachelidae. Other families have been merged, and many genera and species have been added, reclassified or renamed.

The taxonomy and classification used in this guide follows that of The World Spider Catalog (Version 22.5., Natural History Museum Bern, online at http://wsc.nmbe.ch). Many classifications are still to be resolved, however, and this book is sure to be revised even further as new data become available.

The digital camera and macro-photography have opened a new world for science. The beautiful colours, intricate webs and interesting behaviour of spiders are now documented daily. I hope this book will influence and stimulate photographers to record our spider fauna so that that we will eventually have an image of every species in the country.

At present 72 spider families and 2,282 species are known from South Africa. It is impossible to capture all of these species in one book. Instead, representative genera and species have been chosen to give the reader an overview of South African spider diversity and to enable the identification of the more common spiders encountered in the field and in and around the home.

To give serious spider watchers a comprehensive overview of all known South African spiders, a series of online *Spider Photo Identification Guides* have been prepared for each of the 72 families. These contain information on all known genera and species. The guides are free and can be requested from the author or downloaded from several sites, including Zenodo at **https://zenodo.org/communities/sansa/**.

Ansie Dippenaar-Schoeman
dippenaaransie@gmail.com

CONTENTS

Menneus sp.

Stasimopus sp.

INTRODUCTION

Spiders are found everywhere, in and around houses, in every garden and on every farm, and in all outdoor spaces. Despite being widely feared, very few South African spiders have venom harmful to humans, and no spider-related death has ever been recorded in the region.

Spiders have great natural and academic significance. They are important predators in all terrestrial ecosystems. They display a range of fascinating behaviours, and are excellent subjects to teach the younger generation about nature. They produce silk stronger than any human-made fibre, using it to construct intricate webs, to build retreats, to encase eggs, to trap and wrap prey, and even as a sail to fly through the air.

South Africa has a rich spider fauna: at present 72 families and 2,282 species are known. Endemism is high, with 60% of species found in no other country. The most diverse families are Salticidae (jumping spiders) with 353 species, followed by Gnaphosidae (ground spiders) with 212 species and Thomisidae (crab spiders) with 143 species.

This field guide features some 780 of the more common species found in South Africa, with notes on identification, behaviour, distribution, and biological and conservation significance.

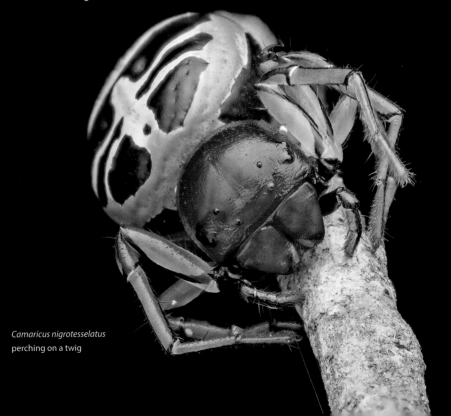

Camaricus nigrotesselatus
perching on a twig

WHAT ARE SPIDERS?

All spiders belong to the phylum **Arthropoda**, a name meaning 'jointed legs'. This diverse group of terrestrial, marine and aquatic organisms includes insects, crustaceans, millipedes and centipedes.

The subphylum **Chelicerata** falls within Arthropoda and comprises the class **Arachnida**, which includes all animals with eight walking legs, as well as the marine Pycnogonida (sea spiders) and Merostomata (horseshoe crabs).

Arachnida is a diverse group of primarily terrestrial arthropods, and is represented by 11 extant orders. Arachnids are second only to insects in abundance and diversity among the terrestrial animals. The following orders are known from South Africa: Acari (mites and ticks), Amblypygi (whip spiders), **Araneae (spiders)**, Opiliones (harvestmen), Palpigradi (micro whip-scorpions), Pseudoscorpiones (false scorpions), Scorpiones (scorpions) and the Solifugae (wind spiders).

All spiders have two body segments, consisting of a fused head and thorax (known as a cephalothorax) and an abdomen. They have eight legs, a pair of specialised appendages known as pedipalpi, and six or eight eyes (occasionally two or none).

Also unique to spiders is their ability to secrete various types of silk. These tough, flexible strands have an astounding variety of applications: from webs and burrow linings to tripwires and trapdoors.

Poltys furcifer, a web dweller

At the time of print, the World Spider Catalog lists 50,622 described species of spider, making Araneae the sixth most species-rich order of animals.

SPIDER GUILDS

Spiders are found in a variety of habitats, and display a range of adaptations to their surroundings. Since most live in a defined environment with limitations set by physical conditions and biological factors, species can be grouped into guilds based on their habitat preferences and predatory methods. The main guilds for spiders are **web dwellers**, which use silk threads to catch their prey, and **wanderers** (plant and ground dwellers), which use force to overpower their prey.

As a starting point to identification, this book is divided into three sections:

- **Web dwellers** p. 24
- **Plant dwellers** p. 148
- **Ground dwellers** p. 269

Peucetia pulchra, a plant dweller

Harpactira tigrina, a ground dweller

A *Trichopagis* female. All spiders have a fused head and thorax (cephalothorax).

SPIDER MORPHOLOGY

Spiders belong to the class Arachnida, which includes all creatures with eight legs. The following characteristics distinguish spiders from other members of this class:

CEPHALOTHORAX The head and thorax are fused, forming a single unit: the **cephalothorax**. The upper or dorsal side is covered with a shield, the **carapace**, on which two to eight simple but well-developed **eyes** occur. Ventrally, the following structures are discernible from anterior to posterior:
■ The **chelicerae**, which typically comprise a sturdy basal segment and a fang. A venom gland resides in the basal segment. Venom is secreted through an opening at the tip of the fang.
■ Sucking mouth parts, which consist of a **labium** and **endites** (maxillae).
■ The shield-like **sternum**.

APPENDAGES Five pairs of appendages are present: four pairs of **legs** and one pair of **pedipalpi** or palpi. The palpi, which resemble legs, are situated on either side of the mouth. In adult males the palp tibia is usually enlarged to contain the secondary copulatory organs, which are species-specific. Each leg has seven segments: the **coxa, trochanter, femur, patella, tibia, metatarsus** and **tarsus**. The tarsi are provided with claws. Web-dwelling

spiders typically have three claws, while most ground- and plant-living spiders have two claws, along with a dense tuft of hair (**scopula**) that facilitate climbing.

ABDOMEN The abdomen is joined to the cephalothorax by a thin **pedicel** through which the circulation and feeding systems are canalised. The abdomen's exoskeleton is much thinner than that of the cephalothorax, allowing great expansion when prey is eaten, or when eggs develop. In many spiders, the dorsal surface of the abdomen is provided with complex and often brightly coloured patterns, tubercles and knobs.

A number of structures are present on the ventral surface of the abdomen. An **epigastric furrow** runs transversely across it near the pedicel. The external openings of the sexual organs are situated in the middle of this furrow. In adult females this opening is known as the **epigynum**, the shape of which is species-specific. The external openings of the **booklungs** – the respiratory system of spiders – are present on either side of the epigastric region. Three pairs of **spinnerets** are located on the posterior part of the abdomen, and are provided with small **spigots** from which silk emerges. A number of families have an accessory spinning organ, the **cribellum**, just anterior to the spinnerets. These are known as cribellate spiders.

DORSAL VIEW OF SPIDER

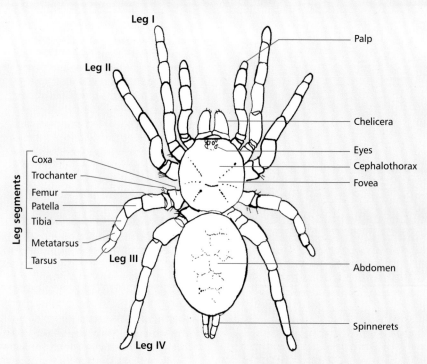

Leg I

Leg II

Palp

Chelicera

Eyes

Cephalothorax

Fovea

Coxa

Trochanter

Femur

Patella

Tibia

Metatarsus

Tarsus

Leg segments

Leg III

Abdomen

Spinnerets

Leg IV

VENTRAL VIEW OF SPIDER

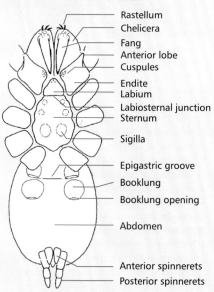

Rastellum
Chelicera
Fang
Anterior lobe
Cuspules

Endite
Labium
Labiosternal junction
Sternum

Sigilla

Epigastric groove

Booklung

Booklung opening

Abdomen

Anterior spinnerets
Posterior spinnerets

SPIDER INFRA-ORDERS

In South Africa the order Araneae can be subdivided into two infra-orders:

■ The primitive **Mygalomorphae** includes the various baboon and trapdoor spiders. They are also known as mygalomorph or four-lunged spiders. Their chelicerae are positioned so that the fangs swing forward into the prey, like an axe (paraxial).

■ The **Araneomorphae**, a much larger group, contains all other spiders. Their chelicerae swing in towards each other, like a pincer (diaxial). They are also known as two-lunged or 'true' spiders.

Paraxial

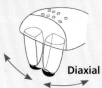

Diaxial

Cluster of *Cyrtophora citricola* webs

SILK

Spiders are famed for secreting silk – the strongest and most flexible fibre in the natural world. Humans have not been able to reproduce the remarkable qualities of silk.

Silk production starts when a protein-rich fluid is formed in specialised glands within the abdomen. This fluid hardens when it oozes out of the spigots situated on the spinnerets, forming a solid thread. The spider uses its legs to reel the silk out of its body and manipulates the thread with the claws on its tarsi.

Spiders are known to recycle old webs, rolling up and eating 80–90% of the used silk threads. This 'meal' is partially broken down by digestive enzymes, then swiftly re-absorbed by the silk glands. The recycled silk is available within 30 minutes. Spiders therefore use very little body protein in the daily production of silk.

WHAT IS SILK USED FOR?

- **Construction:** The ability to spin a web evolved over millions of years. These lightweight silk structures are used to catch prey, and come in many shapes and sizes. Some webs are simple, others very intricate.
- **Movement:** Silk enables spiders to move around freely and to retrace their steps. As a spider travels, it may lay down a trail of silk so that it can find its way home. These guiding threads are often used as droplines enabling spiders to jump from heights, either to escape or in pursuit of prey. By using droplines, spiders are able to land poised and ready to pounce. They return to their shelter by clambering back up the thread.
- **Prey wrapping:** After injecting their prey with venom, spiders may further immobilise the victim by swathing it in silk.
- **Dispersal:** Spiders are among the few wingless animals that can 'fly'. The spider produces a thread that gets caught in an air current and lifts the spider into the air. Distances covered vary from a few

Argiope australis with wrapped prey

Neoscona blondeli in the hub of an orb-web

metres to thousands of kilometres. Small ballooning spiders have been observed on ships far out at sea. Typically immature spiderlings disperse in this fashion, but mature spiders of some small species and the small males of web builders may also use this dispersal technique.

- **Scaffolding:** Some spiders use silk threads as a scaffold when they shed their skin.
- **Mating:** Silk has many uses during the reproductive process. Males transfer sperm to silk webbing before mating. Mating often takes place while the spiders are supported by silk threads, and some males even 'tie' their partner down.
- **Egg sacs:** After laying eggs, the female spider uses several layers of silk to protect the eggs from harsh weather and predators.
- **Retreats:** Spiders construct a variety of shelters, such as sac-like silken retreats in plants or structures made of a mixture of silk and pebbles. Burrow-living spiders line their tunnels with silk threads and construct trap doors from silk.

Uloborus plumipes female atop egg sac

Rhene lingularis female in silk retreat

Four-lunged spiders, such as this *Stasimopus* female, have the longest lifespan.

A small *Thomisus citrinellus* male perches on a female's abdomen, ready to mate.

Argiope australis mating

LIFE CYCLE

Most spiders live for only one year. A female that hatches in autumn will hibernate as an immature spider, mature in spring, lay her eggs during summer and die in late summer. Males typically have a shorter lifespan, as they have no role to play after the mating season.

Certain families such as Lycosidae (wolf spiders) and Salticidae (jumping spiders) live longer than a year – about 18 months. The greatest longevity is found in primitive four-lunged spiders, such as baboon spiders. The female reaches sexual maturity only after 12 years, after which she lives a further five or more years.

COURTSHIP AND MATING

Spiders usually mate in spring and summer. To prepare for mating, the male transfers sperm from the genital opening beneath his abdomen to the secondary sexual organs on the palpi. This is done by depositing sperm on a small sperm web and then absorbing it with the palpal organ, where it is stored until mating. After this, many males change their lifestyle completely. Male web builders, for example, abandon the web and become free living, in search of a female.

Sexual dimorphism is found in many species, the male often being smaller than the female and with a completely different appearance. In these species, the male must approach his mate carefully to ensure that she does not mistake him for prey.

Courtship behaviour varies too. In some species where sight is well developed, the male performs an intricate courtship ritual that involves raising and waving the palpi. Some of the burrowing spiders, such as Cyrtaucheniidae (trapdoor spiders), see the male announcing his presence by tapping rhythmically against the sides of the female's burrow with his palpi. When the female emerges, the male uses the mating spurs on his front legs to force open her jaws and quickly overpower her. This prevents her from attacking him during mating.

EGG LAYING

Spiders typically lay eggs during summer. The number of eggs produced varies greatly between families. Some of the small ant-eaters of Oecobiidae (round-headed spiders) lay only a few eggs, while females of the genus *Argiope* (garden orb-web spiders) lay up to 9,000 eggs. However, since the latter spiders permanently inhabit webs and are more exposed to predators, only some 2% of the offspring survive to maturity.

Eggs are usually deposited in a waterproof sac made of silk. Sacs vary in size, shape and colour, and are usually well camouflaged. Most females produce multiple egg sacs per season. Some web builders string several egg sacs beneath one another in the web. Plant and ground dwellers may attach their egg sacs to nearby bark, leaves and rocks.

While some females lay their eggs and then leave, others tend to the eggs and the young hatchlings. The female may sit close to the egg sac and watch over it, as is the case with Thomisidae (crab spiders). Pholcidae females (daddy long-legs spiders) carry the

A *Quamtana* female carries an egg sac held together by a few silk threads.

egg sac in their mouth. Wolf spiders attach the egg sac to their spinnerets and pull it behind them, and then allow newly hatched spiderlings onto their back, where they reside in safety for a few days. Pisauridae females (nursery-web spiders) make a nursery of silk for their young. The hatchlings remain in this shelter until they have grown strong enough to care for themselves.

Lycosidae female carrying spiderlings on her back

DISPERSAL

Once hatched, some spiderlings simply walk away from the nest to settle somewhere else, but others have the ability to disperse using air currents, a technique known as **ballooning**. This type of dispersal occurs on warm days rather than windy ones. The spiderling climbs to the highest point it can reach – the tip of a blade of grass or a branch – then stands on the tips of its legs with its abdomen tilted upwards. It releases a stream of silk, which is drawn upwards by the warm air current. When the silk stream is pulled taught, the spiderling loosens its grip and floats away. Ballooning is usually restricted to a height of 70m or less above the surface, but some spiders have also been found in air samples taken at a height of 1,500m. Naturally, the spiderlings are at the mercy of air currents. Many lose their lives while ballooning or land in unsuitable places, but many find a new home, often far away from where they hatched.

Local overpopulation can occur when many spiderlings emerge from a nest simultaneously. Competition for food increases rapidly, and cannibalism frequently occurs.

MOULTING

To grow in size, spiders must shed their skin in a process known as moulting. The first moult takes place inside the egg sac, and emerging spiderlings closely resemble adults in all but size. A few days before further moulting, the spider stops eating. In most cases, it hangs from a short silk thread while it sheds. The process begins with the skin under the carapace, just above the coxae of the legs, parting. The carapace then lifts off like a lid, but remains attached at the pedicel. Next, the skin of the abdomen splits at the side and the abdomen comes free. The legs, palpi and chelicerae are pulled free from the skin with rhythmic movements and the spider finally swings free. At this stage the spider is soft and defenceless until the new skin hardens. In young spiders, moulting is completed within a few minutes, but as the spider matures, the process may last for an hour or more. If a leg is lost between moults, the spider is capable of growing a new one, which appears after the next moult. Initially, the new leg is shorter and thinner than the others.

Small species may moult only three times during their life, whereas larger species may moult nine or ten times.

Dispersing *Cladomelea longipalpis* hatchlings

Synema imitatrix moulting

SPIDERS AS PREDATORS

From the time they hatch, all spiders are predators, feeding on live prey. Ground-living spiders feed mainly on ground insects and larvae hibernating in the soil. Many plant-dwelling spiders are wandering nocturnal hunters, actively moving around in search of food. Web-building spiders prey on any flying or crawling insects that come in contact with their silk threads.

During periods of prey abundance, spiders will often consume large amounts of food in a relatively short period of time. The abdomen is able to distend to accommodate the additional load.

Palystes superciliosus female feeding

During periods of low prey availability, spiders are able to decrease their metabolic rate, enabling them to survive and maintain normal reproduction.

Spiders have a significant impact on insect control on farms, in houses and in gardens. Besides feeding directly on pest prey, they also cause indirect mortality: the movement of spiders could dislodge larvae that then drop to the ground and die. Webs spun over leaves also limit insect food sources and make them less suitable for egg laying.

Neoscona female wrapping prey

SPIDERS AS PREY

BIRDS Spiders are among the favourite prey items of insectivorous birds, such as fiscal shrikes. Some birds, such as the brubru, do not eat spiders but use the silk of hundreds of webs to build a single nest.

MITES Several predatory mite families parasitise and prey on spiders. These tiny creatures can occasionally be seen with the naked eye on larger species such as baboon spiders. They are usually found on the carapace, especially in the fovea.

NEMATODES Many species of spider have been recorded as hosts of nematodes (roundworms).

MAMMALS Vervet monkeys are fond of feeding on spiders. They're known to snatch orb-web spiders from their web.

Older individuals train the younger ones how to catch these spiders.

WASPS Adult wasps typically feed on sugars, such as nectar, but their larvae are carnivorous. Several wasp species are able to overpower spiders and immobilise them with venom. The wasp drags the paralysed spider to its burrow and lays an egg on or in the spider. The spider then serves as food for the developing wasp larva.

SPIDERS The families Archaeidae, Mimetidae and Palpimanidae specialise in the predation of other spiders. Large web spiders are often subject to kleptoparasites – small spiders that live on the edge of the webs and steal food (and may even hunt the host itself).

Some button spiders, such as this *Latrodectus geometricus* female, are easily recognised by the hourglass marking under the abdomen.

VENOM

Whatever their hunting strategy – stalking, trapping or ambushing – the vast majority of spider species follow the same killing and feeding procedure. Their primary weapon is their chelicerae, a pair of jointed jaws with a set of sharp, retractable fangs. The fangs have a small hole at the tip, and are hollow inside. A duct connects the fang tip to the spider's venom gland, which is typically situated in the basal segment of the chelicerae or deeper inside the cephalothorax.

When a spider attacks its prey, it swings its fangs into the animal's body. The fangs work like hypodermic needles, injecting the animal with enough venom to paralyse or kill it. With the exception of the Uloboridae (hackled orb-web spiders), all spiders produce venom to subdue or kill prey.

The potency of the venom varies from family to family. In most cases, the venom is strong enough to kill insects. In some cases, it is potent enough to immobilise small reptiles and mammals.

Many people fear being bitten by a spider. Since a variety of spider species are found in houses and outbuildings, it is inevitable that they will come in close contact with humans. Most spiders will avoid physical contact, but if accidentally touched or squeezed, they might deliver a bite in self-defence. However, of the 2,282 spider species found in South Africa, only a few have venom of medical importance (i.e. harmful to humans), and no fatalities have ever been reported in the country.

The region's medically important spiders can be classified by the type of venom they produce: **neurotoxic** or **cytotoxic**.

After envenomation, spiders don't eat their prey whole. Instead, they expel digestive enzymes onto or into the animal. Some species do this by biting the prey into pieces using the serrated 'teeth' on their chelicerae. They then eject digestive fluids onto the remains. Others use their fangs to inject digestive fluids directly into the prey. This causes the animal's insides to liquefy, leaving the exoskeleton more or less intact.

Once its meal is liquefied, the spider will suck the fluid into its stomach through the hairs on the chelicerae and mouth, which act as a filter.

Neurotoxic venom

This venom affects the central nervous system. Bites from spiders having this venom are usually accompanied by severe pain.

BUTTON SPIDERS
(Theridiidae: *Latrodectus*)
In South Africa, it is only the button spiders that have this venom. Eight species are known to occur here and are divided into the **black button complex** (more venomous) and **brown button complex** (less venomous).

SYMPTOMS AND SIGNS The term latrodectism is used to describe the effects of envenomation by button spiders. Only the female spider is able to pierce human skin and, in most cases, a full dosage of venom is not administered.

A bite from a **black button** spider is usually very painful and causes generalised muscle pain and cramps, stiffness of the stomach muscles, limb pain (especially in the legs), weakness of the legs, profuse sweating, raised blood pressure and restlessness. Although no fatalities have been recorded, the venom can potentially cause severe symptoms, with small children and elderly people being most at risk.

Symptoms of a **brown button** spider bite are milder and tend to be restricted to the bite site, characterised by a local burning sensation which may spread to the surrounding tissue and lymph nodes. The bite site is often identified by a red spot or blanched area surrounded by a localised rash. It usually clears up within a day or two.

TREATMENT The administration of black button antivenom is the only effective treatment for severe latrodectism. A dose of 10ml is administered intravenously. Patients usually respond within 10–30 minutes, but a follow-up dose of 5ml is occasionally necessary after four to six hours.

Spiders of the black button complex. From left to right: *Latrodectus cinctus*, *L. pallidus*, *L. renivulvatus*, *L. karooensis* (top) and *L. indistinctus*. These spiders are more venomous than those of the brown button complex.

Spiders of the brown button complex. From left to right: *Latrodectus umbukwane*, *L. rhodesiensis* and *L. geometricus*. These spiders vary from cream, grey and brown to black.

Hospitalisation may be required, and the patient should be kept under observation for at least 6–12 hours after treatment in case of allergic reaction (uncommon) to the refined equine antivenom serum. The only effective agent for the relief of muscular pain and cramps is intravenous calcium gluconate, the effects of which last only 20–30 minutes. Care should also be taken to prevent and treat secondary infections.

Black button spider antivenom is made by the South African Vaccine Producers Institute in Edenvale and can also be obtained from the South African Institute for Medical Research in Johannesburg.

Cytotoxic venom

This venom affects the tissue around the bite. Considerable tissue damage can ensue and lesions of up to 10cm in diameter may develop. Symptoms develop gradually and the person is often unaware that they have been bitten until the area around the bite becomes painful. It is therefore usually difficult to establish which spider species delivered the bite, especially since bites often occur while people are sleeping. In South Africa three genera are of particular medical importance. Two genera, *Cheiracanthium* and *Loxosceles*, produce cytotoxic venom. The venom of a third genus, *Hexophthalma*, has a combination of cytotoxic and haemotoxic (affecting the blood) components. However, no confirmed cases of human envenomation by *Hexophthalma* spiders are known in South Africa and clinical evidence is inconclusive.

SAC SPIDERS
(Cheiracanthiidae: *Cheiracanthium*)

The sac spiders are commonly found outdoors and only one species, *C. furculatum*, is regularly found in houses. These spiders spend the day in a soft silk sac-like retreat, often made in folds of curtains, bedding and clothing.

Cheiracanthium furculatum. Sac spiders are readily recognised by their pale colour and distinct dark face.

SYMPTOMS AND SIGNS Medical records indicate that most patients are bitten while asleep. The bite is painless and the person is usually not aware of being bitten. Sometimes two fang bite marks (4–8mm apart) are visible. A typical bull's eye lesion may form and the surrounding area gradually becomes red, swollen and painful. The centre of the wound undergoes necrotic changes, leaving an ulcerating wound. The severity of the lesion varies from patient to patient, and local tissue damage and necrosis may be minimal or extensive. Systemic symptoms such as tender lymph nodes, a rash, low-grade fever, headaches, muscle and joint pain may occasionally develop.

TREATMENT The majority of bites are self-limiting and heal spontaneously. Treatment of the bites should be directed at preventing and treating secondary infection using local antiseptics and systemic antibiotics. Occasionally an infected wound may develop into rapidly spreading cellulitis, which requires aggressive antibiotic therapy. The patient should receive a tetanus toxoid booster.

VIOLIN SPIDERS
(Sicariidae: *Loxosceles*)
Violin spiders usually live in grassland and caves, with only *L. simillima* and *L. parrami* known to enter houses. These spiders are usually brown or reddish brown in colour,

with dark markings on their bodies. They are characterised by violin-shaped markings on the carapace and are quite often confused with Pholcidae (daddy long-legs spiders), which do not produce venom of medical importance. Violin spiders are nocturnal and may find their way into pyjamas, beds and shoes.

SYMPTOMS AND SIGNS The superficial bite is painless and initially goes unnoticed. About two hours after the bite, a red swollen lesion, sometimes with a purple centre, develops. During the next day or two bleeding into the site causes a blackened lesion. By day four the swelling and inflammation subside, while cutaneous necrosis continues to spread slowly. Necrotic tissue sloughs off, leaving a deep ulcerating wound, which is slow to heal and leaves a scar.

TREATMENT At present no antivenom is available. Treatment should focus on preventing and treating secondary infection using local antiseptics and systemic antibiotics. Timely surgical cleaning may arrest a spreading lesion. Dapsone treatment in low doses for 14 days may control extension of the ulceration. Plastic surgery may be necessary to repair tissue damage, and scars may require reconstructive surgery with skin grafting at a later stage. The patient should receive a tetanus toxoid booster.

Loxosceles simillima

Loxosceles parrami

COLLECTING SPIDERS

Spiders are found in a variety of habitats and in all field layers – from ground level to tree canopy. Different methods are used to collect spiders, depending on the species' habits, habitat and field layer.

HAND COLLECTION A wide variety of species can be collected by carefully looking under leaves and by lifting logs, stones and bark. Once located, the spiders are gently scooped into a jar.

SWEEP NETTING The most effective way of collecting large numbers of spiders in grass and small shrubs is by using a sweep net to dislodge specimens. Once collected, the contents of the net are emptied onto a tray and the specimens removed with a pooter or paintbrush dipped in alcohol.

BEATING SHEETS Foliage dwellers are best caught using a beating sheet. In this method, a sheet is placed beneath the vegetation and then the branches are shaken or hit with a stick to knock specimens down from the bushes onto the sheet.

FOGGING Some collectors use sprays to collect spiders from inaccessible parts of a tree. A sheet is placed beneath the tree to catch spiders that succumb to the fogging spray and fall to the ground.

Cyphalonotus larvatus. Many species are nocturnal and well camouflaged, making it tricky to find and collect these spiders.

PITFALL TRAPS These traps are effective for collecting ground-dwelling spiders. A container is buried in the ground, its upper rim placed level with the ground surface. Containers need to be checked regularly and any spiders collected before they can be taken by spider predators.

PAPER TRAPS These are used to attract spiders living in crevices on trees and species that migrate upwards after overwintering in the ground. Strips of brown corrugated paper, about 15cm wide, are tied around the tree trunk, fastened with string, and left for up to a month before being carefully removed.

Hand collecting

Sweep netting grass

Pitfall trap to be buried

The corrugations (ideally 3mm in diameter) provide refuge for spiders who settle in the protective grooves.

SIEVES Spiders that live among leaf litter and rotting wood can be effectively collected using a sieve. Any frame with a wire mesh is suitable. Loose debris is collected and placed in the sieve. Shaking

the sieve over a white surface will separate the spiders from the debris, releasing the spiders and leaving loose debris in the sieve.

LEAF LITTER AND HUMUS EXTRACTION DEVICES Plant and ground dwellers can be sampled with a fuel-powered leaf blower set to vacuum mode with a fine mesh bag attached.

BIOMES OF SOUTH AFRICA

South Africa is divided into nine different biomes based on dominant vegetation type and prevailing climate, among other factors. The biomes are depicted in the map below. In this book, each species entry lists the biomes within which the spider has been collected, giving an indication of the species' preference or adaptation to one or more

vegetation types. Spiders display a range of adaptations to their surroundings and may occur in one or across several different biomes. As such, biomes are a useful tool when predicting spider distribution.

Within these biomes, spiders inhabit various niches or micro-habitats (e.g. leaf litter, rock crevices, bark, flowers).

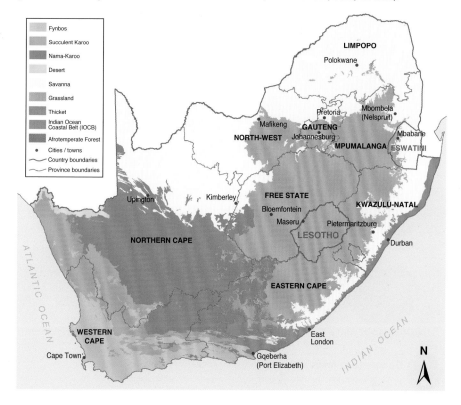

HOW TO USE THIS BOOK

This book is divided into three sections:
web dwellers, **plant dwellers** and **ground dwellers**.
Each section features a **Quick Key** to the spider
families in that section.

Some spider families are not confined to a single
guild. For example, some plant-dwelling families
also include ground dwellers, so be sure to check
the other sections' Quick Keys should your specimen
not feature in the expected group.

❶ Family account
❷ Typical morphology
❸ Genus account
❹ Scientific name
❺ Common name
❻ Distribution map
❼ Species description
❽ Conservation status
❾ Footer: Family name

SPIDER SIZES: Spiders are measured
from the tip of the chelicerae to the
end of the abdomen. In this book, the
following size categories are used to
describe spiders:

Very small: <3mm

Small: 3–6mm

Medium-sized: 7–15mm

Actual size

Large: 16–30mm

Very large: >30mm

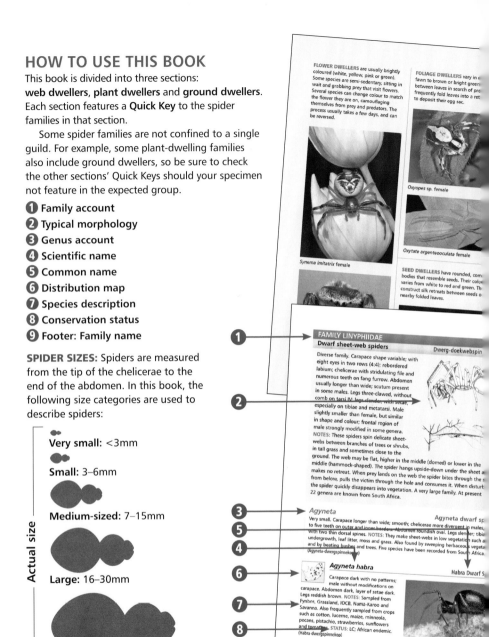

FLOWER DWELLERS are usually brightly
coloured (white, yellow, pink or green).
Some species are semi-sedentary, sitting in
wait and grabbing prey that visit flowers.
Several species can change colour to match
the flower they are on, camouflaging
themselves from prey and predators. The
process usually takes a few days, and can
be reversed.

FOLIAGE DWELLERS vary in c
fawn to brown or bright green
between leaves in search of pre
frequently fold leaves into a ret
to deposit their egg sac.

Oxyopes sp. female

Oxytate argenteooculata female

Synema imitatrix female

SEED DWELLERS have rounded, com
bodies that resemble seeds. Their colo
varies from white to red and green. Th
construct silk retreats between seeds o
nearby folded leaves.

FAMILY LINYPHIIDAE
Dwarf sheet-web spiders   Dwerg-doekwebspin

Diverse family. Carapace shape variable; with
eight eyes in two rows (4:4); rebordered
labium; chelicerae with stridulating file and
numerous teeth on fang furrow. Abdomen
usually longer than wide; scutum present
in some males. Legs three-clawed, without
comb on tarsi IV; legs slender, with setae,
especially on tibiae and metatarsi. Male
slightly smaller than female, but similar
in shape and colour; frontal region of
male strongly modified in some genera.
NOTES: These spiders spin delicate sheet-
webs between branches of trees or shrubs,
in tall grass and sometimes close to the
ground. The web may be flat, higher in the middle (domed) or lower in the
middle (hammock-shaped). The spider hangs upside-down under the sheet a
makes no retreat. When prey lands on the web the spider bites through the s
from below, pulls the victim through the hole and consumes it. When disturb
the spider quickly disappears into vegetation. A very large family. At present
22 genera are known from South Africa.

Agyneta   Agyneta dwarf sp
Very small. Carapace longer than wide; smooth; chelicerae more divergent in males,
to five teeth on outer and inner borders. Abdomen roundish oval. Legs slender; tibia
with two thin dorsal spines. NOTES: They make sheet-webs in low vegetation such a
undergrowth, leaf litter, moss and grass. Also found by sweeping herbaceous vegeta
and by beating bushes and trees. Five species have been recorded from South Africa.
(Agyneta-dwergspinnekop)

Agyneta habra   Habra Dwarf S
Carapace dark with no patterns;
male without modifications on
carapace. Abdomen dark, layer of setae dark.
Legs reddish brown. NOTES: Sampled from
Fynbos, Grassland, IOCB, Nama-Karoo and
Savanna. Also frequently sampled from crops
such as cotton, lucerne, maize, minneola,
pecans, pistachio, strawberries, sunflowers
and tomatoes. STATUS: LC; African endemic.
(Habra-dwergspinnekop)

> ⓘ **Danger to humans** Spiders with venom of medical importance have been
> indicated with this symbol 🜍 and are discussed in greater detail on page 16.

EYE FORMULA Eye arrangement differs between families and genera. An eye formula lists the number of eyes in each row. A species with an eye formula of 6:2 has six eyes in the front row and two in the back, whereas one with a formula of 2:2:2:2 has four rows of two eyes.

Eye formula: 4:4

Eye formula: 2:2:4

LEG FORMULA The relative lengths of a spider's legs are useful for identification. A leg formula ranks the legs from longest to shortest. The spider below has a leg formula of 1-2-4-3, indicating that the first leg is the longest and the third leg is the shortest.

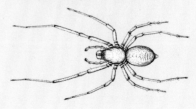

WEB DWELLERS

Whereas plant and ground dwellers are typically 'wanderers' that move about in search of prey, web-dwelling spiders build and inhabit webs. These highly specialised structures can be considered an extension of the spider's tactile sense organs. The use of a web to capture prey developed long after spiders came into existence – it took more than 200 million years for the first simple orb-webs to appear. The great diversity of webs observed today suggests that this predation strategy is very successful.

Though some webs seem to be a chaotic arrangement of silk threads, most threads serve a definite purpose:

- **Mooring threads** anchor and support the web. The uppermost threads are called bridge lines.
- **Pilot threads** guide the spider as it moves about in the web.
- **Signal threads** or triplines betray the presence of prey or predators.
- **Catch threads** ensnare victims and are often strong and sticky.

Prasonica nigrotaeniata in the hub of its orb-web

Spiders construct many different web types – they vary within genera and even within a species. Among the more common families, the following web types can be recognised:

ORB-WEBS consist of bridge lines, radii and a circular spiral of adhesive threads. These webs are typically vertical. The shape of the web, its orientation and the number of radii vary greatly between genera. Garbage-line orb-webs, for instance, have a typical circular shape, but contain a line of prey remains and detritus. Adapted cribellate orb-webs include cast-webs (held with the front legs and flung over prey) and triangle-webs. Reduced orb-webs consist of a few strands of silk. In these webs, prey capture requires active involvement from the spider, e.g. *Cladomelea* spiders that 'fish' for flying insects by swinging a sticky bolas thread.

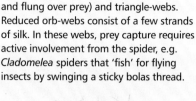

Tropical tent-web

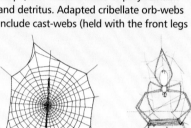

Garbage-line orb-web   Cast-web

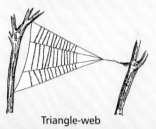

Triangle-web

Asianopis sp. with cast-web. This adapted cribellate orb-web is used as a net to capture prey.

FUNNEL-WEBS consist of a slightly concave, non-adhesive sheet made from a mesh of silk threads. The sheet is spun over the ground (or any horizontal area) and is often clearly visible in the early morning when covered with droplets of dew. Typically, the web is permanent and is repaired and enlarged as the spider grows. A funnel-shaped retreat is situated on one side of the web. This retreat usually incorporates a second escape opening.

GUMFOOT-WEBS typically consist of a central cluster of silk, small stones and debris (with or without a retreat), as well as mooring, signal and catch threads. The lower catch threads are secured to the ground under high tension, and are studded with sticky droplets. When running or jumping insects collide with these threads, the threads dislodge and insects adhering to the droplets are left swinging helplessly. The spider then hoists the victim up.

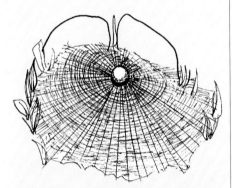

Funnel-web

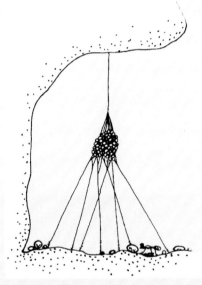

Gumfoot-web

Funnel-web of *Benoitia* sp.

Spider and prey at core of gumfoot-web

SPACE-WEBS are open, without a distinct structure. They are frequently built between different surfaces and fill whatever space is available. Space-web are usually found close to the ground, in corners, under overhanging rocks, or in old mammal burrows. None of the threads are adhesive.

RETREAT-WEBS are not true webs. They comprise a retreat with triplines, used to alert the spider to approaching prey. The triplines are generally non-adhesive, serving as signal threads rather than catch threads. More primitive web builders tend to use triplines as a hunting strategy. These spiders use their legs and chelicerae to overpower prey.

Space-web

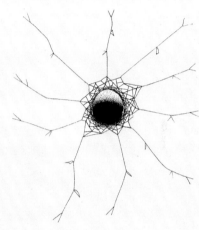

Retreat-web

SHEET-WEBS are complex three-dimensional structures. They vary markedly in shape and size, but typically consist of a horizontal sheet, which may be flat, concave or convex. Domed webs are more effective at catching prey approaching from below, while hammock-webs are well suited to catching prey moving downwards. The spider usually hangs from the underside of the web.

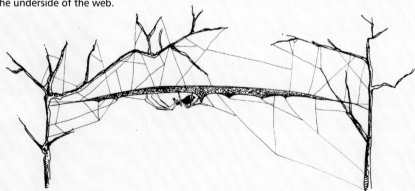

Sheet-web

Family Agelenidae p. 32

Medium-sized; three-clawed; eight eyes in two rows (4:4); posterior spinnerets two-segmented, long, slender, with apical segment tapering towards tip. Coloration various shades of brown and grey. **Web type:** Funnel-web.

Spinnerets

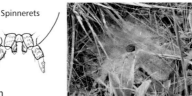

Funnel-web

Benoitia sp.

Family Amaurobiidae p. 35

Small to medium-sized; three-clawed; eight eyes in two rows (4:4); with or without cribellum. Coloration shades of fawn to dark, abdomen with chevron pattern or with a shield. **Web type:** Retreat-web or free running.

Chumma sp.

Chresiona sp.

Family Araneidae p. 38

Morphologically diverse family. Small to very large; three-clawed; eight eyes in two rows (4:4); labium rebordered; shape of abdomen variable. Diurnal species usually more brightly coloured than nocturnal species. **Web type:** Orb-web.

Caerostris sp.

Araneus sp.

Argiope sp.

Family Cyatholipidae p. 76

Very small, delicate; three-clawed; eight eyes in two rows (4:4); legs long, slender; posterior tracheal spiracles widely spaced, linked externally by transverse groove sclerotised at each end ①. Abdomen may have dorsal markings. **Web type:** Horizontal sheet-web.

Abdomen

Cyatholipus sp.

Family Deinopidae p. 79

Medium-sized to large; three-clawed; eight eyes in three rows; posterior median eyes enlarged ①; cribellate; bodies usually elongated; legs I and II very long; abdomen with one or two humps, or triangular. Coloration various shades of silvery white, grey, brownish black or olive-green. **Web type:** Cast-web.

Eye region

Menneus sp.

Family Dictynidae p. 82

Very small to small; three-clawed; eight eyes in two rows (4:4); cribellate with wide cribellum; carapace usually with white setae rows. Coloration pale to dark brown or grey; abdomen usually pale with dark pattern. **Web type:** Retreat-web.

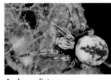

Archaeodictyna sp.

Family Drymusidae p. 84

Medium-sized; three-clawed, tarsi with onychium; six eyes in three diads. Carapace and legs brown with darker patches; abdomen with distinct brown or purple hue, dorsum decorated with pattern of pale chevrons. **Web type:** Loose space-web.

Eye region

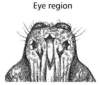 

Izithunzi sp.

Family Eresidae p. 85

Morphologically a very diverse family; small to large; three-clawed; eight eyes, with median eyes situated close together and lateral eyes widely spaced; cribellate; carapace convex, rectangular. Body usually clothed in dense layer of short setae; various hues of brown or grey. **Web type:** Retreat-web.

Paradonea sp.

Family Euagridae p. 91

Medium to large mygalomorph spiders; three-clawed; eight eyes in compact group; body hairy; median spinnerets short, posterior spinnerets longer than carapace with terminal segment longer than basal or middle segment. **Web type:** Large funnel-web.

Allothele sp.

Family Filistatidae p. 93

Small; three-clawed; eight eyes in compact group, situated on small eye tubercle; cribellate; labium fused to sternum. Coloration variable, pale yellow to light brown, dark brown or black. **Web type:** Tubular retreat-web.

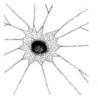 

Andoharano sp.

Family Hahniidae p. 94

Small; three-clawed; eight eyes in two rows (4:4); spinnerets situated in transverse row ①; tracheal spiracles open midway on abdomen. Carapace light to dark brown with dark pattern. **Web type:** Sheet-web on ground surface.

Spinnerets

Hahnia sp.

Family Ischnothelidae p. 95

Medium-sized to large mygalomorph spiders; three-clawed; eight eyes on eye tubercle; posterior spinnerets very long, median and posterior spinnerets widely spaced. Coloration medium to dark brown, sometimes with purplish tint; abdomen with markings. **Web type:** Large funnel-web.

Thelechoris sp.

Family Linyphiidae p. 96

Morphologically a very diverse family; very small to small; three-clawed; eight eyes (4:4); slender legs with setae, especially on tibiae and metatarsi; labium rebordered. Coloration usually dark, shiny. **Web type:** Sheet-web spun in vegetation or close to the ground.

Sheet-web

Mecynidis sp.

Family Mysmenidae p. 99

Very small; three-clawed; eight eyes in two rows (4:4); male with mating spur on metatarsus I (sometimes on tibia I as well). Coloration varies from yellow-brown to grey, sometimes with greenish tinge. **Web type:** Small modified orb-web.

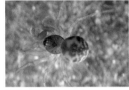
Isela sp.

Family Nesticidae p. 100

Very small to medium-sized; three-clawed; eight eyes (4:4); tarsi IV with row of serrated bristles ①; labium rebordered; abdomen decorated with pale symmetrical spots. **Web type:** Three-dimensional cob-web.

Nesticella sp.

Family Oecobiidae p. 101

Morphologically diverse family; small to medium-sized; three-clawed; six or eight eyes; includes cribellate and ecribellate genera; anal tubercle large, two-segmented with double fringe of curved setae. Coloration variable. **Web type:** Retreat-web or layered web under stones.

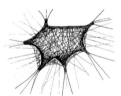

Uroctea sp.

Family Penestomidae p. 103

Small; three-clawed; eight eyes in two rows (4:4), posterior eye row slightly recurved, more widely spaced than anteriors; cribellate; carapace subrectangular with shallow ovoid fovea, flattened. Coloration dark brown, abdomen almost black, with white markings in some species. **Web type:** Retreat-web.

Penestomus sp.

Family Pholcidae p. 105

Morphologically a very diverse family; very small to medium-sized; three-clawed; six or eight eyes; legs very long; abdomen shape variable. Coloration varies from cream with few dark markings to greyish brown with dark chevrons. **Web type:** Space-web or no web.

Smeringopus sp.

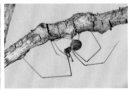
Spermophora sp.

30 Web dwellers

Family Phyxelididae   p. 109

Medium-sized; three-clawed; eight eyes (4:4); cribellate; palp femora with enlarged or modified setae on prolateral side in both sexes ①; metatarsi I of male strongly modified. Coloration various shades of dark brown or grey, abdomen sometimes with ill-defined pattern. **Web type:** Retreat-web.

Palp femur

Themacrys sp.

Family Pisauridae   p. 113

Morphologically diverse family; medium-sized to very large; three-clawed; eight eyes in 2–4 rows; abdomen elongated, oval, tapering towards spinnerets; legs long and slender; trochanters deeply notched. Cryptic carapace frequently marked with bands or patterns. **Web type:** Sheet-web or no web.

Rothus sp.

Family Segestriidae   p. 123

Medium-sized; three-clawed; six eyes closely grouped; leg III directed forwards; tibiae and metatarsi I with double row of spines ventrally; posterior tracheae anteriorly positioned. Coloration variable, brown to reddish black or purplish black. **Web type:** Tube-shaped retreat-web.

Retreat-web   *Ariadna* sp.

Family Symphytognathidae   p. 125

Very small; three-clawed; six eyes arranged in three pairs; lungless; chelicerae fused; sternum broadly truncated posteriorly. Coloration either white, with long, grey setae, or pale grey. **Web type:** Dwarf orb-web in leaf litter.

Family Tetragnathidae   p. 126

Morphologically diverse family; small to large; three-clawed; eight eyes in two rows (4:4); chelicerae variable, long and well developed, with rows of large teeth and strong projecting spurs in males of *Tetragnatha* and *Leucauge*; abdomen shape variable. Coloration fawn to dull brown or grey with silvery markings, sometimes with distinct green, silver, white and bronze pattern. **Web type:** Orb-web.

Chelicerae

Leucauge sp.

Family Theridiidae   p. 132

Morphologically a very diverse family; small to medium-sized; three-clawed; eight eyes (4:4); row of slightly curved, serrated bristles on tarsi IV ①. Coloration variable. **Web type:** Gumfoot-web.

Tarsus IV

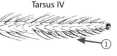

Latrodectus sp.

Family Uloboridae   p. 144

Morphologically diverse family; small to medium-sized; three-clawed; cribellate; eight eyes (4:4); body covered in feathery setae; carapace pear-shaped; posterior lateral eyes not on tubercles; venom glands absent. Body usually dull shades of cream, grey or brown. **Web type:** Orb-web made of cribellate silk, some adapted and reduced.

Uloborus sp.

Funnel-web spiders Tregterwebspinnekoppe

Carapace narrow in eye region; fovea long; eight eyes equal-sized, arranged in two rows (4:4). Abdomen narrow, oval, tapering towards spinnerets; posterior spinnerets two-segmented, long, slender, with apical segment tapering towards tip. Legs three-clawed, of similar length, long, slender. Males slightly smaller than females, with more slender legs. The genera and species found in South Africa are very similar in colour and spinneret morphology and can be distinguished only by their genitalia. NOTES: They build non-sticky funnel-webs, usually in low vegetation. Webs consist of a flat, open sheet with a horizontal, funnel-shaped retreat made close to the soil surface. The dew-covered webs are easily spotted early in the morning. Five genera and 10 species have been recorded in South Africa.

Agelenid funnel-web in grass

Agelena

Agelena grass funnel-web spiders

Medium-sized. Carapace with lateral bands. Abdomen with median band bordered by rows of spots; heart mark sometimes distinct. Two-segmented posterior spinnerets longer than anterior pair. Legs mottled or faintly banded. NOTES: These spiders build funnel-webs. Prey includes a variety of jumping and flying insects, such as beetles, grasshoppers, locusts and termites. Two species are known from South Africa. (Agelena-grastregterwebspinnekoppe)

Agelena australis

Southern Grass Funnel-web Spider

Carapace with broad dark lateral bands. Abdomen with brownish median band; latter bordered by white spots; first spot yellowish white and larger than rest. Legs mottled brown and yellowish. NOTES: Funnel-webs sampled from Grassland and Savanna. STATUS: LC; African endemic. (Suidelike Grastregterwebspinnekop)

Agelena gaerdesi

Gaerdes's Grass Funnel-web Spider

Carapace sports dark lateral bands with four small paired pale patches. Abdomen with reddish-brown median band; latter bordered by darker spots; heart mark distinct. Legs yellowish with irregular brown bands. **NOTES:** Funnel-webs made in most biomes, as well as Northern Cape pistachio orchards. **STATUS:** LC; southern African endemic. (Gaerdes se Grastregterwegspinnekop)

Benoitia

Benoit's funnel-web spiders

Medium-sized. Carapace with broad lateral bands. Abdomen with spots. Male palpal structure large, with screw-like conductor bearing apical membranous lamella. Female epigyne has epigynal pit with paired pits and septum with rounded lobes. **NOTES:** Funnel-webs very commonly seen early in the morning in field and often found in abandoned mammal burrows. Three species are known from South Africa. (Benoit se Tregterwebspinnekoppe)

Benoitia deserticola

Desert Funnel-web Spider

Carapace pale yellow-brown with dark lateral bands, with four paired pale patches. Abdomen yellowish brown above, marked with paler median band bordered by four pair of black spots. Legs pale yellow, banded. **NOTES:** Funnel-webs found in Fynbos, Grassland, Savanna and Succulent Karoo. **STATUS:** LC; southern African endemic. (Woestyn-tregterwebspinnekop)

Benoitia ocellata

Spotted Funnel-web Spider

Carapace yellow-brown with dark lateral bands and paired white patches. Abdomen grey with dark median band; latter bordered by row of paired white spots; first pair yellowish and larger than rest. Legs mottled, faintly banded. **NOTES:** Found in all biomes except the more arid ones. Also sampled from maize fields in the North West province. **STATUS:** LC; African endemic. (Gekolde Tregterwebspinnekop)

Family Agelenidae 33

Mistaria
Mistaria funnel-web spiders

Medium-sized. Carapace with lateral bands. Abdomen with dark central band dorsally; sides with pale spots. Female epigyne with horseshoe-shaped epigynal pit. Male palp bears two tibial apophyses. NOTES: Frequently found in conglomerate of funnel-shaped webs made in shrubs and trees. Older, abandoned webs often covered by dust. Only one species is known from South Africa. (Mistaria-tregterwebspinnekoppe)

Mistaria zuluana
Zululand Funnel-web Spider

Carapace creamy brown with dark lateral bands and few pale patches. Abdomen dark dorsally, with darker, median band bordered by several pairs of yellow oblique spots. Legs with broad dark bands. NOTES: Sampled from Fynbos, Grassland, Nama-Karoo and Savanna. STATUS: LC; South African endemic. (Zululandse Tregterwebspinnekop)

Olorunia
Olorunia funnel-web spiders

Medium-sized. Only male known. Carapace sports broad lateral bands; eye region narrow. Abdomen narrow, oval, with median band bordered by paired pale patches. Legs long, slender. NOTES: They build funnel-webs. Monotypic. (Olorunia-tregterwebspinnekoppe)

Olorunia punctata
Lehtinen's Funnel-web Spider

Carapace yellow-brown with dark lateral bands; bands with small pale patches. Abdomen with reddish-grey median band bordered by five paired pale small patches. Coxae and femora banded. NOTES: Sampled from Grassland, Nama-Karoo, Savanna and Thicket. STATUS: LC; African endemic. (Lehtinen se Tregterwebspinnekop)

Tegenaria
House funnel-web spiders

Medium-sized. Cephalic region slightly elevated, with short lateral bands; sternum with median band and lateral spots. Abdomen with light spots or indistinct chevrons; distal segment of posterior pair of spinnerets varies in length: longer or slightly shorter than basal segment. Legs armed with spines. Male more slender than female, with very long legs. NOTES: They build funnel-webs in dark corners of outbuildings. Three synanthropic species were introduced to South Africa. (Huistregterwebspinnekoppe)

Tegenaria domestica   Common House Funnel-web Spider

One of the smaller species in the genus *Tegenaria*. Carapace greyish brown. Abdomen roundish oval, with indistinct chevrons. Legs often banded. NOTES: Synanthropic. STATUS: LC; Cosmopolitan. (Gewone Huistregterwebspinnekop)

FAMILY AMAUROBIIDAE
Mesh-web spiders   Maaswebspinnekoppe

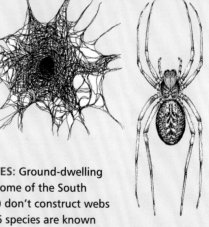

Very small to medium-sized. Carapace slightly longer than wide, narrower in eye region; eight eyes arranged in two rows (4:4); lateral bands present in some genera (absent in *Chumma*). Abdomen oval in some genera, with ill-defined chevron or mottled patterns; scutum present in *Chumma*; cribellate or ecribellate genera. Legs three-clawed, slender, of medium length. NOTES: Ground-dwelling spiders. Despite the name 'mesh-web', some of the South African genera (*Chresiona* and *Chumma*) don't construct webs and are free running. Five genera and 16 species are known from South Africa.

Chresiona   Chresiona mesh-web spiders

Small. Carapace brown, with lateral bands. Abdomen patterned, with distinct heart mark; sometimes with white reticulation. Cribellum absent. Legs banded. NOTES: Free-living ground dwellers sampled while sweeping and beating low vegetation. Three species are known, all endemic to South Africa. (Chresiona-maaswebspinnekoppe)

Chresiona invalida Invalida Mesh-web Spider

Carapace pale brown, with dark lateral and marginal bands. Abdomen ash-grey, with dark heart mark, followed by a row of chevrons in posterior half. Legs faintly banded. **NOTES:** Sampled from Fynbos, Grassland and Savanna. **STATUS:** LC; South African endemic. (Invalida-maaswebspinnekop)

Chumma **Chumma spiny-backed spiders**

Very small. Carapace oval; cephalic region well separated by cervical groove; fovea absent; chelicerae strong. Abdomen slightly flattened; field of stiff macrosetae with large sockets present anteriorly; well-developed dorsal scutum present in both sexes. Cribellum absent. Legs short, spineless or bearing only one or two spines on femora. **NOTES:** Free-living ground dwellers collected from litter layer. Eight species have been recorded in South Africa. (Chumma-stekelrugspinnekoppe)

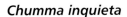

Chumma inquieta Inquieta Spiny-backed Spider

Carapace orange; eye region dark. Abdomen with dark oval scutum. Legs same colour as carapace; distal leg segments darker. **NOTES:** Some specimens sampled from dunes in the litter layer in Fynbos and Thicket. **STATUS:** Endangered; South African endemic. (Inquieta-stekelrugspinnekop)

Chumma interfluvialis — Free State Spiny-backed Spider

Carapace cream to orange-yellow; eye region dark. Abdomen bears oval scutum. Legs same colour as carapace. **NOTES:** Sampled while sifting leaf litter in the Grassland biome. **STATUS:** DD; South African endemic. (Vrystaatse Stekelrugspinnekop)

Macrobunus — Macrobunus mesh-web spiders

Small to medium-sized. Only female known. Carapace oval; fovea long; anterior median eyes larger than posterior lateral eyes. Abdomen oval. Cribellum present, undivided. Legs of medium length. **NOTES:** Ground dwellers sampled from pitfall traps. One species is known from South Africa. (Macrobunus-maaswebspinnekoppe)

Macrobunus caffer — Fynbos Mesh-web Spider

Carapace yellowish brown; cephalic region bordered by short dark bands; thoracic region bears three black spots on each side. Abdomen with dark heart mark and scattered black patches. Legs same colour as carapace, faintly banded. **NOTES:** Sampled from the Fynbos biome. **STATUS:** LC; South African endemic. (Fynbos-maaswebspinnekop)

Pseudauximus — Pseudauximus mesh-web spiders

Small to medium-sized. Carapace with long and narrow fovea. Abdomen with darker patches; layer of short, fine setae present; white reticulation visible through integument. Cribellum present, undivided. Legs long, especially in males. **NOTES:** Represented by three species endemic to South Africa. (Pseudauximus-maaswebspinnekoppe)

Family Amaurobiidae

Pseudauximus pallidus — Pallidus Mesh-web Spider

Carapace fawn; cephalic region bordered by dark bands; thoracic region with black patches. Abdomen bears distinct heart mark; faint chevrons present posteriorly. Legs faintly banded. NOTES: Collected from Fynbos and Nama-Karoo. STATUS: LC; South African endemic. (Pallidus-maaswebspinnekop)

FAMILY ARANEIDAE
Araneid orb-web spiders — Araneid-wawielwebspinnekoppe

Members of the Araneidae are very diverse. Eight eyes arranged in two rows (4:4); labium rebordered. Abdomen shape varies greatly, usually globose, overhanging the carapace, frequently covered in humps and with distinct patterns. Legs three-clawed, kept close to the body when at rest, of medium length, usually bearing numerous spines; third leg the shortest. NOTES: All make orb-webs. The spider usually hangs head down in the middle of the orb-web or is found in a tunnel-shaped retreat of silk close by. The web can be either horizontal or vertical. Some genera also make adapted or reduced orb-webs to catch specific types of prey. In South Africa the family is represented by 39 genera and 95 species.

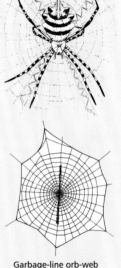

Tropical tent orb-web   Stone nest orb-web   Garbage-line orb-web

Acantharachne — Acantharachne orb-web spiders

Medium-sized. Carapace elevated, as long as wide; several short horn-like tubercles present in cephalic region; median eyes situated on low tubercle; lateral eyes widely spaced from median eyes. Abdomen wider than long; shoulders decorated with two large circle-shaped, hump-bearing, wart-like processes. Front legs only slightly longer than hind legs. NOTES: Nothing is known about their behaviour. Females rest on vegetation during the day. There are suggestions that they may forage using a bolas. One species has been recorded from South Africa. (Acantharachne-wawielwebspinnekoppe)

Acantharachne seydeli — Seydel's Orb-web Spider

Carapace brown with scattered white setae. Abdomen creamy brown with mottled brown humps; wart-like processes darker. Legs same colour as carapace; legs I and II with banded distal segments. **NOTES:** Only known from KwaZulu-Natal. **STATUS:** LC; African endemic. (Seydel se Wawielwebspinnekop)

Aethriscus — Aethriscus orb-web spiders

Medium-sized. Carapace smooth, shiny, with small tubercle level with cephalic region; eye region narrower in front. Abdomen shiny, triangular; anterior border straight with 11 sigilla; blunt round humps present on lateral borders. Legs very short, folding around the body when resting. **NOTES:** Nocturnal orb-web dwellers. When at rest on vegetation the shiny body resembles bird droppings. Endemic to Africa; only one species is known from South Africa. (Aethriscus-wawielwebspinnekoppe)

Aethriscus olivaceus — Bird-dropping Orb-web Spider

Carapace olive-brown. Abdomen olive-yellow with darker humps; posterior area paler. Legs olive-brown. **NOTES:** Sampled from Forest, Grassland, Savanna and Thicket and from avocado orchards. **STATUS:** LC; African endemic. (Voëlmis-wawielwebspinnekop)

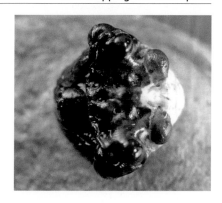

Afracantha — Afracantha orb-web spiders

Small to medium-sized. Carapace broad, with slight indentation between cephalic and thoracic region; lateral eyes close together, situated on carapace border but widely spaced from median eyes. Abdomen elevated, hard; anterior edge rounded, bearing 14 sigilla; two prominent humps posterolaterally, with another two on posterior edge. Legs short, arranged around carapace. **NOTES:** They make dense orb-webs. An African genus known from only one species. (Afracantha-wawielwebspinnekoppe)

Afracantha camerunensis — Camerunensis Orb-web Spider

Carapace dark brown with scattered white setae. Abdomen brown, mottled with white and yellow-brown, bearing scattered white setae; two humps present posterolaterally, yellowish brown, bearing dense long white setae; two humps on posterior edge, darker. Legs yellow-brown, bearing white setae. NOTES: The dense orb-web (>32 radii) is made about two metres above ground level. Known to occur in the shrub and tree layer of IOCB and Savanna. STATUS: LC; African endemic. (Camerunensis-wawielwebspinnekop)

Arachnura — Arachnura tailed spiders

Medium-sized. Carapace broad, narrower anteriorly; eyes in two rows, with posterior median eyes closely spaced. Abdomen broad; anteriorly with two V-shaped horn-like projections extending over carapace; abdomen tapers into long tail with soft humps on the tip. Legs I and II stronger than rest. NOTES: The orb-web is suspended at an angle, and has a V-shaped section missing from the top of the web. A series of woolly, brownish egg sacs are strung together and arranged in a line from the centre of the web to fill the missing section. Only one species has been recorded in South Africa. (Arachnura-stertspinnekoppe)

Arachnura scorpionoides — Scorpion-tailed Orb-web Spider

Body coloration varies between specimens, ranging from fawn to yellow. Carapace pale brown with white setae; thin dark median band extends from eyes to posterior edge. Abdomen mottled yellow with broad paler area, bordered by darker band that extends from abdominal horns to hump on tail tip. Legs same colour as carapace, faintly banded; leg II sometimes with dark longitudinal stripes along length. NOTES: Sampled from Fynbos, IOCB, Savanna and Thicket. Also sampled from macadamia orchards. STATUS: LC; African and Madagascan endemics. (Skerpioenstert-wawielwebspinnekop)

Araneus
Araneus hairy field spiders

Small to medium-sized. Species variable in colour. Carapace hairy, moderately arched, without horny outgrowths. Abdomen hairy, round to oval, overlapping carapace; shoulder humps present in some species. Legs spiny; tibiae II have ventral spines in males. **NOTES:** They make orb-webs at night. Most do not hang in the middle of the web, instead staying in retreats made to the side of the web, often between leaves. A signal thread connects them to the hub of the web. A large genus, represented by 11 species in South Africa. (Araneus-harigeveldspinnekoppe)

Araneus apricus　　　　　　　　　　Green Pea Spider

Carapace dark brown with scattered white setae. Abdomen round, soft, bright green, anteriorly with dark band that has yellowish tint. Legs paler than carapace, sometimes with distinct bands. Cryptic coloration helps it blend with the environment. Male sampled, but yet undescribed. **NOTES:** Makes an orb-web with a retreat to one side. Sampled from all biomes except the more arid ones. Also sampled from avocado, citrus and macadamia orchards and tomato fields. **STATUS:** LC; African endemic. (Groen Ertjiespinnekop)

Araneus coccinella　　　　　　　　　Coccinella Spider

Carapace fawn with scattered white setae; eye region dark. Abdomen elongated, oval, rounded posteriorly, projecting slightly past spinnerets, orange-yellow above, decorated with eight large black spots which meet posteriorly to form a dark band. Legs same colour as carapace, short, with few setae; tarsi of legs dark. **NOTES:** Orb-web dweller sampled mainly from Grassland and Savanna. **STATUS:** LC; South African endemic. (Coccinella-spinnekop)

Araneus nigroquadratus　　Black-spotted Hairy Field Spider

Carapace dark brown with white setae. Abdomen yellowish grey with dark U-shaped marking, ventrally with yellow markings bordered by white. Legs bear white setae dorsally, darker at tips. **NOTES:** Makes a large orb-web at night. Sampled from Fynbos, Grassland, IOCB and Thicket. Also sampled from pine plantations and tomato fields. **STATUS:** LC; southern African endemic. (Swartkol-harigeveldspinnekop)

Araniella
Araniella orb-web spiders

Small orb-weavers recognised by the 1–4 pairs of small black spots posterolaterally on abdomen. Carapace narrower in eye region; eyes small. Abdomen oval, slightly longer than wide. Legs with scattered erect setae, not banded but darker distally.
NOTES: Constructs an orb-web in shrubs and bushes. No retreat is made. Only one species is known from South Africa. (Araniella-wawielwebspinnekoppe)

Araniella cucurbitina
Cucumber Spider

Carapace and legs yellowish green. Abdomen with light green folium; posteriorly with three pairs of small black spots around edge; abdominal venter green; yellow or brown stripe laterally. Legs not banded, but darker distally.
NOTES: Constructs an orb-web between grasses in the Grassland biome. STATUS: LC; Cosmopolitan. (Komkommerspinnekop)

Argiope
Agriope garden orb-web spiders

Medium to large. Strong sexual dimorphism in shape and size, males being much smaller. **Female** Carapace narrower anteriorly, rounded laterally; sternum heart-shaped with wavy margin. Abdomen oval, often with lateral extensions or lobes, usually brightly coloured with distinct patterns. Legs long, slender; leg III the shortest; legs usually banded. **Male** Abdomen without lobes. NOTES: These spiders make large orb-webs in open grassland areas and gardens. Webs are usually placed low, and found in nearly any vegetation sturdy enough to bear the weight. The spider hangs in the hub, head down, throughout the day. The web is sometimes decorated with a stabilimentum. In some species the males make their own webs, in others they are found on the edge of a female's web. Eight species are known from South Africa. (Agriope-tuinwawielwebspinnekoppe)

Argiope aurocincta
Aurocincta Garden Orb-web Spider

Only female known. Carapace dark with silver setae. Abdomen sports distinct colour pattern consisting of five yellow and dark bands of varying breadth. Legs yellow to brown with distinct bands.
NOTES: Sampled from Forest, Grassland, IOCB, Nama-Karoo and Savanna. STATUS: LC; African endemic. (Aurocincta-tuinwawielwebspinnekop)

Argiope australis

Female Carapace silvery. Abdomen with bluntly rounded lobes laterally; sometimes with tail-like extension; distinct broad yellow and grey horizontal bands. Legs with dark bands. **Male** Abdomen narrow, without lobes, with two lateral bands. NOTES: Makes dense orb-webs in grassland, sometimes with one or two stabilimentum bands. Sampled from all the biomes. Also collected from crops such as avocado, peach and pistachio orchards, pine plantations and pumpkin fields. STATUS: LC; African endemic. (Australis-tuinwawielwebspinnekop)

Argiope flavipalpis

Flavipalpis Garden Orb-web Spider

Female Carapace fawn, with dense layer of setae; darker markings sometimes radiate from fovea. Abdomen has distinctly shaped lobes with sharp edges, very similar to *A. levii*. The two species differ only in the shape of the epigynum; colour varies from yellow to mottled white with grey spots. Legs banded. **Male** Abdominal dorsal pattern consists of five transverse, irregular, dark stripes on non-pigmentated white background. NOTES: Spins a new orb-web daily, sometimes with a stabilimentum along the length. Stabilimentum shape differs each day. Recorded in Forest and Savanna. STATUS: LC; African endemic. (Flavipalpis-tuinwawielwebspinnekop)

Argiope levii

Levi's Garden Orb-web Spider

Female Carapace greyish white with dense layer of setae. Abdomen distinct in shape, with pointed lateral tubercles, colour varies from yellow to mottled white with grey markings. **Male** Abdominal dorsal pattern almost absent or consists of few transverse dark bars on white background; ventrum without pattern or few faint markings on median line. NOTES: Makes orb-webs, sometimes with a stabilimentum along the length. In juveniles the stabiliment is dense, covering the central area. Sampled from Forest, Grassland, IOCB and Savanna. STATUS: LC; African endemic. (Levi se Tuinwawielwebspinnekop)

Argiope lobata
Lobata Garden Orb-web Spider

Female Carapace pale brown, covered in dense setae, giving it a silvery appearance. Abdomen has distinct yellow and grey bands, with pattern formed by dark patches present on anterior edge of each lateral blunt lobe. Legs banded. **Male** Abdominal dorsal pattern consists of two longitudinal light brown bands with darker lateral edges on white background. **NOTES:** Sampled from Fynbos, Grassland, Nama-Karoo and Savanna. **STATUS:** LC; Cosmopolitan. (Lobata-tuinwawielwebspinnekop)

Argiope tapinolobata
Long-bodied Garden Orb-web Spider

Female Carapace silvery with two dark bands; eye region darker. Abdomen almost cylindrical, twice as long as wide, with very shallow lobes, few brown transverse bands present laterally; posterior end of abdomen extends tail-like past spinnerets. Legs banded. **Male** Abdomen without bands. **NOTES:** Sampled from the Grassland biome in Gauteng. **STATUS:** LC; southern African endemic. (Langlyf-tuinwawielwebspinnekop)

Argiope trifasciata
Trifasciata Garden Orb-web Spider

Female Carapace silvery with markings radiating from fovea; eye region darker. Abdomen sports dorsal pattern with numerous transverse brown lines, bordering fawn and silver bands; sides of carapace undulating; ventrum dark, bordered by white bands. Legs banded. **Male** Abdomen without any lateral extensions; dorsal abdominal pattern consisting of numerous transverse brown lines on yellowish white background. **NOTES:** Sampled from all biomes except the more arid ones. Also sampled from crops such as cotton, kenaf, lucerne and tomato. **STATUS:** LC; Cosmopolitan. (Trifasciata-tuinwawielwebspinnekop)

Bijoaraneus
Bijoaraneus hairy field spiders

Small to medium-sized. Carapace longer than wide. Abdomen round to oval, overlapping the carapace. Legs of medium length, spiny. **NOTES:** Makes an orb-web with a silk retreat in a folded leaf next to web. A signal thread from the retreat leads to the hub of the web. One species is known from South Africa. (Bijoaraneus-harigeveldspinnekoppe)

Bijoaraneus legonensis
Bum-eyed Hairy Field Spider

Carapace brown, sometimes with green tint; eye region dark. Abdomen mottled white dorsally, bottle-green ventrally, dorsally distinctly decorated with kindney-shaped dark marking anteriorly and four dark spots on posterior edge. Leg colour similar to carapace. **NOTES:** Makes an orb-web with a silk retreat in a folded leaf next to web. When in danger the spider tilts its abdomen upwards, showing a row of dark spots. Sampled from Fynbos, Savanna and Thicket. **STATUS:** LC; African endemic. (Kolstert-harigeveldspinnekop)

Caerostris
Caerostris bark spiders

Large. Body with dense layer of setae with horny or leathery protuberances on carapace and abdomen. Carapace with transversal row of four conical humps in upper cephalic region; median eyes closely grouped on small tubercles; sternum variable, in some species covered in white or black setae. Abdomen roundish oval; dorsal plane varies in shape between species or even in the same species, bearing tubercles that resemble bark structure; abdomen venter also variable, with four, two or no white spots. Legs with dense rows of long setae that fit snugly around the body when resting; femur IV bearing spatulate or slender setae. Males rare, resemble females but are much smaller. **NOTES:** They construct large, complete vertical orb-webs, with many radii and viscid spirals. The web is made between trees, and the bridge line can be several metres across. It is constructed when the sun sets and removed early in the morning. The bridge line is usually left intact and used again the next night. During the day these spiders rest on the bark of a nearby tree. On cloudy days, they are sometimes found in the web. Four species are known from South Africa. (Caerostris-basspinnekoppe)

Caerostris sexcuspidata

Family Araneidae 45

Caerostris corticosa

Bare-legged Bark Spider

Carapace greyish brown, hairy; sternum covered in dense white setae. Abdomen resembles *C. sexcuspidata* in colour and general character, but has a uniformly dark ventral surface. Legs same colour as carapace; femur IV without spatulate setae. **NOTES:** Makes a large orb-web between shrubs and trees. Sampled from Fynbos, Grassland, Savanna and Succulent Karoo. **STATUS:** LC; southern African endemic. (Kaalbeen-basspinnekop)

Caerostris sexcuspidata

Horned Bark Spider

Carapace greyish brown. Abdomen dorsally variable with differently shaped tubercles; ventrally variable with either no markings or two or three distinct white spots. Legs greyish brown; femur IV with spatulate setae on posterior edge. **NOTES:** A very common species widespread throughout South Africa. Found in all biomes except Desert. Also sampled from various crops, including apple, citrus, pine plantations and tomato fields. **STATUS:** LC; African endemic. (Horingbasspinnekop)

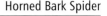

Caerostris vicina

Vicina Bark Spider

Carapace greyish brown with tubercles in eye region. Abdomen dorsally flattened, with small tubercles; ventrally without distinct white spots. Femur IV with spatulate setae on posterior edge. **NOTES:** Makes a large orb-web. Sampled in Forest and Savanna. **STATUS:** LC; African endemic. (Vicina-basspinnekop)

Cladomelea
African bolas spiders

Small to medium-sized. Carapace with three long, sharp-tipped protuberances arranged in median row. Abdomen decorated with humps, tubercles and tufts of strong setae. Legs I and II longer than rest, densely covered in long, thin setae. Sexes differ in colour, size and shape. Males much smaller, darker and without humps. NOTES: Female bolas spiders construct a reduced orb-web at night. The web consists of a strand of silk terminating in 1–3 sticky droplets, known as a bolas. The silk thread is held by one of the second pair of legs, while the spider hangs, using the fourth pair of legs, from a trapeze line constructed in foliage. It then swings the bolas rapidly until it contacts flying prey, usually a moth. The spider rapidly reels in the thread, drawing in its prey. These spiders usually rest in a retreat in foliage during the day. The egg sacs are round, brown, and attached to twigs close to the trapeze line. Three species are known from South Africa. (Afrika-bolasspinnekoppe)

Cladomelea akermani
Akerman's Bolas Spider

Carapace yellow-brown, three protuberances dark. Abdomen triangular, yellowish brown, with >20 small blunt yellow humps, each bearing a tuft of setae. Legs same colour as carapace, covered by dense layer of setae. NOTES: Has a restricted distribution in KwaZulu-Natal. Found in open grasslands. STATUS: Vulnerable; South African endemic. (Akerman se Bolasspinnekop)

Cladomelea debeeri
Debeer's Bolas Spider

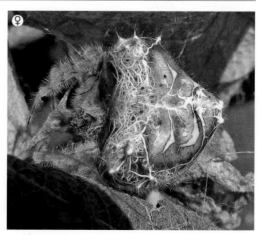

Carapace yellow-brown, covered in dense setae; protuberances dark. Abdomen fawn, mottled with yellow and rose-coloured patches, triangular, anterolateral corners studded with five prominent humps; latter cream at base and dark at tip and bearing a tuft of long white setae. Legs creamish white with dark bands, covered in long white woolly setae. NOTES: It has a restricted distribution in KwaZulu-Natal. STATUS: Vulnerable; South African endemic. (Debeer se Bolasspinnekop)

Cladomelea longipes Pink Bolas Spider

Carapace broad, greyish pink, covered in dense setae, giving it a woolly appearance, with three dark protuberances. Abdomen triangular, dorsally pink, with silky setae, giving it a woolly appearance; decorated with >20 round white humps, each bearing a tuft of white setae; humps vary in size between specimens; two humps laterally larger and yellow in colour. Legs yellowish with dense setae, banded. **NOTES:** Found in shrubland in the Savanna biome. **STATUS:** LC; African endemic. (Pienk Bolasspinnekop)

Clitaetra Clitaetra tree orb-web spiders

Medium-sized. **Female** Carapace round, slightly flattened; lateral eyes widely separated, posterior lateral eyes larger than posterior median eyes. Abdomen pentagonal, flattened, with five pairs of dorsomedian sigilla. Legs slender with scattered setae. **Male** Abdomen oval, with three pairs of dorsal sigilla and scutum. **NOTES:** These spiders typically spin elongated orb-webs over tree trunks. The hub of the orb is reinforced with fine silk mesh. The spider rests at the hub, often with prey remains suspended above the hub. One species is known from South Africa. (Clitaetra-boomwawielwebspinnekoppe)

Clitaetra irenae Irene's Tree Orb-web Spider

Carapace and chelicerae yellow-grey with white marginal band. Abdomen pale grey with brown and white pattern and pair of red patches laterally. Legs whitish yellow, with dark brown spine sockets and spines; tarsi brown. **NOTES:** Restricted to Savanna biome in KwaZulu-Natal. **STATUS:** LC; African endemic. (Irene se Boomwawielwebspinnekop)

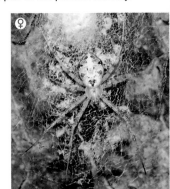

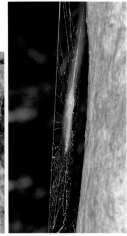

Cyclosa
Garbage-line spiders

Small to medium-sized. Carapace longer than wide, narrowed anteriorly; eight eyes in two rows (4:4). Abdomen longer than wide, overhanging carapace; posterior end decorated with tubercles in female, blunt in male. Legs of medium length. NOTES: They make a complete, vertical, closely woven orb-web in vegetation. A stabilimentum of the bodies of dead prey and other debris passes vertically through the hub. The spider often sits amid this structure, or at one end of it, thus achieving a remarkable degree of camouflage. Three species are known from South Africa. (Afvallynspinnekoppe)

Cyclosa elongatus
Long-tailed Garbage-line Spider

Carapace dark. Abdomen elongated, cryptic, with mottled brown and white patches; blunt tubercle extends tail-like past spinnerets. Legs same colour as abdomen, with darker bands. NOTES: Its orb-web is commonly found in Forest, Fynbos, Grassland and Savanna. Also sampled from citrus and pistachio orchards, and cotton fields. STATUS: LC; South African endemic. (Langstert-afvallynspinnekop)

Cyclosa insulana
Insulana Garbage-line Spider

Carapace brown. Abdomen with broad longitudinal silvery white band that extends to posterior tip; posterior end tail-like, extending past spinnerets, with three tubercles in female, blunt in male. Legs with dark bands. NOTES: This common species has been sampled from all biomes. Also recorded in crops such as avocado, citrus orchards and tomato fields. STATUS: LC; Cosmopolitan. (Insulana-afvallynspinnekop)

Cyclosa oculata
Oculata Garbage-line Spider

Carapace dark brown to black. Abdomen dark red-brown to black, sometimes with paler pattern; posterior end with three dorsal tubercles, anterior end with two. Legs banded. NOTES: Sampled from Forest, Fynbos, Grassland and Savanna as well as from citrus, cotton, macadamia and potatoes. STATUS: LC; cosmopolitan. (Oculata-afvallynspinnekop)

Cyphalonotus
Twig spiders

Small to medium-sized. *Cyphalonotus* can be recognised by the abdomen being much higher than wide. Carapace hairy; eight eyes slightly separated on a forward-protruding eye tubercle; lateral eyes close together at base of eye tubercle. Abdomen hairy, same colour as carapace; with numerous anterodorsal humps and tubercles. Legs I and II longer than rest; legs protruding upwards. NOTES: Makes a large vertical orb-web at night. One species is known from South Africa. (Takkiespinnekoppe)

Cyphalonotus larvatus
Larvatus Twig Spider

Carapace cryptic greyish brown. Abdomen triangular in lateral view, dorsal part with large hump; abdomen same colour as carapace. Legs same colour as body, with scattered dark setae. NOTES: The spider hangs in the centre of the large orb-web with the legs spread out. When disturbed, the web is pulled together with the legs. The spider takes the web down during the day, when it rests on bark with the legs protruding into the air, resembling a twig. Sampled from Forest, Fynbos, Grassland and Savanna. STATUS: LC; African endemic. (Larvatus-takkiespinnekop)

Cyrtarachne
Cyrtarachne bird-dropping spiders

Small to medium-sized. **Female** Carapace convex with rugged surface; fovea absent; both eye rows recurved; lateral eyes contiguous. Abdomen large, triangular, wider than long, with paired sigilla; dorsum shiny, appearing hard and shell-like. Legs short; integument leathery, with bands and spots. **Male** Much smaller. NOTES: During the day these spiders rest on nearby vegetation mimicking bird droppings. They construct a 'spanning thread-web': a basic orb-web, but the web diameter, sticky spiral spacing, and viscid thread diameter are larger than that of typical orb-webs. Only one species is known from South Africa. (Cyrtarachne-voëlmisspinnekoppe)

Cyrtarachne ixoides female on leaf

Cyrtarachne ixoides — White-banded Bird-dropping Spider

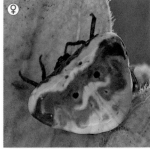

Female Carapace brown, shiny. Abdomen decorated with irregular horizontal bands of white and brown, paired sigilla present centrally; dorsum shiny. Legs short.
NOTES: Sampled from Fynbos, Grassland, Savanna and Thicket.
STATUS: LC; Cosmopolitan.
(Witband-voëlmisspinnekop)

Cyrtophora — Cyrtophora tent-web spiders

Small to medium-sized. Carapace longer than wide; eight eyes in two rows (4:4), with lateral eyes on small tubercles. Abdomen longer than wide, overhanging the carapace, decorated with six blunt tubercles. Legs moderately long, stout, usually pulled close to

the body. Males much smaller, without abdominal tubercles.
NOTES: The adapted orb-web consists of a fine-meshed sheet, similar to the enlarged central area of orb-webs, but made of dry silk and arranged horizontally. It is positioned in an irregular support system consisting of silk threads above and below the mesh. The top structure is denser than the bottom structure. Two species are known from South Africa.
(Cyrtophora-tentwebspinnekoppe)

Tropical tent-web

Cyrtophora citricola — Tropical Tent-web Spider

Female Carapace almost flat dorsally, dark, but covered in dense layer of white setae. Abdomen varies in colour from reddish brown to black with white spots to almost creamish brown. Legs banded.
NOTES: The spider hangs upside-down in the web's centre. Insects flying into the top support system are knocked down and grasped by the spider, hence the name 'knock-down trap'. Sampled from all the biomes except the more arid ones. **STATUS:** LC; cosmopolitan.
(Tropiese Tentwebspinnekop)

Cyrtophora petersi

Peters' Tent-web Spider

Carapace dark, covered in a dense layer of white setae. Abdomen overhangs carapace; longer than wide, slightly flattened, bearing tubercles near edge; varies in colour from black with white spots to almost creamish brown. Legs banded. NOTES: The female's tent-webs have a dead leaf suspended from the hub of the web. Females were found resting beneath the leaf, whereas males tend to rest on other parts of the tent-web. Sampled from a citrus orchard in the Savanna biome. STATUS: LC; southern African endemic. (Peters se Tentwebspinnekop)

 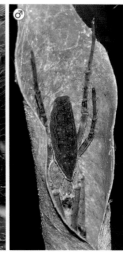

Eriovixia

Eriovixia araneid spiders

Small. Carapace as wide as long; cephalic region raised, bearing dense setae; eyes on tubercles more distinct in males. Abdomen hairy, almost round, save for pronounced, easily visible, round humps that vary from small humps to pointed extensions. Male abdomen decorated with setae and white spots. Legs short, grouped together around carapace; male legs with long spines. NOTES: These spiders spin typical orb-webs between vegetation. Web renewed daily. During the day they take up position on top of a leaf. This is possibly another bird-dropping mimic. One species has been recorded from South Africa. (Eriovixia-araneidspinnekoppe)

Eriovixia excelsa

Humpback Spider

Female Carapace dark, covered in dense layer of white setae. Abdomen usually brownish grey to dark brown; integument covered in short stiff setae; abdomen with yellow spots ventrally. Legs same colour as carapace, with white setae. **Male** Carapace dark, with few setae. Abdomen dark, decorated with setae and white spots. Legs with long spines. NOTES: Sampled from Grassland and Savanna. STATUS: LC; Cosmopolitan. (Boggelrugspinnekop)

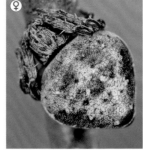 

Gasteracantha
Gasteracantha kite spiders

Small to medium-sized. Brightly coloured with striking patterns. Carapace usually as wide as long, partly covered by abdomen; eyes in two rows (4:4), widely spaced. Abdomen wider than long, with hard, shell-like flattened area; variation in colour and shape between species; dorsally decorated with modified lateral and posterior spines that differ in length and shape between species; number of small sigilla present. Sexes differ in appearance. Males are smaller in size and the abdomen is without spines. NOTES: The web is a complete orb, made either vertically or on an inclined plane, with an open hub, many radii, and viscid spirals. The orb-webs are usually made high in trees or tall shrubs above the observer's eye level, giving the impression that the spider is floating in space. The bridge line is frequently longer than the orb section. These spiders are active during the day and do not remove their webs. Four species are known from South Africa. (Gasteracantha-vlieërspinnekoppe)

Gasteracantha falcicornis
Long-wing Kite Spider

Carapace reddish brown. Abdomen reddish brown, decorated with yellow bands; abdominal spines with spine II very long, curving backwards; longer than width of abdomen. Legs short, darker than carapace. NOTES: Commonly found in the warmer tropical regions. Sampled from the Savanna biome. STATUS: LC; African endemic. (Langvlerk-vlieërspinnekop)

Gasteracantha milvoides
Medium-wing Kite Spider

Carapace orange-brown, bearing white setae. Abdomen white or yellow, decorated with red; sigilla with dark spots; dorsum wider than long; abdominal spines with spine II directed sideways. Legs short, darker than carapace. NOTES: Commonly found in the warmer tropical regions. Sampled from Forest, Grassland, Savanna and Thicket. STATUS: LC; African endemic. (Mediumvlerk-vlieërspinnekop)

Gasteracantha sanguinolenta — Short-wing Kite Spider

Carapace dark. Abdomen yellow or white, decorated with dark patterns, wider than long; abdominal spines with spine II short, directed sideways. Legs short, same colour as carapace. **NOTES:** Very common in South Africa. Sampled from all biomes except the more arid ones. **STATUS:** LC; African endemic. (Kortvlerk-vlieërspinnekop)

Gasteracantha versicolor — Common Kite Spider

Carapace reddish brown. Abdomen yellow or white, decorated with broad dark red bands; abdominal spines present; spine II long. Legs short, dark in colour. **NOTES:** Sampled from Forest, Fynbos, Grassland, IOCB and Savanna. Also sampled from citrus orchards. **STATUS:** LC; African endemic. (Gewone Vlieërspinnekop)

Gastroxya — Gastroxya kite spiders

Small. Carapace wider than long, covered in white setae; fovea longitudinal; lateral eyes closely spaced near lateral edge; cheliceral furrow with two rows of teeth; sternum with curved tip. Dorsum of abdomen with double row of 18 marginal sigilla; four sigilla form trapezoid medially with double row on posterior border; ventrum without protuberances. **NOTES:** Rare orb-web spiders; poorly known. One species has been recorded in South Africa. (Gastroxya-vlieërspinnekoppe)

Gastroxya benoiti Benoit's Kite Spider

Only female known. Carapace dark, covered in dense white setae. Abdomen dark, mottled with brown and white setae; marginal sigilla white. NOTES: Rare orb-web spiders; nothing is known about their behaviour. Sampled from Savanna and Thicket. STATUS: DD for taxonomic reasons. South African endemic. (Benoit se Vlieërspinnekop)

Gea Gea orb-web spiders

Medium-sized. These spiders differ from most araneid genera by having a strongly procurved posterior eye row. Carapace round, narrower in eye region, clothed in white setae; anterior eyes evenly spaced; posterior median eyes large. Abdomen shield-shaped, anteriorly truncated, with slight shoulders, narrowing towards spinnerets. Legs long, banded. NOTES: They build vertical webs in open spaces among shrubs or low herbs. The spider is typically found at the hub of the web with legs I and II spread forward and legs III and IV directed backward. The web consists of closely spaced radii and spirals. One species has been recorded in South Africa. (Gea-wawielwebspinnekoppe)

Gea infuscata Infuscata Orb-web Spider

Carapace reddish brown with dense white setae. Abdomen with white, reddish-brown and dark bands, dark patch present posteriorly. Legs resemble carapace, with white setae, faintly banded. NOTES: Sampled from Forest, Fynbos and Savanna. STATUS: LC; African endemic. (Infuscata-wawielwebspinnekop)

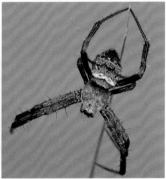

Hypsacantha Hypsacantha box kite spiders

Small. Carapace broad; median eyes on small tubercles; lateral eyes situated near border of carapace. Abdomen hard, leathery; anterior edge slightly rounded, with two small tubercles and six sigilla; abdomen slopes slightly to the rear, with two pairs of small tubercles, median pair pointing upwards. Legs short, same colour as carapace. NOTES: Orb-web spiders. Nothing more is known about their behaviour. A monotypic African genus. (Hypsacantha-boksvlieërspinnekoppe)

Hypsacantha crucimaculata
Crucimaculata Box Kite Spider

Carapace dark brown with strong white setae. Abdomen brown, mottled, with spots and short white median band; anterior edge slightly rounded with two small tubercles. Legs same colour as carapace. NOTES: Sampled from Nama-Karoo and Savanna. STATUS: LC; African endemic. (Crucimaculata-boksvlieërspinnekop)

Hypsosinga
False pyjama spiders

Small. Carapace smooth, shiny; *Hypsosinga* eyes differ from those of *Singa*: posterior median eyes are the largest; ocular quadrangle wider behind than in front, or rectangular; no thoracic depression. Abdomen oval, widest in the middle; dorsal pattern consists of paired dark longitudinal bands or large paired spots. NOTES: Makes a complete orb-web, usually with a retreat. They live on low plants where their small orb-webs frequently go unnoticed. Three species are known from South Africa. (Valspajamaspinnekoppe)

Hypsosinga holzapfelae
Black-spot False Pyjama Spider

Carapace yellow; eye region dark. Abdomen white, sometimes tinted with red, with two pairs of black spots. Legs uniformly yellow; distal segments tinted. NOTES: Orb-web spiders sampled from Grassland and Savanna. Also sampled from macadamia, avocado and tomato fields. STATUS: LC; African endemic. (Swartkol-valspajamaspinnekop)

Hypsosinga lithyphantoides
Banded False Pyjama Spider

Female Carapace dark, shiny. Abdomen dorsum shiny black with white median band bordered by dark lateral bands; irregular orange band on lateral edge. Legs same colour as carapace. **Male** Dark, without orange markings. NOTES: Sampled from Grassland, IOCB and Savanna. Also sampled from agroecosystems. STATUS: LC; African endemic. (Streep-valspajamaspinnekop)

Hypsosinga pygmaea

Spotted False Pyjama Spider

Carapace fawn with two dark lateral bands; eye region dark. Abdomen dorsum shiny, white with faint lateral bands and black spots. Legs same colour as carapace, banded. NOTES: Commonly sampled from Grassland and Savanna. STATUS: LC; Cosmopolitan. (Gekolde Valspajamaspinnekop)

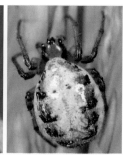

Ideocaira

Ideocaira triangle orb-web spiders

Medium-sized. Recognised by the triangular shape of the abdomen. Carapace pear-shaped; eye region narrowed, more so in males; median eyes grouped together; posterior median eyes larger than anterior median eyes; cephalic region slightly elevated; fovea longitudinal. Abdomen truncated anteriorly. Front legs strong, with strong setae on tibiae; when resting the legs are pulled close to the body. NOTES: These spiders make orb-webs at night, but little else is known about their behaviour. Two endemic species are known from South Africa. (Ideocaira-driehoek-wawielwebspinnekoppe)

Ideocaira transversa

Brown Triangle Orb-web Spider

Carapace dull brown, with scattered white setae; eye region paler; fovea dark. Abdomen brown with greenish tint; anterior edge with long white setae; shoulder with paired short white bands; white V-shaped marking on posterior edge. Legs same colour as carapace. NOTES: Recorded from Fynbos, Savanna and Thicket. STATUS: LC; South African endemic. (Bruin Driehoek-wawielwebspinnekop)

Ideocaira triquetra

Orange Triangle Orb-web Spider

Carapace orange-brown, covered in pale setae; fovea dark; eyes on tubercle in males. Abdomen same colour as carapace; white V-shaped marking on posterior edge; dorsum with pale setae cover. Legs same colour as body. NOTES: An orb-web spider recorded from Fynbos, Savanna and Thicket. STATUS: LC; South African endemic. (Oranje Driehoek-wawielwebspinnekop)

Isoxya

Box kite spiders

Small to medium-sized. Carapace as wide as long. Abdomen brightly decorated with yellow, red or black and white patterns; dorsal part hardened to form rigid scutum with spots and depressions, prolonged laterally and posteriorly with spine-like extensions; spinnerets surrounded by sclerotised ring. Legs relatively short. Sexes differ in size, shape and colour. NOTES: These spiders make large orb-webs, usually high up in trees. They are found in the web during the day. The web spiral is usually decorated with small silk tufts. The egg sacs are covered in loosely woven silk threads, and attached to vegetation near the web. Six species are known from South Africa. (Boksvlieërspinnekoppe)

Isoxya stuhlmanni in web

Isoxya cicatricosa

Black-and-white Box Kite Spider

Carapace dark, with dense layer of white setae. Abdomen dark, decorated with white patches that vary in size and are arranged in vertical and horizontal rows; spine-like extensions dark. Legs dark, same colour as carapace, bearing scattered white setae. NOTES: Found in all biomes except Desert and Succulent Karoo. STATUS: LC; African endemic. (Swart-en-wit Boksvlieërspinnekop)

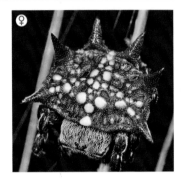

Isoxya mossamedensis

Angola Box Kite Spider

Carapace dark, with dense layer of white setae. Abdomen dark with closely grouped white patches; six reddish-brown, spine-like extensions, sharply pointed; abdomen slightly narrower towards rear. Legs same colour as carapace. NOTES: Sampled from Fynbos and Grassland. STATUS: LC; southern African endemic. (Angolese Boksvlieërspinnekop)

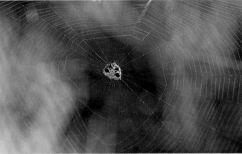

Isoxya mucronata

Mucronata Box Kite Spider

Carapace dark, with scattered white setae. Abdomen dull orange-brown, decorated with white median band; spine-like extensions short and darker than rest of abdomen. Legs same colour as carapace; distal leg segments reddish brown. NOTES: Sampled from Forest, Grassland and IOCB. STATUS: LC; African endemic. (Mucronata-boksvlieërspinnekop)

Isoxya tabulata

Yellow Box Kite Spider

Carapace dark brown with white setae. Abdomen bright yellow-orange; bearing numerous narrow spots and depressions; spine-like extensions short and dark. Legs same colour as carapace. NOTES: Sampled from Forest, Grassland, IOCB, Savanna and Thicket. STATUS: LC; African endemic. (Geel Boksvlieërspinnekop)

Kilima

Kilima grass orb-web spiders

Medium-sized. Carapace elongated, eyes in two rows (4:4). Abdomen elongated oval, with median and lateral bands. Legs slender, of medium length. NOTES: Common grassland spiders. Found in their large orb-webs when the sun sets. At sunrise they leave the web intact, resting on nearby grasses during the day. One species is known from South Africa. (Kilima-graswawielwebspinnekoppe)

Kilima decens

Kilima Grass Orb-web Spider

Carapace fawn with dark median band that is covered in long white setae. Abdomen with narrow orange median band bordered by thin bands that vary from white to brown, followed by broader dark brown lateral bands with scalloped edge; abdomen with long setae. Leg colour like carapace. NOTES: Sampled from Fynbos, Grassland, IOCB and Savanna. Also collected from potato and pumpkin fields. STATUS: LC; African endemic. (Kilima-graswawielwebspinnekop)

Larinia Larinia grass orb-web spiders

Medium-sized. Carapace longer than wide, with short, grooved longitudinal fovea; anterior median eyes largest. Abdomen elongated. Leg I longest, leg III shortest. NOTES: Typical grassland species, resembling grass in shape and colour. These spiders construct loosely woven orb-webs. During the day they rest with their body and legs stretched along a blade of grass. Three species are known from South Africa. (Larinia-graswawielwebspinnekoppe)

Larinia bifida Bifida Grass Orb-web Spider

Carapace fawn with broad dark median band and dark marginal bands. Abdomen with curvy longitudinal bands consisting of narrow reddish band bordered by white bands with a thin black scalloped edge. Legs same colour as carapace, faintly banded, with strong setae, especially on legs I and II. Easily confused with *Kilima decens*, but the median lines on the abdomen differ in shape. NOTES: Sampled from Fynbos and Grassland. STATUS: LC; African endemic. (Bifida-graswawielwebspinnekop)

Larinia chloris Chloris Grass Orb-web Spider

Carapace fawn with dark median band. Abdomen with several longitudinal white, maroon and grey bands; anterior edge has small hump; abdomen with numerous scattered white setae. Legs fawn with longitudinal reddish band, bear strong setae. NOTES: Sampled from Fynbos, Grassland, Thicket and Savanna. STATUS: LC; Cosmopolitan. (Chloris-graswawielwebspinnekop)

Lipocrea Lipocrea grass orb-web spiders

Medium-sized. Carapace elongated, pear-shaped, narrower in eye region; fovea elongated, with narrow longitudinal band dorsally. Abdomen oval, elongated with narrow tip anteriorly and slight hump above spinnerets. Legs very long, decorated with spots and setae. NOTES: They make orb-webs in grass at night and rest on nearby blades during the day. They typically do not remove the web in the morning. Monotypic; African endemic. (Lipocrea-graswawielwebspinnekoppe)

Lipocrea longissima female at rest

Lipocrea longissima Long-tailed Grass Orb-web Spider

Carapace straw-coloured with median band. Abdomen straw-coloured with several longitudinal bands, some with pinkish colour; frequently with five paired black spots. Legs same colour as body, bear setae with dark spots at their base. NOTES: Makes orb-webs in Forest, Fynbos, Grassland, IOCB and Savanna. Also sampled from avocado and pecan orchards, as well as tomato fields. STATUS: LC; African endemic. (Langstert-graswawielwebspinnekop)

Mahembea Mahembea grass orb-web spiders

Medium-sized. Carapace elongated oval; lateral eyes closely grouped. Abdomen elongated, extends past spinnerets, covered in long setae, with thin paired longitudinal bands. Legs same colour as body, bear setae with dark spots at their base. NOTES: They make orb-webs in grass at night and remove them early in the morning. Monotypic; African endemic. (Mahembea-graswawielwebspinnekoppe)

Mahembea hewitti Hewitt's Grass Orb-web Spider

Carapace narrow, straw-coloured with dark median band; median area clothed in long white setae. Abdomen orange with spotted appearance, four narrow yellow bands curve over length of abdomen. Legs same colour as carapace, with faint reddish bands. NOTES: Makes webs in the Forest, IOCB and Savanna. Also sampled from sugarcane fields. STATUS: LC; African endemic. (Hewitt se Graswawielwebspinnekop)

Megaraneus Megaraneus tree orb-web spiders

Females large; males small. Carapace longer than wide; narrower in eye region; fovea a median indentation; integument covered by minute, round, wart-like tubercles. Abdomen has three pairs of blunt lateral sub-angular tubercles and one on anterior edge; posterior abdomen with blunt extension; dorsum with two pairs of large round sigilla and about 50 smaller pit-like impressions. Leg I shorter than IV. NOTES: These spiders make orb-webs in herbaceous plants at a height of 1–1.5m. The web consists of 25–30 radii with 25 viscid spirals. The free zone is narrow, and the hub is a fairly small, rounded area. Monotypic; African endemic. (Megaraneus-boomwawielwebspinnekoppe)

Megaraneus gabonensis Gabon Tree Orb-web Spider

Carapace blackish brown, covered in short golden setae; pale marginal band present; eye tubercles sometimes partly reddish. Abdomen dark with variable pattern of yellow markings. Legs black. **NOTES:** Sampled from the IOCB biome. **STATUS:** LC; African endemic. (Gaboenese Boomwawielwebspinnekop)

Nemoscolus Stone-nest spiders

Small spiders. Carapace pear-shaped, narrower in eye region. Abdomen roundish oval. Legs same colour as carapace, kept tight against the body. Males slightly smaller than females. **NOTES:** Their adapted orb-webs are known as stone-nest webs because of the tube-like retreat made of small stones and silk in the centre of the horizontal orb-web. It serves as a retreat and a repository for eggs. The spider sits in the entrance of the retreat waiting for prey. The webs are usually made in grass and lack a stabilimentum. Prey usually comprises jumping insects like second-instar locusts. Four species are known from South Africa. (Klipnessiespinnekoppe)

Nemoscolus obscurus at rest

Nemoscolus cotti Cott's Stone-nest Spider

Only male described. Carapace dark, shiny. Abdomen roundish oval, fawn, with two lateral bands originating from anterior edge and merging near posterior edge. Legs pale brown. **NOTES:** Sampled from Grassland, Nama-Karoo and Savanna. **STATUS:** LC; South African endemic. (Cott se Klipnessiespinnekop)

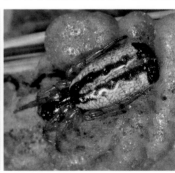

Nemoscolus obscurus

Brown Stone-nest Spider

Carapace dark brown; eye region dark. Abdomen dark with four oblique lateral spots on each side; 10 smaller spots arranged in pairs along length of abdomen. Legs same colour as carapace. **NOTES:** The stone-nest consists of a long silk tube covered in small stones. Sampled from the Savanna biome. **STATUS:** LC; South African endemic. (Bruin Klipnessiespinnekop)

Nemoscolus tubicola

Tube Stone-nest Spider

Carapace brown; eye region dark. Abdomen creamy white with paired brown patches. Legs same colour as carapace. **NOTES:** The stone-nest of this species is short and U-shaped. Sampled from Desert, Fynbos, Grassland, Nama-Karoo, Savanna, Succulent Karoo and Thicket. **STATUS:** LC; southern African endemic. (Buisweb-klipnessiespinnekop)

Nemoscolus vigintipunctatus

Spotted Stone-nest Spider

Carapace dark. Abdomen elongated, creamy white, with dark spots of varying size arranged in paired rows. Legs dark, banded. **NOTES:** Sampled from Forest, Fynbos, Grassland, IOCB, Savanna and Succulent Karoo. **STATUS:** LC; southern African endemic. (Gekolde Klipnessiespinnekop)

Neoscona — Neoscona hairy field spiders

Small to medium-sized, males smaller. Very diverse in shape and colour. Carapace as wide as long, usually with dense layer of setae. Abdomen oval, elongated or triangular, sometimes with paired anterolateral humps; abdomen overhangs carapace. Legs of medium length, kept close to body at rest. Sexes differ in size and colour; males bear cluster of stout macrosetae prolaterally on tibiae I and II. **NOTES:** The orb-webs are usually vertical, with an open hub except for a few cross threads. The spider hunts at night, and remains in a retreat, usually within a curled leaf, near the web during daylight hours. Represented by 17 species in South Africa. (Neoscona-harigeveldspinnekoppe)

Neoscona alberti — Albert's Hairy Field Spider

Carapace brown to greyish black, covered in dense white setae. Abdomen longer than wide, with distinct shoulders overhanging carapace; heart mark distinct; folium pattern in posterior part; ventrum has broad median band with two pale spots. Legs of medium length, banded. **NOTES:** Known from Grassland and Thicket. **STATUS:** LC; African endemic. (Albert se Harigeveldspinnekop)

Neoscona blondeli — Blondel's Hairy Field Spider

Carapace cream to brown to greyish black, bears dense white setae. Abdomen longer than wide, with round shoulders; variable dark folium pattern; in juveniles dark triangular. Legs banded. **NOTES:** Sampled from all the biomes except Desert and Succulent Karoo. Also found in crops such as avocado, cotton, pecans, pistachio, tomatoes and vineyards. **STATUS:** LC; African endemic. (Blondel se Harigeveldspinnekop)

Neoscona hirta — Hirta Hairy Field Spider

Carapace creamy brown to greyish red with dense white setae. Abdomen covered in dense setae and scattered long dark setae; folium pattern faint or absent. Legs same colour as body. **NOTES:** Sampled from Fynbos, Grassland, Savanna and Thicket. Also found in vineyards. **STATUS:** LC; African endemic. (Hirta-harigeveldspinnekop)

Neoscona moreli   Morel's Hairy Field Spider

Carapace dark, sporting lateral bands with dense white setae. Abdomen elongated oval, with distinct broad white median band bordered by scalloped darker bands, followed by dark band with white patches. Legs same colour as carapace, banded. **NOTES:** Sampled from Forest, Grassland, IOCB, Nama- and Succulent Karoo, Savanna and Thicket. Also sampled from avocado, pecan and pistachio orchards, and cotton, lucerne, maize and tomato fields. **STATUS:** LC; Cosmopolitan. (Morel se Harigeveldspinnekop)

Neoscona penicillipes   Large Hairy Field Spider

Carapace reddish brown; covered in dense short white setae. Abdomen as wide as long, with round shoulders, variable in colour, sometimes with folium pattern or spotted appearance. Legs same colour as carapace, with scattered short erect setae. **NOTES:** Sampled from Grassland, Nama-Karoo, Savanna, Succulent Karoo and Thicket. **STATUS:** LC; African endemic. (Groot Harigeveldspinnekop)

Neoscona quincasea   Quincasea Hairy Field Spider

Carapace brown, covered in short white setae. Abdomen fawn to brown, sometimes with green tint, longer than wide, with round shoulders; folium pattern varies between specimens and sexes. Legs of medium length, banded. **NOTES:** Sampled from Forest, Fynbos, Grassland, IOCB, Nama-Karoo and Savanna. Also sampled from pine plantations and vineyards. **STATUS:** LC; African endemic. (Quincasea-harigeveldspinnekop)

Neoscona rapta — Rapta Hairy Field Spider

Carapace brown with darker markings and dense layer of white setae. Abdomen uniformly grey to brown with dark triangular pattern on anterior border. Legs brown, banded. **NOTES:** Sampled from all biomes, except the more arid ones. Also sampled from pistachio orchards. **STATUS:** LC; African endemic. (Rapta-harigeveldspinnekop)

Neoscona rufipalpis — Rufipalpis Hairy Field Spider

Carapace dark brown with white setae. Abdomen as wide as long; colour varies from fawn to pale green; dark band at anterior edge; folium pattern absent or faint; dark sigilla and faint transverse bands formed by dense setae. Legs brown and faintly banded. **NOTES:** Makes an orb-web, usually in trees. The silk threads have a golden sheen. The spider constructs a funnel-shaped retreat using leaves and silk. Sampled from most biomes except the more arid ones. Also collected from avocado, citrus and macadamia orchards. **STATUS:** LC; African endemic. (Rufipalpis-harigeveldspinnekop)

Neoscona subfusca — Subfusca Hairy Field Spider

Colour very variable. Carapace dark with patches of white setae. Abdomen usually decorated with folium; juveniles with 'shoulders' as well as broad white band, absent in adults. Legs same colour as carapace. **NOTES:** A very common species sampled from all biomes except Desert, as well as from crops such as avocado, citrus, grapefruit, macadamia, pecan and pistachio orchards, pine plantations, cotton, tomato fields and vineyards. **STATUS:** LC; cosmopolitan. (Subfusca-harigeveldspinnekop)

Neoscona theisi theisiella — Theisi Hairy Field Spider

Carapace brown with dense white setae. Abdomen longer than wide, with round shoulders; very distinct dark folium with paler central longitudinal band. Legs same colour as carapace, posterior legs banded. NOTES: Commonly sampled from Fynbos, Grassland, Thicket and Savanna. STATUS: LC; African endemic. (Theisi-harigeveldspinnekop)

Neoscona triangula — Red-spotted Hairy Field Spider

Carapace varies from creamish brown to dark grey; densely covered in setae. Abdomen as wide as long. Species distinguished by red marking on ventral surface of abdomen, resembling that of *Latrodectus geometricus* (brown button spider). Legs faintly banded. NOTES: Sampled from Forest, Grassland, IOCB, Nama- and Succulent Karoo, Savanna and Thicket. Also sampled from crops such as avocado, macadamia and pecan orchards, onion, sorghum and tomato fields. STATUS: LC; Cosmopolitan. (Rooikol-harigeveldspinnekop)

Neoscona vigilans — Vigilans Hairy Field Spider

Carapace varies from creamish brown to dark grey; densely covered in creamy white setae. Abdomen as wide as long; dorsum has distinct dark heart mark. Legs mottled, faintly banded, with short erect creamy setae. NOTES: Sampled from Forest, Grassland, IOCB, Nama-Karoo and Savanna. STATUS: LC; Cosmopolitan. (Vigilans-harigeveldspinnekop)

Nephilingis

Hermit spiders

Females large; males much smaller. Carapace longer than wide; eyes in two evenly spaced rows. Abdomen ovoid to cylindrical. Legs very long and slender. NOTES: These spiders build large asymmetrical white orb-webs. One species has been recorded in South Africa. (Kluisenaarspinnekoppe)

Nephilingis cruentata female in funnel

Nephilingis cruentata

Cruentata Hermit Spider

Carapace dark, shiny; sternum bright yellow. Abdomen ovoid to cylindrical; varies from very dark with only a yellow band anteriorly to creamy yellow mottled with grey and white. Legs vary from dark to banded in yellow. NOTES: Builds an asymmetrical white orb-web, often against tree trunks, walls or large rocks, with a funnel-shaped retreat on the side. Frequently found under the overhangs of roofs. Sampled from Forest, Grassland, IOCB and Savanna. STATUS: LC; Cosmopolitan. (Cruentata-kluisenaarspinnekop)

Paralarinia

Paralarinia orb-web spiders

Medium-sized. Carapace as wide as long; cephalic region elevated, bearing dense setae; Abdomen roundish oval. Legs brown. NOTES: Web dwellers that construct typical orb-webs in and between vegetation at night. One species is known from South Africa. (Paralarinia-wawielwebspinnekoppe)

Paralarinia bartelsi

Bartel's Orb-web Spider

Carapace yellow-brown, eyes on black spots. Abdomen marked with paler folium, with scalloped edges and brown spots. Legs banded. NOTES: Sampled from Forest, Fynbos, IOCB and Savanna. STATUS: LC; South African endemic. (Bartel se Wawielwebspinnekop)

Paraplectana   Lady beetle spiders

Medium-sized. Females distinguished by their round body and bright coloration. Carapace uniformly pale brown. Abdomen round and almost completely covering carapace, shiny, with bright red, yellow or orange patches on a dark background, resembling a lady beetle. Legs thin, arranged around carapace. Males unknown. **NOTES:** These spiders make spanning thread orb-webs in vegetation at night. They feed on moths. During the day they rest on vegetation, mimicking a lady beetle. Sampled from Fynbos, Grassland and Savanna. Only two species have been recorded from South Africa. (Skilpadkewerspinnekoppe)

Paraplectana thorntoni   Thornton's Red Lady Beetle Spider

Carapace yellow-brown. Abdomen round, almost completely covering carapace, shiny black, leathery, decorated with scattered bright red patches. Legs dark, faintly banded. **NOTES:** Found in the Fynbos, Grassland and Savanna. **STATUS:** LC; African endemic. (Thornton se Rooi Skilpadkewerspinnekop)

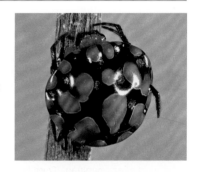

Paraplectana walleri   Waller's Yellow Lady Beetle Spider

Carapace uniformly orange-brown. Abdomen shiny, yellow, marked with numerous small black spots around dorsal and ventral edges. Coxae and part of femora yellowish, rest of leg segments dark. **NOTES:** Sampled from Grassland and Savanna. Also found in citrus orchards. **STATUS:** LC; African endemic. (Waller se Geel Skilpadkewerspinnekop)

Pararaneus   Pararaneus spiny field spiders

Medium-sized. Carapace pear-shaped; anterior eyes slightly protruding; cephalic region with dense layer of setae, especially in male. Abdomen shield-like, dorsally rounded, in some species with a pair of small white spots, in most species with four or five transverse bands. Legs strong, bearing numerous strong erect spines. Males have a stronger build than females and dense setae on the body. **NOTES:** These spiders make a typical vertical orb-web. Three species are known from South Africa. (Pararaneus-stekelrigeveldspinnekoppe)

Araraneus cyrtoscapus   Cyrtoscapus Spiny Field Spider

Carapace varies from brown to reddish yellow, with dense layer of setae. Abdomen has four or five transverse bands dorsally, faintly spotted. Legs same colour as carapace, bearing strong spines. **NOTES:** Sampled from Forest, Fynbos, Grassland, IOCB, Nama-Karoo, Savanna and Thicket. Also sampled from avocado, citrus and pistachio orchards and tomato fields. **STATUS:** LC; African endemic. (Cyrtoscapus-stekelrigeveldspinnekop)

Araraneus perforatus   Perforatus Spiny Field Spider

Carapace varies from brown to creamy yellow. Abdomen has four or five transverse bands dorsally, with dense layer of setae. In males the abdomen is covered in numerous strong erect setae. Legs same colour as carapace, with strong spines. **NOTES:** Makes orb-webs in open grass. Commonly sampled with a sweep net from the Thicket biome. **STATUS:** LC; African endemic. (Perforatus-stekelrigeveldspinnekop)

Araraneus spectator   White-spot Spiny Field Spider

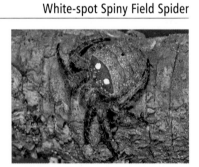

Carapace dark brown to creamy yellow. Abdomen dorsum orange-brown with spotted appearance; anteriorly with oval dark area bearing two distinct white spots; posteriorly with four or five transverse bands. Legs same colour as carapace. **NOTES:** Known from Grassland, IOCB, Savanna and Thicket. Also sampled from crops such as maize and strawberries. **STATUS:** LC; Cosmopolitan. (Witkol-stekelrigeveldspinnekop)

Pasilobus   **Pasilobus bird-dropping spiders**

Medium-sized. Carapace round, slightly broader than long, shiny; ocular quadrangle subquadrate and slightly raised. Abdomen twice as broad as long, smooth, with low tubercles. Legs slender; legs I and II longer than rest. **NOTES:** These spiders build an orb-web at night. Observed during the day while resting on the upper surfaces of leaves, fully visible and strongly resembling bird droppings. A specimen was observed resting on a thin covering of silk threads. Only one species is known from South Africa. (Pasilobus-voëlmisspinnekoppe)

Pasilobus dippenaarae   Dippenaar's Bird-dropping Spider

Carapace yellow-brown, shiny, with dark markings; surface coarsely rugose. Abdomen surface smooth, yellow-brown with broad white transverse band; anterior margin with five pairs of small tubercles followed by pair of large anterolateral tubercles. NOTES: Sampled from the Savanna biome. STATUS: LC; South African endemic. (Dippenaar se Voëlmisspinnekop)

Poltys   Poltys orb-web spiders

Medium-sized. Carapace pear-shaped; lateral eyes widely spaced; eye tubercle present as frontally elevated projection. Abdomen anteriorly elevated, with irregular tubercles. Legs I and II long, with flat, curved and spinulose tibiae and metatarsi. NOTES: These spiders build finely meshed orb-webs at night and remove them around dawn. Moths are the most frequent prey. During the day they hide motionless on vegetation with the legs drawn tightly around the body. Only one species is known from South Africa. (Poltys-wawielwebspinnekoppe)

Poltys furcifer   Green Poltys Orb-web Spider

Carapace creamish white, covered in dense grey setae. Abdomen elevation creamish white, posterior areas with irregular green markings. Legs with reddish tint; dorsal area covered in dense grey setae. NOTES: Sampled from Grassland, Savanna and Thicket. STATUS: LC; African endemic. (Groen Poltys-wawielwebspinnekop)

Prasonica   Prasonica leaf weaver spiders

Medium-sized. Carapace pear-shaped, narrower in eye region, bears white setae; median eyes grouped together; posterior median eyes largest; lateral eyes close together. Abdomen oval, slightly flattened, with varied yellow, white or dark brown patterns and white setae; sometimes with black spots posteriorly. Legs slender, same colour as carapace. NOTES: Found mainly in forest clearings, where they weave their orb-webs between leaves and flowers. These webs are only about 10cm in diameter. They also weave a retreat in the folds of leaves. Freshly hatched spiderlings are red and change to brown. Mature spiders are green. Three species are known from South Africa. (Prasonica-blaarweefspinnekoppe)

Prasonica albolimbata   Albolimbata Leaf Weaver Spider

Carapace uniformly green with white setae. Abdomen green with varied yellow patches. Legs same colour as carapace. **NOTES:** Sampled from Grassland and Savanna. **STATUS:** LC; African endemic. (Albolimbata-blaarweefspinnekop)

Prasonica nigrotaeniata   Black-spot Leaf Weaver Spider

Carapace uniformly green. Abdomen green, with blackish area with white patches dorsally and black spots posteriorly. Legs green. **NOTES:** Sampled from Grassland, IOCB and Savanna. **STATUS:** LC; African endemic. (Swartkol-blaarweefspinnekop)

Prasonica seriata   Two-spot Leaf Weaver Spider

Carapace uniformly green. Abdomen varies from pale green to brownish dorsally with white patches; two distinct black spots present posteriorly. Legs same colour as carapace. **NOTES:** Sampled from Fynbos, Grassland, IOCB, Savanna and Thicket. **STATUS:** LC; African endemic. (Tweekol-blaarweefspinnekop)

Pycnacantha
Hedgehog spiders

Medium-sized. Carapace slightly longer than wide, narrower in eye region; eyes situated on small humps. Abdomen round, overhangs carapace, bears numerous sharply pointed tubercles. Legs of medium length to long; legs I and II much longer and stronger than posterior ones. NOTES: These spiders make reduced orb-webs. In the evening they spin a triangular trapezium between two adjacent grass stems. Here they hang upside-down, with their legs streched out to catch flying insects. They rest on grass during the day. One species is known from South Africa. (Krimpvarkiespinnekoppe)

Pycnacantha tribulus
Tribulus Hedgehog Spider

Carapace fawnish brown, paler around edge; lateral areas darker. Abdomen straw-coloured, bearing >30 sharply pointed tubercles of varying length; tip of tubercles dark; some specimens with dark band over length of tubercle. Legs same colour as carapace. NOTES: Sampled from Desert, Fynbos, Grassland, IOCB, Savanna and Thicket. STATUS: LC; southern African endemic. (Tribulus-krimpvarkiespinnekop)

Singa
Singa striped orb-web spiders

Small. Carapace longer than wide; anterior median eyes largest, median ocular quadrangle wider in front than behind. Abdomen oval, longer than wide, overhangs carapace; legs moderately long, kept close to body when at rest. NOTES: Very little known about their behaviour. The small orb-webs are made in low-growing vegetation, herbs or grasses. Two species recorded from South Africa. (Singa-streepwawielwebspinnekoppe)

Singa albodorsata
Pyjama Spider

Carapace dark brown; darker around eyes. Abdomen dark with white median band and two white lateral bands. Legs with orange-brown tone. NOTES: Sampled from low-growing vegetation in Grassland, IOCB and Savanna. STATUS: LC; southern African endemic. (Pajamaspinnekop)

Singafrotypa   Singafrotypa orb-web spiders

Medium-sized. Cephalic region wide; median and lateral eyes widely separated. Abdomen cylindrical, longer than wide, with parallel sides, caudally overhanging spinnerets. Legs stout, spiny. NOTES: Natural history unknown. Cylindrical body with advanced spinnerets might suggest utilisation of rolled leaves or grass stems as a retreat on the web. Only one species is known from South Africa. (Singafrotypa-wawielwebspinnekoppe)

Singafrotypa mandela   Mandela's Orb-web Spider

Carapace shiny, dark brown. Abdomen creamy with broad median band with scalloped border bordered by two darker lateral bands; eight sigilla in two rows on median band. Legs banded. NOTES: Sampled from Fynbos and Savanna. STATUS: LC; South African endemic. (Mandela se Wawielwebspinnekop)

Trichonephila   Golden orb-web spiders

Large to very large spiders with colourful bodies. Each species is recognised by its colour pattern, which may show considerable intraspecific variation. Carapace longer than wide, with short, horn-like protuberances in females; eight eyes in two evenly spaced rows. Abdomen large, cylindrical. Legs long, slender; two species with conspicuous tufts of setae on at least tibiae of legs I, II and IV. Sexes differ in size, shape and colour. NOTES: They build large (1–1.5m) orb-webs between trees and shrubs. The viscid spiral of the web is yellowish, and the radii are pulled out of their direct course, giving the web a notched appearance. The spiders make use of the same web over long periods, replacing only the viscid lines. In the older specimens the web may be only half a circle, while younger individuals have more complete orbs. Four species are known from South Africa. (Goue Wawielwebspinnekoppe)

Trichonephila fenestrata   Black-legged Golden Orb-web Spider

Carapace dark, silvery. Abdomen usually with distinct yellow and blueish pattern dorsally. Legs black; brushes of setae on legs I, II and IV. Males without distinct patterns. NOTES: Sampled from all the biomes except the arid ones. Also sampled from citrus and prickly pear orchards. STATUS: LC; southern African endemic. (Swartpoot-gouewawielwebspinnekop)

Trichonephila inaurata madagascariensis Red-legged Golden Orb-web Spider

Carapace dark, silvery. Abdomen silvery grey towards front; dark yellow-spotted pattern towards rear. Legs dark with reddish tint, brushes of setae less distinct. NOTES: Sampled from Forest, Fynbos, IOCB and Savanna. STATUS: LC; African endemic. (Rooipoot-gouewawielwebspinnekop)

Trichonephila komaci Giant Golden Orb-web Spider

Carapace silvery. Abdomen with distinct bold black and pale yellow patterns. Legs are blackish with no bands; brushes of short setae on legs I, II and IV. NOTES: Sampled from the IOCB biome. STATUS: LC; African endemic. (Reuse Gouewawielwebspinnekop)

Trichonephila senegalensis Banded-legged Golden Orb-web Spider

Carapace silvery. Abdomen with distinct yellow-and-black pattern dorsally; yellow with black patterns ventrally. Legs strongly banded. Male without distinct patterns. NOTES: Common species sampled from all the biomes except the arid ones. STATUS: LC; African endemic. (Streepbeen-gouewawielwebspinnekop)

Ursa
Ursa orb-web spiders

Small. Carapace pear-shaped; eyes in two rows; anterior and posterior median eyes close together; lateral and anterior median eyes larger than posterior lateral eyes. Abdomen round, decorated with faint whitish markings. Legs same colour as carapace; leg IV shortest; leg I with rows of lined setae. **NOTES:** Nothing is known about their behaviour. Sampled while sweeping grass. Represented by one species in South Africa. (Ursa-wawielwebspinnekoppe)

Ursa turbinata
Spiny-legged Orb-web Spider

Carapace fawn with wide darker V-shaped marking in cephalic region. Abdomen fawn with brown and yellow spots. Legs pale yellow. **NOTES:** Sampled from Fynbos and Savanna. **STATUS:** DD; South African endemic. (Stekelpoot-wawielwebspinnekop)

FAMILY CYATHOLIPIDAE
Tree sheet-web spiders
Boomdoekwebspinnekoppe

Carapace convex, heart-shaped to oval; eight eyes in two rows (4:4), situated close to anterior margin. Abdomen with two widely spaced posterior tracheal spiracles linked by transverse groove sclerotised at each end; abdomen globular, ovoid, triangular to long, sometimes extends past spinnerets. Legs three-clawed, long, slender; leg I the longest. **NOTES:** Nocturnal. They make small horizontal sheet-webs in low vegetation between tree trunks, low shrubs, or tree buttresses. The web consists of a fine sheet spun close to the tree trunk. The spider hangs beneath the sheet. When prey lands on the web the spider bites through the sheet. Typically found in cool, moist tropical montane and temperate lowland forests in the south. Represented by 16 endemic species in South Africa.

Cyatholipus
Cyatholipus tree sheet-web spiders

Very small. Carapace domed, short, smooth to weakly rugose, glabrous, with median row of long setae between posterior eye row and thoracic fovea; fovea a broad, deep pit. Abdomen nearly spherical, with rows of stout bristles on dorsal and posterolateral surfaces; strong sclerotisations surround spinnerets and area between epigastric furrow and pedicle; usually marked with spots. Legs relatively short. **NOTES:** They build small horizontal sheet-webs between tree trunks and surrounding low shrubs. Known from six species in South Africa. (Cyatholipus-boomdoekwebspinnekoppe)

Cyatholipus isolatus
Hanglip Tree Sheet-web Spider

Carapace and sternum orange-brown; black around eyes. Abdomen orange with black spots. Legs dark. **NOTES:** Builds sheet-webs in the understorey of moist forest. Sampled from Forest and Savanna. **STATUS:** NT; South African endemic. (Hanglip-boomdoekwebspinnekop)

Cyatholipus quadrimaculatus
Spotted Tree Sheet-web Spider

Carapace yellowish brown with dark patch over eye region. Abdomen white, with two pairs of dorsolateral spots, markings slightly smaller in female; spherical to ovoid. Legs same colour as carapace. **NOTES:** They build small horizontal sheet-webs 30cm to 2m above the ground between buttresses of tree trunks, in grass, or in foliage of low shrubs or trees. Sampled from Fynbos, IOCB and Thicket. Also occurs in vineyards around Stellenbosch in the Western Cape. **STATUS:** LC; South African endemic. (Gekolde Boomdoekwebspinnekop)

Isicabu
Isicabu tree sheet-web spiders

Small. Carapace inclined to weakly domed, narrow, weakly rugose to granulate; fovea a shallow to deep ovoid pit; eye region wider than long; anterior eye row strongly recurved; posterior eye row nearly straight; sternum longer than wide; strongly rugose. Abdomen triangular, extends past spinnerets, with scattered fine setae. Legs slender, very long. **NOTES:** They make sheet-webs in the understorey of forests. Some specimens were found in caves. Known from two South African species. (Isicabu-boomdoekwebspinnekoppe)

Isicabu zuluensis
Zululand Tree Sheet-web Spider

Carapace red-brown, black around eyes; dark markings radiate anteriorly, laterally and posteriorly from fovea. Abdomen yellow-orange with bright white subcutaneous deposits; paired dark median bands join behind middle. Legs dark. **NOTES:** Found in Forest, IOCB and Savanna. Also sampled from pine plantations at Ngome State Forest in KwaZulu-Natal. **STATUS:** Vulnerable; South African endemic. (Zululandse Boomdoekwebspinnekop)

Ubacisi   Ubacisi tree sheet-web spiders

Small. Carapace oval, evenly curved in profile, with truncated posterior margin. Abdomen triangular when viewed laterally. Abdomen without coarse setae; pedicel present. Legs long. **NOTES:** Hang beneath sheet-webs in shaded areas of forests. Monotypic, known from a single South African species. (Ubacisi-boomdoekwebspinnekoppe)

Ubacisi capensis   Cape Tree Sheet-web Spider

Carapace, chelicerae, sternum, labium and palpal coxae dark brown. Abdomen dark grey, dorsum with longitudinal rows of three median and four dorsolateral light grey spots; sides paler, venter dark. **NOTES:** Some specimens have been collected from moist, wooded canyons on the slopes of Table Mountain and at the entrance of bat caves. Sampled from Fynbos and Thicket. **STATUS:** LC; South African endemic. (Kaapse Boomdoekwebspinnekop)

Ulwembua   Ulwembua tree sheet-web spiders

Small. Carapace with texture finely rugose to granular; evenly curved with posterior margin truncated to weakly concave. Abdomen triangular when viewed laterally, without coarse setae, with pedicel. Legs long. **NOTES:** Abundant in wet, closed-canopy forest; found hanging from sheet-webs less than 50cm from ground in low vegetation and tree buttresses. Seven species are known in South Africa. (Ulwembua-boomdoekwebspinnekoppe)

Ulwembua denticulata   Limpopo Tree Sheet-web Spider

Carapace brown with dark median patch. Abdomen yellow-white, mottled with grey and brown dorsal markings. Legs pale; femora and patellae darker. **NOTES:** Sampled from Forest, Fynbos, Grassland, IOCB and Savanna. Also sampled from avocado and citrus orchards. **STATUS:** LC; South African endemic. (Limpopo-boomdoekwebspinnekop)

Ulwembua pulchra   Dlinza Tree Sheet-web Spider

Carapace dark brown with red-brown longitudinal band from mid-cephalic region to posterior margin; granulate, rugose. Abdomen yellow-white, mottled with grey dorsal markings. Legs yellow-brown. **NOTES:** Builds small horizontal sheet-webs in vegetation. Sampled from Forest, IOCB and Savanna. **STATUS:** LC; South African endemic. (Dlinza-boomdoekwebspinnekop)

FAMILY DEINOPIDAE
Net-casting spiders
Netgooispinnekoppe

Carapace longer than wide; fovea varies from a deep oval pit to a shallow depression; eight eyes arranged in three rows; posterior median eyes enlarged (especially in *Asianopis*, less so in *Menneus*). Abdomen elongated, with one or two humps, which vary in shape and size; humps typically reduced in males.

Menneus sp. with expandable web

Asianopis sp., showing the enlarged posterior median eyes

Legs three-clawed; legs I and II long and slender, up to three times or more the length of the body; tarsus IV with short erect macrosetae.

NOTES: Constructs an adapted cribellate orb-web. The spider hangs upside-down above the substrate, supported by a scaffold of non-sticky silk. It holds a small, elastic web with its long front legs, gripping it at the corners. By moving its legs, it can expand the web. When prey comes within reach, the spider stretches the web five to six times the original size and casts it over its victim. It then uses its hind legs to wrap the prey victim with silk. These spiders are procryptic by day, resting with their bodies adpressed against the bark of a branch. Two genera and seven species have been recorded from South Africa.

Asianopis
Ogre-face spiders

Medium-sized. Carapace twice as long as wide, flat, narrowed in region of anterior legs; posterior median eyes very large, with encircling fringe of short, broad, modified setae forming a horn; distinct, dark V-shaped marking present in male. Abdomen elongated; twice as long as wide. Legs very long, slender, three times the length of the body. NOTES: They live in low vegetation in coastal Forest and Fynbos and humid Savanna, and construct a small, expandable web that they cast over prey. Procryptic by day, resting with their bodies appressed against the bark of a branch. Four species are known from South Africa. (Monsterspinnekoppe)

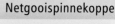

Eye pattern

Asianopis anchietae

Angola Ogre-face Spider

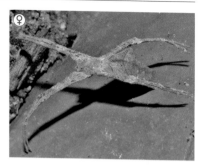

Body grey-brown, clothed in dense setae. Carapace with V-shaped white bands; frontal eye with dark dorsal horns. Abdomen with two humps. Femur I has large basal enlargement in female. NOTES: Sampled from IOCB and Savanna. STATUS: LC; African endemic. (Angolese Monsterspinnekop)

Asianopis aspectans

Aspectans Ogre-face Spider

Carapace yellowish brown, covered with white setae; reddish setae around eyes; without white bands, unlike *A. anchietae*. Abdomen yellowish brown; posterior blunt. Legs yellow-brown. NOTES: Sampled from IOCB and Savanna. STATUS: LC; African endemic. (Aspectansmonsterspinnekop)

Asianopis cylindrica

Long-palp Ogre-face Spider

Carapace dark olive, with silver V-shaped marking; chelicerae with two silver bands. Abdomen elongated; with pair of tubercles centrally; abdomen end blunt with very broad cribellum. Legs brown. NOTES: Lives in low vegetation. Has been sampled from Fynbos, Grassland, IOCB and Savanna. STATUS: LC; southern African endemic. (Langpalpmonsterspinnekop)

Menneus

Medium-sized. Carapace longer than wide, clothed in minute spinules; fovea a deep oval pit. Posterior median eyes not as large as in *Asianopis*. Abdomen longer than wide, with one unpaired hump or two humps; humps absent in males. Coloration resembles that of bark. Legs I and II longer than others. **NOTES:** Procryptic by day, resting with their bodies adpressed against vegetation. Makes a rectangular expandable web with cribellate silk at night, holding it with the front legs. Most species are associated with vertical grass stems and twigs near the ground and are more commonly found in Grassland and Savanna regions. Three species are known from South Africa. (Boggelrugspinnekoppe)

Eye pattern

Menneus camelus

Camelus Net-casting Spider

Carapace dark dorsally, various shades of greyish brown, unmarked. Abdomen same colour as carapace; males generally darker than females. Legs dark, same colour as carapace. **NOTES:** Sampled from Fynbos, Grassland, IOCB, Savanna and Thicket. Synanthropic, frequently found in and around houses in South Africa. Also sampled from avocado orchards. **STATUS:** LC; South African endemic. (Camelus-netgooispinnekop)

Menneus capensis

Cape Net-casting Spider

Carapace olive-green or olive-brown; white V-shaped median band expands over posterior part of head, up to each posterior lateral eye; anterior surface of head darker. Abdomen triangular with lateral humps; thin white horizontal band. Legs dark, same colour as carapace. **NOTES:** Typically found under boulders adjacent to water. Sampled from the Fynbos biome as well as from *Eucalyptus* plantations. **STATUS:** LC; South African endemic. (Kaapse Netgooispinnekop)

Menneus dromedarius

Dromedari Net-casting Spider

Carapace dark dorsally, marked with various shades of greyish brown. Abdomen same colour as carapace; males generally darker than females. Legs same colour as carapace. **NOTES:** Sampled from Forest, Fynbos, Grassland and Thicket. **STATUS:** LC; Madagascan and South African endemic. (Dromedarius-netgooispinnekop)

FAMILY DICTYNIDAE
Mesh-weavers   Maaswebspinnekoppe

Carapace with eight eyes in two rows (4:4); cephalic region typically elevated. Abdomen oval, slightly overlapping carapace; cribellate spiders with uniseriate calamistrum and cribellum. Legs of moderate length and equal size, three-clawed, usually without true spines. **NOTES:** Most mesh-weavers live in retreat-webs made with cribellate silk on branches, in crevices, in grass inflorescences or between twigs. They construct a retreat within a larger mesh-web. Prey remains are typically retained in the web, presumably as a form of camouflage, and giving a good indication of diet and size-range of prey. This is a large cosmopolitan family. To date three genera and four species are known from South Africa.

Archaeodictyna

Archaeodictyna mesh-web spiders

Small. Carapace elevated, with longitudinal rows of white setae; eyes large, subequal in size; chelicerae bow-shaped in males. Abdomen oval, slightly overlapping carapace; usually bearing dense cover of setae. **NOTES:** The retreat in which the spider resides is made within the parameters of a mesh-web that consists of cribellate silk strands attached to the vegetation. Only two species are known from South Africa. (Archaeodictyna-maaswebspinnekoppe)

Archaeodictyna female in web

Archaeodictyna condocta   Common Mesh-web Spider

Carapace dark brown with rows of white setae dorsally. Abdomen with dense white setae; dark central area with pattern. Legs pale with dense setae and faint bands. Male slightly smaller than female. **NOTES:** Solitary, lives in mesh-like retreats made in vegetation, usually along the sides of branches or among dried stalks. Sampled from Fynbos, Grassland and Savanna. **STATUS:** LC; Cosmopolitan. (Gewone Maaswebspinnekop)

Brigittea   Brigittea mesh-web spiders

Small. Carapace narrowed in eye region; cephalic region elevated, with longitudinal rows of white setae. Abdomen oval; slightly overlapping carapace. Legs slender; leg I stronger than others. **NOTES:** Makes retreat-webs consisting of sticky threads radiating outwards on walls. The spider takes up position in the middle of the web. One species was recently introduced to South Africa. (Brigittea-maaswebspinnekoppe)

Brigittea civica   Civica Mesh-web Spider

Carapace dark brown; cephalic region with rows of white setae. Abdomen dark brown with scattered white setae; dark central area with pattern stretching from anterior border to spinnerets. Legs pale with white setae and faint bands. Male slightly smaller than female. **NOTES:** Sampled from buildings in Gauteng. **STATUS:** LC; Cosmopolitan. (Civica-maaswebspinnekop)

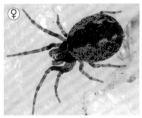

Mashimo   Mashimo mesh-web spiders

Small. Carapace pear-shaped; groove separates cephalic region from thoracic region, radiating depressions present; eye region broad; eyes small, in two rows; chelicerae strong. Abdomen long, oval, with white setae. Calamistrum consists of 18 or 19 strongly curved setae. **NOTES:** Nothing is known about their behaviour. Monotypic. The type specimen was described in Zambia, but has since been recorded in South Africa. (Mashimo-maaswebspinnekoppe)

Family Dictynidae   83

Mashimo leleupi — Leleupi Mesh-web Spider

Carapace orange; eye region with white setae. Abdomen same colour as carapace. Legs whitish; other segments yellow. **NOTES:** Some specimens have been sampled from pitfall traps and low vegetation in Fynbos, Grassland, IOCB, Savanna and Thicket. **STATUS:** LC; African endemic. (Leleupi-maaswebspinnekop)

FAMILY DRYMUSIDAE
False violin spiders — Valsvioolspinnekoppe

The family Drymusidae is recognised by the six eyes being arranged in three diads, the booklung slits with chitinous depressions, and long legs with three claws and onychium. It is known from a single genus, *Izithunzi* from South Africa. Morphology discussed below.

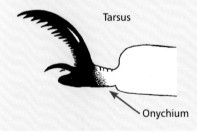

Tarsus

Onychium

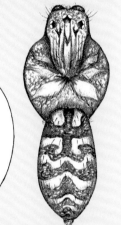

Abdomen
(ventral view)

Booklungs
with chitinous
depressions

Izithunzi — Izithunzi false violin spiders

Medium-sized. This genus resembles *Loxosceles* (violin spiders). Carapace slightly depressed; only thoracic region elevated; numerous long, dark setae present; six eyes arranged in three diads in a recurved row. Abdomen round to oval with light covering of short stiff setae. Legs three-clawed, with onychium, very long, slender, without spines; leg formula 1-2-4-3. **NOTES:** These cryptic nocturnal spiders hang beneath loose space webs hidden in wall crevices or below leaf litter. Frequently found in forests and occasionally in caves. Represented by five endemic species in South Africa. (Izithunzi-valsvioolspinnekoppe)

Izithunzi capense   Cape False Violin Spider

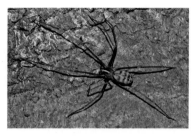

Carapace dark with faint, dull pattern medially. Abdomen dark, marked with about four pale wavy bands. Legs similar in colour to carapace. **NOTES:** Found under exfoliated bark or in crevices between boulders, always in cool shaded areas, where it hangs beneath loose space webs, sometimes with sheet- or tube-like extensions. Sampled from Afromontane forest and pine plantations as well as caves in the Fynbos biome. **STATUS:** Rare habitat specialist; South African endemic. (Kaapse Valsvioolspinnekop)

Izithunzi silvicola   Knysna False Violin Spider

Carapace dark with two black marks medially. Abdomen same colour as carapace, with yellow transverse band. Legs same colour as carapace. **NOTES:** A rare species found on the ground under debris or in tree hollows in indigenous forests. Sampled from the Forest biome. **STATUS:** Rare habitat specialist; South African endemic. (Knysna-valsvioolspinnekop)

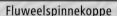

FAMILY ERESIDAE
Velvet spiders   Fluweelspinnekoppe

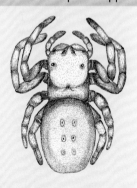

Diverse family. Carapace rectangular, eight eyes; median eyes situated close together; lateral eyes widely spaced; fovea circular, but variable in depth. Abdomen rounded to oval, thickly clothed in setae, frequently with patterns. Legs three-clawed, short, stout, thickly clothed in setae; tarsi usually connected to metatarsi with almost rigid joints. Distinct sexual dimorphism in shape and colour. **NOTES:** Velvet spiders have a diverse lifestyle. Webs differ between genera: usually a sheet-like signal-web radiating from a retreat made of cribellate silk; shape of retreat varies between genera. Five genera and 30 species are known from South Africa.

Dresserus — Ground velvet spiders

Medium-sized to large. Carapace elevated in cephalic region, densely clothed in setae; fovea circular; eight eyes in two rows (4:4); male has distinct horns on anterior carapace edge. Abdomen oval, thickly clothed in setae, sometimes spotted; cribellum 3- or 4-partite. Legs short and stout. NOTES: Sluggish spiders that make retreat-webs of blueish-white silk. The capture section consists of shroud-like, loosely woven silk trap-lines extending outwards. Webs are usually made in dark, sheltered places. Found in a variety of habitats. Represented by 11 species in South Africa. (Grondfluweelspinnekoppe)

Dresserus collinus — Collinus Ground Velvet Spider

Carapace dark brown, almost black, longer than wide. Abdomen grey with pale spots; cribellum 4-partite. Legs same colour as carapace. NOTES: Found in retreat-webs, mainly under stones in the Fynbos biome. STATUS: DD; South African endemic. (Collinus-grondfluweelspinnekop)

Dresserus colsoni — Colsoni Ground Velvet Spider

Carapace dark; chelicerae and mouthparts dark. Abdomen dull brown, covered with dense short setae. Legs dark. NOTES: Commonly found in retreat-webs, mainly under stones and sometimes in compost heaps in gardens. Sampled from Grassland, IOCB and Savanna. STATUS: LC; South African endemic. (Colsoni-grondfluweelspinnekop)

Dresserus kannemeyeri — Kannemeyer's Ground Velvet Spider

Carapace dark red, clothed in short setae; long dark setae on lateral and posterior border; chelicerae reddish brown, darker anteriorly. Abdomen dull red-brown with moderately dense grey setae. Legs reddish brown. NOTES: Sampled from the Grassland biome. STATUS: LC; South African endemic. (Kannemeyer se Grondfluweelspinnekop)

Gandanameno   Tree velvet spiders

Large. Resemble *Dresserus* but cribellum is a different shape. Carapace densely clothed in setae, fovea circular. Abdomen oval, densely clothed in setae; cribellum bipartite. Legs short and stout. NOTES: They usually live under loose bark and build a funnel-like retreat with the entrance sheltered under a tarpaulin-like signal-web. Some specimens have been found near the ground. Three species are known from South Africa. (Boomfluweelspinnekoppe)

Gandanameno fumosa   Fumosa Tree Velvet Spider

 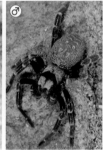

Carapace dark; sternum thickly covered with minute sharp spinules. Abdomen dark with small white spots; sigilla white-ringed. Legs dark, with velvet-like, dense setae. NOTES: Usually lives under loose bark and builds a funnel-like retreat. Sampled from Desert, Fynbos, Grassland, Savanna and Succulent Karoo. STATUS: LC; southern African endemic. (Fumosa-boomfluweelspinnekop)

Gandanameno purcelli   Purcell's Tree Velvet Spider

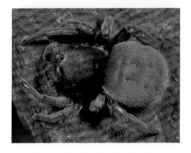

Carapace dark reddish brown; chelicerae dark; carapace clothed in flat dark setae. Abdomen dull red-brown, with short setae; no white rings around dorsal sigilla, unlike closely related species. Legs reddish brown; posterior legs slightly paler; anterior legs darker distally. NOTES: Builds a retreat-web under bark. Sampled from Fynbos, Grassland, IOCB, Savanna and Thicket. STATUS: LC; South African endemic. (Purcell se Boomfluweelspinnekop)

Gandanameno spenceri   Spencer's Tree Velvet Spider

Carapace dark, clothed in white setae; chelicerae reddish black. Abdomen fawn, white setae giving it a spotted appearance; dorsal sigilla white-ringed. Legs dark. NOTES: Commonly found under bark and occasionally under ground debris. Sampled from Fynbos, Grassland and Savanna. STATUS: LC; southern African endemic. (Spencer se Boomfluweelspinnekop)

Paradonea
Paradonea velvet spiders

Medium-sized. Carapace rectangular, elevated, densely clothed in short setae; cephalic region raised above thoracic region; anterior lateral eyes situated on distinct tubercles. Abdomen roundish oval, densely clothed in setae; cribellum bipartite. Legs short and stout, densely setose; anterior legs longer than posterior legs. Sexes differ in shape and colour; males usually more brightly coloured. NOTES: They make retreat-webs with a funnel-shaped retreat consisting of arrays of radiating threads covered with hackled bands of cribellate silk. Represented by five southern African endemic species. (Paradonea-fluweelspinnekoppe)

Paradonea presleyi
Presley's Velvet Spider

Only male known. Carapace dark, covered in white setae, which are denser in eye and thoracic regions; cephalic region elevated. Abdomen has two longitudinal bands of white setae dorsally that may merge into one; bands diverge posteriorly. Legs with longitudinal bands of white setae. NOTES: Sampled from the Savanna biome. STATUS: LC; southern African endemic. (Presley se Fluweelspinnekop)

Paradonea striatipes
Black-and-white Velvet Spider

Only male known. Carapace black with broad white marginal bands; anterior margin of clypeus and chelicerae white. Abdomen black with four transverse white bands. Legs II to IV with narrow longitudinal white bands, other than tarsi; leg I has white spots dorsally and is longer than others. NOTES: Builds silken tube-like nests under stones or shrubs in the Savanna biome. STATUS: LC; southern African endemic. (Swart-en-wit Fluweelspinnekop)

Paradonea variegata
Spotted Velvet Spider

Female Body densely mottled with white and olivaceous setae. Abdomen with olivaceous spots. Legs clothed in white and olivaceous setae. Male Carapace with dense black setae. Abdomen covered with black setae dorsally with broad creamy lateral bands. Legs covered with dense white setae dorsally. NOTES: Builds a round web approximately 10cm in diameter, which may be covered with sand and debris. Sampled from Desert, Fynbos, Nama-Karoo, Savanna and Succulent Karoo. STATUS: LC; southern African endemic. (Bont Fluweelspinnekop)

Seothyra

Buck-spoor spiders

Medium-sized. Carapace thickly clothed in dense setae; lateral eyes wide apart; posterior lateral eyes usually positioned far back on carapace. Abdomen roundish oval and clothed in short setae; spinnerets modified; only anterior pair well developed. Sexes differ in appearance. Males mimic Formicidae and Mutillidae ants with their decorative patterns. **NOTES:** Ground dwellers. They construct retreat-webs consisting of a burrow lined with silk. The entrance is covered with a lobed silk flap that serves as a signal-web. The upper part of the silk flap resembles a hoof print (buck-spoor) in the sand, hence the common name. The shape of print can vary. Juveniles and females permanently inhabit these

The capture webs covering the burrow of a *Seothyra fasciata* female have a buck-spoor shape.

burrows, whereas males run on the soil surface in search of females during mating season. This African genus is represented by five species in South Africa. (Bokspoorspinnekoppe)

Seothyra fasciata

Fasciata Buck-spoor Spider

Female Brown to dark brown. Carapace clothed in black setae; eyes circled with black. Abdomen grey to charcoal. Legs same colour as carapace. **Male** Cephalic region elevated, with dense bright red setae. Abdomen black with yellow markings. Leg I strong, with some black segments. **NOTES:** Constructs burrow retreat-webs in Desert, Nama-Karoo, Savanna and Succulent Karoo. **STATUS:** LC; southern African endemic. (Fasciata-bokspoorspinnekop)

Seothyra longipedata

Northern Cape Buck-spoor Spider

Female Carapace yellowish brown, darker laterally; cephalic region covered with fine setae; eyes circled with black. Abdomen pale without patterns. Legs similar in colour to carapace; femora slightly darker. **Male** Carapace dark reddish brown; cephalic region marked with circular patch of dark setae. Abdomen dark with broad fawn band covering almost entire dorsal area. Legs have white longitudinal bands dorsally. **NOTES:** Constructs burrow retreat-webs in Desert, Fynbos and Savanna. **STATUS:** LC; southern African endemic. (Noord-Kaapse Bokspoorspinnekop)

Stegodyphus

Stegodyphus velvet spiders

Medium-sized. Carapace rectangular, elevated, thickly clothed in setae; lateral eyes wide apart; posterior lateral eyes usually positioned far back on carapace. Abdomen roundish oval, clothed in dense setae. Legs short, stout, thickly clothed in setae. Males smaller and more brightly coloured than females. NOTES: Different species have different lifestyles, with two living in large community nests. Known from six species in South Africa. (Stegodyphus-fluweelspinnekoppe)

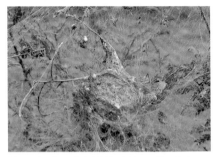

Stegodyphus dumicola community nest

Stegodyphus dumicola

Dumicola Community Nest Spider

Female Carapace covered with white or yellow setae; face dark, bisected by median line of white setae. Abdomen pale yellow, other than sigilla, which have black spots. Legs yellow, some banded. **Male** Darker. Abdomen clothed in rusty red or brownish setae dorsally and dorsolaterally. NOTES: Lives in community nests made of cribellate silk and debris in trees. The nest consists of numerous tunnels and chambers and several sheet-like webs. Parallel threads criss-crossed with cribellate silk form a ladder-like structure used to catch prey. All inhabitants of this community nest work together to catch prey and to repair the web. Sampled from all biomes except Desert. STATUS: LC; southern African endemic. (Dumicola-versamelnesspinnekop)

Stegodyphus mimosarum

Mimosarum Community Nest Spider

Male Very dark, almost black, with white marginal bands and white setae on chelicerae. Abdomen black with white median bands and white marking near spinnerets. Front legs banded, modified, bearing fringe of setae. **Female** Orange-cream; carapace with triangular eye pattern; transverse band over chelicerae; cephalic region very low. NOTES: Makes retreat-webs and lives in community nests in trees in Fynbos, Grassland, IOCB and Savanna. STATUS: LC; African endemic. (Mimosarum-versamelnesspinnekop)

Stegodyphus tentoriicola — White Tentoriicola Velvet Spider

Female Carapace covered with white or yellow setae; thoracic region largely reddish, yellow at sides. Abdomen pale yellow, sigilla with black spots. Legs yellow, some banded. **Male** Carapace often with some yellow setae on each side of thoracic region and yellowish-brown ones on face. Abdomen clothed in rusty red or brownish setae above and on upper part of sides. NOTES: Makes retreat-webs and has been sampled from grass heads. Sampled from Fynbos, Grassland, Nama-Karoo and Savanna. STATUS: LC; southern African endemic. (Wit Tentoriicola-fluweelspinnekop)

FAMILY EUAGRIDAE
Curtain-web spiders   Gordynwebspinnekoppe

Mygalomorph spiders. Eight eyes, closely grouped; cephalic region low; thoracic region elevated; labium without cuspules. Abdomen oval, with dense setae; posterior spinnerets very long; median and posterior spinnerets widely spaced. Legs three-clawed; leg III usually longer than I or II. NOTES: They make very large sheet-webs also called curtain-webs with funnel retreats in subterranean cavities, under rocks, in rotten logs, in leaf litter or under bark. Two genera are known from South Africa.

Allothele   Allothele curtain-web spiders

Medium-sized to large. Carapace integument with dense setae cover; eyes in compact group; fovea a deep transverse groove with radiating striae; two erect setae side-by-side in front of fovea. Abdomen oval, with dense setae. Legs with dense setae and scattered long erect setae. NOTES: These spiders appear to be adapted to Forest and Savanna habitats. They typically build curtain-webs in cool, shady places such as on tree trunks and in abandoned animal burrows. The males abandon their webs in search of mates during the wet summer months. Five species have been recorded in South Africa. (Allothele-doekwebspinnekoppe)

Allothele female showing the long spinnerets

Allothele australis　　　Eastern Cape Curtain-web Spider

Carapace yellowish brown, covered with dense brown setae. Abdomen brown, without markings; posterior spinnerets longer than carapace. Legs same colour as body. Males have a well-developed mating spur on tibia II with stout tooth-like apical and subapical spines. **NOTES:** Lives in curtain-webs with a funnel retreat beneath stones and in rock crevices. Sampled from Fynbos and Thicket. **STATUS:** LC; South African endemic. (Oos-Kaapse Doekwebspinnekop)

Allothele caffer　　　Dark Curtain-web Spider

Carapace dark brown, covered with dense setae. Abdomen with pale spots, medium to dark brown. Legs same colour as carapace, with numerous setae. **NOTES:** Makes curtain-webs with a funnel retreat. Sampled from Grassland and Savanna. **STATUS:** LC; South African endemic. (Donker Doekwebspinnekop)

Allothele malawi　　　Malawi Curtain-web Spider

Carapace covered with dense, brown, shiny setae; fovea a deep transverse groove. Abdomen medium to dark brown, with faint markings. Legs same colour as carapace. **NOTES:** Makes its curtain-webs in Grassland and Savanna. **STATUS:** LC; African endemic. (Malawiese Doekwebspinnekop)

92 **Web dwellers**

FAMILY FILISTATIDAE
Crevice weavers   Skeurspinnekoppe

Small, three-clawed, cribellate spiders; eight
eyes in compact group, situated on small
eye tubercle with labium fused to sternum;
chelicerae with laminae, basally fused. They
can cover large areas with their cribellate
silk. These spiders are known from only a
single genus, *Andoharano* from South Africa.
Morphology discussed below.

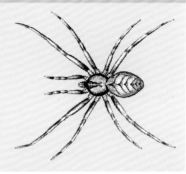

Andoharano   Andoharano crevice-web spiders

Carapace circular; cephalic region distinctly narrowed anteriorly; chelicerae with
laminae; carapace densely covered with fine setae; fangs short. Abdomen oval;
spinnerets set slightly forward; median spinnerets two-segmented with large basal
spigot; cribellum divided. Legs long, especially in males, three-clawed, with numerous
spines; paired setae ventrally on tibiae and metatarsi; calamistrum on metatarsus IV.
NOTES: Webs consist of a tubular retreat made in crevices in rocks and walls, with
triplines radiating from the entrance. Only one species is currently known from South
Africa. (Andoharano-skeurwebspinnekoppe)

Andoharano ansieae   Ansie's Crevice-web Spider

Carapace and legs almost uniformly
reddish brown with weakly
developed darker brownish bands; eye tubercle
with blackish spot. Abdomen yellowish brown
with slightly darker and diffuse dorsal pattern
consisting of a few almost indistinct transverse
markings. Leg I very long in male; femora with
dense setae ventrally. **NOTES:** Their webs can be
seen on tree trunks without bark, on walls, and
on or behind decorative articles in the house.
During the day this spider sits in its retreat under
the bark. It guards its eggs, which are covered
loosely by a silk sheet. **STATUS:** LC; southern
African endemic. (Ansie se Skeurwebspinnekop)

FAMILY HAHNIIDAE

Comb-tailed spiders   Kamstertspinnekoppe

Small, three-clawed spiders recognised by
the spinnerets situated in a transverse row
and the tracheal spiracles opening midway
on abdomen. This family is known from only
a single genus, *Hahnia* from South Africa.
Morphology discussed below.

Hahnia   Hahnia comb-tailed spiders

Small spiders. Carapace longer than wide; narrowed in cephalic region; fovea short,
with striae; eyes equal in size, in two rows (4:4). Abdomen oval; tracheal spiracles open
midway on abdomen; spinnerets situated in transverse row; posterior spinnerets long,
two-segmented; respiratory system with two booklungs. Legs three-clawed, short,
robust, with few setae. Stridulatory organs are present on chelicerae, composed of a
series of ridges on the lateral side and completed by the spur on the palpal patella. These
are more strongly developed in males. Females are darker than males. NOTES: They make
small, delicate sheet-webs in depressions such as hoof prints on the soil surface and in
crevices on tree trunks. In the early morning these small webs are clearly visible when
dew collects on them. The spider hangs beneath the web and, if disturbed, disappears
into vegetation or beneath sand particles. Eight species are known from South Africa.
(Hahnia-kamstertspinnekoppe)

Hahnia clathrata   Clathrata Comb-tailed Spider

Carapace pale yellowish cream with dark
radiating striae; border with dark patches.
Abdomen pale with dark median stripe and lateral bands.
Legs faintly banded. NOTES: Makes small sheet-webs
in leaf litter. Sampled from Fynbos, IOCB, Savanna and
Thicket. STATUS: LC; southern African endemic. (Clathrata-
kamstertspinnekop)

Hahnia lobata   Lobata Comb-tailed Spider

Carapace brown; fovea a faint dark line
with darker radiating striae; eye region dark.
Abdomen greyish brown with long setae; dark chevrons
medially near posterior edge. Legs paler than carapace, with
faint bands. NOTES: Makes small sheet-webs in leaf litter;
has also been collected from forest litter, pine plantations
and caves in Forest, Fynbos, Grassland, IOCB and Savanna.
STATUS: LC; South African endemic. (Lobata-kamstertspinnekop)

Hahnia tabulicola

Tabulicola Comb-tailed Spider

Carapace pale yellowish cream; fovea a distinct dark line with darker radiating striae; eye region dark; dark marginal band. Abdomen pale with dark area forming distinct chevrons over medial area. Legs same colour as carapace, with faint bands. NOTES: Makes small sheet-webs in litter and has been collected using pitfall traps. Sampled from all biomes except Desert and Nama- and Succulent Karoo. Also sampled from cotton and maize. STATUS: LC; African endemic. (Tabulicola-kamstertspinnekop)

FAMILY ISCHNOTHELIDAE
Curtain-web spiders
Gordynwebspinnekoppe

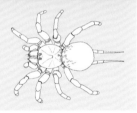

Medium-sized to large mygalomorph spiders recognised by very long and widely spaced posterior spinnerets. They are known from only a single genus, *Thelechoris* from South Africa. Their morphology is discussed below.

Thelechoris

Thelechoris curtain-web spiders

Medium-sized to large. Carapace flat; cephalic region low; thoracic region elevated; with soft, downy setae; fovea pit-like and short; eye group wider than long, close to clypeal edge; endites with cuspules. Abdomen clothed in setae, long setae dorsally, shorter ones ventrally; posterior spinnerets long, tapering. Legs long, spinose; leg formula 4-3-2-1; tibia I of male with elongated distal process and thorn-like spine; metatarsi I with proximal process; paired claws with one S-shaped row of teeth; scopulae absent. NOTES: The capture web is laid over the ground or any horizontal area. It usually remains in the same place and is repaired and enlarged as the spider grows. In some species the three-dimensional capture webs consist of interconnected sheets funneling towards the retreat. A protective tubular or funnel-shaped silk retreat is made on the side of the sheet. Only one species is known from South Africa. (Thelechoris-gordynwebspinnekoppe)

Thelechoris striatipes

Striatipes Curtain-web Spider

Carapace medium to dark brown, sometimes with purplish tint; one to three strong setae around fovea. Abdomen same colour as carapace. Mating spur on male tibia I small and terminal; metatarsus I straight, smooth; same colour as carapace. NOTES: Sampled from IOCB, Savanna and Thicket. STATUS: LC; African endemic. (Striatipes-gordynwebspinnekop)

FAMILY LINYPHIIDAE
Dwarf sheet-web spiders Dwerg-doekwebspinnekoppe

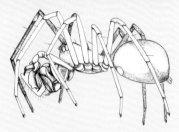

Diverse family. Carapace shape variable; with eight eyes in two rows (4:4); rebordered labium; chelicerae with stridulating file and numerous teeth on fang furrow. Abdomen usually longer than wide; scutum present in some males. Legs three-clawed, without comb on tarsi IV; legs slender, with setae, especially on tibiae and metatarsi. Male slightly smaller than female, but similar in shape and colour; frontal region of male strongly modified in some genera. **NOTES:** These spiders spin delicate sheet-webs between branches of trees or shrubs, in tall grass and sometimes close to the

ground. The web may be flat, higher in the middle (domed) or lower in the middle (hammock-shaped). The spider hangs upside-down under the sheet and makes no retreat. When prey lands on the web the spider bites through the sheet from below, pulls the victim through the hole and consumes it. When disturbed the spider quickly disappears into vegetation. A very large family. At present 22 genera are known from South Africa.

Agyneta Agyneta dwarf spiders

Very small. Carapace longer than wide; smooth; chelicerae more divergent in males; three to five teeth on outer and inner borders. Abdomen roundish oval. Legs slender; tibiae with two thin dorsal spines. **NOTES:** They make sheet-webs in low vegetation such as undergrowth, leaf litter, moss and grass. Also found by sweeping herbaceous vegetation and by beating bushes and trees. Five species have been recorded from South Africa. (Agyneta-dwergspinnekoppe)

Agyneta habra Habra Dwarf Spider

Carapace dark with no patterns; male without modifications on carapace. Abdomen dark, layer of setae dark. Legs reddish brown. **NOTES:** Sampled from Fynbos, Grassland, IOCB, Nama-Karoo and Savanna. Also frequently sampled from crops such as cotton, lucerne, maize, minneola, pecans, pistachio, strawberries, sunflowers and tomatoes. **STATUS:** LC; African endemic. (Habra-dwergspinnekop)

Limoneta   Limoneta dwarf spiders

Very small. Carapace longer than wide, evenly rounded. Abdomen elongated, oval, with markings. Legs long, slender; leg I longest. Chelicerae with stridulating ridges in males. **NOTES:** These spiders make sheet-webs close to the ground. Commonly found in pasture. Only one species is known from South Africa. (Limoneta-dwergspinnekoppe)

Limoneta sirimoni   Sirimon's Dwarf Spider

Carapace chestnut-brown, smooth, without markings. Abdomen fawn with dark grey and white spots and bars. Legs pale yellowish with bands on joints. **NOTES:** Makes sheet-webs close to the ground in Fynbos, Grassland and Savanna. Also sampled from maize, lucerne and strawberries. **STATUS:** LC; African endemic. (Sirimon se Dwergspinnekop)

Mecynidis   Tree dwarf spiders

Small. Carapace longer than wide; cephalic region elevated; chelicerae with stridulating file posteriorly in male. Abdomen elongated; in some species the female has a dorsal tubercle posteriorly. Legs slender. **NOTES:** They make sheet-webs in trees. Only one species is known from South Africa. (Boomdwergspinnekoppe)

Mecynidis dentipalpis   Dentipalpis Tree Dwarf Spider

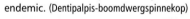

Carapace and sternum dark brown, smooth, without markings. Abdomen dark with broad median dark band bordered by white lateral band. Legs pale brown. **NOTES:** Sampled from Fynbos, Savanna and Thicket. **STATUS:** LC; southern African endemic. (Dentipalpis-boomdwergspinnekop)

Microlinyphia
Microlinyphia dwarf spiders

Small. Carapace elongated; posterior median eyes on dark tubercles; chelicerae of male elongated, slanting backwards, with large protrusion proximally on posterior surface. Abdomen elevated, elongated. Legs slender. Male with thinner abdomen. NOTES: They make sheet-webs low in vegetation. Only one species is known from South Africa. (Microlinyphia-dwergspinnekoppe)

Microlinyphia sterilis
Black-and-white Dwarf Spider

Carapace dark, shiny. Abdomen dark, elevated, marked with white spots. Legs dark. NOTES: Common. Found in all biomes except Desert. STATUS: LC; African endemic. (Swart-en-wit Dwergspinnekop)

Ostearius
Ostearius dwarf spiders

Small. Carapace longer than wide; eyes large, closely grouped; anterior eyes in straight row; posterior eyes in slightly recurved row; fang groove with five promarginal teeth. Abdomen oval, shiny, with layer of setae. Legs slender. NOTES: They make sheet-webs in a variety of habitats. Only one introduced species is known from South Africa. (Ostearius-dwergspinnekoppe)

Ostearius melanopygius
Black-tail Dwarf Spider

Carapace dark brown with faint striae; sternum brown. Abdomen orange with small black circle around spinnerets. Legs yellow-brown. Male slightly smaller than female. NOTES: Sampled from all biomes except Desert. Frequently sampled from crops. STATUS: LC; Cosmopolitan. (Swartstert-dwergspinnekop)

Pelecopsis
Horned dwarf spiders

Small. Carapace elevated, longer than wide in males; eye region 'deformed' in males, with the eyes situated high on large eye tubercles; tubercles not present in females. Abdomen oval; shield covers dorsal part in male. Legs of medium length. NOTES: They make sheet-webs close to the soil surface. Three species are known from South Africa. (Horingdwergspinnekoppe)

Pelecopsis janus
Janus Horned Dwarf Spider

Carapace light brown, darker in cephalic region, finely reticulate. Abdomen dark. Legs yellow; femora I and II darker. NOTES: Common in all biomes except Desert and Thicket. Also sampled from crops and orchards such as cotton, kenaf, lucerne, maize, pistachio, sorghum and vineyards. STATUS: LC; southern Africa. (Janus-horingdwergspinnekop)

FAMILY MYSMENIDAE
Dwarf orb-web spiders
Dwergwawielwebspinnekoppe

Small spiders with round bodies recognised by the sclerotised subdistal ventral spot on femur I in the female and the mating spur on metatarsus I of the male. Known from only a single genus, *Isela* from South Africa. Morphology discussed below.

Isela
Isela dwarf orb-web spiders

Very small. Carapace glabrous; usually elevated, highest point behind eyes; eight eyes. Abdomen soft; spherical to higher than long; usually bearing scattered, long setae. Mating spur on metatarsus I in male; female with sclerotised subdistal ventral spot on femur I; cymbium of male palp with lobes or apophyses. NOTES: These spiders build highly modified small orb-webs. Some species are sedentary, living in webs in leaf litter, others live as kleptoparasites on the webs of other spiders. This African genus is represented by two species, with only one known from South Africa. (Isela-dwergwawielwebspinnekoppe)

Isela okuncana
Okuncana Dwarf Orb-web Spider

Carapace yellow-brown to grey, fovea and striae darker with dark marginal band; smooth. Abdomen dark grey with pale markings. Legs yellow-grey. NOTES: Sampled from the web of Dipluridae specimens (curtain-web spiders) as well as from pitfall traps. STATUS: DD; South African endemic. (Okuncana-dwergwawielwebspinnekop)

Comb-footed spiders Kamvoetspinnekoppe

Small spiders with round bodies. Recognised by the globular abdomen, long, three-clawed legs and the row of serrated bristles on tarsi IV. Known from a single genus, *Nesticella* from South Africa. Morphology discussed below.

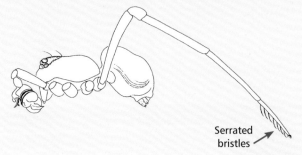

Serrated bristles

Nesticella Cave comb-footed spiders

Very small to medium-sized. Carapace short, pear-shaped; fovea a wide depression; eight eyes in two rows (4:4); labium rebordered; cheliceral fang furrow toothed. Abdomen globular. Legs long; three-clawed; tarsi IV with row of serrated bristles. NOTES: Their webs are three dimensional but not as regular as in the Theridiidae (comb-footed spiders). Collected from plants, but often inhabit dark places. Only one species is known from South Africa. (Grot-kamvoetspinnekoppe)

Nesticella female

Nesticella benoiti Benoit's Comb-footed Spider

Carapace fawn with irregular dark median band. Abdomen fawn, marked with dark symmetrical spots and transverse bands. Legs banded. NOTES: Sampled from Grassland and Savanna and from crop fields, including maize, sunflowers and tomatoes. STATUS: LC; southern Africa. (Benoit se Kamvoetspinnekop)

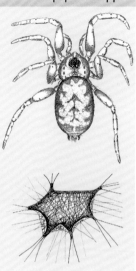

Diverse family. Recognised by the large, two-jointed anal tubercle with a double row of fringed setae. Carapace subcircular, wider than long; six or eight eyes arranged in compact group near centre of carapace; posterior median eyes variable; chelicerae short; fangs short; fovea absent. Abdomen flattened, oval to round; anterior spinnerets short, domed, two-segmented, with short distal segment; posterior spinnerets two-segmented, with long, curved distal segment. Some genera with cribellum. Legs three-clawed, short, subequal in length, arranged around body in star-like fashion. NOTES: They live in star-shaped mesh-webs made over cracks and crevices or in corners of rocks or walls. Some are found on the ground under stones. Four genera and five species are known from South Africa.

Oecobius
Dwarf round-headed spiders

Small. Carapace with eight eyes arranged in two rows; posterior median eyes subcircular. Abdomen oval, slightly overlapping carapace; cribellum present. Legs short. NOTES: They construct irregular, star-shaped sheets as retreats anchored to the substrate with threads that serve as triplines. The sheet is small, about 10mm in diameter, creamy white, and has several entrances. Retreats are built over small crevices, indentations in rocks, and in corners of man-made structures such as windowsills. Two species are known from South Africa. (Dwerg-rondekopspinnekoppe)

Oecobius navus
House Round-headed Spider

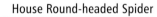

Carapace pale with dark median band and dark marginal band; posterior median eyes oval. Abdomen pale with darker markings and white guanine granules. Legs same colour as carapace. NOTES: Synanthropic. Known to feed on ants. Sampled from Fynbos, Grassland, IOCB, Nama-Karoo, Savanna and Thicket. STATUS: LC; Cosmopolitan. (Huisrondekopspinnekop)

Paroecobius
Large-eyed round-headed spiders

Small. Carapace dome-shaped, wider than long; fovea absent; can be distinguished from other genera by large, dark anterior median eyes. Abdomen flattened, oval, slightly overhanging carapace, with layer of setae; cribellum present. Legs with few or no spines; calamistrum of female in single row, situated on proximal half of metatarsus IV, calamistrum absent in males. NOTES: They live in shallow crevices covered with a silk sheet and triplines. The sheet is usually open on two sides. Retreats have been found on outer walls of buildings. Represented by five species in southern Africa and Madagascar. (Grootoog-rondekopspinnekoppe)

Paroecobius nicolaii
Nicolai's Round-headed Spider

Carapace yellowish brown with dark marginal band; anterior median eye the largest. Abdomen slightly elongated, fawn, with darker irregular markings and layer of strong setae. Legs pale. NOTES: Lives inside shallow rock crevices and bark. The crevice is covered with a silk hammock, which is usually open at two ends. Sampled from the Savanna biome. STATUS: DD; South African endemic. (Nicolai se Rondekopspinnekop)

Uroctea
Desert round-headed spiders

Medium-sized. Recognised by their larger size, colour and spots on the abdomen, and eye pattern. Carapace subcircular; clypeal snout distinct; eight eyes; anterior median eyes largest, remainder arranged in compact group around them. Abdomen flattened, oval to round; large, anal tubercle two-jointed with double row of fringed setae; abdominal markings variable between adults and juveniles; cribellum absent. Legs short. NOTES: Ground dwellers that make an easily recognised web under stones. The retreat is a multi-layered sheet and consists of a flat part facing the stone, with a dome-shaped part facing the ground. The round, scalloped edge is fastened to the stone with stiff threads radiating in all directions. Small objects such as stones and bits of debris are frequently attached to the silk threads. Three species are known from South Africa. (Woestyn-rondekopspinnekoppe)

Uroctea quinquenotata
Five-spot Round-headed Spider

Carapace orange-yellow; eye region darker. Abdomen varies from dark with yellow spots to dark with orange or dark spots on dorsum; spots more prominent in young, tending to disappear in adults, though variation occurs. Legs same colour as carapace. NOTES: Occurs in more arid areas. Sampled from Desert, Fynbos, Nama-Karoo and Succulent Karoo. STATUS: LC; South African endemic. (Vyfkol-rondekopspinnekop)

Uroecobius   Six-eyed round-headed spiders

Small. Carapace subcircular, wider than long, without fovea; six eyes arranged in two rows in compact group near centre of carapace; posterior median eyes reduced; anterior median eyes large, circular. Abdomen somewhat flattened, oval, tapering posteriorly, slightly overlapping carapace, dark, with spots; cribellum absent. Legs short. **NOTES:** Usually found on rock surfaces, under a small star-shaped web very similar to that of *Oecobius*. This genus is monotypic and known from only one endemic South African species. (Sesoog-rondekopspinnekoppe)

Uroecobius ecribellatus   Rock Round-headed spider

Carapace black. Abdomen black with two pairs of white spots. Legs distally paler, only femora dark. **NOTES:** Makes star-shaped web retreats on rocks over small crevices and indentations. The spider sits on the substrate with its back to the sheet. Ants seem to be its main prey, but it eats minute flies as well. Sampled from Grassland and Savanna. **STATUS:** LC; South African endemic. (Rots-rondekopspinnekop)

FAMILY PENESTOMIDAE
Flat velvet spiders   Platfluweelspinnekoppe

Small to medium-sized cribellate spiders recognised by their flattened bodies and eye arrangement: eight eyes in two rows; anterior row procurved; posterior eye row slightly recurved, more widely spaced than anterior row. They make silk retreats in tunnels in boulders and under debris on the ground. This family is known from only a single genus, *Penestomus* from South Africa. Their morphology is discussed overleaf.

Penestomus

Small to medium-sized. Carapace rectangular, flattened, with shallow circular fovea; eight eyes in two rows; posterior eye row slightly recurved, more widely spaced than anteriors; sternum ovoid, longer than wide, not fused to labium; endites parallel, with serrula; promargin of fang furrow armed with four to six teeth increasing in size from base of fang to penultimate tooth. Abdomen rounded to oval, thickly clothed in fine setae, frequently with white markings. Legs short, stout, thickly clothed in setae. NOTES: Retreat-webs are made underneath rocks lying on the soil surface. The webs follow a winding path that varies in length. Eight endemic species occur in South Africa. (Penestomus-platfluweelspinnekoppe)

Penestomus flat velvet spiders

Penestomus male

Penestomus egazini
Egazini Flat Velvet Spider

Carapace dark, rugose, covered in fine black setae; thick white setae concentrated in thoracic region; sternum dusky pale yellow; chelicerae dark. Abdomen dark dorsally with pair of narrow dorsolateral patches of white setae, rest of dorsum covered in fine black setae. Legs dark with bands of white setae. NOTES: Prey remains dominated by ants, especially *Camponotus* and *Lepisiota*, with some beetles (Coleoptera) and bugs (Hemiptera). STATUS: Rare; South African endemic. (Egazini-platfluweelspinnekop)

Penestomus stilleri
Stiller's Flat Velvet Spider

Carapace dark brown, darker in eye region; cephalic region with scattered white setae. Abdomen dark with two paired patches of white setae and one patch above the spinnerets. Legs brown with narrow bands of white setae. NOTES: The type species was found in a silk-lined tunnel under an exfoliated section of a boulder. Sampled from the Fynbos biome. STATUS: DD; South African endemic. (Stiller se Platfluweelspinnekop)

FAMILY PHOLCIDAE
Daddy long-legs spiders
Langbeenspinnekoppe

Carapace varies from short, broad and almost circular to sometimes reniform; cephalic region usually raised, with deep striae; thoracic region sometimes with deep, longitudinal fovea; clypeus elevated, sometimes concave beneath eyes; six or eight eyes with anterior median eyes smallest or absent, with other eyes in two triads or on tubercles; eyes occupy entire width of carapace; chelicerae chelate, in males often with modifications; labium fused to sternum. Abdomen shape variable. Legs extremely long and slender, with flexible tarsi and short, membranous onychium; three-clawed. **NOTES:** These spiders live in tangled space-webs with very different configurations. Some webs are irregular, with long threads haphazardly criss-crossing. In others, the centre of the web consists of a large, more compactly woven sheet, with a network of irregular threads above and below. These spiders typically hang upside-down from their webs. They vibrate the web rapidly when it is touched. The female carries her eggs in the chelicerae – unprotected, as they lack an enveloping sac. Several species have been collected from caves and dwellings. Seven genera and 45 species are known in South Africa.

Artema
Giant daddy long-legs spiders

Medium-sized. Recognised by their large size, very long legs and round abdomen. Carapace flat, broad, with deep fovea; eyes situated on small tubercles; four anterior eyes well separated; median eyes smaller than lateral eyes; sternum heart-shaped; male chelicerae have large black protrusions with modified setae. Abdomen globular. Legs very long. **NOTES:** Sometimes found in human habitations where they weave a convex, dome-shaped web with an irregular network of threads that extend in all directions. Only one species is known from South Africa. (Groot langbeenspinnekoppe)

Artema atlanta
Artema Long-legs Spider

Carapace shiny brown with dark areas. Abdomen round, pale, with large spots covering dorsal surface. Legs same colour as carapace, very long. **NOTES:** Not abundant in South Africa. Sampled from houses in Mpumalanga. **STATUS:** LC; throughout Africa and Madagascar. (Artema-langbeenspinnekop)

Crossopriza
Crossopriza long-legs spiders

Small to medium-sized. Carapace with deep round depression between head and thorax. Abdomen has triangular appearance in lateral view, with caudal end tapering to a point above spinnerets; marked with dark irregular pattern. Legs extremely long. NOTES: Found in human settlements, in houses, sheds and outdoors. Only one introduced species has been recorded from South Africa. (Crossopriza-langbeenspinnekoppe)

Crossopriza lyoni — Lyoni Long-legs Spider

Carapace pale ivory with brown median dorsal depression. Abdomen grey with white lateral stripes and dark irregular pattern. Legs similar in colour but with numerous brown spots. NOTES: Mainly sampled from buildings in South Africa. STATUS: LC; Cosmopolitan. (Lyoni-langbeenspinnekop)

Leptopholcus
Leptopholcus long-legs spiders

Small. Carapace low, flattened; lacking a fovea; six eyes in two widely separated triads on margin of carapace; anterior median eyes represented as a pair of specks between triads. Abdomen vermiform; longer than wide. Legs very long. Sexual dimorphism slight. NOTES: Relatively rare in collections, which is probably mainly due to their cryptic habits. Most appear to be restricted to relatively humid areas where they live cryptically on the underside of large leaves. Only one species has been recorded from South Africa. (Leptopholcus-langbeenspinnekoppe)

Leptopholcus gracilis — Gracilis Long-legs Spider

Carapace green with dark patches over eye region. Abdomen parallel-sided; anteriorly nearly square, with round posterior margin; dorsum pale green, almost translucent. Legs very long, same colour as carapace. NOTES: Little is known about its behaviour. Sampled from IOCB and Savanna. STATUS: LC; African endemic. (Gracilis-langbeenspinnekop)

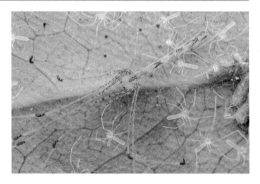

Quamtana

Quamtana long-legs spiders

Small. Carapace oval or round, without median groove or pit; six or eight eyes; distinguished from other genera by the pair of long modified setae on the male's cheliceral apophyses. Abdomen globular, oval or elevated. Legs very long. Sexual dimorphism slight. NOTES: They live in space-webs close to the ground under litter or stones, and have been sampled with litter-sifting, pitfall-trapping and sweep-netting. Represented by 20 species in South Africa. (Quamtana-langbeenspinnekoppe)

Quamtana entabeni
Entabeni Long-legs Spider

Carapace fawn, slightly darker medially; sternum pale. Abdomen grey with darker spots shining through cuticle. Legs fawn; patellae, tibiae and metatarsi joints darker. NOTES: Sampled from litter and pitfall traps in forest areas in Forest and Savanna. STATUS: Rare; South African endemic. (Entabeni-langbeenspinnekop)

Quamtana hectori
Hector's Long-legs Spider

Carapace reddish brown with brown markings medially. Abdomen reddish brown. Legs same colour as carapace. NOTES: Lives in space-webs and commonly found under stones. Sampled from Grassland and Savanna. STATUS: LC; South African endemic. (Hector se Langbeenspinnekop)

Quamtana knysna
Knysna Long-legs Spider

Carapace fawn with broad brown median band, which also runs over eye region and clypeus. Abdomen fawn with large dark spots; genital region brown ventrally. Legs pale; patellae and tibia-metatarsi joints brown. NOTES: Sampled from leaf litter in forest areas in the Forest biome. STATUS: LC; South African endemic. (Knysna-langbeenspinnekop)

Quamtana lotzi
Lotz's Long-legs Spider

Carapace fawn with light brown median band. Abdomen fawn, dorsum with many black spots. Legs brown, with slightly darker bands on femora and tibiae. NOTES: Sampled from leaf litter in the Grassland biome. STATUS: DD; South African endemic. (Lotz se Langbeenspinnekop)

Smeringopus
Smeringopus long-legs spiders

Medium-sized. Carapace with deep thoracic pit; eye region slightly raised; eye triads close together. Abdomen elongated, posteriorly pointed, with distinct dark pattern dorsally. Legs long, thin. NOTES: They build space-webs. The sheet part of the web is domed, with the spider hanging from the apex of the dome. Prey (mostly ants) that land on the silk threads or move below the web are caught with the extended front legs. The egg sac contains about 40 eggs, clearly visible through the thin layer of silk. Fourteen species are known from South Africa. (Smeringopus-langbeenspinnekoppe)

Smeringopus koppies
Koppies Long-legs Spider

Carapace fawn with dark median and lateral bands and narrow dark marginal band; clypeus with pair of indistinct dark bands. Abdomen brown with irregular dark median band dorsally, bordered by fawn band. Legs banded. NOTES: Makes space-webs in leaf litter. Also found in houses, mainly in Grassland and Savanna. STATUS: LC; southern African endemic. (Koppies-langbeenspinnekop)

Smeringopus natalensis
Natal Long-legs Spider

Carapace fawn with irregular dark median band, lateral bands and narrow marginal band. Abdomen with dark median band dorsally; laterally with irregular bands, three dark lines ventrally. Legs banded subdistally on femora and tibiae. NOTES: A very common species sampled throughout South Africa, including in built-up areas. Found in all biomes except Desert and Succulent Karoo. Also sampled from cotton and pistachio orchards. STATUS: LC; southern African endemic. (Natalse Langbeenspinnekop)

FAMILY PHYXELIDIDAE

Hackled mesh-web spiders   Maaswebspinnekoppe

Carapace longer than wide; thoracic fovea long, deep, narrow; eight eyes in two rows (4:4), usually all pale in colour. Abdomen oval, usually with dense layer of fine setae; spinnerets short; cribellum present. Legs three-clawed, long. Male has mating spur on metatarsus. Female has darker markings. NOTES: Typical ground-dwelling retreat-web spiders that inhabit damp and dark places beneath logs and stones, in holes in trees or under stones in caves. They make cribellate funnel-like signal-webs in shady places close to the soil surface. Nine genera and 30 species are known from South Africa.

Malaika   Malaika hackled band spiders

Small to medium-sized spiders. Carapace longer than wide; cephalic region with broad, faint, dusky V-shaped mark anterior to thoracic fovea. Abdomen with anterior longitudinal dark bands. Legs covered with feathery setae; legs III and IV banded. NOTES: They live in retreat-webs under stones and ground debris. Two species have been recorded in South Africa. (Malaika-maaswebspinnekoppe)

Malaika longipes   Table Mountain Hackled Band Spider

Carapace pale yellow-brown; dusky V-shaped mark anterior to thoracic fovea; faint reticulations extending to eye region; black pigment surrounding each eye. Abdomen yellow-white, dorsum with anterior longitudinal dark bands, median and broad dark chevrons. Legs same colour as carapace. NOTES: Ground-living cryptic spiders. Inhabit retreat-webs in damp and dark places. Sampled from the Fynbos biome. STATUS: Rare; South African endemic. (Tafelberg-maaswebspinnekop)

Phyxelida   Phyxelida hackled band spiders

Medium-sized. Carapace wider than long; thoracic fovea usually broad and deep, but may be rectangular or narrowed posteriorly. Abdomen with variable dorsal markings; venter with longitudinal bands that may be faint or very broad and elaborate. Legs long. NOTES: Ground-living cryptic spiders. Inhabit retreat-web in damp and dark places. Only one species is known from South Africa. (Phyxelida-maaswebspinnekoppe)

Phyxelida makapanensis — Makapans Cave Hackled Band Spider

Carapace fawnish brown; dark pigment surrounds each eye and extends between anterior median eyes. Abdomen greyish with layer of setae. Legs same colour as carapace. NOTES: Sampled from deep within Makapans Cave in Limpopo. Also sampled outside caves in the Grassland biome. Spins very irregular cribellate webs beneath stones or in cracks on the walls. STATUS: LC; South African endemic. (Makapansgrot se Maaswebspinnekop)

Pongolania — Pongolania hackled band spiders

Medium-sized. Only females known. Carapace with elevated cephalic region; fovea long, deep; anterior eye row slightly recurved; posterior eye row straight. Abdomen oval with short layer of setae. Legs long with layer of setae. NOTES: Ground-dwelling cryptic spiders that inhabit retreat-webs in dark places. Known from two South African species. (Pongolania-maaswebspinnekoppe)

Pongolania chrysionaria — Gauteng Hackled Band Spider

Carapace yellow-brown; cephalic region slightly darker with scattered dark setae; faint striae extend to posterior eyes; black pigment surrounds each eye. Abdomen grey-brown with faint markings and dark setae. Legs similar to carapace. NOTES: Sampled from the Grassland biome. Also recorded in citrus orchards and maize fields. STATUS: LC; South African endemic. (Gautengse Maaswebspinnekop)

Themacrys — Themacrys hackled band spiders

Medium-sized. Carapace sparsely setose; fovea long, deep; chelicerae smooth, or with weak lateral and ventral wrinkles, or with strong, deep anterior, lateral and ventral wrinkles or striae. Abdomen with light median band and crossbars. Legs short to elongated. NOTES: These spiders are found in dark, shady places. Known from five South African species. (Themacrys-maaswebspinnekoppe)

Themacrys irrorata — Irrorata Hackled Web Spider

Carapace orange-brown; cephalic region with dusky, dark, V-shaped border; margin of thoracic region dusky; eyes surrounded by black pigment. Abdomen fawn, dorsum with transverse dark bars, posteriorly with two or three chevrons. Legs same colour as carapace. NOTES: Common in coastal forests in IOCB and dense, moist bushveld in Savanna. STATUS: LC; South African endemic. (Irrorata-maaswebspinnekop)

Themacrys silvicola — Pietermaritzburg Hackled Band Spider

Carapace dark brown; eyes surrounded by black pigment. Abdomen dark; dorsum with light longitudinal heart mark and three light transverse bars. Legs and palps yellow-brown distally. Recorded from Grassland, IOCB and Savanna. STATUS: Vulnerable under criterion B; South African endemic. (Pietermaritzburgse Maaswebspinnekop)

Vidole — Vidole hackled band spiders

Medium-sized. Fovea long, deep, narrowed posteriorly; anterior eye row slightly recurved; posterior eye row straight. Abdomen oval; dorsum with variable markings and layer of setae; venter with paired narrow longitudinal bands. Legs long, tarsi densely setose ventrally. NOTES: Ground-dwelling cryptic spiders that inhabit retreat-webs in damp and dark places. Known from five species, all from South Africa. (Vidole-maaswebspinnekoppe)

Vidole capensis — Cape Hackled Band Spider

Carapace dark brown; eye region dusky, eyes surrounded by black pigment. Abdomen greyish brown, with anterior and median pairs of faint light spots and short light longitudinal median band; dense layer of setae. Legs pale brown. NOTES: Sampled from Fynbos, Grassland, IOCB, Nama-Karoo, Savanna and Thicket. Also sampled from citrus orchards in the Eastern Cape. STATUS: LC; South African endemic. (Kaapse Maaswebspinnekop)

Vidole sothoana

Sothoana Hackled Band Spider

Carapace brown; eyes surrounded by black pigment. Abdomen uniformly grey with light heart mark and faint median chevrons. Legs and palps coloration similar to carapace. NOTES: Found in open vegetation, in Grassland and Savanna, and in cultivated fields such as maize and cotton. STATUS: LC; southern African endemic. (Sothoana-maaswebspinnekop)

Xevioso

Xevioso hackled band spiders

Medium-sized. Carapace slightly longer than wide; thoracic fovea long, usually deep, narrowed posteriorly; anterior eye row recurved; posterior eye row straight. Abdomen dorsum with variable markings; venter with paired longitudinal bands narrow to absent. Leg formula 1-4-2-3. NOTES: The commonest cribellate spiders found in coastal dune forests and swamp forests. Collected beneath rocks, logs and tree bark. Eight species are known from South Africa. (Xevioso-maaswebspinnekoppe)

Xevioso colobata

Colobata Hackled Band Spider

Carapace dark brown, with dark, sclerotised radii on thoracic region margin; eyes surrounded by black pigment. Abdomen grey-brown, dorsum with faint chevrons. Leg coloration similar to carapace. NOTES: A ground-dwelling cryptic spider that inhabits retreat-webs in damp and dark places. Sampled from the Savanna biome as well as citrus orchards. STATUS: LC; South African endemic. (Colobata-maaswebspinnekop)

Xevioso orthomeles

Kruger Park Hackled Band Spider

Carapace reddish brown; eyes surrounded by black pigment. Abdomen greyish brown with anteromedian longitudinal light area and paired light median spots. Legs and palps same colour as carapace. Markings darker in female. NOTES: Sampled from Grassland and Savanna where it was primarily found in bushveld. It makes retreat-webs on the ground. STATUS: LC; southern African endemic. (Krugerwildtuin-maaswebspinnekop)

FAMILY PISAURIDAE
Nursery-web spiders
Babakamerspinnekoppe

A diverse group of spiders. Carapace longer than wide; in some genera with blunt tubercles on anterolateral edge of clypeus; eight eyes, but pattern variable: two rows (4:4), three rows (4:2:2) or four rows (2:2:2:2), with at least one pair of eyes on shallow tubercles. Abdomen variable, from elongated to roundish oval. Legs three-clawed. NOTES: This diverse family contains free-living plant and ground dwellers as well as web dwellers. The female carries the egg cocoon beneath her sternum, held by her chelicerae and palps. Just before the young emerge, the female constructs a nursery web, in which she deposits the egg cocoon with emerging spiderlings. After emerging, the young stay in this nursery web before they disperse. This large cosmopolitan family is represented by 13 genera and 37 species in South Africa.

Afropisaura
Afropisaura nursery-web spiders

Medium-sized. Recognised by the straight anterior eye row. Carapace as wide as long; narrower in eye region; eight eyes in two rows (4:4); anterior eye row slightly procurved; posterior row recurved; anterior median eyes smallest; chelicerae with three equal-sized cheliceral teeth. Abdomen elongated, tapering posteriorly, usually with plumose setae. Legs three-clawed, relatively long, sometimes slightly laterigrade, with setae on patellae, femora, tibiae and metatarsi; tarsi with trichobothria in two rows or scattered; trochanters deeply notched. NOTES: Free-living plant dwellers. Frequently sampled by sweeping grass and low vegetation. Two species have been recorded in South Africa. (Afropisaura-babakamerspinnekoppe).

Afropisaura ducis
Ducis Nursery-web Spider

Carapace cryptic with grey background and brown and white longitudinal bands. Abdomen fawn with dark longitudinal wavy median band with white border. Legs pale with faint bands. NOTES: Sampled from Grassland, IOCB, Savanna and Thicket. STATUS: LC; African endemic. (Ducis-babakamerspinnekop)

Afropisaura rothiformis
Common Grass Nursery-web Spider

Carapace grey with dark broad longitudinal bands bordered with thin white stripe. Dark band with white border extends over length of abdomen. Legs pale with faint bands. NOTES: Sampled from Grassland, IOCB, Savanna and Thicket. STATUS: LC; African endemic. (Gewone Babakamerspinnekop)

Charminus
Charminus nursery-web spiders

Medium-sized. Resemble *Cispius*. Recognised by recurved anterior eye row. Carapace longer than wide; narrower in eye region; eyes in two rows (4:4), both rows recurved; anterior row only slightly shorter than posterior row; anterior eyes slightly smaller than posterior eyes. Abdomen oval. Legs pale or banded. Female slightly larger than male, but male with longer legs. NOTES: Most inhabit grasses, herbs and low-growing shrubs, especially in shaded areas. These plant-living nursery-web spiders are commonly found on vegetation at night. Four species are known from South Africa. (Charminus-babakamerspinnekoppe)

Female *Charminus* with egg sac

Charminus ambiguus
Ambiguus Nursery-web Spider

Carapace mottled brown with narrow white rim. Abdomen same mottled brown as carapace; lateral borders white; with two paler spots medially. Legs colourless. NOTES: Specimens have been observed early in the morning, when they run through and over the grass while taking tremendous leaps. They retreat during the warmer parts of the day. Sampled with sweep nets from IOCB and Savanna. STATUS: LC; African endemic. (Ambiguus-babakamerspinnekop)

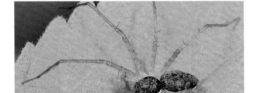

Charminus atomarius   Atomarius Nursery-web Spider

Carapace dark; symmetrical patterns of black on brown or grey background with narrow pale median band. Abdomen with dark broad median band bordered by wavy white narrow band. Legs pale with markings. **NOTES:** Sampled from IOCB and Savanna, usually with sweep nets. **STATUS:** LC; African endemic. (Atomarius-babakamerspinnekop)

Charminus natalensis   Natal Nursery-web Spider

Carapace dark with symmetrical patterns, pale narrow median band as well as one near lateral border; striae pale. Abdomen with dark broad median band bordered by wavy white narrow band. Legs dark, banded. **NOTES:** Sampled from Forest and IOCB. **STATUS:** LC; South African endemic. (Natalse Babakamerspinnekop)

Chiasmopes   Chiasmopes nursery-web spiders

Medium-sized. Carapace longer than wide, with longitudinal bands; eight eyes arranged in four rows (2:2:2:2); anterior lateral eyes close together on shallow tubercles on edge of clypeus; posterior margin of chelicerae with three teeth. Abdomen elongated oval, tapers posteriorly. Legs slightly laterigrade, with numerous spines. **NOTES:** They construct their sheet-webs in vegetation close to the ground. The web consists of many criss-crossing silk threads. Known from four African species, all recorded in South Africa. (Chiasmopes-babakamerspinnekoppe)

Chiasmopes lineatus   Striped Nursery-web Spider

Carapace with broad pale median band, extending between eyes as tuft of setae; rest of carapace marked with symmetrical black patterns on brown or grey background. Abdomen with dark longitudinal bands. Legs with faint markings and spots. **NOTES:** Sampled from Forest, Fynbos, Grassland, IOCB, Savanna and Thicket; also sampled from maize fields. **STATUS:** LC; African endemic. (Gestreepte Babakamerspinnekop)

Family Pisauridae   **115**

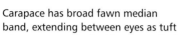

Chiasmopes signatus
Grahamstown Nursery-web Spider

Carapace has broad fawn median band, extending between eyes as tuft of setae; rest of carapace marked with symmetrical patterns of black on a brown or grey background. Abdomen with dark longitudinal bands. Legs with faint markings and spots. NOTES: Sheet-web spiders sampled from the Thicket biome. STATUS: DD; South African endemic. (Grahamstadse Babakamerspinnekop)

Cispius
Cispius nursery-web spiders

Medium-sized. Carapace and abdomen only slightly elongated, marked with symmetrical patterns or longitudinal bands. Carapace slightly longer than wide, narrower in eye region; eyes in two rows (4:4); anterior row recurved; anterior eyes smaller than posterior eyes; three cheliceral teeth in most species. Abdomen oval, with patterns. Legs strong, frequently banded. NOTES: The capture web is sheet-like and composed of dense criss-crossing threads. At one end the web is drawn into a long funnel that descends into the base of a plant. The spider runs on top of the web using scaffold lines. Three species have been recorded in South Africa. (Cispius-babakamerspinnekoppe)

Cispius problematicus
Zaire Nursery-web Spider

Carapace with broad pale wavy median band; rest of carapace with symmetrical patterns of black on a brown or grey background. Abdomen with broad pale wavy median band and two white spots near posterior edge. Legs banded. NOTES: Sampled from the Savanna biome. STATUS: LC; African endemic. (Zaïrese Babakamerspinnekop)

Cispius variegatus
Variegated Nursery-web Spider

Carapace with broad pale median band extending between eyes; band bordered by dark lateral bands. Abdomen with median band bordered by dark lateral bands. Legs banded. NOTES: Sampled from Forest, Savanna and Thicket. STATUS: LC; African endemic. (Bont Babakamerspinnekop)

Euprosthenops
Euprosthenops nursery-web spiders

Medium-sized. Carapace longer than wide; eyes in four rows (2:2:2:2); clypeus with blunt projection; anterior lateral eyes situated on projection; chelicerae with four posterior teeth. Abdomen elongated, tapering posteriorly. Legs laterigrade with strong setae. **NOTES:** They make large webs in vegetation, or sometimes in hollows in trees, with a funnel at the bottom. Three species have been recorded in South Africa. (Euprosthenops-babakamerspinnekoppe)

Euprosthenops australis African Nursery-web Spider

Carapace silver-grey with pale median band bordered by broad dark lateral bands, with radiating striae. Abdomen golden-brown dorsally with short dark heart mark. Legs dark grey with paler bands. **NOTES:** Sampled from Grassland, IOCB, Savanna and Thicket. **STATUS:** LC; African endemic. (Afrika-babakamerspinnekop)

Euprosthenops bayaonianus Decorated Nursery-web Spider

Carapace pale with narrow median band bordered by broad brown lateral bands, with radiating striae; two half-circles behind eye region. Abdomen brown with darker markings. Legs dark brown with paler bands. **NOTES:** Sampled from Grassland, Savanna and Thicket. **STATUS:** LC; African endemic. (Bont Babakamerspinnekop)

Euprosthenops proximus Tanzania Nursery-web Spider

Carapace pale grey with narrow pale median band bordered by two dark lateral bands, followed by white bands and narrow marginal band. Abdomen with several brown and white longitudinal bands and dark brown heart mark. Legs dark brown with spots. **NOTES:** Sampled from Grassland and Savanna. **STATUS:** LC; African endemic. (Tanzaniese Babakamerspinnekop)

Euprosthenopsis   Euprosthenopsis nursery-web spiders

Medium-sized. Carapace as wide as long; eyes in four rows (2:2:2:2); clypeus with blunt projection; anterior lateral eyes situated on projection; posterior margin of chelicerae with three teeth. Abdomen oval, tapering posteriorly. Legs relatively long, sometimes slightly laterigrade; three-clawed. NOTES: These spiders forage on sheet-webs made low in vegetation. The spiders run on top of the sheet. Four species are known from South Africa. (Euprosthenopsis-babakamerspinnekoppe)

Euprosthenopsis armata   Armata Nursery-web Spider

Carapace dark with two thin white submarginal bands extending to peduncles of anterior lateral eyes; thin white median band penetrates eye group and is connected by white band to lateral bands. Abdomen dark with two lateral white bands. Legs same colour as carapace. NOTES: Makes sheet-webs in Grassland and Savanna. STATUS: LC; African endemic. (Armata-babakamerspinnekop)

Euprosthenopsis pulchella   Pulchella Nursery-web Spider

Carapace dark with two thin white median bands connecting with white band between eyes. Abdomen dark with narrow white median band and two lateral white bands. Legs mottled with white. NOTES: Sampled from Desert, Fynbos, Grassland, Nama-Karoo and Savanna. STATUS: LC; southern African endemic. (Pulchella-babakamerspinnekop)

Euprosthenopsis vuattouxi   Vuattouxi Nursery-web Spider

Carapace creamy brown with white marginal band connecting with white band between eyes, bordered by two thin white lateral bands and narrow white marginal band. Abdomen creamish with two lateral pale bands. Legs same colour as carapace. NOTES: Sampled from Grassland, IOCB, Nama-Karoo and Savanna. STATUS: LC; African endemic. (Vuattouxi-babakamerspinnekop)

Hygropoda
Hygropoda nursery-web spiders

Medium-sized. Carapace flat in profile; eyes in two rows, subequal in size; eyes of posterior eye row larger than those of anterior row; anterior lateral eyes smallest. Abdomen long, slender, tapering posteriorly. Legs very long; tarsi of males and females curving, pseudo-segmented; trochanters with shallow notches. NOTES: Aboreal spiders that hunt on small sheet-webs made over leaves in forest areas. Only one species is known from South Africa. (Hygropoda-babakamerspinnekoppe)

Hygropoda tangana
Green Nursery-web Spider

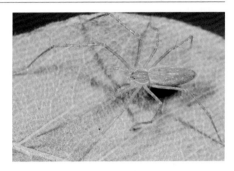

Carapace green, flat, with thin white marginal band; chelicerae yellowish. Abdomen green with faint longitudinal white spots and lines; sides yellowish. Legs same colour as abdomen. NOTES: Free-living plant dweller sampled from foliage in IOCB and Savanna. STATUS: LC; African endemic. (Groen Babakamerspinnekop)

Maypacius
Maypacius nursery-web spiders

Medium-sized. Recognised by their elongated bodies. Carapace longer than wide, narrower in eye region; anterior eye row strongly procurved; anterior lateral eyes not on tubercles but located nearly below anterior median eyes; posterior eye row strongly recurved; cheliceral furrow with two teeth of equal size. Abdomen elongated, tapering posteriorly. Legs long. NOTES: They make sheet-webs in vegetation. Four species are known from South Africa. (Maypacius-babakamerspinnekoppe)

Maypacius roeweri
Roewer's Nursery-web Spider

Carapace with broad dark median band extending from between eyes to posterior edge; band bordered by thin white lateral bands and pale marginal band. Abdomen sports dark median band bordered by thin pale bands; heart mark pale brown; sides fawn. Legs greyish with faint markings and spots. NOTES: Makes sheet-webs in vegetation. Active at night. Sampled from Grassland and Savanna. STATUS: LC; African endemic. (Roewer se Babakamerspinnekop)

Nilus — Fish-eating spiders

Large. Carapace longer than wide, marked with narrow white longitudinal bands; eyes arranged in two rows (4:4); chelicerae with three teeth on lower margin. Abdomen has variable patterns, with white or yellow longitudinal bands or spots. Legs relatively long, sometimes slightly laterigrade, with numerous spines. Males slightly smaller than females. NOTES: Free-running ground dwellers associated with freshwater bodies. Known to catch small fish, tadpoles and large aquatic invertebrates, including insect nymphs or larvae. Five species are known from South Africa. (Visvreterspinnekoppe)

Nilus curtus — Curtus's Fish-eating Spider

Carapace colour variable, sometimes with white or brown bands. Abdomen colour variable, with broad dark brown median band and white spots bordered by yellow-brown lateral bands. Legs usually banded. NOTES: Sampled from Forest, Fynbos, Grassland, IOCB and Savanna. STATUS: LC; African endemic. (Curtus se Visvreterspinnekop)

Nilus margaritatus — Margarita's Fish-eating Spider

Carapace dark brown with marginal white bands, sometimes with dark margin extending to clypeal edge. Abdomen brown with thin white band and row of spots on lateral border. Legs mottled grey. NOTES: Sampled from Grassland, IOCB and Savanna. STATUS: LC; African endemic. (Margarita se Visvreterspinnekop)

Nilus massajae — Massaja's Fish-eating Spider

Carapace with submarginal white band. Abdomen dark brown with submarginal white band and small paired white spots. Legs same colour as carapace. NOTES: Sampled from Forest, Fynbos, Grassland, IOCB and Savanna. STATUS: LC; African endemic. (Massaja se Visvreterspinnekop)

Nilus radiatolineatus　　　　Radiatolineatus Fish-eating Spider

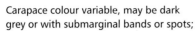

Carapace colour variable, may be dark grey or with submarginal bands or spots; abdomen same as carapace with yellow spots or dark transverse bands. Legs banded. **NOTES:** Sampled from the Savanna biome. **STATUS:** LC; African endemic. (Radiatolineatus-visvreterspinnekop)

Nilus rossi　　　　Ross's Fish-eating Spider

Carapace brown, variable, with broad yellow lateral bands; abdomen mottled brown with faint folium marking on posterior border. Legs with spots. **NOTES:** Sampled from the Savanna biome. **STATUS:** LC; African endemic. (Ross se Visvreterspinnekop)

Perenethis　　　　Perenethis nursery-web spiders

Medium-sized. Carapace low, almost flat in lateral view; eye region curves down to chelicerae; eyes not on tubercles, unlike in some other genera; anterior eye row slightly procurved; posterior row recurved; eyes rather small and subequal. Abdomen elongated, oval, tapering to posterior end; with indistinct brownish bands. Legs of median length. **NOTES:** Free-living plant dwellers. Two species have been collected from South Africa. (Perenethis-babakamerspinnekoppe)

Perenethis symmetrica　　　　Symmetrica Nursery-web Spider

Carapace fawn, with thin white median band bordered by brown lateral bands with white border; lateral bands extend to clypeal edge. Abdomen fawn with broad wavy brown median band with white border. Legs fawn. **NOTES:** It makes funnel-webs in open grass. Sampled from Fynbos and Savanna. **STATUS:** LC; African endemic. (Symmetrica-babakamerspinnekop)

Rothus
Rothus nursery-web spiders

Medium-sized. Carapace longer than wide, clothed in plumose setae; tufts of setae between anterior eyes; eight eyes arranged in two rows (4:4); posterior eye row recurved; teeth on cheliceral furrow. Abdomen elongated, tapers posteriorly, with plumose setae, decorated with longitudinal bands. Body colour variable. Legs relatively long, with strong setae; spines present on patellae, femora, tibiae and metatarsi. NOTES: Free-running spiders found in vegetation. Their movements are swift and erratic, as they sometimes jump while moving across the substrate. Some·species may wander into houses. Represented by three African species, all known from South Africa. (Rothus-babakamerspinnekoppe)

Rothus aethiopicus
Aethiopicus Nursery-web Spider

Carapace usually with broad pale median band ending in tuft of setae between eyes. Abdomen with bands that vary in shape and colour. Legs same colour as carapace. NOTES: Sampled from Fynbos, Grassland, Nama-Karoo, Savanna and Succulent Karoo. Also sampled from lucerne fields, pecan orchards and vineyards. STATUS: LC; African endemic. (Aethiopicus-babakamerspinnekop)

Walrencea
Walrencea nursery-web spiders

Medium-sized. Carapace slightly longer than wide, narrower in eye region; eight eyes in two rows (4:4); anterior eye row recurved; cephalic region broad; fovea short; two to four teeth on posterior margin of chelicera. Abdomen with slightly dark folium. Legs of medium length. NOTES: Free-living plant dwellers. Monotypic, known from one South African species. (Walrencea-babakamerspinnekoppe)

Walrencea globosa
Lawrence's Nursery-web Spider

Carapace with thin white median band that continues onto abdomen, band bordered by two darker lateral bands; rest of carapace mottled grey. Abdomen with dark folium, bordered by wavy white bands. Legs banded. NOTES: Sampled from silk retreats made in dried branches in Fynbos and IOCB. STATUS: DD; South African endemic. (Lawrence se Babakamerspinnekop)

FAMILY SEGESTRIIDAE
Tube-web spiders — Buiswebspinnekoppe

The family Segestriidae is recognised by the six closely grouped eyes, the fact that leg III is directed forwards, and by the double row of spines on the ventral surface of tibiae and metatarsi I. The family is known from a single genus, *Ariadna* from South Africa, and their morphology is discussed below.

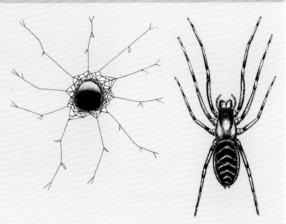

Ariadna
Ariadna tube-web spiders

Medium-sized. Carapace longer than wide, hairy to smooth; fovea a small depression; six eyes arranged in groups of two; chelicerae long and slender; fangs small; cheliceral furrow with few teeth. Abdomen longer than wide, cylindrical, setose; spinnerets short; anterior spinnerets contiguous. Legs three-clawed; third pair of legs directed forwards along with legs I and II; front legs with a double row of spines ventrally. NOTES: They construct a signal-web. The entrance of the tube has a small collar of regular white silk with triplines. The latter have no adhesive elements and are used to signal the arrival of prey. The spider uses the tube part of the web as a retreat. Some species are common in indigenous forest where they make their tube retreats in fallen tree trunks, while others are adapted to drier regions, such as Savanna, Nama-Karoo, Succulent Karoo and Desert. At present, 15 species are known from South Africa. (Ariadna-buiswebspinnekoppe)

Ariadna bilineata
Bilineata Tube-web Spider

Carapace dark red-brown to purplish black. Abdomen greyish brown. Legs same colour as carapace. Juveniles paler than adults. NOTES: They make webs in crevices of walls, rocks, fallen tree trunks or bark. Sampled from Fynbos and Savanna. STATUS: LC; South African endemic. (Bilineata-buiswebspinnekop)

Ariadna corticola — Bow-legged Tube-web Spider

Carapace colour varies from yellowish brown to dark red-brown or purplish black. Abdomen greyish brown. Front legs same colour as carapace; hind legs paler. Juveniles paler than adults. **NOTES:** Sampled from Forest, Grassland, IOCB, Savanna and Thicket. **STATUS:** LC; South African endemic. (Boggelbeen-buiswebspinnekop)

Ariadna jubata — Jubata Tube-web Spider

Carapace light brown; cephalic region darkened on each side; chelicerae dark reddish brown. Abdomen purplish black, with narrow mark on underside posteriorly. Anterior legs reddish or reddish yellow; posterior legs pale yellow. **NOTES:** Found under stones in Desert and Succulent Karoo. **STATUS:** LC; South African endemic. (Jubata-buiswebspinnekop)

Ariadna umtalica — Umtalica Tube-web Spider

Carapace dark brown; eye region black; chelicerae reddish black; sternum and labium brown, latter paler at apex. Abdomen pallid, suffused with purple. Legs infuscate, reddish above; anterior tibiae and metatarsi blackish red. **NOTES:** Found under stones in the Savanna biome. **STATUS:** LC; southern African endemic. (Umtalica-buiswebspinnekop)

Dwarf orb-web spiders　　　　　　　　Dwergwawielwebspinnekoppe

Very small (<2mm) lungless spiders. Clypeus and cephalic region elevated; four or six eyes; chelicerae fused; sternum broadly truncated posteriorly. Abdomen soft, globose, without scuta. Legs three-clawed. **NOTES:** Cryptozoic spiders found in the litter layer of forests. One genus is known from South Africa.

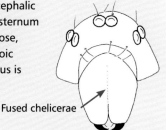

Fused chelicerae

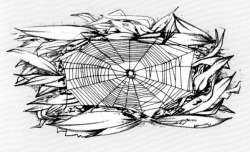

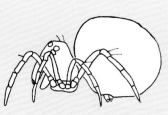

Symphytognatha　　　　　　　Symphytognatha orb-weavers

Very small. Chelicerae fused over most of their length; six eyes arranged in three diads. Abdomen spherical, soft. Legs three-clawed, sometimes with erect setae; spines absent; claws sometimes long and multidentate. **NOTES:** The smallest spiders ever described belong to this genus. They are found in temperate regions where they live in the litter of rainforests and similar moist habitats. Some species construct two-dimensional orb-webs with modification of the hub and radii. Owing to their minute size, they are easily overlooked and rarely collected. More species likely await discovery across the world. One species has been described from South Africa. (Symphytognatha-wawielwebspinnekoppe)

Symphytognatha imbulunga　　　Dwarf Sheet-Web Spider

Carapace yellow-white with dark pigment around eyes; chelicerae and sternum pale yellow-brown. Abdomen globose, pale grey-white, sparsely covered with simple setae; venter with two large, dark spots anterior to spinnerets. Legs pale yellow-brown. **NOTES:** The species was sampled from the litter layer of indigenous forest in the IOCB biome. **STATUS:** DD; South African endemic. (Dwergwawielwebspinnekop)

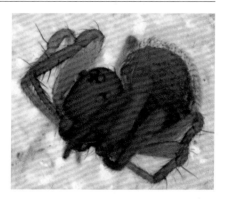

FAMILY TETRAGNATHIDAE
Long-jawed orb-web spiders   Langkaakwawielwebspinnekoppe

A very diverse family. Carapace
usually longer than wide;
chelicerae variable, from short
and stout to very long and well
developed, with rows of large
teeth and strong projecting spurs
(*Tetragnatha*); eight eyes in two
rows (4:4); lateral eyes contiguous
or set apart. Abdomen shape
variable, elongated and cylindrical or round to
ovoid; in some species abdomen extends beyond
spinnerets. Legs long, slender, with or without
spines. NOTES: Orb-web weavers that occupy a
variety of habitats. They frequently construct their
webs in vegetation, sometimes near or above
streams and ponds. The incline of the web can vary
from vertical to horizontal, but is typically vertical
or at a sharp angle. Five genera and 27 species are known from South Africa.

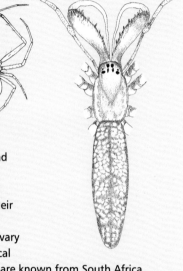

Diphya   Diphya large-eyed orb-web spiders

Small. Carapace pear-shaped, shiny; sides usually darker; eye region elevated, usually
darker; eyes prominent, in two rows, posterior row the widest; clypeus steep; sternum
heart-shaped. Abdomen stout, rounded, pale to dark, patterned. Legs long, slender;
front legs longer than others, bear row of thin spines. NOTES: Little is known about their
behaviour. One specimen was collected close to the ground, in an orb-web made in grass.
At present five species are known from South Africa. (Diphya-grootoog-wawielwebspinnekoppe)

Diphya simoni   Simon's Large-eyed Orb-web Spider

Carapace shiny, yellowish
brown, darker in male;
sides dark; border between head
and thoracic region with dark brown
patch; eye region dark; clypeus
paler. Abdomen mostly dark with
white patches. Legs honey-coloured;
femora III and IV sometimes with darker
bands. NOTES: Sampled from Fynbos,
Savanna and Thicket. STATUS: LC;
South African endemic. (Simon se
Grootoogwawielwebspinnekop)

Leucauge — Silver marsh spiders

Medium-sized. Recognised by their bright colours. Carapace slightly flattened; eyes in two rows. Abdomen elongated, overhangs carapace, truncated anteriorly, tapers posteriorly, sometimes past spinnerets. Legs slender, with double row of long, strong trichobothria on femora IV. Males slightly smaller than females. NOTES: They spin large vertical to almost horizontal webs in vegetation in a variety of habitats, frequently in damp places such as marshes or rainforests. They are found in their webs during the day. Eight species are known from South Africa. (Silwervleispinnekoppe)

Leucauge auronotum — Green-banded Silver Vlei Spider

Carapace shiny, with green median and marginal bands; chelicerae reddish. Abdomen elongated, silver-white, dorsum with heart mark; green lateral bands originate from posterior end. Legs same colour as carapace, with green tint. NOTES: Builds large orb-webs in Fynbos, Grassland and Savanna. STATUS: LC; South African endemic. (Groenband-silwervleispinnekop)

Leucauge decorata — Tailed Silver Vlei Spider

Carapace shiny, yellow-green, with green median and marginal bands; chelicerae reddish. Abdomen elongated, silver-white, with long silver and greenish bands on both sides of heart mark; posterior tip of abdomen extends past spinnerets. Femora with green tint; other leg segments yellowish. NOTES: Sampled from Forest, Fynbos, IOCB, Grassland, Nama-Karoo and Savanna and crops, including citrus orchards, maize fields and commercial pine plantations. STATUS: LC; Cosmopolitan. (Stertsilwervleispinnekop)

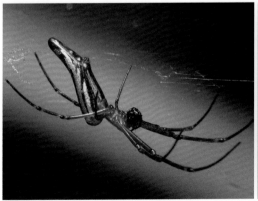

Leucauge festiva

Carapace shiny, yellow-brown. Abdomen elongated with short posterior tip, silver, decorated with red mask-like pattern dorsally, with tints of maroon, yellow, gold and green. Legs yellowish brown. Male chelicerae with protuberances. NOTES: A common species that makes orb-webs in Forest, Fynbos, Grassland, IOCB, Nama-Karoo and Savanna. Also sampled from avocado and macadamia orchards, as well as pumpkin and tomato fields. STATUS: LC; African endemic. (Afrika-maskersilwervleispinnekop)

Leucauge levanderi

Levander's Silver Vlei Spider

Carapace shiny with dark median and marginal bands. Abdomen elongated, short posterior tip with dark patches; dorsum with heart mark and broad silver bands, tinted with red bands; venter with broad green band edged with yellow and red. Legs same colour as carapace. NOTES: Makes orb-webs in Forest, Fynbos, Grassland, IOCB, Savanna and Thicket. STATUS: LC; African endemic. (Levander se Silwervleispinnekop)

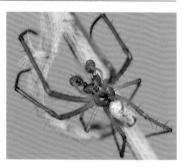

Leucauge medjensis

Black-spotted Silver Vlei Spider

Carapace shiny, reddish brown. Abdomen oval with short extended posterior tip; dorsum silver with two dark patches on anterior edge and single dark patch on posterior tip. Legs with reddish-brown bands. NOTES: A rare species found in the eastern parts of the country. Sampled from Forest, Grassland, IOCB, Savanna and Thicket. Also recorded in citrus orchards. STATUS: LC; African endemic. (Swartkol-silwervleispinnekop)

Leucauge thomeensis

Thomeensis Silver Vlei Spider

Carapace shiny, brown. Abdomen roundish oval; posterior edge rounded and decorated with dark patches; ventrum with red spots. Legs dark. NOTES: Makes orb-webs low in grass. Sampled from Forest, IOCB, Savanna and Thicket. Also sampled in high numbers from avocado, citrus and macadamia orchards. STATUS: LC; African endemic. (Thomeensis-silwervleispinnekop)

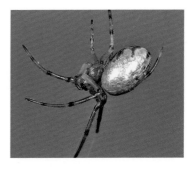

Metellina

Metellina orb-web spiders

Medium-sized. Carapace longer than wide; eyes in two rows (4:4); median eyes with canoe-shaped tapetum; posterior lateral eyes on single tubercle; fovea long. Abdomen longer than wide, oval, without tubercles. Legs long; I and II longer than others. NOTES: Web dwellers found in vegetation. One species is known from South Africa. (Metellina-wawielwebspinnekoppe)

Metellina haddadi

Haddad's Orb-web Spider

Carapace yellow-brown; dark triangular area posterior to eyes extends to form dark median band; dark marginal band. Abdomen mottled, with dark folium. Legs banded. NOTES: Sampled from vegetation in the Fynbos biome. STATUS: DD; South African endemic. (Haddad se Wawielwebspinnekop)

Tetragnatha

Long-jawed water spiders

Medium-sized. Bodies and legs characteristically long. Carapace longer than wide; chelicerae project forwards, more distinct in males and bearing two rows of large teeth along the inside margin; fangs long, with hooked tips. Abdomen elongated, much longer than wide. Legs long and slender. NOTES: These spiders build orb-webs in vegetation, usually near water or horizontally above the water surface. During periods of inactivity the spider will sit on plant stems with the body and legs pressed to the substrate. They prey on flying insects such as mosquitoes. Twelve species are known from South Africa. (Langkaakwaterspinnekoppe)

Tetragnatha bogotensis   Bogotensis Long-jawed Water Spider

Carapace straw-coloured. Abdomen with distinct dark heart mark; blunt tip above spinnerets. Legs same as carapace. NOTES: Sampled from most biomes except Desert and Succulent Karoo. STATUS: LC; Cosmopolitan. (Bogotensis-langkaakwaterspinnekop)

Tetragnatha ceylonica   Humpback Long-jawed Water Spider

Carapace straw-coloured. Abdomen with distinct small hump medially. Legs same colour as carapace. NOTES: Sampled from Fynbos, Grassland, IOCB, Savanna and Thicket. STATUS: LC; Cosmopolitan. (Boggelrug-langkaakwaterspinnekop)

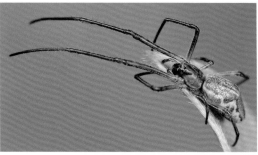

Tetragnatha demissa   Demissa's Long-jawed Water Spider

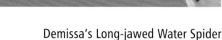

Carapace and legs dark reddish brown; lateral eyes on small humps. Abdomen paler with dark patterns. Legs same colour as carapace. NOTES: Sampled from Fynbos, Grassland, Nama-Karoo, Savanna and Thicket. STATUS: LC; Cosmopolitan. (Demissa se Langkaakwaterspinnekop)

Tetragnatha isidis — Isidis Long-tailed Water Spider

Body and legs straw-coloured. Body very elongated, with abdomen extending tail-like past spinnerets. Legs straw-coloured. **NOTES:** Sampled from Fynbos, Grassland, IOCB and Savanna. **STATUS:** LC; Cosmopolitan. (Isidis-langstertwaterspinnekop)

Tetragnatha subsquamata — Green Long-jawed Water Spider

Carapace green with brown tint. Abdomen green with white patterns; unlike related species, abdomen does not extend past spinnerets. Legs green. **NOTES:** Makes orb-webs in grass. Sampled from Forest, Grassland, IOCB, and Savanna as well as in avocado and macadamia orchards and maize fields. **STATUS:** LC; African endemic. (Groen Langkaakwaterspinnekop)

Tetragnatha vermiformis — Vermiformis Long-jawed Water Spider

Carapace reddish brown with faint median band. Abdomen with broad reddish-brown median band. Legs same colour as carapace. **NOTES:** Sometimes abundant in built-up areas, covering everything with their silk threads. Sampled from Fynbos, Grassland, IOCB and Savanna. **STATUS:** LC; Cosmopolitan. (Vermiformis-langkaakwaterspinnekop)

FAMILY THERIDIIDAE
Comb-footed spiders
Kamvoetspinnekoppe

A diverse family. Carapace variable in profile, from flat to elevated; in some genera the frontal region of the male's carapace has extravagant modifications; eight eyes in two rows (4:4). Abdomen variable in shape, from oval to round and elevated to elongated, sometimes extending past spinnerets; some species have dorsal stridulating plates near pedicel. Legs moderately to very long, three-clawed, ecribellate, with no or few spines; row of slightly curved, serrated bristles on tarsi IV form a comb; tarsi usually tapering. **NOTES:** They build gumfoot-webs, making three-dimensional aerial webs in dark corners in a variety of microhabitats. It's likely they adjust the shape of their web depending on the available space, and add lines, including adhesive threads, on subsequent nights. At present 18 genera and 63 species have been recorded in South Africa.

Argyrodes
Argyrodes dew-drop spiders

Small. Recognised by the silvery patches of variable sizes on the abdomen. Carapace smooth in female; eye region of males usually has characteristic lobes and projections clothed in special setae. Abdomen with prominent hump, latter higher than long and usually silver in colour; length and size of abdomen varies from species to species. Legs slender; legs I and II the longest. **NOTES:** These spiders are generally kleptoparasites, living on the webs of other large orb-weavers and stealing their prey. Some species are commensal, inhabiting another spider's web but not stealing its food. Others steal the host's silk, or prey upon its eggs. Only a few species catch prey in their own webs. Five species are known from South Africa. (Argyrodes-doudruppelspinnekoppe)

Argyrodes argyrodes
Silver Dew-drop Spider

Carapace dark brown. Abdomen of female elevated, cone-shaped, bright silver, with short, black mid-dorsal line and a black spot on posterior tip; abdomen in male triangular with dark median band dorsally. Legs brown. **NOTES:** Sampled from other spiders' webs in Grassland and Savanna. **STATUS:** LC; Cosmopolitan. (Silwer Doudruppelspinnekop)

Argyrodes convivans Convivans Dew-drop Spider

Carapace light brown; eye region smooth in female; male has eye tubercles, upper anterior tubercle blackish brown. Abdomen yellow dorsally, brownish at sides; posterior apex with round blackish spot; black spot on each side. Legs uniformly yellow-brown, distal segments darker. NOTES: Sampled from other spiders' orb-webs in Forest, Fynbos, Grassland, IOCB and Savanna. Also sampled from citrus orchards and cotton fields. STATUS: LC; southern African endemic. (Convivans-doudruppelspinnekop)

Argyrodes sextuberculosus Sextuberculosus Dew-drop Spider

Carapace brown. Abdomen silvery, with longitudinal black median strip adorned with speckles of silver; end of posterior tubercle almost entirely black; venter blackish brown, dotted with white. Legs brown. NOTES: Kleptoparasites known from the Savanna biome. STATUS: LC; African endemic. (Sextuberculosus-doudruppelspinnekop)

Argyrodes stridulator Stridulator Dew-drop Spider

Carapace yellow-brown, infuscate, margins dark. Abdomen silvery at sides, enclosing narrow median band, which is slightly darker than sides. Legs and palps similar in colour to carapace. NOTES: Sampled from IOCB and Savanna. STATUS: LC; South African endemic. (Stridulator-doudruppelspinnekop)

Family Theridiidae **133**

Enoplognatha   Long-jawed comb-foot spiders

Medium-sized. Recognised by enlarged chelicerae in males. Carapace longer than wide. Abdomen suboval; carina present above pedicel in male. Leg I or IV the longest. NOTES: They make cobwebs under stones or ground debris. Some specimens were sampled from vegetation where they build webs on, between and around leaves. Three species have been recorded in South Africa. (Langkaak-kamvoetspinnekoppe)

Enoplognatha molesta   Molesta Long-jawed Spider

Female Carapace yellow-brown with two thin black longitudinal lines centrally, thin black marginal band. Abdomen oval, white with brown median band bordered by spotted area and scalloped black bands. Legs same colour as carapace, marked with numerous black spots. **Male** Body more slender; legs longer; colour of body and legs darker; chelicerae elongated with protuberances. NOTES: Sampled from all biomes. Also sampled from crops, including citrus, cotton, maize, potatoes, sorghum, strawberries, sugarcane and tomatoes. STATUS: LC; South African endemic. (Molesta-langkaakspinnekop)

Episinus   Episinus comb-foot spiders

Small. Carapace slightly longer than wide; eye region roundly elevated or projecting anteriorly; often with a pair of horns between anterior and posterior median eyes. Abdomen usually widest medially; modified with humps. Legs somewhat robust. Males and females similar in appearance, other than for male's slimmer abdomen. NOTES: They can be found at ground level between low vegetation making a very simple H- or Y-shaped web. Three species recorded from South Africa. (Episinus-kamvoetspinnekoppe)

Episinus marignaci   Butterfly Comb-foot Spider

Carapace fawn with two dark V-shaped longitudinal bands; sides brown. Abdomen reddish brown with distinct triangular pattern dorsally; dorsal triangle consists of a yellow area bordered by a thin reddish band; second smaller pink triangle on the yellow triangle. Legs same colour as carapace, but legs I and IV darker. NOTES: Found at ground level in low vegetation in Fynbos, IOCB, Savanna and Thicket. STATUS: LC; southern African endemic. (Skoenlapper-kamvoetspinnekop)

Euryopis Ant-eating comb-foot spiders

Small. Cephalic region elevated; anterior median eyes larger than and wide apart from posterior median eyes; chelicerae very small; fangs long, flattened. Abdomen triangular, pointed posteriorly, sometimes sclerotised, often with silver spots. Leg IV slightly longer than I and III. **NOTES:** Found on ground level and observed to prey on ants. Two species are known from South Africa. (Miervreterkamvoetspinnekoppe)

Euryopis episinoides Black Ant-eating Comb-foot Spider

Carapace shiny brown to black. Abdomen shiny, black. Legs shiny, dark brown. **NOTES:** An introduced species sampled in high numbers from crops. **STATUS:** LC; Cosmopolitan. (Swart Miervreterkamvoetspinnekop)

Euryopis funebris Silver Ant-eating Comb-foot Spider

Carapace pale cream, darker around fovea and eyes. Abdomen silvery with dark pattern dorsally. Legs same colour as carapace; distal segments banded with dark setae. **NOTES:** An introduced species sampled around dwellings. **STATUS:** LC; Cosmopolitan. (Silwer Miervreterkamvoetspinnekop)

Latrodectus Button spiders ☠

Medium-sized. Carapace wide in thoracic region but flat in profile; eight eyes in two rows (4:4) with lateral eyes separated; chelicerae without teeth. Abdomen globular. Legs moderately long and slender, with no or few spines; leg III the shortest; tarsus IV bears typical row of slightly curved, serrated setae, forming a comb. Sexes differ in size and colour, male much smaller and more brightly coloured. **NOTES:** Button spiders construct three-dimensional webs in dark corners in a variety of microhabitats. Six species are known from South Africa. (Knopiespinnekoppe)

L. indistinctus and *L. geometricus* have well-studied venom of medical importance. The venom of other species in this genus may have the same effect. See page 17.

Latrodectus cinctus
Cinctus Button Spider ☠

Carapace pitch-black. Abdomen with bright red transverse abdominal bands dorsally, varying between specimens and fading as females age; abdomen pitch-black ventrally. Legs black. NOTES: More common in IOCB, Savanna and Thicket. STATUS: LC; African endemic. (Cinctus-knopiespinnekop)

Latrodectus geometricus
Brown Button Spider ☠

Carapace varies from cream, brown to black. Abdomen sometimes cream to pitch-black; in paler specimens geometric pattern visible dorsally; distinct orange-red hourglass ventrally. Legs banded. NOTES: Found in a variety of microhabitats and commonly found around houses. The spiked egg sac is distinct. Sampled from all biomes. STATUS: LC; Cosmopolitan. (Bruin Knopiespinnekop)

Latrodectus indistinctus
Indistinctus Button Spider ☠

Carapace pitch-black. Abdomen with bright red abdominal patterns dorsally, frequently with scattered white markings in between, varying between specimens and fading as females age; abdomen pitch-black ventrally. Legs black. NOTES: Found in a variety of microhabitats and more common in Desert, Fynbos, Nama- and Succulent Karoo. STATUS: LC; southern African endemic. (Indistinctus-knopiespinnekop)

Latrodectus renivulvatus
Renivulvatus Button Spider ☠

Carapace pitch-black. Abdomen with bright red transverse abdominal bands dorsally, varying between specimens and fading as females age; abdomen pitch-black ventrally. Legs dark. **NOTES:** Sampled from all biomes and frequently sampled from crops such as cotton, maize, strawberries, sugarcane and vineyards. Sometimes found in houses in Gauteng and the Free State. **STATUS:** LC; African endemic. (Renivulvatus-knopiespinnekop)

Latrodectus rhodesiensis
Zimbabwean Button Spider ☠

Carapace usually brown. Abdomen cream to brown; geometric pattern visible dorsally in specimens; distinct orange-red hourglass ventrally. Legs banded. **NOTES:** Not common in South Africa. Sampled from Grassland and Savanna. The egg sac is distinct in being large and woolly. **STATUS:** LC; southern African endemic. (Zimbabwiese Knopiespinnekop)

Latrodectus umbukwane
Forest Button Spider ☠

Carapace black. Abdomen dorsally black with light-coloured, irregular oval lines laterally extending onto the dorsal surface with a single dorsal posterior red stripe; ventral surface with irregular marking, situated more posteriorly than the orange-red hourglass of the brown buttons. Legs uniformly black. **NOTES:** Egg sac blueish in colour. Rare sample from Savanna and IOCB. **STATUS:** DD; South African endemic. (Woud-knopiespinnekop)

Meotipa

Meotipa comb-foot spiders

Small. Females of *Meotipa* differ from all other theridiids by a combination of the unusual outline of the abdomen, the tip projecting upward and backward over the spinnerets like some *Argyrodes*, and with an apical rounded knob bearing conspicuous black flattened spines or scales; scales often also situated on the rear face of the abdomen. Eyes relatively large. NOTES: They have a strange resting behaviour, pivoting the body axis over 90° so that it rests with one side turned towards the leaf surface, legs wrapped in a semicircle on the leaf surface. Only one species is known from South Africa. (Meotipa-kamvoetspinnekoppe)

Meotipa pulcherrima

Pulcherrima Comb-foot Spider

Carapace fawn with brown median band. Abdomen white with black and red spots. Legs banded, often very long; leg I longer than IV. NOTES: Sampled from Savanna and Thicket. STATUS: LC; Cosmopolitan. (Pulcherrima-kamvoetspinnekop)

Parasteatoda

Parasteatoda comb-foot spiders

Small. Carapace oval. Abdomen nearly spherical, usually with small posterior projection. Leg formula 1-2-4-3 in male, 1-4-2-3 in female. Male with stridulating plate either side of pedicel. NOTES: Sampled from bark. They make a long narrow silk tube retreat. Two species are known from South Africa. (Parasteatoda-kamvoetspinnekoppe)

Parasteatoda lunata

Lunata Comb-foot Spider

Carapace dark, shiny. Abdomen brown to blackish brown on anterior area before projection; narrow white band covers projection; posterior region reddish brown. Legs with dark bands. NOTES: Sampled from the Savanna biome. STATUS: LC; Cosmopolitan. (Lunata-kamvoetspinnekop)

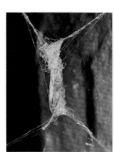

Phoroncidia — Mushroom comb-foot spiders

Very small spiders recognised by round globular abdomen overhanging carapace. Eye region projects anteriorly, overhanging clypeus; chelicerae small. Abdomen heavily sclerotised, leathery with folds or strong spines; sclerotised ring around spinnerets. Legs very short; leg IV longer than leg I. NOTES: They hunt at night, constructing snares consisting of single, more or less horizontal sticky lines. Several species are known from South Africa but most are still unnamed. (Sampioenkamvoetspinnekoppe)

Phoroncidia eburnea — White Mushroom Comb-foot Spider

Carapace dark brown. Abdomen globular with numerous tubercles, mottled white with grey, darker ventrally. Legs same colour as carapace, with dense setae. NOTES: Found in low vegetation. Sampled from Grassland, IOCB and Savanna. STATUS: LC; South African endemic. (Wit Sampioenkamvoetspinnekop)

Phycosoma — Phycosoma comb-foot spiders

Very small spiders. Carapace in female low and not modified; eye region often projecting above clypeus with anterior median eyes sometimes larger than the others; clypeus concave; chelicerae small, without teeth and fangs long and flat; male carapace very elevated, sometimes as high as long, cylindrical in shape with dorsal grooves and depressions. Abdomen sometimes modified, sometimes sclerotised with a dorsal scutum or hump. Leg IV slightly longer than others. NOTES: They construct small cobwebs near the ground where they feed on ants. Also named gallows spiders because they hang their prey until it dies. Several species are known from South Africa, but most are still unnamed. (Phycosoma-kamvoetspinnekoppe)

Phycosoma martinae — Large-spotted Comb-foot Spider

Carapace cream; in male with slight dorsal grooves. Abdomen same colour as carapace, marked with about eight black spots. Legs same colour as carapace; medium to short. NOTES: Sampled from Fynbos, Grassland, IOCB, Savanna and Thicket. Observed feeding on ants. STATUS: LC; Cosmopolitan. (Grootkol-kamvoetspinnekop)

Rhomphaea   Rhomphaea comb-foot spiders

Small. Recognised by boomerang-shaped abdomen; tip of abdomen in air, bearing modified sturdy setae. Carapace elongated; slightly flattened clypeus strongly projecting. Abdomen elongated triangular or cylindrical; female abdomen tapering to a single tip, usually four to six times as long behind as anterior to spinnerets. Legs very long and thin. Male may have eye region with projection. NOTES: Solitary spiders that prey on other spiders. They venture onto other spiders' webs to capture the resident. They have been observed to catch their spider prey with a web held in their hind legs. Several species are known from South Africa but most are still unnamed. (Rhomphaea-kamvoetspinnekoppe)

Rhomphaea affinis   Tailed Comb-foot Spider

Carapace creamy brown. Abdomen elongated, mottled white with silver spots; tip of abdomen with small hook. Legs pale yellow, very long, with dorsal longitudinal bands. NOTES: Sampled from Grassland, IOCB, Savanna and Thicket. STATUS: LC; southern African Endemic. (Stertkamvoetspinnekop)

Rhomphaea nasica   Nasica Comb-foot Spider

Carapace creamy with brown markings. Abdomen mottled white with silver and brown spots. Legs pale yellow, very long, with longitudinal dorsal bands. NOTES: Sampled from Fynbos, Grassland, Savanna and Thicket. STATUS: LC; Cosmopolitan. (Nasica- kamvoetspinnekop)

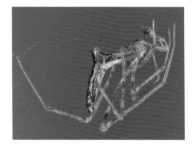

Steatoda   False button spiders

Medium-sized. They resemble members of *Latrodectus*. Carapace longer than wide, with distinct fovea; in male sometimes rugose, with stridulatory ridges on posterior sides of carapace; lateral eyes touching or separated by less than their diameter; chelicerae sometimes enlarged in male, with one or two teeth on anterior margin. Abdomen suboval; in the male abdomen suboval with sclerotised ring around pedicel; colulus large. Leg I or IV longest, III shortest. NOTES: They build their webs beneath logs, stones, other debris under bark or in crevices in boulders, rock faces and tree trunks up to a height of 2m. There is no retreat, and the spiders hide in crevices or under stones. The round white fluffy egg sacs are deposited in the web. Nine species are known from South Africa. (Valsknopiespinnekoppe)

Steatoda capensis — Cape False Button Spider

Carapace dark brown to pitch-black. Abdomen similar in colour with white band on anterior edge; sometimes extending laterally. Legs uniformly black. Males with white markings on abdomen. **NOTES:** They make webs in open grass in all biomes except the more arid ones. **STATUS:** LC; South Africa and Lesotho. (Kaapse Valsknopiespinnekop)

Theridion — False house button spiders

Small spiders. Carapace smoothly curved and widest near the rear. Abdomen raised, roundish, but more oval in the male. Characteristic is the broad longitudinal band running over the abdomen. Legs long, slender. **NOTES:** They build a conical retreat of twigs and leaves in their three-dimensional labyrinth web. The pear-shaped papery egg sac and the youngsters are protected in this retreat and guarded by the female. Youngsters are fed by mouth by their mother until their first moult. Twelve species are known from South Africa. (Valshuisknopiespinnekoppe)

Theridion pictum — Brown False House Button Spider

Carapace yellowish brown, with brown margin and median bands; sternum yellowish, with brown margin. Abdomen with dorsal longitudinal band, ventrally spotted with white, with dark points anterior to the spinnerets. Legs reddish yellow, annulated with brown. **NOTES:** Sampled with pitfall traps from the Savanna biome. Also sampled from avocado and macadamia orchards. **STATUS:** LC; Cosmopolitan. (Bruin Valshuisknopiespinnekop)

Theridion purcelli — Purcell's False House Button Spider

Carapace yellowish brown, with brown marginal and median bands; sternum yellowish, with brown margin. Abdomen with dorsal longitudinal band, laterally white and brown spots. Legs yellow with brown bands. NOTES: Sampled from all biomes except the more arid ones. STATUS: LC; South African endemic. (Purcell se Valshuisknopiespinnekop)

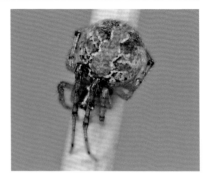

Theridula — Theridula comb-foot spiders

Very small spiders. Carapace wider than long; eyes slightly elevated; shiny. Abdomen shiny, wider than long, sometimes with hump on each side; in male abdomen more oval; some individuals with small, sclerotised spots on venter of abdomen or sclerotised ring around basal segment of anterior pair of spinnerets. Leg I the longest. NOTES: Frequently found on the underside of leaves, on bushes or in tall grass. They have a web with long viscid lines that help capture flying prey. With their threads they bend leaves under which they live, mate, guard their eggs and raise their youngsters. Several species have been recorded from South Africa, but only one species has been named at present. (Theridula-kamvoetspinnekoppe)

Theridula gonygaster — Yellow-spotted Comb-foot Spider

Carapace creamy with black median band; sternum usually black. Abdomen black with a variable number of dorsal white or yellow spots. Legs creamy. NOTES: Sampled from the Fynbos biome. STATUS: LC; Cosmopolitan. (Geelkol-kamvoetspinnekop)

Thwaitesia — Thwaitesia comb-foot spiders

Small. Carapace nearly circular; posterior median eyes separated by their diameter or less; chelicerae small, without teeth. Abdomen usually higher than wide, with silvery spots. Legs long, first patella and tibia two to three times carapace length. NOTES: They make small, tangled webs and hide under leaves during the day. Their mirrored surfaces seem to scatter light, probably helpful in making them hard to see. At least one species has been sampled from South Africa. (Thwaitesia-kamvoetspinnekoppe)

Thwaitesia meruensis Meru Comb-foot Spider

Carapace pale with narrow median dark band; narrow marginal band. Abdomen usually higher than wide, with silvery spots; colulus replaced by two setae. Legs long, first patella and tibia two to three and a half times carapace length; pale with dark bands. NOTES: Sampled from the Savanna biome. STATUS: LC; Cosmopolitan. (Meru-kamvoetspinnekop)

Tidarren One-palp tidarren spiders

Small. Carapace longer than wide, without modifications; clypeus elevated in male, with eye region protruding; concave in female; eyes about equal in size. Abdomen higher than long, in many species with dorsal tubercle, sometimes with white lines on sides and a white band from apex to spinnerets. Males are dwarfs with a total body length of approximately 1mm; stridulatory organ on posterior border of prosoma present, but inconspicuous; adult males possess only one palp. NOTES: Their webs consist of a retreat and a scaffold of threads extending to the side of a wall, not or rarely reaching the ground. Web dimensions depend on the space available: in the field large female webs may measure up to half a metre in height. The retreat is a densely spun area into which prey remnants and other debris are incorporated. Three species are known from South Africa. (Eenpalp-tidarrenspinnekoppe)

Tidarren scenicum Cameroon Tidarren Spider

Carapace wide, dark, shiny. Abdomen mottled brown and yellow; abdomen tip ends in a high tubercle. Legs banded. NOTES: Sampled from vegetation in Fynbos, Grassland and Savanna. STATUS: LC; African endemic. (Kameroense Tidarren-spinnekop)

FAMILY ULOBORIDAE
Hackled orb-web spiders
Maaswawielwebspinnekoppe

Diverse family. Carapace either long and narrow, pear-shaped, or more triangular; eight eyes in two rows (4:4) with anterior eye row reduced in *Miagrammopes*. Abdomen slender or with one or two humps (*Hyptiotes* and *Uloborus*); or very narrow and elongated, sometimes extending past spinnerets (*Miagrammopes*). Legs I and IV longer than other legs in *Uloborus* and *Miagrammopes*, while legs are shorter and stouter in *Hyptiotes*; tibiae I sometimes with brush of long setae (*Uloborus*) and metatarsi IV ventrally with row of macrosetae; metatarsi IV dorsally compressed and curved under uniseriate calamistrum; femora with rows of long trichobothria. NOTES: Two of the genera spin adapted orb-webs made of cribellate silk. Their webs are usually made between the leaves of plants. Four genera and nine species are known from South Africa.

Hyptiotes
Hyptiotes triangle-web spiders

Small. *Hyptiotes* have stout and compact bodies and a triangular carapace that is broad posteriorly and narrowed towards the front. Carapace as broad as long; weakly convex above, highest and broadest at second eye row, posterior eye row very widely spaced; carapace narrowed and rounded in front and widely rounded posteriorly; eight eyes arranged in two unequal, transverse rows. Abdomen of female suboval, moderately to strongly arched; cribellum broad; abdomen of males more slender. Legs shorter and thicker than in other uloborids; calamistrum covering entire length of metatarsus IV. NOTES: These spiders produce a rudimentary orb-web consisting of four radii connected to a single thread. The spider rests on the single thread upon which the four radii converge. The thread is held under tension and manipulated by the spider when catching prey. Only one species is recorded from South Africa. (Hyptiotes-driehoekwebspinnekoppe)

Hyptiotes akermani

Hyptiotes akermani　　　Ackerman's Triangle-web Spider

Carapace a dull shade of cream, grey and brown, triangular, broad posteriorly and narrowed towards the anterior. Abdomen and legs same colour as carapace; covered with dense setae and small tubercles. NOTES: Rare and mainly found in the eastern parts of the country. Sampled from Forest, Grassland, IOCB and Savanna. STATUS: LC; South African endemic. (Ackerman se Driehoekwebspinnekop)

Miagrammopes　　　Single-line-web spiders

Medium-sized. The body is much longer than wide, with the sides almost parallel. Carapace long and narrow; anterior eyes reduced or absent; only four posterior eyes present. Abdomen very narrow and elongated, sometimes extending beyond spinnerets. Legs I and IV much longer than others. NOTES: A horizontal, usually single line is made between two branches or twigs, with only the central section consisting of cribellate silk. This line is held under tension and released when prey is close. The attack behaviour consists of rapid jerking and sudden sagging of the catch thread. The spider rests at the end of one of the lines and will only approach the centre as darkness sets in. Three species have been recorded from South Africa. (Enkellynwebspinnekoppe)

Miagrammopes brevicaudus　　　Spotted Single-line-web Spider

Carapace dull brown, without longitudinal paler bands; posterior median eyes are wide apart from each other. Abdomen longitudinal with pale paired patches and two dark patches centrally; tip not extending past spinnerets. Legs same colour as carapace. NOTES: They make single-line webs in vegetation. Sampled from most of the biomes except the arid ones. STATUS: LC; South African endemic. (Gekolde Enkellynwebspinnekop)

Miagrammopes constrictus Feather-legged Single-line-web Spider

Carapace dark olive-brown, yellowish at anterior and lateral margins. Abdomen with dark median band in anterior part. Front legs with short setae, white, but underside of tibia and upper and underside of metatarsus with a thick mane of longer white-tipped brown setae; three posterior pairs of legs are pale yellowish; distal part of femur of fourth pair dark olive or blackened. NOTES: The webs are made in vegetation. Sampled from Fynbos, Grassland, IOCB, Nama-Karoo and Savanna. STATUS: LC; South African endemic. (Veerpoot-enkellynwebspinnekop)

Philoponella Philoponella hackled orb-web spiders

Small. Carapace longer than wide, with broad transverse thoracic groove; eyes small; posterior eye row nearly straight; integument clothed in white setae. Abdomen long oval; posteriorly rounded; with anterior tubercles distinct, posterior tubercles less distinct. In the male, tibiae I have at least four prolateral, four retrolateral and six distal macrosetae. NOTES: A single-line web is produced. Only one species is known from South Africa. (Philoponella-maaswawielwebspinnekoppe)

Philoponella angolensis Angola Hackled Orb-web Spider

Carapace white, bearing white setae. Abdomen with faint, dusky spots on prominent abdominal tubercles. Legs same colour as carapace. NOTES: Sampled from Fynbos, Savanna and Thicket. STATUS: LC; African endemic. (Angolese Maaswawielwebspinnekop)

Uloborus Uloborus hackled orb-web spiders

Small to medum-sized. Carapace pear-shaped to hexagonal, with conspicuously narrowed cephalic region and narrow thoracic depression; posterior eye row recurved. Abdomen usually has one or two humps (absent in males). In the female of some species leg I has tufts of setae on the tibiae, while in the male two or three rows of strong spines are present. Leg I longer and stronger than others; first femur bears numerous trichobothria. NOTES: Members of *Uloborus* build small orb-webs with cribellate silk. The hub is often meshed or strengthened with a stabilimentum that varies in shape. Three species have been recorded from South Africa. (Uloborus-maaswawielwebspinnekoppe)

Uloborus planipedius Planipedius Hackled Orb-web Spider

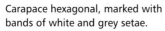

Carapace hexagonal, marked with bands of white and grey setae. Abdomen dull shades of cream, grey or brown; with two low humps. Legs I and IV longer than other legs; same colour as carapace. **NOTES:** Sampled from Forest, Fynbos, Grassland, Nama-Karoo and Savanna. **STATUS:** LC; South African endemic. (Planipedius-maaswawielwebspinnekop)

Uloborus plumipes Feather-legged Spider

Carapace hexagonal, dull shades of cream, grey or brown. Abdomen with two humps; same colour as carapace. Legs I and IV longer than other legs; tibiae I with brush of long setae in female. **NOTES:** Very common. Sampled from all biomes. Its orb-webs are frequently found in and around houses. **STATUS:** LC; Cosmopolitan. (Veerpootspinnekop)

Uloborus walckenaerius Walckenaer's Hackled Orb-web Spider

Carapace with dense layer of cream to white setae. Abdomen wide oval, without humps, with setae that form erect tufts. Legs have faint bands. **NOTES:** This species has been introduced and so far recorded from Fynbos, Grassland and Savanna. **STATUS:** LC; Cosmopolitan. (Walckenaer se Wit Maaswawielwebspinnekop)

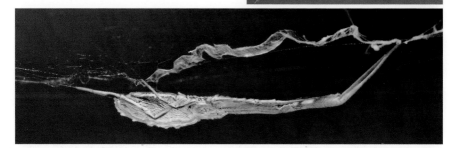

PLANT DWELLERS

Plant-living spiders have a range of characteristic adaptations that facilitate a life on and under bark, in grass, on flowers, among foliage or on seeds. Whereas some web-dwelling spiders use the vibration of silk strands to detect their prey, plant-dwelling spiders typically rely on good eyesight and well-developed tactile sense organs. Claw tufts and brush-like scopulae on the tips of the legs improve their grip on plants and prey. Some plant-dwelling families are nimble wanderers. Others have lost their agility and are semi-sedentary, excelling as ambushers. Plant dwellers can be grouped by the part of the plant they inhabit.

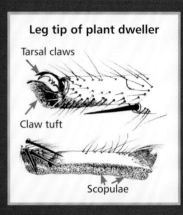

Leg tip of plant dweller

Tarsal claws

Claw tuft

Scopulae

Thomisus spiders often match the colour of the flower they inhabit.

BARK DWELLERS are a cryptic mottled grey-white to dark brown and resemble pieces of bark. Some have a body with large knobbly and spiny protuberances to mimic the growths and thorns commonly found on trees. Others have a flattened body, an adaptation to life in the narrow spaces under bark. When lying adpressed to the bark, their flat body does not cast a shadow. These spiders typically deposit their egg sac under bark or attach it to bark, then camouflage it with bits of bark debris.

GRASS DWELLERS are easily recognised by their elongated body and long, thin legs. They vary in colour from green to fawn or grey. Many are cryptically coloured and sport stripes along the length of their body, imitating the veins in a blade of grass. They are especially difficult to detect while at rest, when the legs are held forward and parallel with the body. Grass dwellers typically tie twisted grass blades and grass seeds together with their silk threads to create a retreat or to deposit their egg sac.

Hamataliwa rufocaligata female

A well-camouflaged *Monaeses austrinus*

Hersilia arborea female

Runcinia flavida female on egg sac

FLOWER DWELLERS are usually brightly coloured (white, yellow, pink or green). Some species are semi-sedentary, sitting in wait and grabbing prey that visit flowers. Several species can change colour to match the flower they are on, camouflaging themselves from prey and predators. The process usually takes a few days, and can be reversed.

Synema imitatrix female

Rhene lingularis male

FOLIAGE DWELLERS vary in colour from fawn to brown or bright green. They move between leaves in search of prey. They frequently fold leaves into a retreat or a site to deposit their egg sac.

Oxyopes sp. female

Oxytate argenteooculata female

SEED DWELLERS have rounded, compact bodies that resemble seeds. Their colour varies from white to red and green. They construct silk retreats between seeds or in nearby folded leaves.

Phoroncidia sp. female

Family Cheiracanthiidae p. 153

Medium-sized; two-clawed; eight eyes in two rows (4:4); front legs longer than hind legs; leg tarsi with dense claw tufts; posterior spinnerets two-segmented, distal segment long ①. *Cheiracanthium* pale yellowish brown with dark face ②; *Cheiramiona* usually with pattern on abdomen ③. In both genera males darker, with longer legs.

Spinnerets

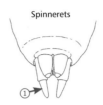

Family Clubionidae p. 157

Medium-sized; two-clawed; eight eyes in two rows (4:4); legs with dense claw tufts ①; front legs shorter than hind legs; anterior spinnerets situated close together. Coloration varies from pale to yellowish green; carapace brownish in some males; abdomen sometimes sports distinct heart mark.

Leg tip

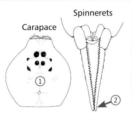

Clubiona sp.

Family Hersiliidae p. 160

Medium-sized; three-clawed; eight eyes closely grouped on eye tubercle (4:4) ①; body flattened; posterior spinnerets long and slender with apical segment strongly tapering ②. Coloration varies from golden-brown to pure white or almost black; mottled.

Carapace

Spinnerets

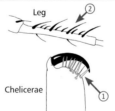

Hersilia sp.

Family Mimetidae p. 163

Small to medium-sized; three-clawed; eight eyes in two rows (4:4); chelicerae with peg teeth ①; prolateral spination on tibiae ②; metatarsi I and II modified. Coloration varies from pale yellowish with dark spots or markings on body to reddish brown; legs frequently banded.

Leg

Chelicerae

Mimetus sp.

Family Oxyopidae p. 165

Small to large; three-clawed; eight eyes arranged in a hexagon (4:4) with the clypeus wide ①; setae prominent on legs ②. Coloration varies from dark brown or yellowish brown (*Hamataliwa* and *Oxyopes*) to bright green (*Peucetia*).

Leg

Carapace

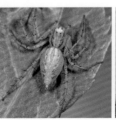

Hamataliwa sp.   *Oxyopes* sp.   *Peucetia* sp.

Family Philodromidae p. 173

Morphologically diverse family; small to medium-sized; two-clawed; eight eyes in two rows (4:4); body covered with soft recumbent setae, usually with dark, heart-shaped mark; abdomen variable in shape, from heart-shaped (*Gephyrota*, *Philodromus*) to oval (*Thanatus*) or elongated (*Tibellus*); legs laterigrade and slender with claw tufts and scopulae. Coloration varies from white to pale cream and reddish brown or greyish brown; frequently mottled with longitudinal bands or chevrons.

Thanatus sp.

Gephyrota sp.

Tibellus sp.

Family Salticidae p. 180

A morphologically very diverse family; very small to large; two-clawed; eight eyes; characterised by square-fronted carapace and four, forwardly directed eyes; anterior median eyes very large. Attractive coloration consisting of bands, stripes or speckles; body clothed in numerous special setae, sometimes iridescent; males more brightly coloured than females.

Carapace

Hyllus sp.

Festucula sp.

Family Sparassidae p. 226

A morphologically diverse family; medium-sized to very large; two-clawed; eight eyes in two rows (4:4); cheliceral margin with teeth; laterigrade legs ①; soft trilobate membranes at apex of metatarsi ② allow hypermobility of tarsi. Colour varies from green, cream and fawn to dark brown or grey, often with dark stripes and mottled pattern.

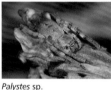

Metatarsus

Palystes sp.

Olios sp.

Family Thomisidae p. 235

A morphologically diverse family; small to large; two-clawed; eight eyes in two rows (4:4) with lateral eyes frequently on tubercles; legs laterigrade, with I and II typically longer than III and IV. Colour varies from brightly coloured (white, pink, green, yellow) to dark brown or grey and mottled; abdomen frequently patterned.

Carapace

Oxytate sp.

Thomisops sp.

Family Trochanteriidae p. 267

Small to medium-sized; two-clawed; eight eyes (4:4); posterior median eyes oval; body flattened; legs laterigrade, folding over the body as in scorpions; fourth trochanters elongated ①; anterior spinnerets with sclerotised subdistal ring. Colour dark brown to grey; abdomen uniform or with pale markings; some species with longitudinal bands.

Platyoides sp.

FAMILY CHEIRACANTHIIDAE
Sac spiders
Sakspinnekoppe

Carapace longer than wide; eight eyes arranged in two rows (4:4). Abdomen oval, with heart mark. Posterior spinnerets two-segmented, distal segment long. Legs two-clawed, with dense claw tuft; legs relatively long,

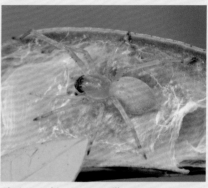

Cheiracanthium sp. on silk retreat

leg I longer than leg IV. Males resemble females, but have a more slender body and longer legs. NOTES: Free-living plant dwellers occasionally found on the ground. They construct sac-like retreats in rolled leaves or grass. Three genera and 47 species have been recorded in South Africa.

Cheiracanthium
Cheiracanthium sac spiders

Medium-sized. Body creamy yellow; face dark. Fovea indistinct to absent; fangs long. Abdomen oval, covered with soft setae; heart mark distinct to indistinct. Legs long; leg formula 1-4-2-3. NOTES: Free-living plant dwellers that make silk retreats in rolled-up leaves. Four types of silken sac retreats can be distinguished: resting, mating, breeding and hibernating. The female encloses herself with the eggs to guard them while they develop. This common genus is found on crops, preying on thrips, mites, insect eggs and butterfly and moth larvae. Some species are found in houses. Ten species have been recorded in South Africa. (Cheiracanthium-sakspinnekoppe)

Cheiracanthium aculeatum
Sudan Sac Spider

Carapace creamy yellow; cephalic region sports faint W-shaped bands; chelicerae and eye region blackish brown. Abdomen yellow to olive-green with distinct heart mark. Legs fawn. NOTES: Sampled from Grassland, IOCB and Savanna. STATUS: LC; African endemic. (Soedanse Sakspinnekop)

Cheiracanthium africanum — African Sac Spider

Cephalic region bears dense setae and faint W-shaped bands; chelicerae and eye region blackish brown. Abdomen yellow to olive-green with distinct heart mark. Legs grey to fawn. **NOTES:** Sampled from gardens, grassland, cultivated crops, shrubs, trees and under stones in all regional biomes except the arid ones. **STATUS:** LC; African endemic. (Afrikasakspinnekop)

Cheiracanthium furculatum — House Sac Spider

Carapace with some fine setae in cephalic region; chelicerae and eye region blackish brown. Abdomen yellow to olive-green with faint heart mark. Legs fawn. **NOTES:** Very common, sampled from grass and trees in all regional biomes except Succulent Karoo. An agrobiont species. Commonly found in houses, especially in Gauteng and the Free State. **STATUS:** LC; African endemic. Introduced to Europe. (Huissakspinnekop)

! This spider is found in houses and has venom of medical importance (see p. 18).

Cheiracanthium vansoni — Vanson's Sac Spider

Carapace fawn; eye region and chelicerae darker, blackish brown. Abdomen yellow to olive-green with distinct heart mark. Legs yellow to fawn. **NOTES:** Sampled from Forest, Grassland, IOCB, Nama-Karoo and Savanna; also from cultivated crops such as cotton and pistachio orchards. **STATUS:** LC; South African endemic. (Vanson se Sakspinnekop)

Cheiramiona   Long-legged sac spiders

Medium-sized. Fovea inconspicuous to absent; eyes dark; in males, chelicerae well developed with long fangs. Abdomen oval, covered with soft setae; heart mark distinct; chevron markings present; apical segment of posterior spinnerets conical. Legs usually banded, relatively long; leg formula 1-4-2-3. Males typically darker in colour and more slender than females, with longer legs. NOTES: Free-living plant dwellers that make silk retreats in rolled-up leaves or grass. Of this African genus, 35 species occur in South Africa. (Langbeensakspinnekoppe)

Cheiramiona amarifontis   Amarifontis Long-legged Sac Spider

Carapace yellowish brown. Abdomen bears distinct dark brown heart mark; chevrons present posteriorly; dark brown ring around spinnerets. Legs bear yellowish-brown bands. NOTES: Sampled from under shrubs in humus and on bushes in Fynbos, Grassland and Thicket. STATUS: LC; South African endemic. (Amarifontis-langbeensakspinnekop)

Cheiramiona clavigera   Zululand Long-legged Sac Spider

Carapace yellowish brown. Abdomen bears distinct dark brown heart mark followed by dark, paired chevrons. Legs yellowish brown. NOTES: Sampled from rehabilitated coastal dune forest at Richards Bay. Occurs in Forest, Fynbos, IOCB, Savanna and Thicket. STATUS: LC; South African endemic. (Zululandse Langbeensakspinnekop)

Cheiramiona debeeri   Debeer's Long-legged Sac Spider

Carapace orange-brown with dark V-shaped median band; chelicerae elongated. Abdomen bears distinct dark brown heart mark; broad dark marking extends to spinnerets. Legs yellowish brown, banded. NOTES: Collected from vegetation in Afromontane forest in the Forest biome. STATUS: DDT; South African endemic. (Debeer se Langbeensakspinnekop)

Cheiramiona florisbadensis Florisbad Long-legged Sac Spider

Female Carapace brown. Abdomen with distinct dark brown heart mark; paired chevrons extend to spinnerets. Legs yellowish with brown bands. **Male** Body dark orange-brown. Legs much longer than those of female, dark brown except on coxae and part of femora. **NOTES:** Sampled from shrubs and forests in Forest, Fynbos, Grassland, Nama-Karoo and Savanna. **STATUS:** LC; South African endemic. (Florisbad-langbeensakspinnekop)

Cheiramiona krugerensis Kruger Park Long-legged Sac Spider

Carapace orange-brown. Abdomen bears distinct dark brown heart mark; chevrons present mid-dorsally on each side; dark brown ring around spinnerets. Legs yellow, banded with brown. **NOTES:** Collected in Forest, Fynbos, Grassland, IOCB, Savanna and Thicket; also from avocado, citrus and mineola orchards and tomato fields. **STATUS:** LC; South African endemic. (Krugerwildtuin-langbeensakspinnekop)

Cheiramiona paradisus Paradisus Long-legged Sac Spider

Carapace reddish brown with dark W-shaped marking posteriorly. Abdomen bears distinct dark brown heart mark, with paired chevrons in female and broad dark band in male. Legs yellowish brown in female; very long and banded in male. **NOTES:** Sampled from Forest, Fynbos, Grassland, IOCB, Savanna and Thicket; also from macadamia orchards. **STATUS:** LC; southern African endemic. (Paradisus-langbeensakspinnekop)

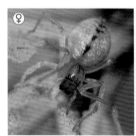

Lessertina

Lessertina sac spiders

Medium-sized. Carapace strongly raised, domed; median eyes closely grouped; carapace surface finely wrinkled, sparsely covered in very short straight white setae; fovea a shallow depression. Abdomen oval, with or without markings, covered in very short, straight, white setae. Legs covered in very short, straight setae; leg formula 4-1-2-3. **NOTES:** Free-living ground dwellers collected from leaf litter. Two species endemic to the eastern and south-eastern parts of South Africa. (Lessertina-sakspinnekoppe)

Lessertina mutica

Lessertina Sac Spider

Carapace black. Abdomen black, with pair of white markings. Legs relatively short, with few spines. **NOTES:** Collected from leaf litter of subtropical coastal and Afromontane forests in Forest, IOCB and Savanna. **STATUS:** LC; South African endemic. (Lessertina-sakspinnekop)

FAMILY CLUBIONIDAE

Grass sac spiders   Grassakspinnekoppe

Carapace longer than wide; fovea shallow to absent; eight small, equal-sized eyes arranged in two rows (4:4), chelicerae of some species strongly developed (especially in males), with long fangs. Abdomen oval; sometimes with small dorsal scutum in males. Legs moderately long, two-clawed, with dense claw tufts; leg I shorter than leg IV. **NOTES:** Wandering hunters found mainly on grass, foliage, loose bark and leaf litter. They make sac-like retreats, often in rolled or folded grass or under loose bark. They also use these retreats during moulting and for depositing their egg sac. These spiders are commonly found during surveys in the Grassland, Nama-Karoo, Savanna and Succulent Karoo. A few species are known from forests. One genus and 26 species are known from South Africa.

Clubiona

Clubiona grass sac spiders

Medium-sized. Species very uniform in colour and shape – difficult to identify to species level without examining genitalia. In males, abdomen sometimes has small scutum. Legs moderately long; leg formula 4-1-2-3. **NOTES:** Free-living plant dwellers represented by 26 species in South Africa. (Clubiona-grassakspinnekoppe)

Clubiona abbajensis

Abbajensis Grass Sac Spider

Carapace and legs creamy brown to fawn; eye region and chelicerae darker. Abdomen silky grey. Legs creamy fawn. NOTES: Sampled from Fynbos, Grassland, Savanna and Thicket; also from avocado, citrus, lemon and macadamia orchards. STATUS: LC; African endemic. (Abbajensis-grassakspinnekop)

Clubiona africana

African Grass Sac Spider

Carapace orange-brown to fawn; eye region and chelicerae darker. Abdomen silky cream. Legs same colour as carapace. NOTES: Sampled from Grassland, Nama-Karoo, Savanna, Succulent Karoo and Thicket; also from avocado, citrus and macadamia orchards, tomato fields and vineyards. STATUS: LC; South African endemic. (Afrika-grassakspinnekop)

Clubiona bevisi

Bevisi's Grass Sac Spider

Carapace high, fawn to dark brown; eye region and chelicerae very dark. Abdomen silky fawn. Legs same colour as carapace. NOTES: Sampled from Grassland and Savanna. STATUS: LC; South African endemic. (Bevisi se Grassakspinnekop)

Clubiona citricolor

Citricolor Grass Sac Spider

Carapace brown with dense setae; eye region and chelicerae darker. Abdomen silky grey. Legs fawn. NOTES: Sampled from the Grassland biome. STATUS: DDT; South African endemic. (Citricolor-grassakspinnekop)

Clubiona durbana

Durban Grass Sac Spider

Carapace brownish to fawn with dense, fine setae; eye region and chelicerae not very dark. Abdomen silky grey, sometimes with greenish tint. Legs same colour as carapace. **NOTES:** Sampled from Grassland, IOCB and Savanna. **STATUS:** LC; South African endemic. (Durbanse Grassakspinnekop)

Clubiona pongolensis

Pongola Grass Sac Spider

Carapace creamy fawn with dense white setae; eye region and chelicerae pale. Abdomen silky grey, with dense setae. Legs same colour as carapace. **NOTES:** Sampled from Grassland and Savanna. **STATUS:** LC; South African endemic. (Pongola-grassakspinnekop)

Clubiona pupillaris

Pupillaris Grass Sac Spider

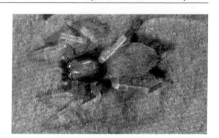

Carapace creamy fawn; dense white setae in U-shape; eye region and chelicerae with brownish tint. Abdomen silky grey, with dense setae. Legs same colour as carapace. **NOTES:** Sampled from Forest, Grassland, IOCB, Savanna and Thicket; also from citrus orchards and cotton fields. **STATUS:** LC; South African endemic. (Pupillaris-grassakspinnekop)

Clubiona sigillata

Pietermaritzburg Grass Sac Spider

Carapace brown; eye region and chelicerae very dark. Abdomen silky grey, with darker scutum. Legs same colour as carapace. **NOTES:** Sampled from Forest, Grassland, Nama-Karoo, Savanna and Thicket. **STATUS:** LC; South African endemic. (Pietermaritzburgse Grassakspinnekop)

FAMILY HERSILIIDAE
Long-spinneret spiders Langspintepelspinnekoppe

Carapace flattened, densely covered with plumose setae; narrow longitudinal fovea present, marked with radiating striae; eight eyes in two strongly recurved rows (4:4), situated on large eye tubercle. Abdomen longer than wide, widest in posterior third, flat, wider behind than in the front, densely covered with plumose setae; posterior spinnerets long and slender with apical segment strongly tapering; inner surface of spinnerets bears series of long tubules that produce thin silk threads. Legs three-clawed; very long, especially in males; leg III shortest in both sexes. NOTES: Free-running spiders commonly found on the bark of trees or on the ground. Those in the genera *Hersilia* and *Neotama* have flattened bodies and are able to lie against the bark without casting shadows. *Tyrotama* spiders build webs under stones. This family is known from three genera and 12 species in South Africa.

Hersilia Hersilia long-spinneret bark spiders

Medium-sized. Carapace ovoid, thoracic region being the widest; chelicerae armed with teeth on pro- and retromargin. Abdomen with four pairs of distinct dorsal muscular pits that vary in size; posterior spinnerets cylindrical. Legs long. NOTES: Free living, cryptic bark dwellers. Remain with their body pressed to the substrate when at rest, moving at great speed when disturbed. They attack prey by circling it while facing away, covering it with bands of silk from their enormously elongated spinnerets. Females construct flat, oval-shaped egg sacs on the surface of tree trunks, camouflaging them with bits of bark. Four species are known from South Africa. (Hersilia-langspintepelbasspinnekoppe)

Hersilia arborea Arborea Long-spinneret Bark Spider

Carapace red-brown with faint black border; clypeus a paler brown; chelicerae pale to dark brown; eye region pale to dark brown. Abdomen mottled white dorsally, lateral border paler; lancet-shaped heart mark present; posterior half of dorsum sports distinct transverse bands; posterior lateral spinnerets banded. Legs same colour as carapace. NOTES: Sampled from trees in Grassland and Savanna. STATUS: LC; southern African endemic. (Arborea-langspintepelbasspinnekop)

Hersilia sericea

Carapace pale brown, covered with black setae; lateral border narrow, black; eye tubercle black with white spot posteriorly. Abdomen mottled black on white background; black, wavy anterolateral border around most of dorsal area; heart mark lancet-shaped; posterior lateral spinnerets and palpi annulated. Legs same colour as carapace. NOTES: Sampled from Forest, Grassland, IOCB, Nama-Karoo, Savanna and Thicket. STATUS: LC; African endemic. (Sericea-langspintepelbasspinnekop)

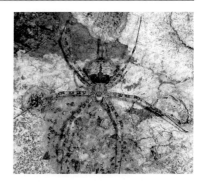

Hersilia setifrons

Setifrons Long-spinneret Bark Spider

Carapace covered with setae that vary from white to dark brown; clypeus pale brown, some specimens with V-shaped mark medially; eye region dark brown or with dark brown patches around eyes. Abdomen dark brown dorsally, black laterally; heart mark lancet-shaped; faint broad transverse bands on either side of heart mark. Femora dark brown; palpi banded. NOTES: Sampled from Forest, Grassland, Nama-Karoo and Savanna. STATUS: LC; southern African endemic. (Setifrons-langspintepelbasspinnekop)

Neotama   Neotama long-spinneret bark spiders

Medium-sized. Posterior spinnerets as long as abdomen. Male closely resembles female, but is smaller, with longer legs. NOTES: Arboreal forest dwellers. Only one species is known from South Africa. (Neotama-langspintepelbasspinnekoppe)

Neotama corticola

Corticola Long-spinneret Bark Spider

Carapace pale yellow to brown with brown and white spots laterally; eye region dark with white mark posterior to the eye tubercle. Abdomen white with dark borders anteriorly; heart mark lancet-shaped; posterior half of abdomen sports dark, V-shaped border; dorsal muscular pits distinct. Legs banded. NOTES: Sampled from Forest, IOCB and Savanna. STATUS: LC; South African endemic. (Corticola-langspintepelbasspinnekop)

Tyrotama — Tyrotama two-tailed ground spiders

Medium-sized. Carapace width equal to or wider than length; eyes on a low tubercle; chelicerae elongated, at least twice as long as wide, unarmed; sternum heart-shaped. Abdomen oval, convex, densely covered with plumose setae, with plain setae scattered in between; posterior lateral spinnerets longer than others. Leg IV longest; leg formula 4-2-1-3. Male smaller than female, with longer legs. NOTES: Found under stones where they construct a circular retreat of closely woven webbing in which small pebbles, chips and vegetable debris are incorporated. Anchor threads attached to the substratum alert the hunter to approaching prey. These spiders move at great speed, overpowering their prey and dragging it back to their retreat, where they feed on it. Their round egg sacs are attached to the underside of a stone and protected with stone chips. Seven species are known from South Africa. (Tyrotama-tweestertgrondspinnekoppe)

Tyrotama abyssus — Abyssus Two-tailed Ground Spider

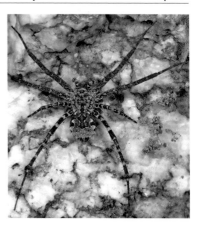

Carapace pale brown, covered with patches of dark setae; border dark; clypeus pale brown; eye tubercle dark around eyes. Abdomen dark brown with pale brown markings; dorsum bears dark, hourglass-shaped heart mark. Legs same colour as carapace. NOTES: Found under stones where it builds circular webs. Webs attach to the underside of the stone, hanging like a veil. The entrance faces north. Sampled from Nama-Karoo and Succulent Karoo. STATUS: LC; southern African endemic. (Abyssus-tweestertgrondspinnekop)

Tyrotama arida — Arida Two-tailed Ground Spider

Carapace pale yellow with dark border; clypeus pale, darker laterally; eye region dark. Abdomen dark brown with dark anterolateral border; heart mark broad; faint transverse bands present posteriorly. Legs same colour as carapace. NOTES: A female was sampled with six egg sacs congregated in a heap, covered with small stone chips. Frequently found in pitfall traps in Desert, Fynbos, Grassland, Nama-Karoo and Savanna. STATUS: LC; South African endemic. (Arida-tweestertgrondspinnekop)

Tyrotama australis   Australis Two-tailed Ground Spider

Carapace testaceous, with thin dark border; clypeus pale brown, dark laterally; eye region pale. Abdomen testaceous, sparsely covered in long, brown setae; border dark. **NOTES:** Most specimens, especially males, were caught in pitfall traps in Desert, Fynbos, Grassland, Nama-Karoo and Savanna. **STATUS:** LC; southern African endemic. (Australis-tweestertgrondspinnekop)

FAMILY MIMETIDAE
Pirate spiders   Rowerspinnekoppe

Carapace with sloping thoracic region; fovea deep; cephalic region varies from long and attenuated to short, sharply convex; carapace bears rows of long setae; eight eyes in two rows (4:4), anterior median eyes usually largest, and raised on small common protuberance; chelicerae fused at base, peg teeth present. Abdomen variable in shape. Legs three-clawed, long and slender; characteristic macrosetae on anterior prolateral surfaces of tibiae and metatarsi on legs I and II, consisting of a series of short spines, interspersed with a series of longer, slightly curved spines. **NOTES:** Most pirate spiders are specialised predators of web-living spiders. They enter the webs of other spiders and, using vibratory patterns that simulate the movement of captured prey or courting males, trick and kill the host. Using the rake-like spines on their legs, they first immobilise the legs of the prey spider. A quick bite is then delivered. Some species are also kleptoparasitic, inhabiting the webs of other spiders and feeding on their eggs as well as their prey. Three genera and four species occur in South Africa.

Anansi   Anansi pirate spiders

Medium-sized. Carapace longer than wide; cephalic region as long as thoracic region; fovea consists of two longitudinal slits whose ends meet posteriorly; anterior eye row straight to slightly recurved; median eyes black, distinctly larger than white lateral eyes; anterior median eyes larger, on tubercle; chelicerae longer than clypeus, with peg teeth. Abdominal humps present. Legs slender, with macrosetae; retrolateral side of femur I and prolateral side of femur II with a longitudinal row of short setae. **NOTES:** A free-living spider found on vegetation, where it preys on other spiders. One species occurs in South Africa. (Anansi-rowerspinnekoppe)

Anansi natalensis　　　　　　　　　　Natal Pirate Spider

Cephalic region with large brown medial marking; chelicerae dark brown. Abdomen sports brown and white spots dorsally, with strong setae. Legs yellow, with spots and bands. **NOTES:** This arboreal species is commonly found in avocado, citrus, cotton and pine plantations, which offer adequate supplies of spiders to prey on. Occurs in all biomes excluding Desert and Succulent Karoo. **STATUS:** LC; South African endemic. (Natalse Rowerspinnekop)

Ero　　　　　　　　　　　　　　　Ero pirate spiders

Small. Carapace elevated in the middle; clypeus concave, about as wide as eye region; eyes in posterior row very slightly procurved; median eyes darker, nearer to each other than to lateral eyes; anterior row very slightly recurved; chelicerae with four or five peg teeth. Abdomen humped, covered with short spines, mottled with dark brown, or black and creamy white, sometimes with reddish tinge. Legs slender, yellow-brown with brown spots; leg I very long; promarginal row of long, slightly curved spines on tibiae and metatarsi of legs I and II. **NOTES:** A free-living spider found on vegetation. Feeds on other spiders. Two species are known from South Africa. (Ero-rowerspinnekoppe)

Ero capensis　　　　　　　　　　　Cape Pirate Spider

Carapace yellow with dark narrow median band and numerous black spots. Abdomen with tubercles and spines; red and white band between tubercles on dorsal surface; rest of abdomen yellow. Legs banded, with numerous spots. **NOTES:** Sampled from Fynbos, Grassland and Thicket. **STATUS:** LC; southern African endemic. (Kaapse Rowerspinnekop)

Ero lawrencei　　　　　　　　　　Lawrence's Pirate Spider

Carapace yellow with dark lateral bands. Abdomen with tubercles and spines; white area on dorsal surface, starting between tubercles and ending at spinnerets; rest of abdomen dark. Legs conspicuously banded. **NOTES:** Sampled from Grassland and Savanna. **STATUS:** LC; southern African endemic. (Lawrence se Rowerspinnekop)

Mimetus
Mimetus pirate spiders

Small. Members of this genus resemble Theridiidae (comb-foot spiders) owing to their globular abdomen. Carapace sometimes bears rows of long spines; distance between anterior edge of carapace and anterior median eyes about a third to half of the distance between anterior and posterior medial eyes. Abdomen broad and angular, with lateral humps. **NOTES:** These specialised spider killers don't spin webs. Slow-moving, they stalk or ambush their prey. They sometimes invade the web of a potential victim, vibrating the silk to mislead the owner. They attack their prey by biting one of its legs and then injecting it with toxin. They then retreat until the victim is paralysed before sucking the fluids from its body. Only one species is known from South Africa. (Mimetus-rowerspinnekoppe)

Mimetus cornutus
Cornutus Pirate Spider

Carapace yellow; whole cephalic region occupied by large brown marking ending at fovea; chelicerae dark brown. Abdomen dorsally divided by a band joining the two abdominal tubercles. Legs yellow, conspicuously banded. **NOTES:** Free-living spider found on vegetation, sampled from IOCB and Savanna. **STATUS:** LC; southern African endemic. (Cornutus-rowerspinnekop)

FAMILY OXYOPIDAE
Lynx spiders
Tierspinnekoppe

Carapace longer than wide, high and convex anteriorly, sloping posteriorly; clypeus wide; eight eyes in form of a hexagon occupy a small area on the edge of carapace; integument bears setae and sometimes scales. Abdomen oval, tapering to a point posteriorly. Legs three-clawed, long and slender, with prominent spines. **NOTES:** Lynx spiders are named for the way they hunt, leaping from leaf to leaf in pursuit of their prey. They catch prey with their legs, often jumping a few centimetres into the air to seize a passing insect in flight. They may also stretch themselves out on the surface of a leaf and drop onto moths

and wasps flying below. These spiders are very common on vegetation and occur in high numbers on trees and grasses. They are also commonly found in agroecosystems. Their egg sacs are fastened to a twig or leaf or suspended in a small irregular web. Three genera and 40 species are known from South Africa.

Hamataliwa

Hamataliwa lynx spiders

Medium-sized. Posterior median eyes further from each other than from posterior lateral eyes; clypeus slopes gradually towards anterior edge; many species sport tufts of setae in eye region. Legs frequently bear longer setae on lateral surface; legs I and II long and more robust than legs III and IV, which are more weakly developed. NOTES: Free-living plant dwellers that occur in high numbers on trees and grasses. Sampled from Fynbos, Grassland, IOCB and Savanna. Some species were collected in agroecosystems. Five species are known from South Africa. (Hamataliwa-tierspinnekoppe)

Hamataliwa kulczynskii

Kulczynski's Lynx Spider

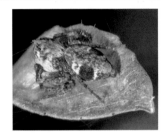

Carapace brownish, with dense layer of setae; strong tufts of setae between eyes. Abdomen bears similar dense setae, with two dark patches on lateral side near posterior end. Legs same colour as carapace. NOTES: Sampled from Fynbos, Grassland, IOCB and Savanna. It has also been found in avocado and macadamia orchards. STATUS: LC; African endemic. (Kulczynski se Tierspinnekop)

Hamataliwa rostrifrons

Rostrifrons Lynx Spider

Carapace dark reddish brown; clypeus lighter; tuft of setae behind posterior row of eyes, projecting forwards and upwards and overhanging the eyes. Abdomen dark reddish brown dorsally, some brown markings centrally; longitudinal whitish bands along side of ventrum, speckled with brown. Legs banded. NOTES: Sampled from IOCB, Savanna and Thicket. STATUS: LC; southern African endemic. (Rostrifrons-tierspinnekop)

Hamataliwa rufocaligata

Rufocaligata Lynx Spider

Carapace short, very high, grey; eye region dark, covered with snow-white, short, lanceolate setae pressed together and inclined downwards. Abdomen short, with long, elevated vertical tubercle, apex blunt with fine setae; covered with white scales. Legs short; metatarsi and tarsi yellow, with dense white setae. NOTES: Found in the Savanna biome. STATUS: LC; African endemic. (Rufocaligata-tierspinnekop)

Hamataliwa strandi — Strand's Lynx Spider

Carapace short, high, mottled with grey, brown, yellow and red setae, giving it a spotted appearance. Abdomen short, mottled with grey and brown setae, apex blunt. Legs short, with dense, long setae of white, grey and red. **NOTES:** Found in the Savanna biome. **STATUS:** LC; African endemic. (Strand se Tierspinnekop)

Oxyopes — Oxyopes lynx spiders

Medium-sized. Carapace almost as wide as long; clypeus vertical, decorated with conspicuous stripes and spots; integument usually clothed in dense scales; posterior eye row strongly procurved. Abdomen oval, tapering to a point posteriorly. Leg IV longer than leg III. **NOTES:** Very common on vegetation and occur in high numbers on grasses. Also commonly found in agroecosystems. They catch prey by jumping a few centimetres into the air and using their legs to seize passing insects in full flight. Their egg sacs are fastened to a twig or leaf, or suspended in a small irregular web. The female guards and defends the eggs. Known from 26 species in South Africa. (Oxyopes-tierspinnekoppe)

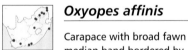

Oxyopes affinis — Tanzania Lynx Spider

Carapace with broad fawn median band bordered by thin white lateral band next to broader brown lateral band; bears dense scales; eye region white. Abdomen with narrow Y-shape median band on broad fawn median band; bordered by dark lateral bands. Legs same colour as carapace, faintly banded. **NOTES:** A common species sampled from grass in Fynbos, Grassland, IOCB, Nama-Karoo and Savanna. **STATUS:** LC; African endemic. (Tanzaniese Tierspinnekop)

Oxyopes angulitarsus — Long-bodied Lynx Spider

Carapace yellowish fawn. Broad median band, bordered by thin white and broader brown lateral bands, run down the length of the carapace and abdomen; short white band in eye region; brown areas covered with scales. Abdomen elongated, narrow, about twice as long as wide, gradually narrowed posteriorly, with lateral edges almost straight. Legs banded and densely clothed with scales. **NOTES:** Sampled from grass in the north-eastern regions of the Savanna biome. **STATUS:** LC; African endemic. (Langlyf-tierspinnekop)

Oxyopes dumonti — Dumont's Lynx Spider

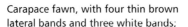

Carapace fawn, with four thin brown lateral bands and three white bands; eye region white. Abdomen short, oval, with broad reddish-yellow band and darker heart mark; darker laterally. Legs same colour as carapace, bearing long spines. **NOTES:** Sampled mainly from Savanna and Thicket. **STATUS:** LC; African endemic. (Dumont se Tierspinnekop)

Oxyopes flavipalpis — Velvet Lynx Spider

Body colour variable, ranging from black to pinkish orange; integument with short dense velvety setae. Abdomen ovoid, sometimes pinkish with dark spots. Legs usually paler. **NOTES:** Makes irregular pinkish egg sac on leaf surfaces. Sampled from Forest, Fynbos, Grassland, IOCB, Savanna and Thicket; also from sugarcane fields. **STATUS:** LC; African endemic. (Fluweel-tierspinnekop)

Oxyopes hoggi — Hogg's Lynx Spider

Carapace yellowish grey; longitudinal median band clothed in pale scales; bordered by broader dark bands on both sides; scales easily rubbed off. Abdomen long, oval, yellowish brown; dorsal area covered with scales; pale markings on side. Legs same colour as carapace, with long spines and dense scales. **NOTES:** A common species sampled from grass in Fynbos, Grassland, Nama-Karoo and Savanna; also from pistachio orchards. **STATUS:** LC; African endemic. (Hogg se Tierspinnekop)

Oxyopes jacksoni — Jackson's Lynx Spider

Recognised by its long body. Carapace fawn; median band bordered by thin white band laterally, followed by broader dark bands on both sides. Abdomen long, oval, yellowish brown; dorsal area sports white longitudinal stripes. Legs same colour as carapace, faintly banded. **NOTES:** A common species sampled from Forest, Fynbos, IOCB, Grassland and Savanna; also from citrus, macadamia, maize and sunflowers. **STATUS:** LC; African endemic. (Jackson se Tierspinnekop)

Oxyopes longispinosus — Long-spine Lynx Spider

Recognised by the very long setae on its legs. Carapace translucent, with scattered black spots; numerous pale scales around eyes; scales easily rubbed off. Abdomen ovoid, mottled yellowish brown, dorsal area covered with white scales. Legs same colour as carapace, faintly banded, with very strong, erect setae. **NOTES:** Sampled from grassy areas in Forest, Fynbos, Grassland, IOCB, Savanna and Thicket; also from macadamia orchards. **STATUS:** LC; South African endemic. (Langstekel-tierspinnekop)

Oxyopes schenkeli
Schenkel's Lynx Spider

Carapace mottled fawn-brown, with numerous scales. Abdomen same colour as carapace, mottled yellow with brown markings forming faint patterns. Legs cream, banded with spots. NOTES: Sampled from grass in Grassland, Nama-Karoo and Savanna; also from avocado, citrus and macadamia. STATUS: LC; African endemic. (Schenkel se Tierspinnekop)

Oxyopes tuberculatus
Humpback Lynx Spider

Carapace mottled grey, with white scales. Abdomen bears blunt tubercle posterior on the abdomen; same colour as carapace; scales easily rubbed off. Legs grey, with bands and spots. NOTES: Found in grassy areas and occurs in both Grassland and Savanna. STATUS: LC; African endemic. (Boggelrug-tierspinnekop)

Oxyopes vogelsangeri
Long-palp Lynx Spider

Carapace yellowish; eye region darker. Abdomen long, ovoid, same colour as carapace. In male, setae covering gives abdomen a shiny appearance. Legs yellowish, with long strong setae. NOTES: Sampled from grass in Grassland, IOCB, Nama-Karoo and Savanna. STATUS: LC; African endemic. (Langpalp-tierspinnekop)

Peucetia
Green lynx spiders

Medium-sized to large. Recognised by their larger size and bright green colour. Cephalic region narrow; thoracic region wider and rounded on sides; anterior eye row recurved and posterior row procurved; clypeus and front of chelicerae frequently decorated with bands. Legs decorated with bands and spots; leg IV longer than leg III. Male resembles female, but is slightly more slender. NOTES: Usually found on green foliage. Some species can change colour to blend in with the colour of the plant. Several species are found on plants with sticky leaves. The female attaches her egg sac to twigs and guards it until the eggs have hatched. Nine species are known from South Africa. (Groentierspinnekoppe)

Peucetia maculifera — Red-legged Green Lynx Spider

Carapace green with scattered brown spots; eye region with white setae; clypeus usually without bands. Abdomen with pale green mediolongitudinal area, speckled with white, sometimes with an indistinct chevron pattern; heart mark often absent or indistinct. Legs yellow-brown, with spots. NOTES: Free-living plant dwellers sampled from Fynbos, Grassland, Nama-Karoo and Savanna. Also sampled from *Helichrysum cooperi*, a common South African plant with very sticky leaves that trap insects. STATUS: LC; southern African endemic. (Rooipoot-groentierspinnekop)

Peucetia nicolae — Nicole's Green Lynx Spider

Carapace green with scattered brown spots; eye region with white setae; clypeus with four broad, dark brown bands extending onto chelicerae. Abdomen bright green dorsally, with irregular cross-like heart mark which varies between specimens; dorsum bordering heart mark dotted with white spots. Legs yellowish brown, becoming darker towards metatarsi and tarsi, bearing numerous spines. NOTES: Sampled from Fynbos and Savanna. STATUS: LC; South African endemic. (Nicole se Groentierspinnekop)

Peucetia pulchra — Pulchra Green Lynx Spider

Carapace green with four clypeal bands present. Abdomen with light green mediolongitudinal area bearing chevron patterns, bordered by two white bands; heart mark indistinct. Legs exceptionally long, with pinkish tint, bearing dark brown spines and numerous dark brown spots. NOTES: Collected in mixed thorn tree veld from grasses and herbs in IOCB and Savanna. STATUS: LC; African endemic. (Pulchra-groentierspinnekop)

Peucetia striata
Striata Green Lynx Spider

Carapace green; eye region with white setae; clypeus with four wavy bands, median band usually extending onto chelicerae for two-thirds of their length; cephalic region with brown spots. Abdomen with irregular cross-like heart mark and series of pale green chevron markings. Legs long, bearing dark brown spines. NOTES: A common species sampled from vegetation in Fynbos, Grassland, Nama-Karoo and Savanna; also from pistachio orchards. STATUS: LC; endemic to Africa and islands. (Striata-groentierspinnekop)

Peucetia transvaalica
Transvaal Green Lynx Spider

Carapace green with scattered dark spots; clypeal bands absent; eye region with white setae. Abdomen green, with olive-green heart mark; median area without patterns, bordered by two white bands. Legs greenish, bearing long, dark brown spines and dark spots. NOTES: A common species sampled from vegetation in Grassland, Nama-Karoo and Savanna. STATUS: LC; African endemic. (Transvaalse Groentierspinnekop)

Peucetia viridis
Viridis Green Lynx Spider

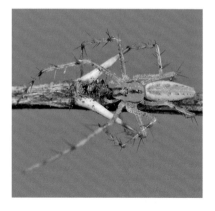

Carapace green with reddish median and lateral bands; eye region with reddish white setae; clypeus with two broad, reddish-brown bands medially. Abdomen pale greyish green, speckled with white; median area grey or green with series of brown obliquely placed longitudinal patterns. Legs with yellowish-brown bands and bearing light brown spines as well as numerous dark brown setae. NOTES: A common species sampled from Forest, Grassland, Nama-Karoo, Savanna, Succulent Karoo and Thicket; also from orchards. STATUS: LC; cosmopolitan. (Viridis-groentierspinnekop)

FAMILY PHILODROMIDAE
Running crab spiders Hardloop-krapspinnekoppe

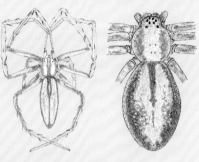

Carapace slightly flattened; shape varies from as long as wide to elongated; eight eyes in two rows (4:4), usually equal in size, not on tubercles; cheliceral furrow usually without teeth; integument clothed in soft recumbent setae. Abdomen variable in shape, from heart-shaped to oval or elongated; covered with soft recumbent setae; heart mark dark, usually distinct. Legs laterigrade; leg II usually longest; others almost equal in length; tarsi two-clawed; tarsi I and II with claw tufts and scopulae. **NOTES:** Free-living hunters. Most genera are found on plants and bark, with only a few found on the ground. Their movements are erratic but swift, their claw tufts and scopulae enabling speedy movement. Their laterigrade legs and flat bodies allow them to hide in crevices. Represented by six genera and 34 species in South Africa.

Gephyrota Gephyrota spiders
Medium-sized. Carapace round, wider than long, slightly narrower in eye region; eyes equal-sized, both eye rows recurved. Abdomen oval, pointed towards spinnerets, covered with pale setae, sometimes with scattered dark markings. Legs almost the same length, leg II slightly longer than others. **NOTES:** Free-living plant dwellers frequently sampled by sweeping vegetation. Only one species is known from South Africa. (Gephyrota-spinnekoppe)

Gephyrota glauca White Gephyrota Spider
Both sexes white. Carapace with distinct white border, slightly darker on sides. Abdomen white with few spots. Legs white, almost translucent. **NOTES:** Sampled from Fynbos, IOCB, Savanna and Thicket. Also found on crops such as macadamia, maize, pistachio, sunflowers and tomatoes. **STATUS:** LC; African endemic. (Wit Gephyrota-spinnekop)

Hirriusa

Hirriusa ground-running spiders

Medium-sized. Agile, ground-dwelling spiders. Carapace as wide as long, sub-oval; thoracic region evenly rounded, sloping gently towards cephalic region; fovea distinct; recognised by recurved anterior eye row and anterior eyes being larger than posterior eyes. Abdomen oval, with light cover of short setae. Legs long and slender, banded. Males have longer legs than females. NOTES: Frequently encountered in sandy regions. Owing to their cryptic coloration, they are well camouflaged and not easily seen on the soil surface. Often collected in pitfall traps, and frequently sampled in areas infested with harvester termites. Since the spiders readily feed on termites under laboratory conditions, they may be an important predator of these insects. The female covers the egg sac with sand and deposits it under stones or debris on the ground. Known from three species in South Africa. (Hirriusa-grondhardloopspinnekoppe)

Hirriusa arenacea
Arenacea Ground Spider

Carapace brown, with broad median stripe and narrow, wavy yellow margin; two broad brown stripes run from posterior median eyes. Abdomen dorsally covered with stout squamous setae, plumose at their base; sides dotted with small brown patches. Legs banded. NOTES: Often collected from pitfall traps in Desert, Grassland, Nama-Karoo, Savanna, Succulent Karoo and Thicket. Also sampled from pistachio orchards. STATUS: LC; southern African endemic. (Arenacea-grondspinnekop)

Hirriusa bidentata
Bidentata Ground Spider

Carapace with broad median pale area bordered by darker bands. Abdomen mottled grey and white, anterior region darker. Legs banded. NOTES: Sampled from soil in Fynbos, Grassland, Nama-Karoo and Savanna. STATUS: LC; South African endemic. (Bidentata-grondspinnekop)

Hirriusa variegata   Banded Ground Spider

Carapace grey to fawn, with white setae. Abdomen pale rusty colour, more reddish ventrally, with feathery white setae on sides. Legs banded. **NOTES:** Sampled from the ground in Grassland, Nama-Karoo and Savanna. **STATUS:** LC; South African endemic. (Gebande Grondspinnekop)

Philodromus   Philodromus running crab spiders

Medium-sized. Carapace shape varies from as long as wide to elongated; clothed in soft recumbent setae; eyes usually equal in size, in two recurved rows. Abdomen heart-shaped to elongated. Body usually mottled. **NOTES:** They capture prey by lying in ambush with their legs extended. Found on tree trunks and in low bushes. Nine species are known from South Africa. (Philodromus-hardloopkrapspinnekoppe)

Philodromus bigibbus australis   Bigibbus Running Crab Spider

Carapace with narrow V-shaped marking between posterior median eyes; clypeus sports white band. Abdomen with dark lateral bands and pair of tubercles near posterior end. Legs banded. **NOTES:** Sampled from vegetation in Grassland, Savanna and Thicket. **STATUS:** LC; South African endemic. (Bigibbus-hardloopkrapspinnekop)

Philodromus brachycephalus   Brachycephalus Running Crab Spider

Carapace with broad pale median band from eyes to posterior edge, bordered by broad darker lateral bands; remainder of carapace darkly speckled. Abdomen with heart mark and darker lateral bands; dorsal area with numerous orange spots. Legs same colour as carapace, lightly banded. **NOTES:** Sampled from Grassland, Savanna and Thicket, as well as from avocado and macadamia orchards. **STATUS:** LC; African endemic. (Brachycephalus-hardloopkrapspinnekop)

Philodromus browningi Browningi Running Crab Spider

Carapace with V-shaped marking behind eyes, median longitudinal band, darker lateral bands and narrow white marginal band. Abdomen with broad pale median band bordered by darker lateral bands; darker patches present posteriorly; dorsal area with pale spots. Legs grey, with numerous spots. **NOTES:** Sampled from vegetation in all biomes except Desert and Succulent Karoo. Also found in pecan and pistachio orchards. **STATUS:** LC; southern African endemic. (Browningi-hardloopkrapspinnekop)

Philodromus grosi Gros's Running Crab Spider

Carapace with fawn median band bordered by broad brown lateral bands; narrow fawn marginal band. Abdomen with heart mark on broad pale median band; bordered by dark lateral bands; posterior area with chevron markings. Legs fawn with numerous spots and bands. **NOTES:** Sampled from soil surface of the Fynbos, Grassland and Savanna. **STATUS:** LC; African endemic. (Gros se Hardloopkrapspinnekop)

Philodromus guineensis Guinea Running Crab Spider

Carapace grey with faint median band; remainder of carapace faintly spotted; narrow dark marginal band. Abdomen grey with broad median band, darker posteriorly, with markings laterally. Legs grey, banded. **NOTES:** Sampled from vegetation in Fynbos, Grassland, IOCB and Savanna, as well as from avocado and citrus orchards. **STATUS:** LC; African endemic. (Guinese Hardloopkrapspinnekop)

Philodromus partitus

Partitus Running Crab Spider

Recognised by its elongated body. Carapace with broad median band bordered by narrower dark bands; clothed in soft, dense, white setae. Abdomen has heart mark on fawn median band, bordered by narrow brown bands; darker laterally; posterior region sports wavy markings. Legs grey with numerous spots. NOTES: Sampled from grasses in Grassland, IOCB, Savanna and Thicket. STATUS: LC; African endemic. (Partitus-hardloopkrapspinnekop)

Suemus

Suemus running crab spiders

Medium-sized. Recognised by their flattened body. Carapace oval, clothed with scattered dark setae; eight eyes in two rows with posterior row strongly recurved. Abdomen elongated oval. Legs long and slender; leg II longer than others. NOTES: Free-living plant dwellers sampled from grasses and occasionally from shrubs. Only one species is known from South Africa. (Suemus-hardloopkrapspinnekoppe)

Eye pattern of *Suemus punctatus*

Suemus punctatus

Punctatus Running Crab Spider

Body orange-yellow, decorated with numerous dark setae and spots. Legs orange-yellow; front legs distally darker, longer than hind legs. NOTES: Sampled with sweep nets from vegetation in Forest, Fynbos, Grassland, IOCB, Nama-Karoo, Savanna and Thicket. STATUS: LC; southern African endemic. (Punctatus-hardloopkrapspinnekop)

Thanatus — Thanatus running crab spiders

Medium-sized. The least flattened members of the Philodromidae family. Carapace with short, dense setae; as wide as it is long; sub-oval in outline; thoracic region evenly rounded, sloping gently towards cephalic region; fovea usually distinct; eight small eyes in two rows, both rows recurved. Abdomen has distinct dark heart mark. Male only slightly smaller than female. NOTES: Found on bare ground or in low vegetation; commonly collected with sweep nets from grass or pitfall traps. Seven species are known from South Africa. (Thanatus-hardloopkrapspinnekoppe)

Thanatus atlanticus — Atlantic Running Crab Spider

Carapace creamy brown with broad pale median band; bordered by darker lateral bands; narrow fawn marginal band; clothed with dense pale setae. Abdomen with distinct heart mark bordered by pale narrow band; chevron markings on posterior edge. Legs spotted. NOTES: Sampled from grass in the Savanna biome. STATUS: LC; African endemic. (Atlantiese Hardloopkrapspinnekop)

Thanatus dorsilineatus — Dorsilineatus Running Crab Spider

Carapace fawn; median band dark, V-shaped; bordered by narrow fawn lateral band and again by broad dark lateral bands. Abdomen fawn, with long dark heart mark and dark chevron marking on posterior end. Legs fawn with distinct dark, longitudinal bands. NOTES: Plant dwellers sampled with sweep nets from Grassland, IOCB and Savanna. Also sampled from maize fields. STATUS: LC; African endemic. (Dorsilineatus-hardloopkrapspinnekop)

Thanatus vulgaris — Vulgaris Running Crab Spider

Carapace yellow-brown, with V-shaped dark median mark bordered by two darker lateral bands. Abdomen greyish yellow-brown with very dark heart mark. Legs uniform yellow, sometimes with spots. NOTES: Introduced species. A common free-living ground dweller sampled from pitfall traps in Fynbos, Grassland, Nama-Karoo, Savanna and Thicket. Also sampled from agroecosystems such as cotton, lucerne, maize, potatoes and strawberries. STATUS: LC; cosmopolitan. (Vulgaris-hardloopkrapspinnekop)

Tibellus Tibellus grass crab spiders

Medium-sized. Recognised by their elongated bodies and strongly recurved posterior eye row. Carapace elongated; eyes small, both eye rows recurved. Abdomen elongated, covered with soft, recumbent setae; usually has dark dorsal heart mark. Legs long. NOTES: Free-living plant dwellers commonly found on grass. The female attaches her egg sacs to grass tufts and guards them. These spiders prey on a variety of insects that live on grass. At present 13 species are known from South Africa. (Tibellus-graskrapspinnekoppe)

Tibellus armatus Armatus Grass Crab Spider

Carapace fawn; with broad reddish-brown median band bordered by thinner paler lateral bands. Abdomen creamy white, mottled; carapace's median band extends onto abdomen, bordered by paler lateral bands. Legs pale yellow, with numerous spots. NOTES: Commonly found on bushes and tall grass in Grassland, IOCB and Savanna. STATUS: LC; African endemic. (Armatus-graskrapspinnekop)

Tibellus gerhardi Gerhard's Grass Crab Spider

Carapace fawn with brown median band composed of brown bands and spots; bordered by lateral bands. Abdomen reddish brown; median band same width from anterior to posterior edges, composed of brown spots. Legs same colour as carapace. NOTES: Commonly found on bushes and tall grass in Grassland and Savanna. STATUS: LC; African endemic. (Gerhard se Graskrapspinnekop)

Tibellus hollidayi Holliday's Grass Crab Spider

Carapace fawn to yellowish brown, with brown median band bordered by fawn lateral bands. Abdomen creamy white, median and lateral bands distinct. Legs pale yellow, with numerous spots. NOTES: Sampled from Fynbos, Grassland, Nama-Karoo and Savanna. STATUS: LC; African endemic. (Holliday se Graskrapspinnekop)

Tibellus minor

Minor Grass Crab Spider

Carapace fawn to yellow; median band pale, bearing short brown setae. Abdomen fawn, mottled in appearance, with longitudinal rows of setae; median band grey. Legs pale yellow with spots. **NOTES:** Commonly found on bushes and tall grass in Fynbos, Grassland, IOCB, Nama-Karoo, Savanna, Succulent Karoo and Thicket. Also sampled from crops such as cotton, maize and vineyards. **STATUS:** LC; African endemic. (Minor-graskrapspinnekop)

Tibellus sunetae

Sunet's Grass Crab Spider

Carapace fawn with distinct brown median and fawn lateral bands. Abdomen creamy white, with brown median and fawn lateral bands. Legs pale yellow with numerous spots. **NOTES:** Commonly found on bushes and tall grass in the Savanna biome. **STATUS:** LC; southern African endemic. (Sunet se Graskrapspinnekop)

FAMILY SALTICIDAE
Jumping spiders

Springspinnekoppe

Carapace square-fronted, short to elongated; cephalic region high in some genera; eye region frequently decorated with clusters of long setae laterally; eight eyes in three or four rows; anterior median eyes characteristicly large. Abdomen varies from round to oval to elongated. Legs two-clawed, short, frequently decorated with tufts of setae. Males differ from females in shape and colour. **NOTES:** Salticids are typically diurnal, cursorial hunting spiders with well-developed vision. Found on vegetation and on the ground. With their large eyes and complex retinas, their sense of sight is unparalleled among animals of similar size. After detecting their prey, they pursue it with a combination of stalking, chasing, leaping and/ or lunging movements. This is the largest spider family in the region, with 355 known species.

Hyllus brevitarsis male

Afraflacilla

Afraflacilla jumping spiders

Small to medium-sized. Carapace rectangular; bears a curved row of 12 or more stridulatory tubercles laterally below eye region; these tubercles correspond with matching structures on the femur of leg I and are used to produce sound. Abdomen oval, somewhat squared-off at the front. Leg I more massive than others, sometimes very hairy and sometimes with very large spur underneath enlarged tibia. Sexes similar in general body shape. **NOTES:** Mostly found on tree trunks, but sometimes on the ground or in foliage. Some species in the region use stridulatory organs for social behaviour (both sexes as well as juveniles). Known from nine species in South Africa. (Afraflacilla-springspinnekoppe)

Afraflacilla venustula

Venustula Jumping Spider

Carapace flattened, dark brown; eye region black with white scale-like setae; eyes circled with reddish-brown setae. Abdomen oval, black, with three pairs of white spots. Leg I stout and stronger than others, bearing numerous scattered long hair-like setae. Female paler than male. **NOTES:** Associated with bark of *Vachellia* and *Ficus* trees in the Savanna biome. **STATUS:** LC; South African endemic. (Venustula-springspinnekop)

Afromarengo

Afromarengo jumping spiders

Small to medium-sized. Male carapace flat, elongated oval, truncated anteriorly and rounded posteriorly. Abdomen long, oval. Leg I long, more robust compared to rest; femur, patella and tibia swollen; tibiae clothed with long, dense setae. Sexes similar in general body shape. **NOTES:** Free-living plant dweller. Only one species is known from South Africa. (Afromarengo-springspinnekoppe)

Afromarengo coriacea

Coriacea Jumping Spider

Carapace dark with dense layer of brown setae; anterior eyes rimmed by white setae; covered dorsally in metallic green and orange scales. Abdomen oval, olive-brown, with some metallic green and orange scales. Legs II–IV yellow; femora, tibiae and metatarsi with blackish stripes at the sides. **NOTES:** This species was collected by beating foliage but also sampled from beneath bark of the fever tree *Vachellia xanthophloea*. Found mainly in IOCB and Savanna. **STATUS:** LC; African endemic. (Coriacea-springspinnekop)

Asemonea

Asemonea jumping spiders

Carapace oval; eyes in four rows, situated on tubercles; eye region covered with dense scale-like setae. Abdomen long, oval. Legs long and slender, bearing numerous long, moderately robust spines. Coloration varies from white to green, with black pattern. Males more colourful. **NOTES:** Found on large green leaves at the edge of forests. Females are often seen tending to their eggs or young on the underside of leaves. Four species are known from South Africa. (Asemonea-springspinnekoppe)

Asemonea amatola

Hogsback Jumping Spider

Female Carapace translucent white, with delicate traces of two dark bands on thoracic region; eye region has white scales. Abdomen whitish, with small blackish spots; light setae cover entire body. Legs translucent white. **Male** Body fawn, with brown lateral bands on carapace and abdomen; eye region with red and white scales. Legs banded. **NOTES:** Collected by beating shrubs in the Forest biome. **STATUS:** DD; South African endemic. (Hogsback-springspinnekop)

Baryphas

Baryphas jumping spiders

Sturdy-looking, medium-sized salticids. Body clothed with dark, erect setae. Carapace as long as wide, dorsally rounded. Abdomen round oval, with dense setae. Legs almost same length. Sexes differ in colour. **NOTES:** One species recorded from South Africa. (Baryphas-springspinnekoppe)

Baryphas ahenus

Ahenus Jumping Spider

Female Carapace dark, covered in pale brown setae; eye region, clypeus chelicerae and palps with dense fawn scales. Abdomen colour variable, usually dark with dense reddish-brown setae; sports white and red markings. Legs black, with pale scales that are especially long on legs I and II. **Male** Darker. **NOTES:** Very common, collected from foliage of shrubs and trees. Sampled from Forest, Fynbos, Grassland, Nama-Karoo and Savanna as well as from agroecosystems, including citrus, maize, pine plantations and strawberries. **STATUS:** LC; African endemic. (Ahenus-springspinnekop)

Belippo
Belippo jumping spiders

Small ant-like spiders with elongated bodies. Carapace shiny, with shallow constriction behind eye region; surface with scattered white setae; eye region black. Abdomen oval with shollow constriction. Legs slender. NOTES: Ground-dwelling spiders usually collected from leaf litter. Three species occur in South Africa. (Belippo-springspinnekoppe)

Belippo calcarata
Calcarata Ant Spider

Carapace brown, darker in eye region, covered with brown setae and scattered white scales. Abdomen brown; constriction with scattered white scales; posterior half shiny brown. Legs brown, faintly banded. NOTES: Collected from leaf litter in Forest. STATUS: LC; African endemic. (Calcarata-mierspinnekop)

Bianor
Bianor jumping spiders

Small to medium-sized. Colour and patterns vary among species. Carapace moderately high, flat on top, with thorax sloping steadily to posterior margin. Abdomen round to oval, can be much wider than carapace. Legs sturdy and not particularly long, with the femora, patellae and tibiae of leg I swollen and much more robust than all the other segments; male has enlarged femora I and sparse to thick white facial setae. NOTES: Found living on the ground, grass, tree trunks and on foliage. Two species are known from South Africa. (Bianor-springspinnekoppe)

Bianor albobimaculatus
Algeria Jumping Spider

Female Carapace dark brown dorsally; clypeus sports band of dense white setae; palps white. Abdomen mottled brown and white, with white spots. Legs banded, with scattered scales. **Male** Carapace dark brown dorsally, with dense yellow white setae laterally on clypeus. Abdomen blackish brown dorsally, with reddish setae; two small white lateral spots. NOTES: Plant dweller sampled from Fynbos, Nama-Karoo and Savanna. Collected at ground level, at base of plants, but also seen to drop from tall trees. Also collected from cotton fields. STATUS: LC; cosmopolitan. (Algeriese Springspinnekop)

Cyrba   Cyrba jumping spiders

Small to medium-sized. Species of this genus can be recognised by the posterior narrowing of the eye region. Carapace high in profile and, when viewed from above, rectangular with curved sides. Abdomen oval. Legs slender, of approximately equal length. Sexes differ in colour. NOTES: Common ground-dwelling salticids, but sometimes sampled from bushes. Known from three species in South Africa. (Cyrba-springspinnekoppe)

Cyrba lineata   White-stripe Jumping Spider

Male Carapace light brown to dark brown at margins; eye region slightly darker than thoracic region, with dense brown scales and setae; clypeus white. Abdomen oval, blackish, with narrow white median band. Legs banded; leg IV longest. Female darker. NOTES: A ground-dwelling salticid common under logs and rocks and in leaf litter. Sampled from Forest, Grassland and Savanna. STATUS: LC; southern African endemic. (Witstreep-springspinnekop)

Cyrba nigrimana   Orange Jumping Spider

Female Carapace brown with orange tint; eye region slightly darker than thoracic region, with dense brown scales and setae; clypeus low, with dense band of yellow-white setae. Abdomen dark grey, covered with dense, short, greyish setae. Legs light brown; only tibiae and metatarsi of first pair black. **Male** Body and legs covered in dense orange setae; clypeus with white dense band; palpi and tibiae I black. NOTES: Ground dweller, usually collected from under logs and rocks in Grassland and Savanna. STATUS: LC; South African endemic. (Oranje Springspinnekop)

Dendryphantes   Dendryphantes jumping spiders

Small spiders with slightly flattened bodies. Carapace oval, flat; eye region with dense white setae on clypeus. Abdomen usually has herringbone pattern. Males darker than females; legs I and II stronger than others. NOTES: Collected from the foliage of shrubs. Nine species occur in South Africa. (Dendryphantes-springspinnekoppe)

Dendryphantes purcelli
Purcell's Jumping Spider

Female Carapace oval, brown, with dense brown and white setae; clypeus has white setae and scales. Abdomen mottled greyish beige, with traces of brown herringbone pattern and rounded brown spots. Legs fawn with darker bands. **Male** Abdomen darker. **NOTES:** Plant dwellers collected from grass and shrubs in Fynbos, Grassland and Savanna. Also sampled from pine plantations. **STATUS:** LC; African endemic. (Purcell se Springspinnekop)

Dendryphantes rafalskii
Rafalskii's Jumping Spider

Carapace brown, covered with short white setae and scales. Abdomen pale, decorated dorsally with dense white setae and irregular brown spots. Legs same colour as carapace, with numerous white scales. **NOTES:** Sampled from Grassland. **STATUS:** LC; southern African endemic. (Rafalskii se Springspinnekop)

Euophrys
Euophrys jumping spiders

Small. Carapace short and high; cephalic region longer than thoracic region. Abdomen oval. Legs relatively short, almost the same length, leg IV being slightly longer. Males more colourful than females. **NOTES:** Often found when sifting litter or at the base of low vegetation. Known from 17 South African species. (Euophrys-springspinnekoppe)

Euophrys leipoldti
Leipoldt's Jumping Spider

Male Carapace covered in dense white setae, decorated with short dark median band and two dark U-shaped lateral bands bordered by red setae; eyes circled with red setae. Abdomen mottled grey with dark median band. Legs sport white and brown bands. **NOTES:** More common in the arid western parts of South Africa. Sampled from Desert, Fynbos and Succulent Karoo. **STATUS:** LC; South African endemic. (Leipoldt se Springspinnekop)

Evarcha

Evarcha jumping spiders

Small to medium-sized. Carapace broad, oval, longer than wide; dorsally flat; sides very steep; rear truncated. Abdomen oval, pointed at spinnerets. Legs moderately long, bear setae; leg I slightly more robust than others. Sexes differ in size and colour. NOTES: Often associated with low vegetation. They hide in silken retreats. Known from 15 species in South Africa. (Evarcha-springspinnekoppe)

Evarcha flagellaris

Blue-lip Jumping Spider

Carapace creamy, mottled with brown, dark submarginal band present; clypeus has blueish tint. Abdomen has broad creamy median band dorsally, latter tapers towards spinnerets and bordered by two dark brown lateral bands. Legs faintly banded. NOTES: Collected with pitfall traps or sweep nets in Grassland and Savanna. Also sampled from agroecosystems, such as apple and citrus orchards and kenaf. STATUS: LC; African endemic. (Bloulip-springspinnekop)

Evarcha ignea

Red-lip Jumping Spider

Carapace with white-and-orange marginal band and scattered white tufts of setae. Abdomen dark, with scattered white spots and bands. Legs dark; distal segments banded with white. Male recognised by broad band of dark red setae on clypeus. NOTES: Collected from the bases of grasses and from leaf litter in Grassland, IOCB and Savanna. Some males have been captured beneath bark and in houses. STATUS: LC; African endemic. (Rooilip-springspinnekop)

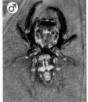

Evarcha prosimilis

Prosimilis Jumping Spider

Carapace dark, clothed in brown and white setae; clypeus high, covered in dark reddish setae; red scales around eyes in males and short white bands in females. Abdomen light brown with mottled yellowish-white pattern. Legs banded. NOTES: Very common in leaf litter. Collected in Forest, Grassland, IOCB, Nama-Karoo and Savanna. Occasionally sampled from the bases of grass tussocks. STATUS: LC; African endemic. (Prosimilis-springspinnekop)

Evarcha striolata
Zebra Jumping Spider

Carapace orange-brown, frequently bald, with white or colourless setae and scales around eyes. In male, abdomen has white median band bordered by lateral dark bands with dense dark setae; bands brown and fawn in female. Legs yellowish. NOTES: Collected from grass tussocks or grassy litter in Fynbos, Grassland and Savanna. Also sampled from vineyards. STATUS: LC; South African endemic. (Sebra-springspinnekop)

Evarcha vittula
White-banded Jumping Spider

Only male known. Carapace dark brown, long median band of white setae; carapace bordered by band of white setae; eye region black, anterior eyes encircled by orange scales. Abdomen ovoid, slightly elongated, dark, with wide median band. Legs dark, mottled with brown; scales present on femora. NOTES: Collected from the base of grasses from Grassland, Nama-Karoo and Savanna. STATUS: LC; South African endemic. (Witband-springspinnekop)

Festucula
Festucula jumping spiders

Small to medium-sized. Body very slender, length four to six times width. Carapace distinctly flattened; sternum narrow. Only leg I longer and thicker than others. Both sexes bear stridulation structures on legs. Sexes sometimes differ in size. NOTES: Elongated body and cryptic coloration indicate adaptation to grass dwellings. Three species are known from South Africa. (Festucula-springspinnekoppe)

Festucula leroyae
Leroy's Grass Jumping Spider

Carapace low, covered in grey-white adpressed setae and brown lateral bands; eye region brown; clypeus narrow, with some white setae. Abdomen with grey-white setae and broad lateral bands, which extend to spinnerets. Leg I long and robust, brown; other legs yellow. NOTES: Present in high numbers in Grassland and Savanna. STATUS: LC; southern African endemic. (Leroy se Grasspringspinnekop)

Festucula robustus
Robust Grass Jumping Spider

Body large compared to other species in genus.
Female Carapace brown with band of reddish-brown setae laterally; clypeus brown, covered with creamy scales and setae. Abdomen covered with creamy dense setae; dorsum sports broad brown lateral bands. Leg I long and robust.
NOTES: Sampled from grasses in Grassland and Savanna. STATUS: DD; South African endemic. (Groot Grasspringspinnekop)

Habrocestum
Habrocestum jumping spiders

Small to medium-sized. Carapace broad, but longer than wide, rounded behind posterior eyes; anterior eye row wider than others. Abdomen smaller than carapace, broad, almost pear-shaped. Leg III longer than I. Male smaller than female, differs in colour.
NOTES: Collected from soil surface and leaf litter. Represented by nine species in South Africa. (Habrocestum-springspinnekoppe)

Habrocestum africanum
African Jumping Spider

Carapace dark brown, reddish brown in vicinity of eyes; short greyish setae in thoracic region; eye region with red setae and scales in male, fawn and white markings in female. Abdomen small, dark yellow with mottled brown pattern. Legs dark yellow with brown spots. NOTES: Sampled from leaf litter, foliage and bark in Fynbos and Savanna. Occasionally collected from foliage of low shrubs and from bark of *Vachellia xanthophloea*. STATUS: LC; South African endemic. (Afrika-springspinnekop)

Harmochirus
Harmochirus jumping spiders

Small. Carapace high, rectangular, with strongly curved sides, widest at posterior lateral eyes; upper surface flattened. Abdomen slightly heart-shaped in female; rounded in male. Leg I with femora, patellae and tibiae massive, much longer and more strongly built than others, with long, thick fringe. Sexes differ in shape and colour. NOTES: Found on flowers and leaves. A single species is known from South Africa. (Harmochirus-springspinnekoppe)

Harmochirus luculentus — Luculentus Jumping Spider

Body dark brown. **Male** Carapace high in cephalic region; posterior thoracic slope very steep; eye region large; short white setae on thoracic region of carapace; long and bushy white setae and scales on clypeus. Dorsal scutum present on abdomen. Leg I larger than others, brown, with long, flattened bristles on patella and tibia. **Female** Body slightly lighter. Carapace brown, with darker eye region, eyes ringed with black. **NOTES:** Found on flowers and buds on leaves, especially their tips. Occasionally seen on walls and on the ground. Sampled from Forest, Fynbos, IOCB and Savanna. **STATUS:** LC; African endemic. (Luculentus-springspinnekop)

Hasarius — Hasarius jumping spiders

Small to medium-sized. Carapace broad, U-shaped, sides virtually parallel, rear moderately truncated, top flat; extending to thorax with rear slope of thorax to margin very steep; sides vertical. Abdomen broad oval, rounded at front and tapering very slightly to the rear. Legs long and spiny, legs I and II being very slightly more robust than others. Sexes differ in colour. **NOTES:** These spiders tend to be found in silken cells in low vegetation in the open. One species is known from South Africa. (Hasarius-springspinnekoppe)

Hasarius adansoni — Adanson's House Jumper

Female Carapace brown, darker around margin. Abdomen with pale brown curved central area bordered by dark bands. **Male** Carapace dark brown; eye region posteriorly bordered by crescent-shaped area of white setae. Palp sports V-shaped white bands. Abdomen mottled dark brown; white crescent-shaped collar present. Legs uniformly darkish brown. **NOTES:** A good traveller that has turned up in many countries. Commonly found in houses. Also sampled from Grassland, IOCB, Savanna and Thicket. **STATUS:** LC; cosmopolitan. (Adanson se Huisspringspinnekop)

Heliophanus

Heliophanus jumping spiders

Small. Carapace moderately high, elongated to broad oval, widest towards rear and slightly truncated at front. Abdomen elongated, broad oval, rounded anteriorly and somewhat tapering posteriorly. Legs short, stocky. Female palpi usually light coloured and sometimes even bright yellow or green. Sexes differ in shape and colour. Characteristic of most males of *Heliophanus* are the large femoral apophyses on the palpi. NOTES: Mainly found on vegetation. A large genus: 44 species are known from South Africa. (Heliophanus-springspinnekoppe)

Heliophanus bisulcus

Intertidal Jumping Spider

Male Carapace oval, dark brown; eyes black; short dense greyish setae and ill-defined longitudinal light band in thoracic region. Abdomen oval, blackish, with broad white median band and lateral bands.
Legs same colour as carapace. **Female** Slightly larger than male; carapace dark brown; eye region black; sides reddish brown.
NOTES: Specimens were found in the intertidal zone along rocky seashores close to the seashore. Sampled from the Fynbos biome. STATUS: LC; southern African endemic. (Tussengety-springspinnekop)

Heliophanus claviger

Four-spotted Jumping Spider

Carapace dark brown; white setae form patch between anterior median eyes; two light bands extend from anterior lateral eyes to thoracic region; carapace border with white marginal band; eyes rimmed with red setae. Abdomen oval, dark brown, with white marginal band in anterior half, extending posteriorly; two pairs of rounded spots present in posterior half. Legs dark, with scattered white setae. NOTES: Free-living plant dweller sampled from leaf litter and low-growing foliage in Forest, Fynbos, IOCB and Savanna. STATUS: LC; South African endemic. (Vierkol-springspinnekop)

Heliophanus debilis — Debilis Jumping Spider

Male Carapace dark; anterior eyes rimmed by black setae; long brown setae in vicinity of anterior row; thoracic region with white T-shaped median band; narrow white marginal band. Abdomen dark with narrow marginal white band and white median band. Legs yellow. **Female** Carapace brown; clothed with white setae. Abdomen brown, with light band on anterior margin. Legs yellow. **NOTES:** A free-living plant dweller sampled from Forest, Fynbos, Grassland, IOCB, Nama-Karoo, Savanna and Thicket. Also sampled from agroecosystems such as cotton and pistachio. **STATUS:** LC; African endemic. (Debilis-springspinnekop)

Heliophanus gramineus — Grass-loving Jumping Spider

Female Carapace covered with dense greyish setae with sparse long bristles scattered between them. Abdomen swollen, greyish beige with faint brown pattern consisting of transverse chain of spots. Legs greyish beige. **Male** Darker than female. **NOTES:** Collected at the base of grass tussocks in grassland and fynbos habitats surrounded by Afromontane forests. Sampled from Grassland, Savanna and Thicket. **STATUS:** LC; South African endemic. (Gras-springspinnekop)

Heliophanus hastatus — Hastatus Jumping Spider

Female Carapace brown, with white setae forming two transverse bands; thin white marginal band present. Abdomen greyish beige, with median fawn band linked to five pairs of spots; abdomen with white marginal band. Legs yellowish, lightly banded. **Male** Carapace dark; white setae form transverse band, at posterior margin of eye region and median white band centrally on carapace. Abdomen dark, with white median band and thin marginal bands. Legs yellow. **NOTES:** Free-living plant dweller found in Grassland, Savanna and Thicket. Also sampled from cotton, kenaf and sorghum. **STATUS:** LC; southern African endemic. (Hastatus-springspinnekop)

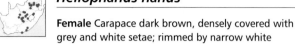

Heliophanus nanus
Nanus Jumping Spider

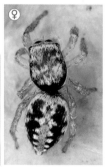

Female Carapace dark brown, densely covered with grey and white setae; rimmed by narrow white marginal band. Abdomen dark, with poorly contrasting fawn median band linked to six pairs of paler patches. Legs creamy, bearing white setae. **Male** Carapace very dark. Abdominal pattern paler than female's. NOTES: Collected from grasses and shrubs in Grassland and Thicket. STATUS: LC; southern African endemic. (Nanus-springspinnekop)

Heliophanus patellaris
Patellaris Jumping Spider

Female Carapace mottled brown; with irregular median band of creamy setae; narrow creamy marginal band; long, creamy setae around eyes. Abdomen creamy yellow, with irregular brown spots and patches in some specimens. Legs grey, banded. **Male** Carapace dark brown, with a few long brown setae in vicinity of anterior eyes; thoracic part with central band of white setae. Abdomen dark brown, with central band of pale setae in some specimens. Leg I brown, others yellow; palpi brown, very dark. NOTES: Found in a wide habitat range: under rocks, in leaf litter, on grass and on walls. Sampled from Fynbos and Grassland as well as maize fields. STATUS: LC; southern African endemic. (Patellaris-springspinnekop)

Heliophanus pauper
Pauper Jumping Spider

Female Carapace dark with white transverse band behind eyes and medially. Abdomen dark with narrow white marginal band and three or four pairs of white spots. Legs brown; palpi pale green. **Male** Dark overall, with brown setae on carapace, setae denser near eyes; white setae form two narrow lateral bands. Abdomen black, covered with dense dark setae. Legs brownish orange, covered by brown setae. NOTES: Free-living plant dwellers sampled from Savanna and Thicket. STATUS: LC; African endemic. (Pauper-springspinnekop)

Heliophanus proszynskii

Proszynski's Jumping Spider

Female Carapace brown; dorsal area covered with dense creamy grey setae with long brown bristles in eye region. Abdomen brown with dense creamy grey lateral bands; median area with paired brown spots. Legs yellow, setae and spines brown. **Male** Carapace dark brown; eye region almost black. Abdomen light brown, lateral surfaces whitish; traces of light median band on abdomen. Legs yellow. **NOTES:** Free-living plant dweller sampled from Fynbos, Grassland, IOCB and Savanna. **STATUS:** LC; southern African endemic. (Proszynski se Springspinnekop)

Heliophanus termitophagus

Termite-feeding Jumping Spider

Female Carapace dark brown; whole surface covered in short brown setae; eye region paler. Abdomen oval, dark brown to blackish, dark area bordered by narrow orange marginal band extending from anterior edge along lateral surfaces of abdomen; two pairs of round spots on dorsum; two white spots next to spinnerets. **Male** Smaller. Cephalic region darker, with pale mark. Abdomen with three pairs of pale spots. **NOTES:** Caught in abandoned snouted harvester termite mounds. **STATUS:** LC; South African endemic. (Termietvreterspringspinnekop)

Heliophanus transvaalicus

Transvaal Jumping Spider

Male Carapace dark brown; whole surface covered in short brown setae; eye region with some red setae; lateral side of clypeus with scattered white scales; eyes encircled by white scales. Abdomen oval, with dense covering of grey to dark brown setae; two pairs of spots near spinnerets. Leg I stronger than others, dark. **Female** Paler than male. **NOTES:** Sampled from Grassland and Savanna. **STATUS:** LC; South African endemic. (Transvaalse Springspinnekop)

Hispo
Hispo jumping spiders

Small. Carapace flat, elongated oval, slightly narrowed near front. Abdomen long, narrow, rounded at front, with long, straight, slightly diverging sides that curve to a point near spinnerets. Femur, patella and tibia of leg I enlarged; legs I and II with few weak ventral spines; leg formula 1-2-3-4. NOTES: Found on bark. One species is known from South Africa. (Hispo-springspinnekoppe)

Hispo georgius
Bark Jumping Spider

Male Abdomen shiny, dark brown, covered in thin, colourless setae; white scales form narrow transverse patches. Leg I enlarged, dark; venter of tibiae and patellae scantily fringed in brown hairs; leg II also thick but paler in colour. **Female** Carapace flattened, brown; cephalic and eye region dark orange, thinly clothed in pale orange hairs. Abdomen whitish yellow, clothed in pale brown setae. Legs pale yellow-orange with scopulae on tarsi IV. NOTES: Sampled from under the bark of large trees in the Savanna biome. STATUS: LC; endemic to southern Africa and Madagascar. (Bas-springspinnekop)

Holcolaetis
Holcolaetis jumping spiders

Medium-sized to large. Carapace low, longer than broad; fovea moderately long, positioned well behind posterior lateral eyes; eyes on low tubercles. Abdomen oval, longer than wide; characteristically marked with broad dorsal dentate median band. Legs I and II hairy and stronger than others. Males usually have longer bodies and more slender legs. NOTES: Mainly plant dwellers. Frequently associated with bark. Two species are known from South Africa. (Holcolaetis-springspinnekoppe)

Holcolaetis vellerea
Vellerea Jumping Spider

Carapace mottled, with reddish-brown setae; eye region blackish; clypeus clothed in dark setae with marginal fringe of long black erect setae; chelicerae dark, reddish, thinly clothed in black setae. Abdomen has dark, broad, irregular median band formed by greyish-yellow setae and scattered bristles. Legs I and II stronger than others, clothed with dense setae; femora and palpi with long pale setae; rest of legs banded. NOTES: Sampled from tree trunks and sometimes found on outside walls. Collected from Grassland and Savanna. STATUS: LC; endemic to Africa and Yemen. (Vellerea-springspinnekop)

Holcolaetis zuluensis — Zululand Jumping Spider

Both sexes have flattened bodies that enable them to crawl into narrow crevices and under bark. **Female** Carapace brown with mottled appearance; broad, yellowish median band bordered by lateral brown bands; clypeus with dense orange setae; white band of setae around eyes. Abdomen brown with broad, irregular yellowish median band bordered by narrow dark brown bands; sides mottled brown. Legs brown, mottled, with small white spots. **Male** Legs longer; body and legs black with creamy white bands. **NOTES:** Frequently associated with bark. Sampled from Forest, Grassland, IOCB and Savanna. **STATUS:** LC; African endemic. (Zululandse Springspinnekop)

Hyllus — Hyllus jumping spiders

Medium-sized, hairy, solid-looking spiders. Carapace high, broad oval, with truncated rear edge, with long sloping thorax and steep sides; cephalic region short, slightly convex. Abdomen oval; rounded at the front and tapering towards the rear. Legs long, stout, leg I being the longest; front legs covered with dense fringes of thin, black setae. Sexes differ in colour and leg length. **NOTES:** Mainly collected from foliage of shrubs and trees where they boldly move around. Represented by five species from South Africa. (Hyllus-springspinnekoppe)

Hyllus argyrotoxus — Argyrotoxus Jumping Spider

Female Hairy; carapace dark brown; with fawn median, lateral and marginal bands. Abdomen dark brown with fawn marginal band; median band consists of chevron patterns. Legs hairy, dark, mottled with fawn. **Male** Carapace black; with transverse and lateral bands of white setae. Abdomen black with narrow white median band ending in series of chevrons and spots; lateral edge with thin white marginal band. Legs sport white bands and spots. **NOTES:** Sampled from Forest, Grassland, IOCB, Savanna and Thicket. Also found in agroecosystems such as avocado, citrus and macadamia orchards and cotton fields. **STATUS:** LC; African endemic. (Argyrotoxus-springspinnekop)

Hyllus brevitarsus
Brevitarsus Jumping Spider

Female Carapace brownish orange with dark lateral bands; tufts of long black bristles near eyes in second row; clypeus with creamy bands. Abdomen dorsally clothed in dense brown and yellow setae; irregular yellow median band present. Legs mottled with dense erect setae. **Male** Carapace rounded; dark brown with short median band of white setae; white setae around eyes and setae form a marginal band. Abdomen narrow oval, with dense grey setae covering. Legs brown, with long, dense, white setae on patellae, tibiae and metatarsi. **NOTES:** Plant dwellers sampled from Forest, Fynbos, Grassland, IOCB, Savanna and Thicket. Also sampled from avocado, lemon and macadamia orchards. **STATUS:** LC; African endemic. (Brevitarsus-springspinnekop)

Hyllus dotatus
Dotatus Jumping Spider

Female Carapace brownish yellow; eye region brown; three transverse bands of fawn setae on clypeus. Abdomen with broad, brown, lateral bands intersected by posteriorly transverse bands. **Male** Dark brown, much darker than female. Carapace round; covered with golden-brown setae; white bands on border; white patches in eye region. Abdomen black, with irregular median band bordered with yellow setae. Legs dark brown with white bands. **NOTES:** Plant dwellers sampled from Forest, Fynbos, Grassland, IOCB, Savanna and Thicket as well as from agroecosystems such as cotton, kenaf and maize. **STATUS:** LC; African endemic. (Dotatus-springspinnekop)

Hyllus treleaveni Treleaveni Jumping Spider

Female Carapace hairy, dark, with median band of white setae; clypeus with transverse bands and dense, erect setae. Abdomen with numerous erect setae, dark with median white band ending in chevrons; laterally with crescent-shaped bands. Legs with dense setae, especially leg I, which has long black and white setae on underside. **Male** Carapace dark brown, with broad median band of white setae; clypeus with pale transverse bands. Abdomen brown with faint median band of white setae. Legs brown, with dense setae. **NOTES:** A large salticid commonly collected from broad-leaved plants in Forest, Fynbos, Grassland, IOCB, Savanna and Thicket. **STATUS:** LC; African endemic. (Treleaveni-springspinnekop)

Icius Icius jumping spiders

Small to medium-sized. Carapace longer than wide. Abdomen elongated. Leg I slightly larger than others. **NOTES:** Ground-dwelling spiders sampled mainly by hand from rocks, the base of grass tussocks and the soil surface. Known from 37 species, five of which occur in South Africa. (Icius-springspinnekoppe)

Icius nigricaudus Black-tailed Jumping Spider

Male Carapace brown, darker around edge; cephalic region dark, bordered by transerve band of creamy scales; four white spots on carapace border. Abdomen elongated oval, anterior two-thirds olive-yellow, posterior third black; white scales form six spots on abdomen. Leg I dark; longer and more robust than others, rest of legs yellowish. Male palp with white scales. **Female** Similar to male, but without white setae patches. **NOTES:** This rare species somewhat resembles *Crematogaster* ants in colour and size. Collected from the base of grasses in the Savanna biome. **STATUS:** Endangered; South African endemic. (Swartstert-springspinnekop)

Icius pulchellus   Pulchellus Jumping Spider

Only male known. Carapace oval, dark brown; eye region with streaks of white setae and scales; clypeus and anterior eye row framed by reddish-fawn setae. Abdomen ovoid, with brown median band bordered by light lateral bands of dense white, yellow and fawn setae. Legs fawn with brown and whitish setae. NOTES: Collected from low vegetation in Grassland and Succulent Karoo. STATUS: DD; South African endemic. (Pulchellus-springspinnekop)

Kima   Kima jumping spiders

Medium-sized. These spiders are ant mimics. Carapace long; sides nearly parallel; cephalic region elevated; upper surface narrow; pedicel long, clearly visible from above. Abdomen long, narrow, with small indentation about a third from the front. Legs thin, slender. NOTES: Free-living plant dwellers. Represented by three species in South Africa. (Kima-springspinnekoppe)

Kima africana   African Jumping Spider

Only male known. Carapace black, elongated, without setae; clypeus black with some short white setae. Abdomen with long pedicel; constriction in the middle; posterior part covered with rich golden-yellow setae. Legs black; front legs have shades of brown at extremities as well as scattered white scales. NOTES: Sampled from Fynbos, Nama-Karoo and Thicket. Also sampled from pistachio orchards in Northern Cape. STATUS: LC; South African endemic. (Afrika-springspinnekop)

198   Plant dwellers

Kima variabilis — Variabilis Jumping Spider

Only male known. Carapace dark, covered with greyish-white setae; pedicel long. Abdomen with same covering as carapace, other than constriction area, which sports a faint white band. Legs long and thin; femora I and II dark with pale bands; legs III and IV dark. **NOTES:** Sampled from Fynbos, IOCB and Savanna. **STATUS:** LC; South African endemic. (Variabilis-springspinnekop)

Langona — Langona jumping spiders

Medium-sized. Carapace longer than wide, narrower in eye region. Abdomen round oval. Abdomen a characteristic striped pattern. Legs short, with scopulae on tarsi; legs I and II shorter than III and IV. **NOTES:** Ground dwellers easily collected in pitfall traps. Known from seven species in South Africa. (Langona-springspinnekoppe)

Langona warchalowskii — Warchalowska's Jumping Spider

Carapace low, dark brown to blackish, with white lateral bands; eye region black with scattered red setae; white bands along lateral edges extend to clypeus. Abdomen black, with narrow white median bands and white lateral bands. Legs short, banded, light brown, distal segments darker. **NOTES:** An exclusively ground-dwelling spider sampled from Fynbos, Grassland and Savanna. **STATUS:** LC; southern African endemic. (Warchalowska se Springspinnekop)

Manzuma — Manzuma jumping spiders

Small. Carapace high; eye region narrowed; fovea present; anterior part of eye region covered with short erect bristles. Abdomen oval. Legs subequal in length, femur III longer than others. Males usually smaller and more brightly coloured. **NOTES:** Ground-dwellers. Two species occur in South Africa. (Manzuma-springspinnekoppe)

Manzuma botswana
Botswana Jumping Spider

Carapace dark brown with lateral bands of scattered reddish-brown setae and scales; eye region dark brown; clypeus covered in short brown scales; central transverse band of paler setae. Abdomen dark brown with irregular median band; narrow bands laterally. Legs same colour as body. NOTES: Sampled from pitfall traps in the Savanna biome. STATUS: LC; southern African endemic. (Botswana-springspinnekop)

Manzuma petroae
Petro's Jumping Spider

Carapace brown with scattered fawn setae; median dark band bordered by lateral fawn bands; clypeus and cheeks covered with long creamy setae; clypeus with diamond-shaped patch of brown setae between anterior median eyes and on upper half of clypeus. Femur I with dense long yellow-white setae. NOTES: Sampled with pitfall traps from Grassland and Savanna. STATUS: LC; South African endemic. (Petro se Springspinnekop)

Massagris
Massagris jumping spiders

Small. Carapace slightly elongated; posterior lateral eyes situated closer to anterior lateral eyes than to posterior eyes. Abdomen elongated oval. Legs almost of equal length. NOTES: Specimens found in leaf litter and low-growing vegetation. Known from seven species, all recorded in South Africa. (Massagris-springspinnekoppe)

Massagris natalensis
Natal's Jumping Spider

Female Carapace brown, mottled with cream, with tufts of setae; long, thick setae form basket-like structure above dorsal surface of chelicerae. Abdomen oval, as narrow as carapace, mottled greyish yellow with tufts of yellow setae; venter yellow. Legs light brown, banded. NOTES: Ground dweller found in leaf litter and low-growing vegetation in the Savanna biome. STATUS: Vulnerable; South African endemic. (Natalse Springspinnekop)

Menemerus
Menemerus jumping spiders

Small to medium-sized. Body flattened, hairy. Carapace longer than wide, with pale lateral margins. Abdomen elongated oval, usually with bands. Femora typically more robust, with big protuberances at base of ventral surface in some species. NOTES: Associated with stones, rocks or bare areas in the open with dead leaves, twigs or leaf litter, provided these habitats are warmed by the sun. Some species found on trees. These sturdy spiders are strong jumpers. Known from 15 species in South Africa. (Menemerus-springspinnekoppe)

Menemerus bifurcus — Bifurcus Jumping Spider

Male Carapace bears mottled brown setae in median area; white marginal band; clypeus sports white band of setae stretching to lateral eyes. Abdomen flat, elongated; most of dorsal area covered with mottled grey and reddish setae. Legs same colour as abdomen, with dark bands. Palpi densely clothed in light greyish setae; femora white. **Female** Paler in colour, without white setae. NOTES: Lives on trees and in leaf litter; sometimes sampled from buildings and gardens in Grassland and Savanna. STATUS: LC; African endemic. (Bifurcus-springspinnekop)

Menemerus bivittatus — Grey Wall Jumping Spider

Male Carapace dark with white marginal band and broad median V-shaped band; clypeus densely covered with band of white setae connecting with marginal band. Abdomen with dark median band; bordered by lateral white bands. Legs hairy; with dark bands. Chelicerae with V-shaped white setae. **Female** Slightly bigger than male. Coloration of abdomen darker. NOTES: Free-living plant dweller recorded from Fynbos, Grassland, IOCB, Savanna and Thicket. STATUS: LC; African endemic. (Grys Muurspringspinnekop)

Menemerus fagei
Fage's Jumping Spider

Carapace brown, with V-shaped median band of creamy setae bordered by two dark lateral bands and narrow bands along lateral margins of carapace; clypeus bears white setae. Abdomen brown, with creamy median band bordered by dark lateral bands. Legs banded. Female larger than male.

NOTES: Plant dwellers sampled from IOCB and Savanna.
STATUS: LC; African endemic.
(Fage se Springspinnekop)

Menemerus transvaalicus
Transvaal Jumping Spider

Carapace dark brown, densely clothed in light grey to fawn setae; light band along lateral margins; clypeus covered with white setae forming transverse bands. Abdomen brown, with ill-defined paler median band. Legs dark orange, marked with dark brown spots.

NOTES: Plant dweller sampled from under bark and rocks in Grassland, Nama-Karoo and Savanna. STATUS: LC; southern African endemic. (Transvaalse Springspinnekop)

Menemerus zimbabwensis
Zimbabwe Jumping Spider

Carapace dark brown with long reddish-brown setae near eyes; median V-shaped band; narrow white band along lateral margins of carapace. Abdomen with broad brown median band; sides greyish white. Legs mottled with brown setae and faint bands.

NOTES: Plant dwellers sampled from under rocks and shrubs in the Savanna biome. Collected from the bark of the fever tree in KwaZulu-Natal. STATUS: LC; southern African endemic. (Zimbabwiese springspinnekop)

Mexcala

Mexcala jumping spiders

Small to medium-sized. Slender spiders with long, thin legs. Carapace longer than wide, rounded posteriorly; cephalic region slightly raised. Abdomen elongated oval. Legs long, especially leg IV. **NOTES:** The spiders are mimics of wasps from the family Mutillidae, also called velvet ants. Some species mimic *Camponotus* ants. Found wandering on the ground, in low-growing plants, on bark and on the walls of houses. Known from four species in South Africa. (Mexcala-springspinnekoppe)

Mexcala elegans

Elegant Jumping Spider

Male Carapace dark with shiny blueish tint; darker striae radiate from fovea. Abdomen slightly elongated; bright silver-grey with black transverse bands. Femora dark with white scales; other leg segments brown with longitudinal bands; tarsi I white. Palp with dense white setae. **Female** Slightly larger; abdominal pattern similar to male's but with thin transverse white band and two pairs of large yellow or white patches. **NOTES:** Found in Forest, Fynbos, Grassland, Nama-Karoo, Savanna and Thicket. **STATUS:** LC; African endemic. (Elegante Springspinnekop)

Mexcala rufa

Rufa Jumping Spider

Only male known. Carapace blueish black; darker striae radiating from fovea; some white scales in vicinity of eyes. Abdomen slender; whole abdomen covered with scale-like setae, orange-yellow; black transverse band at anterior edge; transverse brown band at anterior edge. Legs thin, slender, dark, with some long yellow bands; tarsi I white. **NOTES:** Ground dweller frequently found around ant nests and seen to feed on them. Coloration very similar to the ant *Camponotus fulvopilosus*. Sampled from Fynbos, Grassland, Nama-Karoo and Savanna. **STATUS:** LC; southern African endemic. (Rufa-springspinnekop)

Microbianor
Microbianor jumping spiders

Small beetle-like spiders with stout bodies. Carapace flattened, broad, short, with large trapezoid eye field; clypeus low. Abdomen short, almost round, flattened; dorsum covered with large scutum. Leg I stouter than others. NOTES: Plant dwellers known from three species in South Africa. (Microbianor-springspinnekoppe)

Microbianor furcatus
Furcatus Jumping Spider

Carapace dark brown, almost black, with pitted integument. Abdomen blackish brown, short, almost round, flattened; dorsum covered with large scutum, clothed in small opalescent blue-green and white scales. Femur I black, other segments dark brown. NOTES: Resembles small ladybirds (Coleoptera: Coccinellidae). Collected from low-growing vegetation in Forest and Grassland. STATUS: LC; South African endemic. (Furcatus-springspinnekop)

Myrmarachne
Ant-like jumping spiders

Small to medium-sized. Body shape ant-like. Carapace about twice as long as wide; cephalic region square, raised; narrowed constriction forms characteristic waist where cephalic and thoracic regions join; in male chelicerae thick, long, parallel and projecting forward; fangs about as long as chelicerae, hooked at tip. Abdomen oval or long and thin, with noticeable constricted waist. Legs long, thin. NOTES: Found on shrubs and in leaf litter. Ant-mimicking salticids. Do not prey on ants, but appear to gain protection by living close to them. Known from 12 species in South Africa. (Mieragtige Springspinnekoppe)

Myrmarachne ichneumon
Orange Ant-like Jumping Spider

Female Carapace orange-brown with white wedge-shaped pattern on constriction; eyes on black spots. Abdomen yellowish, tinged with grey, with brownish-orange transverse bands and black and white spots. Legs yellowish orange. Male Slightly paler than female; chelicerae large, same colour as carapace. NOTES: Plant dweller sampled from trees in Forest, Grassland, IOCB and Savanna. Also sampled from citrus orchards. STATUS: LC; African endemic. (Oranje Mieragtige Springspinnekop)

Myrmarachne inflatipalpis   Flat-palp Ant-like Jumping Spider

Carapace reticulate, dark brown with white wedge-shaped band in constriction. Abdomen dark brown, glossy brown scuta separated by scanty white setae. Legs banded. Male chelicerae long, dorsally flattened. NOTES: Free-living plant dweller sampled from Grassland and Savanna. STATUS: LC; southern African endemic. (Platpalp Mieragtige Springspinnekop)

Myrmarachne laurentina   Hairy Ant-like Jumping Spider

Female Carapace black with sparse short, whitish setae and scales. Abdomen yellow-brown, mottled with black, sparsely covered with long white setae. Male Abdomen black with white scales and long white setae on posterior half. Legs dark with some pale segments. NOTES: Mimics *Camponotus* ants. Collected from foliage in IOCB, Savanna and Thicket. STATUS: LC; southern African endemic. (Harige Mieragtige Springspinnekop)

Myrmarachne marshalli   Marshall's Ant-like Jumping Spider

Male Carapace black, with long white setae around eye region; white marking in constriction. Abdomen black with faint vertical bands composed of grey and white setae. Legs pale with black longitudinal bands. Female Resembles male, with more prominent chevron pattern on abdomen. NOTES: Sampled on bark near foraging *Camponotus* ants from Grassland, IOCB, Savanna and Thicket. Abundant in orchards. STATUS: LC; African endemic. (Marshall se Mieragtige Springspinnekop)

Natta

Natta jumping spiders

Small. Body dark, with metallic blue shine. Body scales iridescent, giving metallic appearance. Carapace longer than wide; cephalic region with scales and setae. Abdomen slightly flattened, oval. In males leg I is more robust, bearing fringe of setae on tibiae. NOTES: Usually found in the vicinity of foraging ants, which they mimic in movement by moving the front legs up and down like antennae. Known from two South African species. (Natta-springspinnekoppe)

Natta horizontalis

Red-spotted Jumping Spider

Carapace blackish; cephalic region with dense brownish scales and scattered white setae; narrow white marginal band; eyes circled with red setae; white band below eyes. Abdomen black, covered with black scales in median area and white scales laterally; dorsum with numerous small bright red dots; white spot above spinnerets. Legs brown with creamy patches; leg I with white bands. Male has fewer red spots on abdomen; leg I stronger than others, tibiae with dense black setae. NOTES: Sampled from vegetation in all biomes except Desert and Thicket. STATUS: LC; African endemic; Yemen. (Rooikol-springspinnekop)

Nigorella

Nigorella jumping spiders

Medium-sized. Carapace oval, covered with dark, dense, short setae, convex, gently sloping posteriorly; eye region short; fovea clearly visible; long bristles in vicinity of eyes; clypeus low, dark, clothed in black setae. Abdomen oval, with dense long, dark setae. Leg I slightly thicker than others, with dark scopula on tarsus. NOTES: Free-living plant dwellers sampled from grass tufts. One species recorded from South Africa. (Nigorella-springspinnekoppe)

Nigorella hirsuta

White-spot Jumping Spider

Carapace dark brown; whole body covered in short, dark setae with scattered paler setae in between. Abdomen broader than carapace, brownish grey, with chevron pattern medially; two white spots a third from posterior end. Legs dark brown; leg I slightly thicker than others, with dark scopula on tarsus. Male more slender than female, without white spots on abdomen. NOTES: Recorded from grass in Grassland, Savanna and Thicket. Also sampled from cotton, maize, pecans and strawberries. STATUS: LC; southern African endemic. (Witkol-springspinnekop)

Oviballus

Sheep jumping spiders

Small. Carapace high, as wide as long, densely covered with long white scales and setae; eye region with erect tufts of long setae. Abdomen ovoid, densely covered with short and long white setae. Leg I enlarged; femur and tibia I swollen; all legs covered in long white setae; leg formula 1-4-3-2 in males (legs I and IV equal in length), 4-1-3-2 in females. Sexes similar in coloration, but males slightly darker. NOTES: Free-running plant dweller. Morphologically, it is a very convincing mimic of soft scale insects (Hemiptera: Coccoidea) or larval lacewings (Neuroptera: Chrysopidae), but its movements (short walking bursts) differ from the largely sedentary nature of scale insects, more closely resembling lacewing larvae. Known from only one species endemic to South Africa. (Skapiespringspinnekoppe)

Oviballus vidae

Vida's Sheep Jumping Spider

Carapace integument light brown; covered in short, thin, white scales on eye region; six dense tufts of long white setae, the distal ends of which are dark, two tufts in middle of eye region and two pairs at lateral eyes; rear slope and lateral sides covered with long thin white setae. Abdomen integument white; dorsum covered with dense tufts of white setae. Legs with banded distal segments. Male resembles female, setae tufts less dense. NOTES: A rare species predominantly sampled by beating plants in Forest, Grassland and Thicket. STATUS: LC; South African endemic. (Vida se Skapiespringspinnekop)

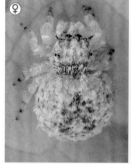

Pachyballus

Beetle jumping spiders

Small and beetle-like. Body very flat, covered with tough, highly sclerotised integument. Carapace rounded, usually slightly wider than long; eye region clearly trapezoid; posterior lateral eyes almost on posterior edge; posterior part of carapace covered by abdomen. Abdomen short, wide, heart-shaped or rounded. Legs short, leg I slightly bigger in males, with enlarged femur. Male sometimes darker in colour. NOTES: Plant dwellers sampled by beating and tree fogging. Known from four species in South Africa. (Kewerspringspinnekoppe)

Pachyballus castaneus

Red Beetle Jumping Spider

Carapace reddish brown, darker around lateral border and eye region; integument pitted with numerous scattered white setae; clypeus narrow; anterior eyes with blueish-white scales. Abdomen round, same colour and type of integument as carapace. Legs pale yellow with white setae. NOTES: Sampled from trees in the Savanna biome. STATUS: LC; African endemic. (Rooi Kewerspringspinnekop)

Parajotus

Parajotus jumping spiders

Medium-sized. Brightly coloured. Carapace high in cephalic region, declining steeply to the rear. Abdomen roundish oval. Legs slender; leg I slightly longer than others. NOTES: Known from two species in South Africa. (Parajotus-springspinnekoppe)

Parajotus obscurofemoratus

Durban Jumping Spider

Only male known. Carapace reddish brown; thoracic region with wide marginal bands of white setae; cephalic region with scattered creamy scales and scattered long black setae; eye region, clypeus and palp black with reddish setae around eyes. Abdomen mottled, with long white and reddish setae. Legs I and II, distal segments reddish brown; rest mottled. NOTES: Collected in the Savanna biome. STATUS: LC; South African endemic. (Durbanse Springspinnekop)

Parajotus refulgens

Dazzling Jumping Spider

Carapace rounded, higher in male; cephalic region with fawn and reddish-brown scales and scattered long setae; five white spots evenly spaced around edge; wide marginal bands; anterior eyes rimmed by red setae; white band on clypeus; when viewed from front, eye region with three long brown scales on both sides; black scales in vicinity of lateral eyes in male. Abdominal pattern composed of reddish, brown and white transverse bands. Legs banded; slightly longer in male. NOTES: Plant dwellers sampled from the Savanna biome. STATUS: LC; African endemic. (Pragtige Springspinnekop)

Pellenes
Pellenes jumping spiders

Small to medium-sized. Carapace moderately high; cephalic and thoracic regions nearly on same plane; cephalic region slants forward slightly; narrower in front than behind; sides parallel in middle; eye region occupies about two-fifths of length. Abdomen oval, usually with dark pattern. Leg I stronger than others; clothed with scales and setae. NOTES: Ground dweller; nine species are known from South Africa. (Pellenes-springspinnekoppe)

Pellenes bulawayoensis
Zimbabwe's Jumping Spider

Carapace bears broad median band of dense white setae bordered by narrower dark lateral bands and narrow marginal band; clypeus narrow, with rows of long white setae. Abdomen brownish with white pattern composed of two transverse streaks and two pairs of small round lateral patches in posterior part. Leg I longer and slightly thicker than others, with scattered scales. Male with less distinct abdominal pattern. NOTES: One of the most common and widespread ground-dwelling jumping spiders in central South Africa. Also collected from the bark of the fever tree. Sampled from Grassland, Nama-Karoo and Savanna. Also recorded in agroecosystems. STATUS: LC; southern African endemic. (Zimbabwiese Springspinnekop)

Pellenes modicus
Creamy Jumping Spider

Carapace with dense, creamy setae; long brown bristles near eyes; anterior eyes rimmed by reddish-fawn setae; clypeus clothed in dense white scales. Abdomen oval; with creamy median band composed of chevron patches. Leg I dark brown, bearing long brown and creamy setae, especially dense ventrally on tibiae; all legs with scattered pale scales. Leg I more robust in male; body lighter. NOTES: Ground dwellers sampled from the Grassland biome. STATUS: LC; African endemic. (Romerige Springspinnekop)

Pellenes tharinae — Tharina's Jumping Spider

Carapace with dense, dark setae; white setae form transverse white band midway down carapace; clypeus with dense pale scales; anterior eye rimmed by red setae. Abdomen decorated with anterior white marginal band followed by seven large white spots. Leg I dark, stronger than others, bearing long setae and club-shaped scales on patella and tibia. Male more reddish brown; legs with longer white setae. NOTES: A widespread species sampled from the ground layer in Fynbos, Grassland, Savanna, Succulent Karoo and Thicket. STATUS: LC; southern African endemic. (Tharina se Springspinnekop)

Phintella — Phintella jumping spiders

Small to medium-sized. Carapace high; cephalic region flat; thorax region sloping; sides more or less vertical. Abdomen oval, wide anteriorly and narrowing to rounded posterior; patterns vary considerably. Legs moderately long and slender; leg I of male marginally longer and stronger than others. NOTES: Commonly found on the leaves of shrubs and trees. Known from three species in South Africa. (Phintella-springspinnekoppe)

Phintella aequipes — Durban Jumping Spider

Female Carapace dark; with vertical bands of white setae; eye region pitted, anterior eyes rimmed by white setae; clypeus low, with brown setae; mouthparts and sternum brownish. Abdomen slightly elongated, sports broad pale median band with darker edges and six white spots; bordered by white marginal bands. Legs translucent, leg setae brown. **Male** Body and legs dark brown with white spots; chelicerae and fangs large; leg I longer. NOTES: Plant dwellers sampled from Forest, Fynbos, Nama-Karoo and Savanna as well as from agroecosystems. STATUS: LC; African endemic. (Durbanse Springspinnekop)

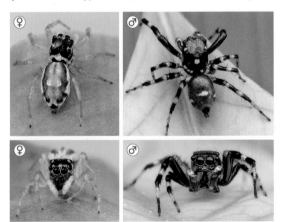

Phintella australis

Australis Jumping Spider

Female Carapace brown with dense layer of creamy setae; side of carapace bears pale brown setae; anterior eyes bordered with creamy setae. Abdomen elongated, brown, with creamy median and marginal bands. Leg I stronger, translucent, with dark femur. **NOTES:** Free-living plant dweller sampled from Fynbos and Grassland. **STATUS:** LC; South African endemic. (Australis-springspinnekop)

Phintella lajuma

Lajuma Jumping Spider

Only female known. Carapace brown, covered in dense white setae, with two faint horizontal bands of brown setae; anterior median eyes rimmed by white scales. Abdomen ovoid, creamy yellow, with indistinct darker pattern composed of broad median band and marginal band. Legs translucent with creamy setae and scales. **NOTES:** Plant dweller collected in the Savanna biome. **STATUS:** LC; South African endemic. (Lajuma-springspinnekop)

Phlegra

Phlegra jumping spiders

Small or medium-sized; majority are dark with characteristic striped pattern: two longitudinal white streaks on carapace and three streaks on abdomen. Carapace longer than wide; slightly flattened. Abdomen elongated; in some males abdomen covered with delicate dorsal scutum. Tibia I with three pairs of ventral spines. Male smaller and more slender. **NOTES:** Ground dwellers found in grass and leaf litter and frequently sampled alongside termites. Known from 12 species in South Africa. (Phlegra-springspinnekoppe)

Family Salticidae **211**

Phlegra bresnieri — Bresnier's Jumping Spider

Cephalic region with dense brown setae and scales and scattered longer setae; thoracic region bears two creamy lateral bands; clypeus with creamy setae and black scales. Abdomen with narrow pale median bands, bordered by two broader brown lateral bands followed by two thin marginal bands laterally. Legs yellow with brown setae; leg IV longest. Male slightly smaller. NOTES: A free-living ground dweller sampled from Fynbos, Grassland, Nama-Karoo and Savanna. STATUS: LC; cosmopolitan. (Bresnier se Springspinnekop)

Phlegra certa — Red-headed Jumping Spider

Only male known. Carapace dark, cephalic region covered in reddish-orange setae; anterior eyes circled with white; clypeus low, dark; mouthparts and sternum dark brown. Abdomen elongated, dark; clothed in thin grey setae. Legs dark brown, with white bands and spots. NOTES: Found in grass and leaf litter and sampled from Grassland and Savanna. STATUS: LC; African endemic. (Rooikop-springspinnekop)

Phlegra karoo — Karoo Jumping Spider

Female Carapace mottled brown; erect black setae in eye region; faint broad brownish median band bordered by creamy faint lateral bands; narrow creamy marginal band. Abdomen with dense setae; broad creamy median band, consisting of faint spots; sides pale. Legs light brown, banded. **Male** Smaller than female. Shape and coloration differ. Carapace with broad brownish median band, bordered by creamy lateral bands and narrow marginal band; eye region greyish blue. Abdomen with fawn median band bordered by brown lateral bands. NOTES: Sampled from pitfall traps in Grassland, Nama-Karoo and Savanna. Also sampled from agroecosystems such as pecan and pistachio orchards. STATUS: LC; southern African endemic. (Karoo-springspinnekop)

Pignus

Pignus jumping spiders

Medium-sized. Carapace oval; large diverging chelicerae with long tooth on retromarginal edge, near base of fang. Leg I with a brush of setae. NOTES: Free-living ground dwellers. Some species associated with termites. Two species are known from South Africa. (Pignus-springspinnekoppe)

Pignus simoni

Simon's Jumping Spider

Carapace has creamy median band bordered by dark brown lateral bands; clypeus with band of white setae; anterior eyes rimmed with red setae. Abdomen ovoid, with broad irregular median white band bordered by brown lateral bands. Legs brown, distal parts of segments darker; legs I and II with tufts of white setae. NOTES: Frequently sampled from areas with high termite populations. Collected from Grassland, Nama-Karoo and Savanna. STATUS: LC; southern African endemic. (Simon se Springspinnekop)

Planamarengo

Planamarengo jumping spiders

Small to medium-sized. Carapace elongated; flat surface with shallow depression in posterior part of thorax; integument with puncture-reticulate sculpturing in cephalic region; clypeus low. Abdomen ovoid, narrow, almost twice as long as wide; integument with poorly developed transverse reticulate pattern. Leg I enlarged. NOTES: Canopy-dwelling and arboreal genus, occasionally recorded from grasslands and thickets. One species recorded from South Africa. (Planamarengo-springspinnekoppe)

Planamarengo bimaculata

Two-spotted Jumping Spider

Carapace rust-orange; surface smooth in cephalic region, punctate on sides and thoracic region, with some white setae laterally. Abdomen elongated, oval, orange, shiny dorsally, with short white setae laterally; pair of large black spots laterally. Leg I long and more robust than others; femur, patella and tibia I swollen and clothed with dense long setae ventrally. NOTES: Free-living plant dwellers. Sampled from Nama-Karoo. STATUS: DD; South African endemic. (Tweekol-springspinnekop)

Plexippus Plexippus jumping spiders

Medium-sized spiders that usually sport a white stripe on the abdomen and carapace. Carapace longer than wide, narrower in eye region. Abdomen elongated, oval. Legs robust. NOTES: Free-living plant dwellers sampled from grass and shrubs. Three species are known from South Africa. (Plexippus-springspinnekoppe)

Plexippus petersi Peter's Jumping Spider

Male Carapace with dense fawn setae; two dark half-moon lateral bands; eye region mottled with reddish-fawn setae; anterior eyes rimmed with white setae. Abdomen fawn with two dark lateral bands; latter interrupted by short white band two-thirds down. Legs fawn with longitudinal bands; femora I dark with scattered white scales. NOTES: Introduced to Africa and Pacific islands. STATUS: LC; cosmopolitan. (Peter se Springspinnekop)

Plexippus tsholotsho Orange Jumping Spider

Only female known. Carapace dark brown, black near eyes; carapace covered with thin brown setae; long brown bristles near eyes; anterior eyes rimmed with red setae; clypeus dark. Abdomen dark brown with wide, light median band, lateral bands dark; dorsum clothed in orange-reddish setae with scattered long brown bristles. Legs brown; leg setae and spines dark. NOTES: Sampled from vegetation in the Savanna biome. STATUS: LC; southern African endemic. (Oranje Springspinnekop)

Portia Portia jumping spiders

Medium-sized, long-legged, ornate spiders with leg fringes and abdominal hair tufts. Carapace high, usually with marked slope; fovea elongated, situated just behind posterior lateral eyes. Abdomen typically ovoid to elongated with tufts of long, erect setae. Leg I long and slender, often with conspicuous setae fringes; spines numerous, generally robust; claw tufts present. Slight sexual dimorphism in colour. NOTES: These spiders do not jump, but move around smoothly and quickly. They prey mainly on other spiders and invade others' webs. One species is known from South Africa. (Portia-springspinnekoppe)

Portia schultzi — Schultz's Dandy Jumping Spider

Carapace brown; eye region, clypeus and face covered with brownish-red setae; thoracic region and sides covered with yellow setae. Abdomen uniformly covered with iridescent yellow setae and a scattering of long black setae. Legs brown with short yellow setae and black spines; leg I bears very heavy black fringe on tibia; shorter, thinner fringe on femur and very thin fringe on patella; palp brown with black setae. **NOTES:** Preys mainly on other spiders. Sampled from Grassland, Nama-Karoo and Savanna. Also collected from macadamia orchards. **STATUS:** LC; African endemic. (Schultz se Spoggerige Springspinnekop)

Pseudicius — Pseudicius jumping spiders

Small. Characterised by slender, flattened bodies and swollen tibia on leg I. Carapace oval, very flat. Abdomen ovoid. Stridulation apparatus on legs and carapace in both sexes is also a distinctive feature. **NOTES:** Plant dwellers sampled from foliage. Represented by 13 species in South Africa. (Pseudicius-springspinnekoppe)

Pseudicius gracilis — Gracilis Jumping Spider

Carapace dark brown with short white transverse band, bordered with narrow white marginal band; white setae on clypeus and around anterior row of eyes; anterior eyes rimmed by white setae. Abdomen brown with three to four white transverse bands; marginal white band of white setae. Leg I brown, larger than others, stout, with swollen femur, patella and tibia; legs II–IV paler. Leg I stronger in male. **NOTES:** Collected from silk retreats constructed in thorns of acacia trees. Sampled from Grassland and Savanna. **STATUS:** LC; South African endemic. (Gracilis-springspinnekop)

Pseudicius maculatus

Maculatus Jumping Spider

Carapace dark, clothed in dense white setae; narrow marginal white band; anterior eyes circled with reddish setae; clypeus and palp with dense white setae. Abdomen dark with numerous white setae on posterior end, sports irregular chevrons. Legs banded with similar white setae as body. **NOTES:** Collected by beating shrubs in Grassland, Savanna and Thicket. **STATUS:** LC; southern African endemic. (Maculatus-springspinnekop)

Rhene

Rhene jumping spiders

Small. Broad, squat, hairy, brownish salticids with flattish bodies. Carapace broader than long, typically thick and flat on top; flat top almost trapezoidal in shape, widest just behind rear eyes and narrowest at front eye row; sides and most of thorax vertical, rear margin very wide and truncated. Abdomen oval, slightly truncated at front, slightly pointed at rear. Legs sturdy; femora, patellae and tibiae noticeably swollen. **NOTES:** Free-living plant dwellers that spin retreats in the seed heads of plants. Known from 14 species in South Africa. (Rhene-springspinnekoppe)

Rhene biguttata

Two-spotted Jumping Spider

Only male known. Carapace reddish brown, pitted, with narrow marginal band of dense creamy setae and scales above first row of eyes. Abdomen reddish brown with creamy setae anteriorly; four dorsal sigilla; two large, irregular creamy white spots, well separated from each other, towards posterior end. Leg I much thickened, especially tibia and patella, which bear long fringe of black setae on the underside; femur I with creamy scales; other legs reddish brown with rings of white setae at joints; palpi dark brown. **NOTES:** A rare arboreal species collected from trees in coastal and Afromontane forests. **STATUS:** DD; South African endemic. (Tweekol-springspinnekop)

Rhene cooperi Cooper's White Jumping Spider

Only female known. Carapace dark, but covered in dense tufts of short and long white setae, giving it a woolly appearance. Abdomen similar, but with denser setae tufts. Legs bear white setae; edges of leg segments sport narrow brown band. **NOTES:** Free-living plant dweller that mimics scale insects or lacewing larvae. Sampled from the IOCB biome. **STATUS:** DD; South African endemic. (Cooper se Wit Springspinnekop)

Rhene facilis Facilis Jumping Spider

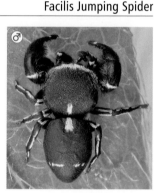

Male Carapace black, pitted, covered in short black setae; creamy white transverse band behind first row of eyes. Abdomen oval, black; short, creamy white median band extends from carapace onto abdomen; two short transverse creamy bands near spinnerets. Leg I almost black, large, with swollen femur and tibia, long black setae on ventral surface of femur, patella and tibia; other legs dark brown with creamy longitudinal bands. **Female** Carapace reddish brown. Leg I orange-brown. **NOTES:** Collected by canopy fogging various trees in Forest and Savanna. **STATUS:** LC; African endemic. (Facilis-springspinnekop)

Rumburak Rumburak jumping spiders

Small to medium-sized. Carapace oval, moderately high, sloping posteriorly. Abdomen oval. First legs stouter than others. The form of the embolus is distinctive in this genus. **NOTES:** Sampled from vegetation. Represented by seven species endemic to South Africa. (Rumburak-springspinnekoppe)

Rumburak laxus Laxus Jumping Spider

Male Carapace dark brown; clypeus covered with sparse brown setae and bristles; anterior eyes rimmed with red setae. Abdomen dark brown dorsally, anterior edge with wide, creamy transverse band; some large light patches and chevrons posteriorly. Leg I black. **Female** White setae on carapace absent. **NOTES:** Sampled from Forest and Savanna. Also found in houses in Gauteng and easily confused with *Hasarius adansoni*. **STATUS:** LC; South African endemic. (Laxus-springspinnekop)

Stenaelurillus

Stenaelurillus jumping spiders

Small to medium-sized. Carapace oblong, slightly narrower in front, curving slightly to broadly truncated rear; dense setae. Abdomen oval, flattened dorsally; spinnerets long. Legs strong; leg IV the longest. NOTES: Free-living ground dwellers known from three species in South Africa. (Stenaelurillus-springspinnekoppe)

Stenaelurillus guttiger

Guttiger Jumping Spider

Carapace dark with white lateral bands and white marginal band; eye region has short, thick bristles; anterior eyes rimmed with white; clypeus with brown setae. Abdomen has large, dark, heart-shaped dorsal pattern with three white spots. Legs dark with white bands. NOTES: Found in warm, dry environments. Sampled from Grassland and Savanna. STATUS: LC; southern African endemic. (Guttiger-springspinnekop)

Stenaelurillus termitophagus

Termite-eating Jumping Spider

Carapace covered in dense setae; broad dark median band bordered by creamy white lateral bands; creamy marginal band; anterior eyes rimmed with reddish setae; white band on clypeus broader in female. Abdomen with narrow creamy median band followed by two dark lateral bands and creamy marginal band. Leg setae brown, mottled. NOTES: Preys on termites, and lives on the outside of open-vented termite mounds of *Odontotermes transvaalensis* and other termite species. Sampled from Grassland and Savanna. STATUS: LC; southern African endemic. (Termietvreter-springspinnekop)

Tanzania

Tanzania jumping spiders

Small spiders. Carapace rather high, longer than wide; clypeus low. Abdomen oval, coloration very variable. Legs same length, often with dark bands. Females sometimes darker than males. NOTES: Ground dwellers represented by five species in South Africa. (Tanzania-springspinnekoppe)

Tanzania parvulus
Parvulus Jumping Spider

Carapace light brown with faint brown median band and brown marginal band. Abdomen rounded, yellowish orange with three irregular brown bands on dorsum and narrow brown bands on sides; median area with scattered white setae. Legs yellow, banded. Male slightly smaller than female. **NOTES:** Sampled from the Savanna biome. **STATUS:** LC; South African endemic. (Parvulus-springspinnekop)

Tenuiballus
Tenuiballus jumping spiders

Small spiders with elongated bodies. Carapace low, flat, with shallow transverse depression on posterior part of carapace; clypeus very low; sternum narrow. Abdomen narrow, three times longer than wide, with dorsal scutum covering entire dorsal surface except small area in caudal part. Leg I dark and enlarged. **NOTES:** Recorded from Grassland. Tenuiballus is known from only the males of two South African species. (Tenuiballus-springspinnekoppe)

Tenuiballus coronatus
Black Jumping Spider

Carapace dark brown, with yellow-orange crown-shaped marking medially. Abdomen dark brown dorsally; shiny scutum covers entire dorsum; two small white spots mediolaterally, just behind midpoint, single small white spot above spinnerets. Leg I long, robust, dark brown, with yellow tarsus; other legs uniformly yellow. **NOTES:** Recorded from the Grassland biome. **STATUS:** DD; South African endemic. (Swart Springspinnekop)

Thyene
Thyene jumping spiders

Small to medium-sized. Carapace rounded posteriorly; in some males the cephalic region is swollen; characterised by the presence of tufts of long black setae near posterior median eyes. Abdomen hairy; varies from roundish oval to elongated. Leg I stronger than others in males; females of several species with transverse stripes on femur I. **NOTES:** Commonly found on grass and trees. Represented by 14 species in South Africa. (Thyene-springspinnekoppe)

Thyene bucculenta
Bucculenta Jumping Spider

Only male known. Carapace round, very broad, reddish brown with large black spots in eye region. Abdomen elongated, oval, with indistinct median silvery stripes. Leg I dark, very strong, with dense layer of setae; rest of legs brown. **NOTES:** Collected from the foliage of shrubs and short trees in Grassland, Nama-Karoo, Savanna and Thicket. Also recorded from lucerne and cotton fields. **STATUS:** LC; African endemic. (Bucculenta-springspinnekop)

Thyene coccineovittata
Spotted Jumping Spider

Female Carapace orange-brown. Abdomen elongated, oval, orange-brown with two darker bands on posterior two-thirds of its length and three pairs of square dark patches. Legs yellow with brown setae and spines; anterior femora with brown stripes. **Male** Carapace reddish brown; anterior eyes rimmed with black setae. Abdomen dark. **NOTES:** Plant dwellers sampled from Fynbos, Grassland, Savanna and Thicket. **STATUS:** LC; African endemic. (Kol-springspinnekop)

Thyene inflata
Orange-banded Jumping Spider

Female Carapace yellowish; white and black transverse bands of dense setae cover eye region. Abdomen elongated, oval, with silvery black median band, bordered by rich orange-red lateral bands followed by creamy white bands. Leg coloration similar to carapace. **Male** Carapace broad, reddish brown with large black spots. Abdomen with indistinct stripes. **NOTES:** Typically associated with foliage of broad-leaved shrubs and trees. Sampled from all biomes except Desert and Succulent Karoo. **STATUS:** LC; African endemic. (Oranjeband-springspinnekop)

220   Plant dwellers

Thyene mutica — Muticus Jumping Spider

Female Pale translucent cream, cephalic region with dark markings; narrow white band of setae below eyes. Abdomen has pair of brown lateral bands. **Male** Dark, with shiny cephalic region. Abdomen has broad pair of longitudinal bands. Legs same colour as carapace; femora I and II with rows of black stripes. **NOTES:** Makes a densely woven barrel silk retreat in dead, curled leaves. Sampled from shrubs in Grassland, IOCB and Savanna, as well as from avocado orchards and cotton fields. **STATUS:** LC; African endemic. (Muticus-springspinnekop)

Thyene natalii — Gold-banded Jumping Spider

Carapace pale brown; cephalic region covered with white scales; eye region with dark spot; anterior eyes white-rimmed. Abdomen roundish oval, marked with transverse bands of reddish-brown setae and silvery iridescent scales; some chevrons present posteriorly. Legs same colour as carapace; femora I with black stripes. **NOTES:** Collected from the foliage of shrubs and short trees in all biomes except Nama- and Succulent Karoo. Commonly found in agroecosystems. The second most abundant species sampled from macadamia orchards. **STATUS:** LC; African endemic. (Goueband-springspinnekop)

Thyene ogdeni — Ogden's Jumping Spider

Female Carapace orange-brown with scattered short white setae and scales in cephalic region; eyes rimmed with white setae. Abdomen elongated, oval, with wide, creamy median band bordered by two brown lateral bands; margins white. Legs yellow, femur I in female with transverse stripes. **Male** Abdomen yellowish medially, brownish laterally, with five pairs of black patches and small white spots between them; brown setae sparsely covers dorsum of abdomen. **NOTES:** Collected from foliage of shrubs and short trees. Sampled from all biomes except Desert, Nama- and Succulent Karoo. Also sampled from citrus orchards. **STATUS:** LC; African endemic. (Ogden se Springspinnekop)

Thyene semiargentea — Long-bodied Jumping Spider

Male Carapace oval, widest at midpoint, dark with white median band and two short lateral bands. Abdomen elongated, oval, clothed in very dense brownish-black hairs with golden metallic sheen; white scales form three pairs of oblique patches laterally and two pairs of small transversal patches posteriorly. Legs dark with scattered white scales. **Female** Lighter in colour. Carapace orange; anterior eyes rimmed with black setae. Abdomen yellowish with dark dots, black pattern in posterior part. Legs yellowish orange. **NOTES:** Commonly found on vegetation in Grassland, IOCB and Savanna. Also sampled from cotton fields. **STATUS:** LC; African endemic.
(Langlyf-springspinnekop)

Thyenula — Thyenula jumping spiders

Small to medium-sized. Carapace rounded, cephalic region moderately high; fovea clearly visible, gently sloping posteriorly; striae usually visible on thoracic region; eye region typically dark with white setae; median eyes rimmed with white or red scales; chelicerae strong, with bicuspid tooth on both margins. Abdomen ovoid. Leg I slightly stouter than others, bearing strong paired setae. **NOTES:** Free-running plant dwellers known from 21 species in South Africa.
(Thyenula-springspinnekoppe)

Thyenula aurantiaca — Aurantiaca Jumping Spider

Male Carapace oval with dense black setae; upside-down U-shaped white band posterior to eye row; white scales between anterior eyes; anterior eyes partially circled with red setae. Abdomen dorsally mottled with median band of small dark patches on pale background. Leg I black, stronger than others; rest of legs banded. **Female** Sports semicircular lighter area on thoracic region anteriorly. Abdomen ventrally yellow with numerous brownish marks. Legs dark yellowish to light brown. **NOTES:** Sampled from all biomes except Desert. Also recorded in avocado and macadamia orchards. **STATUS:** LC; southern African endemic.
(Aurantiaca-springspinnekop)

Thyenula haddadi

Haddad's Jumping Spider

Male Carapace brown with creamy lateral bands and lighter patch on foveal region; anterior eyes rimmed by cream and red scales. Palp with dense creamy red setae. Abdomen with wide brown band medially, bordered by creamy marginal bands. Leg I dark; other legs banded. **Female** Carapace brown with slightly darker eye field. Anterior eyes rimmed by fawn scales. Abdomen generally greyish beige with ill-defined pattern composed of small lighter patches and chevrons, covered with thin, shiny hairs. NOTES: Sampled from leaf litter in clearings in humid forest in Grassland and Savanna. STATUS: LC; South African endemic. (Haddad se Springspinnekop)

Thyenula juvenca

Jelly-baby Jumping Spider

Carapace variable, yellowish orange to green; cephalic region darker; anterior eyes rimmed with white setae. Abdomen oval, light yellow to green, with sparse brown bristles and whitish setae on dorsum. Legs yellow to green with dark brown spines, leg I stouter than others. NOTES: Sampled from the ground layer as well as from vegetation in Savanna and Thicket.
STATUS: LC; South African endemic. (Gompoppie-springspinnekop)

Thyenula leighi

Leigh's Jumping Spider

Male Carapace with broad median band of brown setae bordered by creamy lateral bands and narrow marginal band; clypeus dark; anterior eyes rimmed with red setae. Palp with dense white setae, only distal tip black. Abdomen with V-shaped brown median band bordered by creamy lateral bands. Leg I dark; other legs banded. **Female** Brown with mottled appearance and no distinct bands; legs banded. NOTES: Sampled from leaf litter in forested areas and from pitfall traps in IOCB, Savanna and Thicket. STATUS: LC; South African endemic. (Leigh se Springspinnekop)

Thyenula rufa   Rufa Jumping Spider

Male Carapace brownish orange, shiny; cephalic region darker; anterior eyes rimmed with creamy setae; chelicerae large, robust. Abdomen ovoid; greyish brown with wide light median band with dense reddish setae. Leg I dark brown; other legs with dark distal segments. **Female** Slightly smaller than male. Abdomen varied, from uniformly yellowish brown to ornamented by a few pairs of black patches and reddish setae. NOTES: Sampled by canopy fogging and beating trees in the Savanna biome. STATUS: LC; South African endemic. (Rufa-springspinnekop)

Tusitala   Tusitala jumping spiders

Medium-sized. Recognised by the long chelicerae in males, which have very long and dense bristles, forming a 'basket'. Carapace high, sides slope outward from upper surface and widen in gentle curve from front to back, widest point being behind the posterior eyes; cephalic region slants forward; thoracic region rounds off rather steeply from third row of eyes. Abdomen ovoid. Legs same size. NOTES: Commonly found on vegetation. Three species occur in South Africa. (Tusitala-springspinnekoppe)

Tusitala barbata   Barbata Jumping Spider

Male Carapace brown, covered with red, yellow and white setae, red predominating on sides and white dorsally; face light brown, ornamented with long ridge of stiff setae down front; anterior eyes rimmed with white setae; chelicerae long with erect black setae. Abdomen mottled, clothed in mixture of grey and brown setae; posterior dorsum with indistinct white chevrons. Legs mottled. NOTES: Sampled from all biomes except Desert, Succulent Karoo and Thicket. Also sampled from citrus and pistachio orchards. STATUS: LC; African endemic. (Barbata-springspinnekop)

Veissella
Veissella jumping spiders

Medium-sized. Carapace high with abrupt slope posteriorly; eye field trapezoid, its anterior width slightly larger than posterior width; posterior median eyes relatively large, set on low tubercles; clypeus low. Abdomen ovoid. Legs long and slender; leg I longest; tibia I with dense, long, feathery black setae on ventral surface. NOTES: Plant dwellers. Only one species occurs in South Africa. (Veissella-springspinnekoppe)

Veissella durbani
Durban Jumping Spider

Carapace brown with some short greyish setae, denser near eyes; anterior eyes rimmed with white setae. Abdomen brownish, with traces of darker chevrons posteriorly; dorsum sparsely covered with grey setae. Leg I stronger than others, tibiae I with dense, long, black, feathery setae on ventral surface; other legs same colour as carapace. NOTES: Collected from foliage in IOCB, Savanna and Thicket. Also sampled from macadamia orchards. STATUS: LC; South African endemic. (Durbanse Springspinnekop)

Wandawe
Wanda's jumping spiders

Small spiders. Carapace flattened; integument with small circular pits; clypeus low; chelicerae of medium length. Abdomen roundish oval, brown with transverse yellow patches and bands on brown. Leg I enlarged, femur and tibia swollen, especially in males; tibia I in males with brush of dense unmodified setae ventrally. NOTES: Plant dwellers known from three species, two from South Africa. (Wanda se springspinnekoppe)

Wandawe australis
Wanda's Southern Jumping Spider

Carapace reddish brown with short transverse yellow patches of dense setae; clypeus very low; anterior eyes rimmed with white setae. Abdomen brown with similar transverse patches of dense yellow setae. Legs translucent with dark bands and stripes. NOTES: An arboreal species collected in forest habitats. STATUS: Rare; South African endemic. (Wanda se Suidelike Springspinnekop)

FAMILY SPARASSIDAE
Huntsman spiders
Jagspinnekoppe

Carapace round to oval, narrower in eye region; fovea present; eight eyes in two rows (4:4); size of eyes in anterior row varies between genera, median eyes usually largest. Abdomen hairy, round to oval, often with a dark, median heart mark. Legs long, laterigrade, two-clawed; tarsi with dense claw tufts; scopulae on tarsi and metatarsi moderately dense to sparse. NOTES: Most huntsman spiders are nocturnal. Free living, found mainly on foliage with only a few genera living in silk-lined burrows in the ground or silken retreats under stones. Nine genera and 52 species are known from South Africa.

Eusparassus
Stone huntsman spiders

Medium-sized to large. Carapace as wide as long; eyes in two recurved rows. Abdomen oval. Legs all same size; with two pairs of ventral tibial spines. NOTES: Nocturnal. They build large silk retreats with a papery texture on the underside of stones and in the crevices of rocks, and hide there during the day. Retreats are also used during moulting and as sites to deposit egg sacs. Known from three species in South Africa. (Klipjagspinnekoppe)

Eusparassus borakalalo
Borakalalo Stone Huntsman Spider

Carapace uniformly fawn coloured, with dense layer of yellow-brown setae. Abdomen same colour as carapace, decorated with slightly darker heart mark that extends in narrow band to posterior edge. Legs same colour as body. NOTES: Sampled from silk retreats made on the underside of stones in Grassland and Savanna. STATUS: LC; South African endemic. (Borakalalo-klipjagspinnekop)

Eusparassus jaegeri
Gauteng Stone Huntsman Spider

Carapace and legs uniformly fawn, clothed in pale brownish-grey setae. Abdomen same colour as carapace; heart mark with reddish tint that extends as band to posterior edge; faint red tint laterally. NOTES: Sampled on the ground in Grassland and Savanna. STATUS: LC; southern African endemic. (Gautengse Klipjagspinnekop)

Eusparassus schoemanae   Schoeman's Stone Huntsman Spider

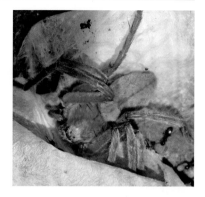

Carapace and legs uniformly yellowish brown. Abdomen brownish grey dorsally, with darker heart mark that extends as band to posterior edge. Legs same colour as body. **NOTES:** Free-living nocturnal spider sampled from Desert, Grassland and Succulent Karoo. **STATUS:** LC; southern African endemic. (Schoeman se Klipjagspinnekop)

May   White huntsman spiders

Medium-sized to large. Carapace as wide as long; eyes in two recurved rows; anterior median eyes largest; chelicerae with two anterior and three posterior teeth, without denticles in between them; fang base bears 1–9 bristles ventrally. Abdomen oval. Leg scopulae on tarsi and metatarsi moderately dense to sparse; tarsi with two claws and claw tuft setae; leg I shortest. **NOTES:** Found in arid regions. Lives in burrows in sand dunes. Known from three Namibian and one South African species. (Wit jagspinnekoppe)

May bruno   Witsand Huntsman Spider

Carapace creamy brown, without distinct pattern; white to shimmering pink setae around eyes, along clypeus and on parts of chelicerae and legs. Abdomen oval. Legs with dense setae on metatarsi and tarsi. **NOTES:** Collected from sand dunes where it digs a burrow leading 20–30cm into the ground. The burrow is closed with a lid. Sampled from Nama-Karoo. **STATUS:** LC; South African endemic. (Witsand-jagspinnekop)

Olios   Olios huntsman spiders

Medium-sized to large. Carapace convex dorsally; eight eyes in two almost straight rows. Abdomen hirsute, round to oval; heart mark usually distinct. Legs long; tarsi with dense claw tufts; scopulae on tarsi and metatarsi moderately dense to sparse. Male slightly smaller than female. **NOTES:** Nocturnal. Wander on trees and shrubs in search of prey. They make silk retreats between two leaves or among seeds, binding everything together with silk strands. Known from 17 species in South Africa. (Olios-jagspinnekoppe)

Olios auricomis
Green Huntsman Spider

Body and legs green. Carapace slightly convex, barely inclined in front; median eyes slightly larger than lateral eyes, posterior eye row very slightly recurved. Abdomen oval, hirsute; heart mark extends towards posterior edge. Legs long, slender. NOTES: Sampled from Grassland, IOCB and Savanna, as well as from avocado and macadamia orchards. STATUS: LC; African endemic. (Groen Jagspinnekop)

Olios correvoni nigrifrons
Black-faced Huntsman Spider

Body fawn, with few spots. Anterior carapace, clypeus, anterior row of eyes and chelicerae black. Abdomen fawn, faintly spotted. Legs same colour as carapace; distal segments darker. NOTES: Sampled from trees and shrubs in Fynbos, Grassland, IOCB, Nama-Karoo and Savanna. STATUS: LC; African endemic. (Swartgesig-jagspinnekop)

Olios freyi
Frey's Huntsman Spider

Carapace fawn with brown spots in cephalic region; eyes on dark spots; chelicerae reddish brown. Abdomen fawn with numerous spots. Legs same colour as carapace, spotted. NOTES: Sampled from trees and shrubs in the Savanna biome. STATUS: LC; African endemic. (Frey se Jagspinnekop)

Olios sjostedti
Sjostedt's Huntsman Spider

Carapace fawn with dark patches, which fuse with darker eye region; chelicerae dark brown distally. Abdomen fawn with dorsal pattern consisting of partly fused triangular patches along heart mark and posterior midline. Coxae and femora pale yellowish brown, rest of legs dark. NOTES: Sampled from trees and shrubs in Forest, Grassland and Savanna, some from bark and under stones. Also sampled from macadamia orchards. STATUS: LC; African endemic. (Sjostedt se Jagspinnekop)

Palystella
Palystella huntsman spiders

Medium-sized. Carapace longer than wide, convex anteriorly; anterior eye row recurved; posterior eyes straight, equidistant. Abdomen oval, hirsute. Tarsi with dense claw tufts; scopulae on tarsi and metatarsi moderately dense to sparse. NOTES: Free-running ground dwellers found in more arid regions. Four species have been described in Namibia, two of which have been recorded in South Africa. (Palystella-jagspinnekoppe)

Palystella namaquensis
Namaqua Huntsman Spider

Carapace uniformly yellow-brown with dark longitudinal marking. Abdomen dark brownish grey, with pair of well-separated white spots near anterior margin and another pair near spinnerets. Legs dark brownish grey. NOTES: Ground dwellers found in more arid regions. Sampled from under rocks in the Nama-Karoo biome. STATUS: LC; southern African endemic. (Namakwa-jagspinnekop)

Palystes
Rain spiders

Large spiders recognised by the broad white clypeal 'moustache' of dense white to yellow setae. Carapace flat; sternum with markings. Abdomen with clearly outlined brown or black heart mark. Legs ventrally decorated with bands and spots; tarsi with dense claw tufts; scopulae on tarsi and metatarsi moderately dense to sparse. Males sometimes smaller than females. NOTES: Nocturnal wandering hunters. The eggs are deposited in a large silk-covered sac attached to vegetation that is guarded by the female. They frequently enter houses, usually one or two days before it starts to rain, hence the common name 'rain spiders'. They are often noticed at night on the walls of rooms where they prey on insects attracted to the light source. Represented by 13 species in South Africa. (Reënspinnekoppe)

Female *Palystes* sp. on egg sac

Palystes castaneus
Cape Rain Spider

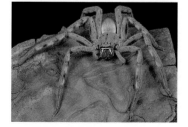

Recognised by black ventrum and sternum. Carapace fawn; clypeus with distinct white band on edge. Abdomen sports broad band ventrally. Legs dorsally similar to carapace. NOTES: Sampled from grass and shrubs in Fynbos, Grassland and Nama-Karoo. Frequently found in gardens and sometimes in houses. STATUS: LC; southern African endemic. (Kaapse Reënspinnekop)

Palystes crawhayi
Crawhay's Rain Spider

Carapace uniformly greyish brown; sternum yellow with two black bands; coxae yellow. Abdomen ventrally with black band behind epigastric furrow, rest of ventrum reddish brown with distinct white spots. Femora spotted with yellowish grey. NOTES: Nocturnal plant dweller that has also been sampled from buildings in the Grassland biome. STATUS: LC; southern African endemic. (Crawhay se Reënspinnekop)

Palystes karooensis
Karoo Rain Spider

Carapace fawn with pale median band; sternum with black bands in line with coxae II, followed by medially interrupted bar at coxae III. Abdomen greyish brown with distinct heart mark; ventrum with dark crescent mark posterior to epigastric furrow followed by reddish area with white spots. Femora with white spots. NOTES: Adults inactive during the day, sheltering under loose bark on vegetation. Sampled from Grassland, Nama-Karoo and Thicket. STATUS: LC; South African endemic. (Karoo-reënspinnekop)

Palystes kreuzmanni
Kreuzmann's Rain Spider

Carapace reddish brown with median band narrowing anteriorly and dark triangular pattern in front of fovea; clypeus with transversal band of dense bright setae. Abdomen fawn with heart mark and white markings medially. Legs dorsally resemble the carapace. NOTES: Builds retreat between apical leaves of bushes in Fynbos vegetation. STATUS: Endangered; South African endemic. (Kreuzmann se Reënspinnekop)

Palystes leppanae — Leppanae Rain Spider

Carapace mottled with paler median band; sternum has two medially interrupted transverse black bands. Abdomen mottled greyish brown with outlined heart mark; latter flanked by paired pale spots; ventrum with dark crescent mark posterior to epigastric furrow, followed by rich reddish-brown background decorated with numerous white spots. Legs banded. NOTES: Sampled from trees and shrubs in Fynbos and Thicket. Also found in buildings. STATUS: LC; South African endemic. (Leppanae-reënspinnekop)

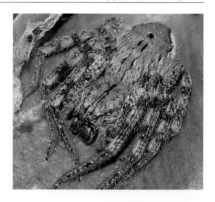

Palystes leroyorum — Leroy's Rain Spider

Carapace mottled greyish brown with two irregular median bands; sternum with solid black band in line with coxae II. Abdomen with dark heart mark. Femora ventrally dark with lacework of fine, irregular white spots. NOTES: Inactive during the day, sheltering in trees. Sampled from Grassland and Savanna. Some specimens were sampled from houses. STATUS: LC; South African endemic. (Leroy se Reënspinnekop)

Palystes perornatus — Eastern Cape Rain Spider

Carapace greyish with pale marginal band; sternum with black band in line with coxae II, followed by medially interrupted band at coxae III. Abdomen fawn-brown with indistinct heart mark; ventrum with dark crescent mark posterior to epigastric furrow followed by reddish area with white spots. Femora spotted with white. NOTES: Sampled from Forest, Grassland, IOCB, Nama-Karoo and Savanna. Some specimens have also been recorded in houses. STATUS: LC; South African endemic. (Oos-Kaapse Reënspinnekop)

Family Sparassidae **231**

Palystes superciliosus — House Rain Spider

Carapace coloration ranges from a nearly uniform pale brown to dark, with dark median band; sternum with dark band in line with coxae II. Abdomen lacks ventral markings other than four longitudinal striations and a dark band posterior to epigastric furrow. Tibiae banded ventrally; coxae dark. NOTES: A very common species found in trees and often also seen in houses. Usually enters houses before rainy spells. Attaches large egg sacs to vegetation. Sampled from all biomes except those that are arid. Also sampled from cabbage, avocado and macadamia orchards. STATUS: LC; South African endemic. (Huisreënspinnekop)

Panaretella — Spotted huntsman spiders

Medium-sized to large spiders. Carapace slightly longer than wide; anterior lateral eyes only slightly larger than rest; posterior eye row wider than anterior eye row. Sternum and coxae have fine black spots ventrally, against a pale white or yellow background. Abdomen with a dark marking on each side of the abdomen posteriorly. Leg tarsi with dense claw tufts; scopulae on tarsi and metatarsi moderately dense to sparse. NOTES: Free living, found in vegetation such as trees. Five species occur in South Africa. (Kol-jagspinnekoppe)

Panaretella immaculata — Immaculata Huntsman Spider

Body reddish brown. Abdomen without markings, other than a fairly narrow, darker median band in anterior half, two distinct black spots circled with white laterally and a paler posterior area. Legs reddish brown. NOTES: Sampled from trees in Savanna. STATUS: LC; South African endemic. (Immaculata-jagspinnekop)

Panaretella minor
Minor Huntsman Spider

Carapace yellow-brown with some indistinct dark spots and stripes radiating from fovea; sternum and coxae yellow with numerous black spots. Abdomen reddish brown dorsally, with some faint, curved, light transverse stripes near spinnerets; ventral surface reddish brown; pair of large black oval markings at the sides of abdomen. Legs yellow-brown with very indistinct dark spots. **NOTES:** Sampled from IOCB and Savanna. **STATUS:** LC; South African endemic. (Minor-jagspinnekop)

Parapalystes
Parapalystes huntsman spiders

Large. Resemble *Palystes* (rain spiders) in having a white band on the clypeal edge. Carapace with domed cephalic region; sternum black except for a white to yellow pattern on the anterior third. Abdomen with solid heart mark. Tarsi with dense claw tufts. **NOTES:** Free-living plant dwellers known from five species endemic to South Africa. (Parapalystes-jagspinnekoppe)

Parapalystes cultrifer
Cultrifer Huntsman Spider

Carapace fawn to brown with numerous dark spots; indistinct band present medially. Abdomen with faint heart mark and triangle-shaped dark markings posteriorly. Legs same colour as carapace. **NOTES:** Sampled from Succulent Karoo and Thicket. **STATUS:** LC; South African endemic. (Cultrifer-jagspinnekop)

Parapalystes euphorbiae
Euphorbia Huntsman Spider

Carapace brownish grey with thin white median band; posterior half dark; sternum black. Abdomen has triangle-shaped dark markings in a central band over abdomen; bright orange area present ventrally. Legs with distinct bands ventrally; coxae bright orange. **NOTES:** Sampled from retreats in low leafless *Euphorbia* shrubs growing on dune hummocks in Desert and Succulent Karoo. **STATUS:** LC; South African endemic. (Euphorbia-jagspinnekop)

Parapalystes lycosinus
Lycosinus Huntsman Spider

Carapace fawn to brown with numerous dark spots; dark V-shaped marking present medially. Abdomen has five triangular-shaped dark markings in a central band. Legs same colour as carapace. NOTES: Sampled from Fynbos, Nama-Karoo and Thicket. STATUS: LC; South African endemic. (Lycosinus-jagspinnekop)

Pseudomicrommata
Grass huntsman spiders

Large. Recognised by an elongated abdomen and a distinct dark band over the carapace and abdomen. Carapace slightly longer than wide, flat dorsally; anterior eye row recurved and posterior row procurved; anterior median eyes smallest. Abdomen elongated with well-defined red-and-brown bands along the body. Three pairs of ventral tibial spines on legs. NOTES: They make large nests in grass and attach papery egg sacs to grass blades. Frequently found in the common African *Eragrostis* grass. Two species are known from South Africa. (Grasjagspinnekoppe)

Pseudomicrommata longipes
African Grass Huntsman Spider

Carapace longer than wide, grey, with broad dark median band bordered by thin white band. These bands extend over abdomen up to spinnerets. Legs grey with some longitudinal bands. NOTES: Grass dwellers. Female constructs a papery egg sac attached to grass blades. Recorded in grass, but also occurs in bushes, small trees and leaf litter. Sampled from Fynbos, Grassland, Savanna and Thicket. STATUS: LC; African endemic. (Afrika-grasjagspinnekop)

Pseudomicrommata vittigera
Vittigera Grass Huntsman Spider

Carapace longer than wide, brown, with thin dark median band and two dark lateral bands. Abdomen cream with dark median band that extends up to spinnerets. Legs same colour as carapace. NOTES: Free-living grass dwellers. Also occurs in bushes, small trees and leaf litter in the Savanna biome. STATUS: LC; southern African endemic. (Vittigera-grasjagspinnekop)

FAMILY THOMISIDAE
Crab spiders
Krapspinnekoppe

Carapace variable, from semicircular to ovoid to elongated, usually with simple erect setae; eight eyes in two rows (4:4); eyes on strong protuberances or tubercles in some genera; lateral eyes usually on tubercles that vary from rounded to distinct. Abdomen variable, from round to ovoid to elongated; sometimes extends past spinnerets. Legs laterigrade; legs I and II usually longer than III and IV; legs I and II frequently bear rows of paired strong macrosetae on the tibiae and metatarsi. In several genera sexes differ in shape, colour and size. **NOTES:** Very common on plants, inhabiting grass, shrubs, flowers and trees and frequently encountered on crops. Only a few genera are ground dwellers. They are semi-sedentary, excelling as ambushers with cryptic coloration. Mainly active during the day. Their gait is sideways or crab-like, hence their common name. They make retreats in vegetation and ground debris when not active or to deposit the egg sac. Speciose; in South Africa 38 genera and 141 species are known.

Ansiea
Ansie's crab spiders

Small to medium-sized. Carapace as wide as long; surface clothed with numerous erect spiniform setae; eyes in two recurved rows; lateral eyes on small tubercles; median ocular quadrangle wider than long. Abdomen round to oval. Legs I and II with macrosetae on tibiae and metatarsi. Males resemble females in size but can differ in colour. **NOTES:** Free-living plant dwellers frequently found on flowers. One species is known from South Africa. (Ansie se krapspinnekoppe)

Ansiea tuckeri
Tucker's Crab Spider

Female Carapace fawn to pale green; eye region white. Abdomen creamy white or with green tint. Legs same colour as carapace; metatarsi and tarsi I and II with brownish tint. **Male** Carapace fawn to pale green, usually with two distinct brown lateral bands and a thin marginal band. Abdomen off-white to green. Legs fawn, distal parts with reddish-brown band. **NOTES:** Sampled from trees and shrubs in Grassland, IOCB, Savanna and Thicket. Also sampled from avocado, macadamia and pine plantations. **STATUS:** LC; African endemic. (Tucker se Krapspinnekop)

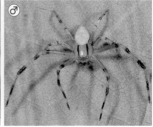

Avelis — Avelis crab spiders

Small. Carapace as wide as long, sides rounded, clothed with numerous white recumbent setae with longer setae scattered in between. Abdomen as wide as long; clothed with long, club-shaped, dark setae. Legs short, of equal length; clothed in the same type of setae as body. Male slightly darker than female. NOTES: Free-living plant dwellers. A monotypic genus endemic to South Africa. (Avelis-krapspinnekoppe)

Avelis hystriculus — Avelis Crab Spider

Carapace varies from tawny to reddish brown to dark brown, with a faint network of paler striae on thoracic region, darker laterally; eyes rimmed with black. Abdomen greyish white to dark, mottled with white and grey. Legs reddish brown to dark brown. Male slightly darker than female, with reddish-brown femora on legs I and II. NOTES: Found on low-growing vegetation in Fynbos, Grassland, Savanna and Thicket. STATUS: LC; South African endemic. (Avelis-krapspinnekop)

Borboropactus — Borboropactus crab spiders

Medium-sized. Recognised by the thick tibiae and metatarsi of leg I, which bear a double row of macrosetae ventrally. Carapace narrower in eye region; fovea longitudinal; integument covered with curly setae. Abdomen triangular, integument bears scales and club-shaped setae, sand particles frequently adhering to latter. Leg I directed to the front and not sideways. NOTES: Free-living ground dwellers found under logs among decaying leaves in damp areas. Three species occur in South Africa. (Borboropactus-krapspinnekoppe)

Borboropactus sp. female

Borboropactus silvicola — Silvicola Crab Spider

Carapace pale brown to grey, slightly darker centrally. Abdomen mottled brown dorsally with some blackish markings. Legs brown, mottled with black spots and bands; leg I stronger than others. NOTES: Sampled from Forest, IOCB, Savanna and Thicket. Also recorded in maize fields. STATUS: LC; South African endemic. (Silvicola-krapspinnekop)

Camaricus
Camaricus crab spiders

Medium-sized. Carapace shiny, evenly convex dorsally. Abdomen oval to subglobular, slightly flattened dorsally. Legs slender, without strong macrosetae. Male smaller than female. **NOTES:** Free-living plant dwellers found in grass and in the herb layer. One species is known from South Africa. (Camaricus-krapspinnekoppe)

Camaricus nigrotesselatus
Nigrotesselatus Crab Spider

Carapace shiny, reddish brown with distinct black spots over lateral eyes. Abdomen has yellow-orange background dorsally, with distinct black patterns; five dorsal sigilla; dark ventrally. Legs have longitudinal bands, sometimes with spots; some leg segments darker in male. **NOTES:** Sampled from grass and shrubs in Forest, Grassland, IOCB, Savanna and Thicket. **STATUS:** LC; African endemic. (Nigrotesselatus-krapspinnekop)

Diaea
Diaea crab spiders

Small to medium-sized. Carapace smooth, bearing simple, isolated setae; moderately convex dorsally, with long setae; lateral eyes on small tubercles; both eye rows recurved and almost the same length. Abdomen round in female, oval to round in males. Legs thin and slender, with numerous erect setae, usually same colour as carapace, sometimes banded. **NOTES:** Free-living plant dwellers very commonly found on grass and shrubs. Four species are known from South Africa. (Diaea-krapspinnekoppe)

Diaea puncta
Puncta Crab Spider

Carapace fawn to green, smooth, bearing simple, isolated setae. Abdomen fawn dorsally, decorated with red spots. Legs same colour as carapace. Legs much longer in male than in female; segments distally banded. **NOTES:** Sampled from grass, shrubs and trees in all biomes except Desert. Also collected from crops such as avocado, cotton, pistachio and strawberries. **STATUS:** LC; African endemic. (Puncta-krapspinnekop)

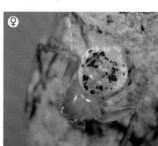

Family Thomisidae 237

Diaea rohani
Rohan's Crab Spider

Only male known. Carapace fawn to pale green, smooth, bearing simple, isolated setae, decorated with two narrow lateral bands. Abdomen fawn to white decorated with paired dark spots. Legs same colour as carapace, distal segments of legs I and II dark. NOTES: Free-living plant dweller found on trees, shrubs and grasses in Grassland and Savanna. STATUS: LC; southern African endemic. (Rohan se Krapspinnekop)

Firmicus
Firmicus crab spiders

Small to medium-sized. Recognised by their flattened body. Carapace very flat and thin; tubercles of anterior lateral eyes shallow, clearly larger than posterior lateral eye tubercles; anterior lateral eyes larger than rest. Abdomen flattened, oval to round. Legs I and II longer and thicker than rest. Males slightly smaller and frequently darker than females. NOTES: Free-living plant dwellers most often found on trees. Represented by three species in South Africa. (Firmicus-krapspinnekoppe)

Firmicus bipunctatus
Green Firmicus Crab Spider

Carapace flattened, narrower anteriorly, pale green, darker around edge. Abdomen greenish with three distinct red markings laterally. Legs same colour as carapace, distal end of each segment banded. NOTES: Plant dwellers sampled from IOCB and Savanna. STATUS: LC; African endemic. (Groen Firmicus-krapspinnekop)

Firmicus bragantinus
White Firmicus Crab Spider

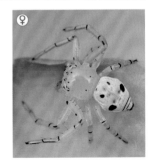

Female Carapace translucent white with two small white spots posteriorly; chelicerae white with large black spot. Abdomen white dorsally with pair of black spots; dark transverse bands on posterior end. Legs same colour as carapace, decorated with black spots. **Male** Smaller in size, reddish brown with four black spots on abdomen. Femora and patellae on legs I and II dark. NOTES: Plant dwellers most commonly found on trees in Forest, Fynbos, IOCB and Savanna. Also sampled from avocado, citrus and grapefruit orchards. STATUS: LC; African endemic. (Wit Firmicus-krapspinnekop)

Geraesta
Geraesta crab spiders

Medium-sized. Carapace semicircular, usually with simple erect setae; eyes in two rows on tubercles. Abdomen ovoid, frequently decorated with patterns, distinct abdominal tubercles present. Legs I and II much longer than rest; tibiae and metatarsi with paired macrosetae. NOTES: Free-living plant dwellers found on trees. Only one species is known from South Africa. (Geraesta-krapspinnekoppe)

Geraesta congoensis
Green Geraesta Crab Spider

Carapace mottled brown, narrowed in eye region, bearing short curly setae. Abdomen decorated with various shades of green; anterior border with yellow tint. Legs same colour as carapace; legs I and II stronger than rest. Male darker than female, with more decoration on abdomen. NOTES: A rare species sampled from plants in IOCB, Savanna and Thicket. STATUS: LC; African endemic. (Groen Geraesta-krapspinnekop)

Heriaeus
Hairy crab spiders

Small. Recognised by the long body setae, which vary from erect to a combination of short, club-shaped or blunt-tipped. Carapace as wide as long. Abdomen round to oval, with indistinct markings. Legs same colour as carapace. NOTES: Most species are free-living plant dwellers, but some are found on the ground. Ten species are known from South Africa. (Harigekrapspinnekoppe)

Heriaeus copricola
Ground Hairy Crab Spider

Carapace with two longitudinal brown bands; eye region white; chelicerae yellow-brown. Abdomen bears long, slender, blunt-tipped setae, fawn, mottled with white, with faint transverse bands posteriorly as well as a number of dark brown markings, some brown spots laterally. Legs with setae and spots. NOTES: Ground dwellers collected in Grassland and Savanna. STATUS: LC; southern African endemic. (Grond-harigekrapspinnekop)

Heriaeus crassispinus　　　　Bushy-leg Hairy Crab Spider

Female Carapace fawn with broad, irregular, lateral bands of brown; numerous strong spines and setae. Abdomen reddish brown, mottled with yellow-brown, bears short, dark brown spiniform setae. Legs fawn with irregular dark bands. **Male** Abdomen blackish brown dorsally, slightly mottled with yellow-brown, sometimes with some white spots. Legs very distinct, with a fringe of long, black setae on tibiae, metatarsi and tarsi of legs I and II. **NOTES:** A free-living plant dweller sampled from a variety of habitats in Grassland, IOCB, Savanna and Thicket. **STATUS:** LC; African endemic. (Veerpoot-harigekrapspinnekop)

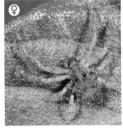
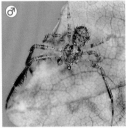

Heriaeus foordi　　　　Foord's Hairy Crab Spider

Carapace dark, with strong setae; eye region mottled with white. Abdomen blackish brown, mottled with red and yellow-brown, bearing short, dark brown spiniform setae. Legs brown with white bands distally on leg segments. **NOTES:** Ground dweller sampled from Grassland and Savanna. **STATUS:** LC; South African endemic. (Foord se Harigekrapspinnekop)

Heriaeus peterwebbi　　　　Peter's Hairy Crab Spider

Carapace has two longitudinal stripes; setae transparent; eye region white. Abdomen bears long spiniform, acute setae; yellow-brown, mottled white, with a central white mark and numerous dark brown spots. Legs have brown spots. **NOTES:** Collected from the ground as well as grasses, thorn trees and crops such as cotton and strawberries in Savanna and Grassland. **STATUS:** LC; southern African endemic. (Peter se Harigekrapspinnekop)

Heriaeus zanii

Zani's Hairy Crab Spider

Carapace has two longitudinal brown stripes medially; setae transparent, some pale brown; eye region yellow-brown. Abdomen with 8–24 long, brown, spiniform setae. Legs lightly spotted. NOTES: Collected in leaf litter and on plants in Fynbos, Grassland and Savanna. STATUS: LC; South African endemic. (Zani se Harigekrapspinnekop)

Hewittia

Hewittia crab spiders

Small. Characterised by the high, anteriorly sloping carapace, longer than wide; eyes arranged in two rows with the median eyes closer to the lateral eyes than to each other. Abdomen oval, a third longer than wide, bluntly truncated anteriorly. Legs slender; legs I and II longer than rest, without macrosetae. Males resemble females, with less sloping cephalic region. NOTES: Free-living plant dwellers. Only one species is known from South Africa. (Hewittia-krapspinnekoppe)

Hewittia gracilis

Hewitt's Crab Spider

Carapace reddish brown; eyes in two rows, covering most of carapace width. Abdomen decorated with lateral white band and dark grey patches. Legs slender, same colour as carapace. NOTES: Sampled from grass and shrubs in Fynbos, Grassland and Savanna. STATUS: LC; African endemic. (Hewitt se Krapspinnekop)

Holopelus

Holopelus crab spiders

Small. Carapace as wide as long, cubic in shape, with rounded sides, anteriorly truncated; dorsal area elevated, flattened, clothed with numerous polyp-like tubercles, each bearing a short club-shaped seta. Legs short, all same size. Male smaller than female. NOTES: Free-living plant dwellers collected from trees and low shrubs. Known from two species in South Africa. (Holopelus-krapspinnekoppe)

Holopelus albibarbis

Cape Holopelus Crab Spider

Carapace reddish brown; clypeus and eye region suffused with yellowish brown; diffuse bands from eyes to posterior edge. Abdomen ivory, sigilla brown. Legs uniform; distal part of each segment yellowish brown. NOTES: Collected from Fynbos, Grassland, Savanna and Thicket. STATUS: LC; African endemic. (Kaapse Holopelus-krapspinnekop)

Holopelus almiae   Almie's Crab Spider

Carapace reddish brown; clypeus and eye region yellowish. Abdomen brown. Legs yellowish brown, distal part of each segment white. NOTES: Sampled from shrubs in Fynbos and Thicket. STATUS: LC; South African endemic. (Almie se Krapspinnekop)

Misumenops   Misumenops crab spiders

Small. Carapace as wide as long, low, slightly convex; surface clothed with numerous erect spiniform setae. Abdomen round; clothed with numerous erect spiniform setae. Legs I and II longer than rest; tibiae and metatarsi with paired macrosetae. Males smaller than females, with much longer legs; setae on body, especially those on the abdomen, are longer and more numerous. NOTES: Inhabits grass, shrubs, flowers and trees. One species is known from South Africa. (Misumenops-krapspinnekoppe)

Misumenops rubrodecoratus   Red-band Crab Spider

Female Carapace yellow with greenish tint; eye region darker. Abdomen greenish white; usually tinted with broad red horseshoe-shaped band anteriorly. Legs sometimes banded. **Male** Smaller; body and legs uniformly yellowish brown. Basal parts of tibiae, metatarsi and tarsi of legs I and II banded. NOTES: One of the most common thomisid species in South Africa. Sampled from all biomes except Desert. Very frequently encountered on crops. STATUS: LC; African endemic. (Rooiband-krapspinnekop)

Monaeses   Monaeses crab spiders

Medium-sized. Recognised by their long bodies, which resemble grass. Carapace elongated. Abdomen long and slender; caudal part varies from short to very long, extending beyond the spinnerets. Legs I and II longer than rest; tibiae and metatarsi with paired macrosetae. Male resembles female, but darker in colour and with longer legs. NOTES: They inhabit grass and low vegetation. Known from seven species in South Africa. (Monaeses-krapspinnekoppe)

Monaeses austrinus   Austrinus Crab Spider

Carapace fawn, suffused with white; two broad brown lateral bands run from eyes to posterior declivity. Abdomen long, fawn, faintly tinted with grey; two white lateral bands extend over length of abdomen; tip long and narrow, extends past spinnerets. Legs faintly banded. Male brown with shorter abdomen. NOTES: Abundant in grass in Forest, Grassland, IOCB, Nama-Karoo, Savanna and Thicket. STATUS: LC; African endemic. (Austrinus-krapspinnekop)

  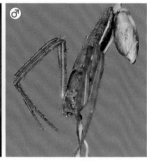

Monaeses fuscus   Brown Crab Spider

Carapace brown; eye region tinted with black; faint white band from posterior lateral eyes to edge of clypeus. Abdomen reddish brown; tip extending slightly past spinnerets. Legs fawn to brown, slightly tinted with black. NOTES: Grass dwellers sampled from Forest, Grassland, IOCB and Savanna. STATUS: LC; South African endemic. (Bruin Krapspinnekop)

Monaeses gibbus   Short-tail Crab Spider

Carapace fawn; eye region and clypeus mottled with white. Abdomen cream to white; creamy broad median band bordered by darker bands and spots; truncated anteriorly but widens posteriorly; posteriorly blunt tip situated above spinnerets. Legs fawn, irregularly spotted with brown. NOTES: Plant dwellers mainly sampled from grass in Grassland, IOCB and Savanna. STATUS: LC; South African endemic. (Kortstert-krapspinnekop)

Monaeses paradoxus
Paradoxus Crab Spider

Carapace varies from fawn to grey, mottled with white and black. Abdomen long, fawn to brown, distinctly marked with two white lateral bands. Legs creamy. **NOTES:** Abundant on grass in Forest, Fynbos, Grassland, IOCB, Nama-Karoo, Savanna and Succulent Karoo. **STATUS:** LC; cosmopolitan. (Paradoxus-krapspinnekop)

Monaeses pustulosus
Pustulosus Crab Spider

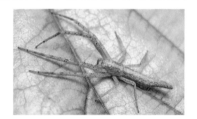

Carapace fawn to grey, with faint lateral bands. Abdomen long, fawn, with numerous dark brown spots. Legs fawn with spots. **NOTES:** Grass dwellers sampled from Forest, Fynbos, Grassland, IOCB, Nama-Karoo and Savanna. **STATUS:** LC; African endemic. (Pustulosus-krapspinnekop)

Monaeses quadrituberculatus
Round-tail Crab Spider

Carapace fawn, mottled with brown and white; tubercles of eyes and edge of clypeus white. Abdomen brown dorsally, with faint grey lateral bands; caudal extension does not extend past spinnerets; small tubercles present posteriorly, each tubercle bears a long seta. Legs fawn, mottled with brown. **NOTES:** Grass dwellers sampled from Desert, Forest, Grassland, IOCB, Nama-Karoo, Savanna and Succulent Karoo. **STATUS:** LC; African endemic. (Rondestert-krapspinnekop)

Mystaria
Mystaria beetle crab spiders

Small, colourful spiders that resemble beetles. Carapace circular to cube-shaped; cephalic and thoracic region elevated; eyes in two rows; median eyes small with the median ocular quadrangle narrower anteriorly than posteriorly. Abdomen circular to oval. Legs slender, without paired macrosetae. Males are smaller than females and differ in colour. Colour can vary between specimens of the same species. **NOTES:** Free-living plant dwellers sampled from trees. A small genus. Nine species are known from South Africa. (Mystaria-kewerkrapspinnekoppe)

Mystaria flavoguttata — Flavoguttata Beetle Crab Spider

Carapace reddish brown; darker around eyes. Abdomen yellowish white with broad brown median band and thin dark lateral bands. Some leg segments same colour as carapace; distal segment with greenish tint. Male body a uniform copper-brown, black or brown. **NOTES:** Sampled from Forest, IOCB and Savanna. **STATUS:** LC; African endemic. (Flavoguttata-kewerkrapspinnekop)

Mystaria lindaicapensis — Linda's Beetle Crab Spider

Carapace varies from mottled copper-brown to bright orange, copper-red or very dark copper. Abdomen varies from uniformly pale dorsally to varying dark patterns, sometimes with thin longitudinal central band; distal segments of legs I and II with greenish tint. **NOTES:** Sampled from grass in Forest and Thicket. **STATUS:** Vulnerable under criterion B; South African endemic. (Linda se kewerkrapspinnekop)

Mystaria rufolimbata — Rufolimbata Beetle Crab Spider

Female Carapace dark reddish brown to almost black. Abdomen dark or sometimes with red U-shaped band and red spots posteriorly. Legs dark. **Male** Uniformly copper-brown, black or brown. **NOTES:** Collected from forest vegetation in Grassland, IOCB and Savanna. **STATUS:** LC; African endemic. (Rufolimbata-kewerkrapspinnekop)

Mystaria savannensis — Striped-leg Beetle Crab Spider

Both sexes can be recognised by dark longitudinal stripes on legs. **Female** Carapace orange-red or dark brown. Abdomen pale with dark patterns dorsally, which vary in shape and colour. **Male** Body dark. **NOTES:** Sampled from a variety of habitats from the Savanna biome. **STATUS:** LC; African endemic. (Streepbeen-kewerkrapspinnekop)

Oxytate

Small to medium-sized. Carapace longer than wide, depressed; eyes in two recurved rows; eyes on small white tubercles; chelicerae wide; hairy band underneath chelicerae. Abdomen elongated and annulated at end. Legs I and II much longer than posterior legs; tibiae and metatarsi with paired macrosetae. NOTES: Free-living tree dwellers. Represented by four species in South Africa. (Oxytate-krapspinnekoppe)

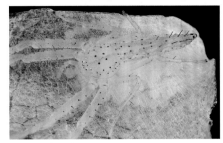

Oxytate female on egg sac

Oxytate argenteooculata

Red-spotted Crab Spider

Body and legs green. Carapace flattened; eyes surrounded with white; darker areas on carapace give spotted appearance; two red spots present centrally on both sides of fovea. Abdomen has similar spotted appearance; provided with transverse rows of 6–8 thick setae on posterior end. Legs spotted. Male darker than female. NOTES: Tree dwellers sampled from Fynbos, Grassland, Savanna and Thicket. STATUS: LC; African endemic. (Rooikol-krapspinnekop)

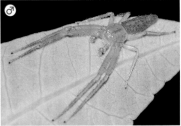

Oxytate concolor

Concolor Crab Spider

Carapace green, slightly flattened, round, with pale marginal band around border; eyes surrounded with white; posterior eye row broader than anterior row. Abdomen oval, with spotted appearance. NOTES: Tree dwellers sampled from Fynbos, Grassland, IOCB and Savanna. Also sampled from avocado, citrus and macadamia nut orchards. STATUS: LC; African endemic. (Concolor-krapspinnekop)

Oxytate ribes
Ribes Crab Spider

Body and legs pale yellowish green. Carapace flattened; eyes surrounded with white; thin red marginal band present. Abdomen with numerous green spots, extends posteriorly. Legs uniformly green. **NOTES:** Tree dwellers sampled from Fynbos, Grassland, IOCB and Savanna. **STATUS:** LC; African endemic. (Ribes-krapspinnekop)

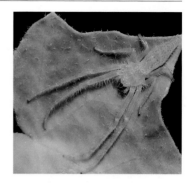

Pactactes
Pactactes crab spiders

Small. Body dark. Abdomen shiny, with white spots. Carapace high, flattened dorsally; numerous long setae on edge of declivity; both eye rows recurved; lateral eyes larger than median eyes, wide apart, close to edge; posterior median eyes very small. Abdomen round. Legs equal in size, with feathered setae; tarsi slightly thickened. **NOTES:** Rare spiders, found on low vegetation. A small genus known from three species endemic to Africa. All three occur in South Africa. (Pactactes-krapspinnekoppe)

Pactactes compactus
Compactus Crab Spider

Carapace dark brown, shiny. Abdomen dark with white markings; two white spots anterolaterally and two on lateral margin; dorsum has scattered long, dark setae. Legs black to reddish brown; thickly covered with short setae. **NOTES:** Plant dwellers sampled from Forest, Fynbos, Grassland, IOCB and Savanna. **STATUS:** LC; South African endemic. (Compactus-krapspinnekop)

Pactactes trimaculatus
Three-spotted Crab Spider

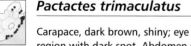

Carapace, dark brown, shiny; eye region with dark spot. Abdomen dark with three yellow (sometimes white) spots; dorsum bears long setae. Legs similar in colour to carapace, thickly covered with short setae. **NOTES:** Plant dwellers sampled from all the biomes except Desert, Nama- and Succulent Karoo. **STATUS:** LC; African endemic. (Driekol-krapspinnekop)

Parabomis

Parabomis crab spiders

Very small to small. Characterised by their small size, short legs, globular bodies and thick, granulous integument. Carapace high with very broad, sloping clypeus and strong posterior declivity; eyes closely grouped, groups set far apart. Abdomen globular, bearing strong striae. Legs very short, without spines. Males slightly smaller than females and darker in colour. NOTES: Free-living plant dwellers mostly sampled from trees. Four species occur in South Africa. (Parabomis-krapspinnekoppe)

Parabomis martini

Martin's Crab Spider

Carapace fawn; clypeus and eye region strongly infused with green; sides dark yellow to fawn with dark brown patches. Abdomen fawn to brown, infused with white or green. Legs reddish brown with darker coxae and femora. NOTES: Recorded from Grassland, IOCB, Savanna and Thicket. STATUS: LC; African endemic. (Martin se Krapspinnekop)

Parabomis megae

Meg's Crab Spider

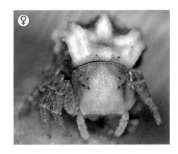

Female Carapace fawn; eye region infused with creamy white. Abdomen white, mottled with green. Legs same colour as carapace, sometimes with darker tint. NOTES: Free living, found on trees in the Savanna biome. STATUS: LC; southern African endemic. (Meg se Krapspinnekop)

Parabomis pilosus

Hairy Crab Spider

Carapace brown; clypeus and eye region strongly infused with fawn; integument thick, granulose, bearing short, thick setae. Abdomen fawn to brown, infused with white. Legs same colour as carapace. Male smaller than female, darker. NOTES: Collected from shrubs in the Savanna biome. STATUS: LC; southern African endemic. (Harige Krapspinnekop)

Parasmodix
Parasmodix crab spiders

Recognised by the distinct shape of the carapace. Cephalic region high, edge bordered by row of strong erect setae, each originating from small tubercle; both eye rows recurved; anterior lateral eyes larger than anterior median eyes. Abdomen rounded, dark. NOTES: Very rare. Monotypic. (Parasmodix-krapspinnekoppe)

Parasmodix quadrituberculata
Crowned Crab Spider

Carapace reddish brown, bearing six well-developed tubercles, each with strong setae on edge. Abdomen dark, mottled with white, bears two oval markings. Legs pale yellow; femora and patellae of legs I and II dark brown; rest of legs with brown spots and lines. NOTES: Sampled with sweep nets in Forest, Grassland and Savanna. Also sampled from maize fields. STATUS: LC. (Kroon-krapspinnekop)

Pherecydes
Pherecydes crab spiders

Small. Characterised by two lateral eyes situated on shared elevated area, which is widely truncated on top. Carapace as wide as long; eyes situated on distinct lateral tubercles; clypeus sloping. Abdomen round. Legs I and II sport numerous dark brown and yellow patches dorsolaterally on the femora and patellae. NOTES: Tree and grass dwellers known from six species in South Africa. (Pherecydes-krapspinnekoppe)

Pherecydes ionae
Iona's Crab Spider

Carapace mottled; clypeus creamy with green tint. Abdomen creamy, mottled with brown; scattered small tubercles each bearing a short dark seta; posterior half with thin wavy brown vertical bands. Legs creamy with dark bands. NOTES: Commonly found on bark in Forest and Savanna. STATUS: LC; African endemic. (Iona se Krapspinnekop)

Pherecydes nicolaasi

Nico's Crab Spider

Carapace fawn to brown; margin, fovea and striae of carapace darker brown, sometimes with green tint; thin yellowish-white band between lateral eyes. Abdomen greyish white; darker median band ventrally. Legs III and IV yellowish white, mottled with black. NOTES: Sampled from trees in Forest, Grassland, Savanna and Thicket. STATUS: LC; South African endemic. (Nico se krapspinnekop)

Pherecydes tuberculatus

Common Crab Spider

Carapace mottled and suffused with yellowish white. Abdomen dull greyish white, speckled with dark brown, very dark ventrally. Legs pale yellow, marked and speckled with dark brown; femur I with dark patches dorso-laterally; tarsi all have dark brown bands apically. NOTES: Plant dweller recorded from Grassland, Forest, Fynbos, Nama-Karoo, Savanna and Thicket. Also sampled from lucerne fields and pine plantations. STATUS: LC; southern African endemic. (Gewone Krapspinnekop)

Phrynarachne

Bird-dropping crab spiders

Small to medium-sized. Carapace as long as wide or longer; two equally recurved eye rows. Abdomen shape variable, integument hard, unequal, grooved and bearing distinct tubercles. Legs thick, robust, angular, grooved; legs I and II stronger than rest; tibiae and metatarsi with paired macrosetae. Males smaller. NOTES: Lives on the surface of leaves. Some make a disc of white silk on which they take up position, mimicking the excrement of birds. Two species are known from South Africa. (Voëlmis-krapspinnekoppe)

Phrynarachne melloleitaoi

Melloleitaoi Crab Spider

Carapace orange-brown; eyes on tubercles; carapace with pale median longitudinal band. Abdomen rich yellow-brown, rugose, with two strong abdominal tubercles directed slightly upwards. Legs dark brown, mottled, with strong setae on tibiae. NOTES: Sampled from trees in Forest, Fynbos, Grassland, IOCB, Savanna and Thicket. Also sampled from citrus orchards. STATUS: LC; southern African endemic. (Melloleitaoi-krapspinnekop)

Phrynarachne rugosa Bird-dropping Crab Spider

Body and legs dull brownish grey with short white longitudinal median band over abdomen. Integument hard, unequal, grooved, bears distinct tubercles. Legs same colour as carapace; thick and robust, angular and grooved. NOTES: Sampled from trees in Forest, Fynbos, IOCB and Savanna. STATUS: LC; African endemic. (Voëlmis-krapspinnekop)

Platythomisus Platythomisus crab spiders

Medium-sized to large. Only females known. Brightly coloured spiders; carapace, abdomen and legs with distinct markings in the form of spots or bands. Carapace shiny, slightly flattened; narrower anteriorly; both eye rows almost straight to slightly recurved; posterior median eyes smallest. Abdomen slightly longer than wide, flattened, decorated with spots. Legs long and slender; tibiae and metatarsi I and II without macrosetae. NOTES: Rare; sampled from trees. Three species known from South Africa. (Platythomisus-krapspinnekoppe)

Platythomisus deserticola Botswana Crab Spider

Carapace fawn; broad black band in eye region; marginal band thin, black. Abdomen creamy white with dark spots over sigilla; few small black spots laterally; edge decorated with yellow and orange markings. Femora I and II with pink tint; remaining leg segments black; hind legs with distal segment dark. NOTES: Sampled from trees in the Savanna biome. STATUS: LC; southern African endemic. (Botswana-krapspinnekop)

Platythomisus jubbi
Jubb's Crab Spider

Carapace orange-brown; broad black band over eye region; carapace bordered with thin white marginal band. Abdomen creamy white with dark spots over sigilla; numerous small black spots laterally; edge decorated with yellow and orange markings. Femora and patellae same colour as carapace; remaining leg segments black. **NOTES:** Sampled from trees in IOCB, Savanna and Thicket. **STATUS:** LC; South African endemic. (Jubb se Krapspinnekop)

Runcinia
Runcinia grass crab spiders

Medium-sized. Recognised by their flattened bodies and eyes on distinct carina. Carapace as wide as long or slightly longer, flattened above; anterior margin straight, posterior margin concave; surface clothed with numerous short irregularly spaced setae. Abdomen shape variable: triangular, oval or long and narrow; posteriorly truncated, rounded or extending caudally; with longitudinal striae following contour of abdomen; rows of setae differ in shape between species. Legs I and II longest; tibiae and metarsi with strong, paired macrosetae. Males more slender than females, with longer legs. **NOTES:** Free-living, very common grass dwellers. Eight species occur in South Africa. (Runcinia-graskrapspinnekoppe)

Female *Runcinia flavida* with spider prey

Runcinia aethiops
Aethiops Grass Crab Spider

Carapace fawn; with narrow white median band and lateral brown bands near border; thin brown marginal band. Abdomen fawn with brown bands laterally; central area with brown markings. Legs fawn. **NOTES:** Common grass dwellers sampled from all biomes except Desert and Succulent Karoo. Also sampled from pine plantations and strawberry fields. **STATUS:** LC; African endemic. (Aethiops-graskrapspinnekop)

Runcinia depressa   Flat Grass Crab Spider

Carapace flattened, fawn with dark marginal band and dark lateral bands; setae short, spiniform. Abdomen oval to slightly elongated; fawn with dark lateral markings. Legs fawn, distal segments darker. Male resembles female, but tarsi I and II and distal part of tibiae I and II dark brown; abdomen with striae bearing rows of alternating short and longer club-shaped setae. **NOTES:** Sampled from Fynbos, Grassland, IOCB, Nama-Karoo and Savanna. Also sampled from agroecosystems. **STATUS:** LC; African endemic. (Plat Graskrapspinnekop)

Runcinia erythrina   Round-head Grass Crab Spider

Carapace fawn with reddish-brown tint; lateral bands; carapace clothed with numerous irregularly spaced, short spiniform setae; carina more rounded in this species than in rest of genus. Abdomen creamy with distinct reddish-brown pattern; slightly longer than wide. Legs fawn. **NOTES:** Free living on plants and commonly found on grass. Sampled from all biomes except Desert and Succulent Karoo. **STATUS:** LC; African endemic. (Rondekop-graskrapspinnekop)

Runcinia flavida   Long-bodied Grass Crab Spider

Carapace fawn; longer than wide; carina and eye region mottled with white; sports pale brown lateral bands. Abdomen elongated, posterior end truncated; fawn, mottled with white; lateral bands sometimes present. Legs fawn; legs I and II mottled with brown and white. **NOTES:** Free living on plants and mostly sampled from grass. Found in all biomes except the more arid ones. Also sampled from pine plantations and strawberry fields. **STATUS:** LC; African endemic. (Langlyf-graskrapspinnekop)

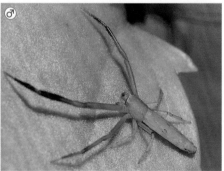

Simorcus

Simorcus crab spiders

Small to medium-sized. Carapace rugose, covered with numerous tubercles, each bearing short clavate or spiniform setae; eyes small, on slightly raised tubercles; eye region elevated, decorated with six tubercles, each bearing setae that can be either short and stout or long and slender. Abdomen longer than wide, caudally obtuse, with 20 or more large tubercles, each bearing a seta. Legs I and II long, with numerous setae, but without paired macrosetae. NOTES: Collected mainly from bark and foliage, although a few were captured in pitfall traps and hand-collected from under rocks or on sand dunes. Four species occur in South Africa. (Simorcus-krapspinnekoppe)

Simorcus cotti

Cott's Crab Spider

Carapace yellow-brown, mottled with white; clypeal edge with 10–14 spiniform setae; eye tubercles distinctly horn-like, with unequally sized, stout, spiniform setae. Abdomen mottled white and grey; species recognised by large abdominal tubercles, each bearing very small spiniform setae. Legs long, with numerous setae. NOTES: Collected by beating and sweeping of grass, trees, shrubs and herbs in Forest, Grassland, IOCB and Savanna. STATUS: LC; African endemic. (Cott se Krapspinnekop)

Simorcus haddadi

Haddad's Crab Spider

Carapace yellow-brown, mottled with white; cephalic region brown; clypeal edge with 12 (10–14) spiniform setae; eye tubercles distinctly horn-like, with unequally sized, stout, spiniform setae. Abdomen mottled white and grey; species recognised by the large abdominal tubercles, each bearing very small spiniform setae. Legs long, with numerous setae. NOTES: Collected with pitfall traps, Winkler leaf litter traps and hand-collecting mainly from the Fynbos biome and coastal dune areas. STATUS: NT; South African endemic. (Haddad se Krapspinnekop)

Simorcus lotzi

Lotz's Crab Spider

Carapace brown, mottled with white; chelicerae dark brown, central third white; clypeus with white lines that run from corner of clypeus towards posterior horns, and horizontally between them. Abdomen mottled white, grey and brown; posterior part of abdomen with irregular white marks. Legs mottled white and yellow-brown. NOTES: Sampled from the Grassland biome. STATUS: LC; southern African. (Lotz se Krapspinnekop)

Smodicinus

Smodicinus crab spiders

Small. Easily recognised by the modified carapace, which is highly elevated to form a crest that is directed posteriorly and divided into six pointed tubercles, flattened above; two tubercles pointed posteriorly and four laterally. Both eye rows recurved; lateral eyes larger than medians. Abdomen round to oval. Legs I and II strong, without macrosetae. **NOTES:** Very rare free-living plant dwellers represented by a single African species. (Smodicinus-krapspinnekoppe)

Smodicinus coroniger

Crowned Crab Spider

Carapace mottled reddish brown, furnished with numerous strongly developed conical apophyses. Abdomen mottled with white markings. All legs with white bands; legs I and II darker than rest. **NOTES:** Free-living plant dweller, sampled mainly from trees in IOCB, Savanna and Thicket. **STATUS:** LC; African endemic. (Kroon-krapspinnekop)

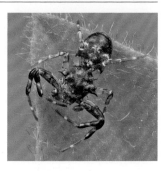

Stiphropus

Stiphropus crab spiders

Small. Carapace as wide as long; eyes in two rows; anterior row almost straight; posterior median eyes smallest; anterior median eyes closer to each other than to the anterior lateral eyes. Abdomen with sigillae that vary in size; sigillae less distinct in males where the abdomen is shield-like. Legs I and II have slightly thickened tarsi; thickly covered with branched setae; tarsi longer than metatarsi but without macrosetae. **NOTES:** Found in low vegetation close to or on ground level. Four species are known from South Africa. (Stiphropus-krapspinnekoppe)

Stiphropus affinis

Red-spot Crab Spider

Carapace shiny, uniformly dark brown; eye region with slight reddish tint over anterior lateral eyes. Abdomen and legs uniformly dark brown, without any distinct markings. Legs I and II have slightly thickened tarsi. **NOTES:** Free living in low vegetation close to ground level. Sampled from Grassland, IOCB, Nama-Karoo, Savanna and Thicket. **STATUS:** LC; southern African endemic. (Rooikol-krapspinnekop)

Stiphropus intermedius — Fat-legged Crab Spider

Carapace uniformly brown. Abdomen brownish, with one pair of sigilla; latter brown and oval. Legs same colour as carapace. NOTES: Recorded in low vegetation close to ground level. Sampled only from the Savanna biome. STATUS: LC; African endemic. (Dikpoot-krapspinnekop)

Stiphropella — Stiphropella crab spiders

Medium-sized. Carapace longer than wide; eyes in two rows; anterior lateral eyes larger than the anterior median eyes; integument slightly leathery. Abdomen round to oval; with distinct large sigilla; without markings. Legs and palpi thickly covered with branched setae; tarsi I and II thickened towards tip; tarsi longer than metatarsi. Resembles *Stiphropus* in their general appearance and in the arrangement of the eyes, but much larger in size. NOTES: Found on ground level, associated with ants. Monotypic and known only from South Africa. (Stiphropella-krapspinnekoppe)

Stiphropella gracilis — Gracilis Crab Spider

Carapace blackish brown with narrow white marginal band. Abdomen blackish brown, shiny; posterior sigilla large; without any other markings. Legs and palpi thickly covered with branched setae. NOTES: Free living on the ground. Observed specimens associated with *Anoplolepis custodiens* ants. STATUS: DDT; South African endemic. (Gracilis-krapspinnekop)

Sylligma — Sylligma crab spiders

Small spiders with ant-like bodies. Carapace slightly longer than wide; round to almost square; elevated in thoracic region; truncated posteriorly and sloping anteriorly; texture smooth to granular; studded with small tubercles, some bearing long erect setae with shorter setae scattered in between. Abdomen round; in some species completely covered dorsally with shiny scutum bearing short, fine, flat-lying setae. Legs long and slender. Males smaller than females. NOTES: Found on plants and ground layer in forest undergrowth, leaf litter and under rocks. Observed preying on ants. Only one species is known from South Africa. (Sylligma-krapspinnekoppe)

Sylligma ndumi — Ndumo Ant-eating Crab Spider

Carapace shiny, smooth, shades of pale to dark copper-brown to rich orange-brown, tinged with black. Abdomen with layer of scattered long setae. Legs same colour as carapace. **NOTES:** Free-living plant dweller sampled from plants and the ground litter layer in Forest, IOCB and Savanna. **STATUS:** LC; southern African endemic. (Ndumo-miervreterkrapspinnekop)

Synema — African mask crab spiders

Small to medium-sized. Carapace shiny; as wide as long or wider than long; convex above; bears numerous scattered setae; eyes in two rows. Abdomen round to oval; smooth integument bears long scattered setae; decorated with bright mask-like patterns. Legs usually same colour as carapace; sometimes banded; femora dorsally with scattered long setae; tibiae and metatarsi I and II with paired macrosetae. **NOTES:** These plant dwellers are occasionally found on flowers. Some species have been found associated with pitcher plants. At present 10 species are known from South Africa. (Afrika-maskerkrapspinnekoppe)

Synema eye pattern

Synema decens — Spotted Crab Spider

Carapace reddish brown. Abdomen fawn with two dark spots and directly below two white spots and dark wavy bands present posteriorly. Legs same colour as carapace; tibiae I and II banded. **NOTES:** Sampled from all the biomes except Desert, Nama-and Succulent Karoo. Collected in agroecosystems such as citrus, cotton and tomatoes. **STATUS:** LC; southern African endemic. (Kol-krapspinnekop)

Synema diana Diana's Crab Spider

Carapace fawn to green; white around eye region. Abdomen fawn with white and black; spots and short lateral bands. Legs same colour as carapace; legs I and II banded with brown. **NOTES:** Sampled from Forest, Grassland, IOCB and Savanna. Also sampled from citrus and macadamia orchards and tomato fields. **STATUS:** LC; African endemic. (Diana se Krapspinnekop)

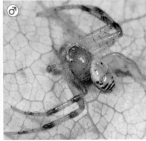

Synema imitatrix Imitatrix Crab Spider

Carapace dark green, usually with darker lateral bands; eye region paler. Abdomen creamy white with dark brown tree pattern. Legs I and II darker and banded; legs III and IV green. **NOTES:** Common species. Sampled from all the biomes except the more arid ones. Also sampled from avocado, citrus and macadamia orchards and tomato fields. **STATUS:** LC; African endemic. (Imitatrix-krapspinnekop)

Synema langheldi Langheld's Crab Spider

Carapace green; eye region yellowish brown. Abdomen yellowish white with dark pattern medially and on posterior half. Legs same colour as carapace; distal segments with more yellowish tint. **NOTES:** Sampled from Grassland, IOCB, Savanna and Thicket. **STATUS:** LC; African endemic. (Langheld se Krapspinnekop)

Synema marlothi

Marloth's Crab Spider

Carapace brown to dark. Abdomen in female with brown pattern and two white spots medially. Abdomen in male fawn, with mask-like dark marking sporting two distinct white spots. Legs I and II dark except tibiae and tarsi; rest of legs green. **NOTES:** Free living on vegetation. Also recorded from parasitic plants such as *Roridula dentata* and *R. gorgonias*. Feeds on the insects these plants catch with their leaf glands. **STATUS:** LC; southern African endemic. (Marloth se Krapspinnekop)

Synema nigrotibiale

Dark-legged Crab Spider

Carapace green with dark tint around eyes. Abdomen white with large dark tree pattern covering almost whole dorsal area. Legs I and II dark, almost black; rest of legs green. **NOTES:** Sampled from all the biomes except the arid ones. **STATUS:** LC; African endemic. (Swartpoot-krapspinnekop)

Synema simoneae

Simon's Crab Spider

Carapace green; eye region with yellowish tint. Abdomen white with small black spots on sides; thin wavy bands near posterior end. Legs same colour as carapace; metatarsi and tarsi I and II with yellow tint. **NOTES:** Occasionally found on flowers. Known from Grassland, IOCB, Savanna and Thicket. **STATUS:** LC; African endemic. (Simon se Krapspinnekop)

Synema vallotoni

Valloton's Crab Spider

Carapace green; eye region with yellowish tint. Abdomen cream with broad dark brown horizontal bands medially and white spots scattered in between. Legs same colour as carapace; metatarsi and tarsi I and II with yellow tint. **NOTES:** Plant dweller sampled from all biomes except the arid ones. Also found in citrus, macadamia and minneola orchards. **STATUS:** LC; southern African endemic. (Valloton se Krapspinnekop)

Family Thomisidae 259

Thomisops

Thomisops crab spiders

Small spiders recognised by their compact body and carapace that is posteriorly truncated, slopes anteriorly and bears small tubercles. Female carapace as wide as long, with sloping clypeus; eyes small, equal in size, arranged in two rows; eye region suffused with white. Abdomen round, usually with a few irregular small black spots dorsally, or covered with dark circular patterns. Legs short, all same size without macrosetae. Distinct sexual dimorphism in shape, size and colour. **NOTES:** Collected from flowering bushes. Seven species are known from South Africa. (Thomisops-krapspinnekoppe)

Thomisops bullatus

Bullatus Crab Spider

Female Carapace dark; eye region suffused with white. Abdomen white to dirty white, usually with a few irregular small black spots dorsally. Legs translucent. **Male** Carapace reddish brown, darker laterally. Abdomen yellow to reddish brown, usually with faint black border and a few black spots dorsally. Legs pale yellow. **NOTES:** Collected from small bushes in the herbaceous layer and grass from Forest, Grassland, IOCB, Savanna and Thicket. **STATUS:** LC; southern African endemic. (Bullatus-krapspinnekop)

Thomisops granulatus

Granulated Crab Spider

Female Carapace and legs pale yellow-green; eye region suffused with yellow; integument rugose and studded with small tubercles. Abdomen white to dirty white, usually with a few irregular small black spots dorsally. **Male** Body and legs reddish brown. **NOTES:** Sampled from Forest, Savanna and Thicket. **STATUS:** LC; southern African endemic. (Growwe Krapspinnekop)

Thomisops pupa

Pupa Crab Spider

Female Carapace fawn, sometimes with greenish tint. Abdomen fawn with irregular greyish-brown concentric circles. **Male** Carapace brown, paler around eyes. Abdomen reddish brown with dark areas. **NOTES:** Free living on plants. Both sexes occasionally found together on flowers. Sampled from Forest, Grassland, IOCB, Savanna and Thicket. **STATUS:** LC; African endemic. (Pupa-krapspinnekop)

Thomisops sulcatus
Sulcatus Crab Spider

Female Carapace brown; clypeus and eye region mottled with yellow and white. Abdomen yellowish brown dorsally with ill-defined blackish-brown spots giving it a mottled appearance. All leg segments have white rims distally. **Male** Smaller than female, usually darker. NOTES: Free living on plants, occasionally found in low vegetation and sampled with sweep nets and pitfall traps. Sampled from Forest, Grassland, IOCB, Savanna and Thicket. STATUS: LC; African endemic. (Sulcatus-krapspinnekop)

Thomisus
Flower crab spiders

Small to medium-sized. Recognised by their brightly coloured bodies. Carapace as wide as long, high and convex, with distinct eye tubercles; integument varies from smooth to rugose and studded with small tubercles; each tubercle provided with a club-shaped or spiniform seta or entire body may be covered with numerous long, spiniform setae. Abdomen partly overhangs carapace. Legs I and II robust, distinctly longer than III and IV; tibiae and metatarsi I and II with paired macrosetae. Sexes with distinct difference in shape, size and colour in most species. NOTES: Commonly found on vegetation such as grass and flowering herbs. Some species are able to change colour and are commonly found on flowers of the same colour. At present 15 species are known from South Africa. (Blomkrapspinnekoppe)

Thomisus sp. waiting for prey

Thomisus australis
African Flower Crab Spider

Female Carapace yellowish; cephalic region white; brown triangular pattern between eyes. Abdomen yellow with faint transverse tinted areas. Legs same colour as carapace. **Male** Carapace brown. Abdomen fawn with darker fawn patterns. Legs brown; tibiae, metatarsi and tarsi of front legs reddish brown. NOTES: Sampled from all the biomes except the arid ones. Also sampled from various crops. STATUS: LC; African endemic. (Afrika-blomkrapspinnekop)

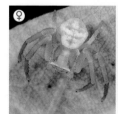

Thomisus blandus — Masked Flower Crab Spider

Female Carapace translucent white, with two broad brown lateral bands; eyes with distinct triangular pattern between them. Abdomen usually white, with transverse brown band over widest part. Legs translucent white, with markings that vary between individuals; femur and tibia I usually have black spots dorsolaterally. **Male** Carapace dark brown, with mediolateral bands which are a shade darker. Abdomen yellow to orange-brown. Legs brown; only half of femora I and II pale. NOTES: Collected from all the biomes except the more arid ones. Also sampled from crops such as citrus, cotton, maize, papaya, pumpkin and strawberries. STATUS: LC; African endemic. Yemen. (Masker-blomkrapspinnekop)

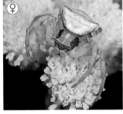

Thomisus citrinellus — Pink Flower Crab Spider

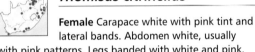

Female Carapace white with pink tint and lateral bands. Abdomen white, usually with pink patterns. Legs banded with white and pink. **Male** Carapace brown. Abdomen fawn with faint white and brown markings dorsally. Legs brown with white joints between segments; tibiae and metatarsi I and II slightly darker than other segments. NOTES: Free living on grass and trees from Fynbos, Grassland, Nama-Karoo, Savanna and Thicket. Also sampled from pecan orchards. STATUS: LC; African endemic. (Pienk Blomkrapspinnekop)

Thomisus daradioides — Two-spotted Flower Crab Spider

Female Can change colour from white to yellow. Carapace with pale pattern between eyes. Abdomen white or yellow; tips of tubercles of abdomen each with a dark spot. Legs same colour as carapace. **Male** Carapace yellowish brown. Abdomen fawn, bearing erect setae. Legs I and II with tibiae and metatarsi dark brown to black. NOTES: Free living on plants and sampled from all the biomes except the more arid regions. Also sampled from citrus and macadamia orchards. STATUS: LC; widespread throughout Africa to India. (Tweekol-blomkrapspinnekop)

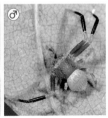

Thomisus granulatus — Hairy Flower Crab Spider

Female Carapace and abdomen cream to fawn, covered with small cream-tipped tubercles, giving it a spotted appearance; white median band present. Legs fawn; prolateral sides of legs sometimes tinged with brown. **Male** Carapace yellowish brown to dark grey, tinged with black. Abdomen yellowish brown, clothed with brown setae. Legs banded. **NOTES:** Free living on shrubs and grasses and sampled from all the biomes except the arid ones. Also known from citrus orchards. **STATUS:** LC; African endemic.
(Harige Blomkrapspinnekop)

Thomisus scrupeus — Brown Flower Crab Spider

Body varies from off-white to dark brown. Abdomen bell-shaped. Legs I and II robust; tibiae and metatarsi I sometimes banded or with darker tint. Males smaller, with dark granulated integument; covered with small tubercles, polyp-like in appearance. **NOTES:** Free living on plants, mainly found on trees and grass from Forest, Fynbos, Grassland, IOCB, Savanna and Thicket. Also sampled from the following crops: avocado, citrus, cotton, minneola and sunflowers. **STATUS:** LC; African endemic.
(Bruin Blomkrapspinnekop)

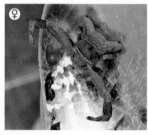

Thomisus stenningi — Stenning's Flower Crab Spider

Female Can change colour, usually white or yellow; occasional specimens with pink patches; eye region and cephalic region suffused with white. Abdomen and legs similar in colour to carapace; tubercles on abdomen sometimes with a black or brownish spot. **Male** Colour varies between individuals; body fawn to off-white; carapace and legs occasionally decorated with red markings. Legs I and II with darker distal segments. **NOTES:** A common species sampled from flowers in all the biomes. Frequently sampled from crops: cotton, potatoes, lucerne, pecans, pine plantations, pistachio orchards. **STATUS:** LC; African endemic. Also occurs in the Seychelles and in Yemen. (Stenning se Blomkrapspinnekop)

Tmarus — Tree crab spiders

Small to medium-sized. Carapace as wide as long or sometimes elongated; clypeus slanting; lateral eyes situated on well-defined tubercles; both eye rows almost straight or only slightly recurved; lateral eyes larger than median eyes. Abdomen often with posterior tubercle dorsally or sometimes elongated; clothed with numerous short stiff setae, which are sometimes situated on small tubercles. Legs spinous; I and II almost the same length, longer than rest; tibiae and metatarsi with paired macrosetae. Males slightly smaller than females, with longer legs. NOTES: Most of the species were sampled from trees where their cryptic coloration enables them to blend in. Eight species are known from South Africa. (Boomkrapspinnekoppe)

Tmarus africanus — Africanus Tree Crab Spider

Carapace, abdomen and legs cryptic greyish fawn, mottled with black. Recognised by the elongated abdomen; front legs much longer than rest. Male more slender and darker than female. NOTES: Sampled from trees in Grassland, IOCB, Savanna and Thicket. STATUS: LC; African endemic. (Africanus-boomkrapspinnekop)

Tmarus cameliformis — Camelback Tree Crab Spider

Carapace usually brown to greyish white, with network of paler striae on thoracic region. Abdomen short, tip giving it a triangular appearance when seen from the side. NOTES: Sampled from all the biomes except the arid ones. Also been sampled from avocado, citrus, cotton and macadamia. STATUS: LC; African endemic. (Bolrug-boomkrapspinnekop)

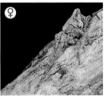

Tmarus foliatus — Short-bum Tree Crab Spider

Colour varies from greyish white to creamy brown. Carapace usually brown to greyish white, with network of paler striae on thoracic region. Abdomen distinct in being longer than wide, tip appears tail-like just above spinnerets. NOTES: Commonly found in Forest, Fynbos, Grassland, IOCB and Savanna. STATUS: LC; African endemic. (Kortstert-boomkrapspinnekop)

Trichopagis — Trichopagis crab spiders

Medium-sized. Recognised by the large, dark, club-shaped setae situated in the eye region. Carapace ovoid to elongated; eight eyes in two rows (4:4), with lateral eyes usually on tubercles that vary from rounded to distinct. Abdomen ovoid to elongated; widest posteriorly; bearing large, dark, club-shaped setae on posterior tip; abdomen frequently decorated with patterns. Legs I and II longer than rest; tibiae and metatarsi with paired macrosetae; legs banded. **NOTES:** Found on trees and low vegetation. Known from a single species. (Trichopagis-krapspinnekoppe)

Trichopagis manicata — Manicata Crab Spider

Female Carapace white with dark triangular markings in eye region. Abdomen white, longer than wide, with greater width in the posterior third, whole dorsal area covered by fawn markings; bearing large, dark, club-shaped setae on posterior tip. **Male** Legs white, with only metatarsi dark; palp yellowish. **NOTES:** Free living on plants; occasionally found inside flower corollas. Also found on trees and low vegetation. Sampled from IOCB and Savanna. **STATUS:** LC; African endemic. (Manicata-krapspinnekop)

Xysticus — Ground crab spiders

Small to medium-sized. Smooth or granulated integument. Body cryptic to blend in with the soil surface. Body and legs covered with simple blunt setae. Legs I and II longer than rest; tibiae and metatarsi I and II each with paired macrosetae ventrally. **NOTES:** Free-living ground species. Eleven species are known from South Africa. (Grondkrapspinnekoppe)

Xysticus fagei — Fage's Ground Crab Spider

Carapace greyish to reddish brown, with narrow white marginal band. Abdomen mottled brown and grey above, uniformly dull brown below. Leg colour similar to carapace. **NOTES:** Sampled from Grassland and Savanna. **STATUS:** LC; African endemic. (Fage se Grondkrapspinnekop)

Xysticus havilandi   Haviland's Ground Crab Spider

Carapace brown; few darker streaks radiating from cephalic striae; narrow white marginal band; clypeus, including anterior row of eyes, mottled brown. Abdomen mottled brown and grey above. Legs mottled. NOTES: Ground dwellers sampled from Fynbos, Grassland and Savanna. STATUS: LC; South African endemic. (Haviland se Grondkrapspinnekop)

Xysticus natalensis   Natal Ground Crab Spider

Carapace brown, mottled with black and yellow. Abdomen mottled brown with irregular transverse bars. Legs mottled, with black spots; femora yellow below. NOTES: A common species found under stones during the day. Sampled from Fynbos, Grassland and Savanna and from crops such as avocado, macadamia, cotton, strawberries and sugarcane. STATUS: LC; southern African endemic. (Natalse Grondkrapspinnekop)

Xysticus urbensis   Urbensis Ground Crab Spider

Carapace dark with faint V-shaped marking defining cephalic region. Abdomen dark above; variegated cream at sides forming irregular transverse bars posteriorly. Legs dark. NOTES: Found under stones during the day. Sampled from Forest, Fynbos, Grassland and Savanna. Also collected from maize fields. STATUS: LC; southern African endemic. (Urbensis-grondkrapspinnekop)

FAMILY TROCHANTERIIDAE
Scorpion spiders   Skerpioenspinnekoppe

Small to large spiders; eight eyes (4:4); posterior median eyes oval.
Abdomen flattened. Legs laterigrade. NOTES: Free living, found beneath
bark or under stones. Occurs in a wide temperature range, from dry arid
regions to humid forest areas. Only one genus known in South Africa.

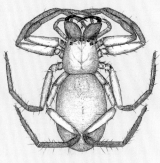

Platyoides   Platyoides scorpion spiders

Medium-sized. Body flattened. Carapace longer than wide; widest between coxae II and
III; eight eyes are in two rows (4:4), with both rows almost straight; posterior median
eyes flattened, pale and irregular; chelicerae enlarged, projecting forward, with long,
curved fangs. Abdomen ovoid; pale with dark markings or with longitudinal bands.
Legs with trochanters elongated, especially IV, folding over the body; tarsi with two
claws. NOTES: Free-living wanderers commonly found under bark or under stones. Their
flattened bodies allow them to live in narrow crevices. Known from ten species in South
Africa. (Platyoides-skerpioenspinnekoppe)

Platyoides leppanae   Leppan's Scorpion Spider

Carapace mahogany-
brown, darker anteriorly;
chelicerae darker and redder.
Abdomen greyish white with dark grey
median and lateral stripes connected
across anterior and posterior
surface. Legs greyish brown, slightly
infuscate ventrally, redder distally;
sternum reddish brown, dark-edged.
NOTES: Sampled from bark in Fynbos,
Grassland, Nama-Karoo, Savanna and
Thicket. STATUS: LC; African endemic.
(Leppan se Skerpioenspinnekop)

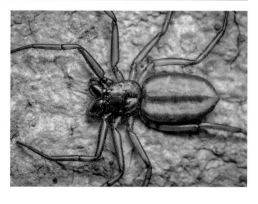

Platyoides pictus
Grahamstown Scorpion Spider

Carapace, chelicerae and legs dark orange-brown; sternum and coxae slightly paler; sternum dark-edged. Abdomen pale yellow with lateral dark grey longitudinal stripes and median dark grey area, divided anteriorly, forming an outline of the heart mark. NOTES: Free-living wanderers sampled from Fynbos and Thicket. STATUS: DD; South African endemic. (Grahamstadse Skerpioenspinnekop)

Platyoides pirie
Pirie's Scorpion Spider

Carapace, abdomen and legs dark. Abdomen with faint paler longitudinal paramedial bands. NOTES: Free-living wanderers sampled from Forest, Fynbos and Savanna. STATUS: LC; South African endemic. (Pirie se Skerpioenspinnekop)

Platyoides walteri
Walter's Scorpion Spider

Carapace and abdomen dark brown; fovea a distinct round area with faint striae and indentations. Abdomen uniform in colour; mouthparts same dark colour. Legs with bright orange coxae, trochanters and femora; remainder of legs darker. NOTES: The most common species, found on bark but also frequently around houses under potted plants. Sampled from Forest, Grassland, Nama-Karoo, Savanna and Thicket. Also sampled from avocado orchards and commercial pine plantations. STATUS: LC; African endemic. Introduced into Australia. (Walter se Skerpioenspinnekop)

GROUND DWELLERS

Ground dwellers are usually robustly built, with stout legs that enable them to move swiftly over the surface and to forcefully overpower and subdue their prey. They are typically cryptically coloured, varying from fawn to brown or black, depending on whether they are diurnal or nocturnal. Most ground-dwelling species are active at night and spend the hottest part of the day in the soil or hiding under rocks. Egg sacs are frequently buried or covered with sand particles. These spiders are usually collected by hand or using pitfall or litter traps.

Ground dwellers can be classified as either free living or burrow dwelling. The shape and size of underground burrows vary between genera.

Trapdoor spider burrows

Hogna female, a free-running ground dweller

BURROW DWELLERS inhabit silk-lined tunnels. The burrow may be a single tunnel, or it may lead to a number of side passages or chambers. Some burrows have a single entrance, while others are U- or Y-shaped. Burrows may lead directly from the soil surface and vary in depth, or consist of silk-lined tunnels and chambers under rocks. Entrances can be either open or closed with trapdoors, which also vary in shape and size. The outside is usually well camouflaged with sand particles or bits of vegetation. Burrows occasionally extend above ground, and have silken signal threads. Some families live permanently in burrows, with only the males being free-roaming. Other genera in families such as Lycosidae (wolf spiders) and Sparassidae (huntsmen spiders) use burrows only as a retreat, and roam about in search of prey.

FREE-LIVING GROUND SPIDERS are associated with sand, rocks, litter or water. Many of them are nocturnal, spending daylight hours hiding beneath the soil surface, under rocks, in litter or underwater. A number of genera have morphological adaptations that enable them to dive beneath the soil surface, while others rapidly cover themselves with sand using their legs. Those that live on rocks and in cracks usually have flattened bodies. Genera associated with water have special body setae that enable them to capture air and 'breathe' underwater.

Nilus sp. on freshwater pond

Augacephalus sp. in entrance of an open burrow

Stasimopus sp. in entrance of a burrow with a trapdoor

Hexophthalma sp. disappearing beneath the surface by throwing sand over itself

QUICK KEY GROUND-DWELLING FAMILIES

Family Anyphaenidae p. 277

Medium-sized to large; two-clawed, claw tufts with lamelliform setae ①; eight eyes in two rows (4:4). Coloration various shades of brown; abdomen with pattern. Intertidal hunters, hiding under limpet shell or in crevices during high tide.

Tarsal claw tufts

Amaurobioides sp. Hiding under limpet shell

Family Archaeidae p. 278

Small; three-clawed; eight eyes situated on greatly elevated cephalic region ①; chelicerae enlarged, long and slender; fangs relatively short and strongly curved, with rows of peg teeth ②. Coloration reddish brown to yellow-brown; abdomen with pattern.

Cephalothorax

Chelicerae

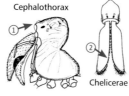

Afrarchaea sp.

Family Atypidae p. 279

Medium-sized to large mygalomorph spiders (sexual dimorphism: males smaller than females); three-clawed; eight eyes on a compact transverse tubercle; chelicerae large, dorsally expanded ①. Coloration of female yellowish brown, male darker.

Cephalothorax

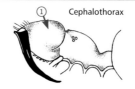

Calommata sp.

Family Barychelidae p. 280

Medium-sized to large mygalomorph spiders; two-clawed; eight eyes situated on eye tubercle; body and legs hairy; apical segment of posterior spinnerets short and dome-shaped ①; tarsi with 4–6 clavate trichobothria restricted basally. Coloration brown to dark brown.

Spinnerets

Pisenor sp.

Family Bemmeridae p. 282

Medium-sized to large mygalomorph spiders; three-clawed; eight eyes situated on eye tubercle (4:4); males with S-shaped row of teeth on paired claws ① and females with two rows ②; endites rectangular without heel but with numerous cuspules ③. Coloration chestnut-brown to reddish yellow.

Teeth row(s) on claw

Endite with cuspules

Homostola sp.

Family Caponiidae p. 283

Medium-sized; three-clawed; two eyes (*Diplogena* ①) or eight eyes (*Caponia* ②) closely grouped, covered with black spot; booklungs replaced by tracheae ③; legs and carapace yellow-orange; abdomen silky grey.

Carapace

Caponia sp.

Quick Key: Ground-dwelling families **271**

Family Cithaeronidae p. 285

Medium-sized; two-clawed; eight eyes with posterior median eyes flattened ①; tarsi long with two strong claws, when dead then legs curl up ②. Coloration pale yellow with markings.

Eye region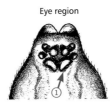

Leg

Cithaeron sp.

Family Corinnidae p. 286

Morphologically a very diverse family; small to medium-sized; two-clawed with distinct claw tufts; eight eyes in two rows (4:4); abdomen with a strong tendency towards sclerotisation, especially in booklung region ①; many species are ant-like in appearance; tibiae and metatarsi of anterior legs with two rows of strong spines ②. Coloration dark to yellowish brown.

Abdomen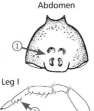

Leg I

Apochinomma sp.

Family Ctenidae p. 296

Medium-sized to large; two-clawed; eight eyes arranged in two rows (4:4) ① or three rows (2:4:2) ②; anterior tibiae with 3–6 pairs of ventral spines; abdomen with patterns. Coloration brown to fawn, with patterns or spots on abdomen.

Carapace

Eye region

Ctenus sp.

Family Cyrtaucheniidae p. 298

Medium-sized to very large mygalomorph spiders; three-clawed; eight eyes in compact group; cephalic region raised; fovea broad and pro- or recurved; rastellum present ①. Coloration varies from dark chestnut-brown to reddish yellow; abdomen sometimes with bands or spots.

Rastellum

Ancylotrypa brevipalpis

Family Desidae p. 301

Large; three-clawed; eight eyes in two rows (4:4) that occupy little more than half the head width; chelicerae very large, almost as long as the carapace, directed to the front. Coloration pale yellow to dark brown. Intertidal hunters, hiding under limpet shell during high tide.

Limpet shell shelter

Desis formidabilis

Hiding under limpet shell

Family Dysderidae p. 302

Medium-sized; two-clawed; six eyes in compact group near clypeal edge ①; chelicerae well developed; fangs long and well developed; carapace and legs deep red to orange; abdomen pinkish grey.

Clypeal edge

Well-developed chelicerae of *Dysdera* sp.

Family Entypesidae p. 303

Large mygalomorph spiders; three-clawed, with dense scopula on tarsi I–III; eight eyes closely grouped on raised eye tubercle (4:4) ①; labium lacks cuspules; rastellum weak (or absent); long, digitiform spinnerets ②. Coloration various shades of yellow to dark brown.

Eye region

Spinnerets

Afropesa sp.

Family Gallieniellidae p. 305

Small to medium-sized; two-clawed; eight eyes in two rows (4:4); chelicerae moderately to greatly elongated; posterior median eyes flattened and irregular in shape or oval ①; anterior spinnerets bear a small apical segment ②. Coloration varies from orange-brown to bright red or darker, sometimes with white bands and spots.

Eye region

Spinnerets

Drassodella sp.   *Drassodella* sp.

Family Gnaphosidae p. 307

Morphologically a diverse family with several subfamilies; small to medium-sized; two-clawed; eight eyes in two rows (4:4), posterior median eyes flattened ①; endites obliquely depressed ventrally ②; anterior spinnerets parallel, large, cylindrical and usually well separated ③. Coloration variable, typically different hues of brown; abdomen sometimes with markings.

Eye region

Chelicerae

Spinnerets

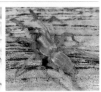

Zelotes sp.   *Drassodes* sp.

Spinnerets

Family Idiopidae p. 322

Morphologically a diverse family; medium-sized to very large mygalomorph spiders; three-clawed; eight eyes with anterior lateral eyes in front of other eyes, close to clypeal edge ①; strong rastellum ②; abdomen with shield in *Galeosoma*; fovea strongly procurved; various shades of brown, yellow, red, olive or purplish.

Carapace   Rastellum

Segregara sp.   *Galeosoma* sp.   *Galeosoma* sp.

Family Liocranidae p. 328

Small to medium-sized; two-clawed; eight eyes (sometimes six); female with median spinnerets flattened ①; tibiae and metatarsi I and II armed with biseriate row of numerous long spines ②. Coloration varies from pale yellow to brownish with indistinct pattern on abdomen, or uniform reddish yellow, or blackish brown.

Spinnerets

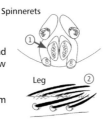

Leg

Rhaeboctesis sp.

Family Lycosidae p. 330

Morphologically a diverse family; small to very large; three-clawed; eight eyes in three rows (4:2:2). Coloration cryptic, ranging from dull yellowish brown to grey or almost black, with broad bands over cephalothorax; dorsum usually with pattern. Some genera include plant dwellers.

Eye region

Hippasa sp.   *Hogna* sp.   *Hippasosa* sp.   *Pirata* sp.   *Zenonina* sp.

Family Microstigmatidae p. 343

Small to medium-sized mygalomorph spiders; three-clawed; eight eyes closely grouped; booklung openings small, oval ①; body covered with blunt-tipped or clavate setae ②; thoracic region elevated behind fovea; various shades of brown.

Abdomen venter

Microstigmata sp.

Family Migidae p. 344

Small to large mygalomorph spiders; three-clawed; eight eyes in two rows; chelicerae short with fangs directed obliquely ①; two distinct, longitudinal keels present on outer surface of cheliceral fang ②; various shades of brown to black, legs and/or abdomen frequently patterned.

Chelicerae

② Fang

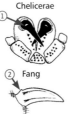

Poecilomigas sp.   *Moggridgea* sp.

Family Oonopidae p. 346

Very small; two-clawed; biserially dentate with onychium; six eyes closely grouped ① or absent; tibiae and tarsi I and II with series of paired macrosetae in some species ②; abdomen in some genera with dorsal and ventral scuta. Often brightly coloured: orange, yellow, greenish or pink; species without scuta paler in colour.

① Eye region

Leg

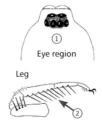

Gamasomorpha sp.

Family Orsolobidae   p. 348

Small; two-clawed; six eyes in two
rows; paired tarsal claws biserially
dentate with an onychium and
spatulate claw tufts; tarsal organ
elevated ①; posterior tracheae
anteriorly positioned; abdomen dorsally suffused with
purplish pigment, with pale hairline chevrons or markings absent.

Paired tarsal claws

Leg

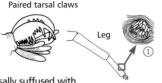

Azanialobus sp.

Family Palpimanidae   p. 350

Medium-sized; three-clawed; eight
eyes in two rows (4:4); leg I enlarged
and stronger than rest; metatarsi
and tibiae with strong prolateral
scopulae ①; carapace heavily
sclerotised; reduced number
of spinnerets; uniformly red to
orange carapace and pale silky-
grey abdomen.

Leg I

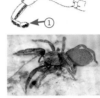

Palpimanus sp.   *Diaphorocellus* sp.

Family Prodidomidae   p. 352

Small to medium-sized;
two-clawed; eight eyes,
arrangement varies: in two
rows (4:4) or circular; anterior
spinnerets wide apart and
positioned far forward of
others ①. Coloration fawn
to orange-brown.

Spinnerets

Eleleis sp.

Family Scytodidae   p. 354

Small to medium-sized; three-
clawed; six eyes small, arranged in
three well-separated diads, each
pair contiguous ①; thoracic region
domed ②; legs long and slender. Coloration pale
yellow to brown to almost black; carapace with dark stripes, bands or
spots joined to form symmetrical pattern on carapace and abdomen.

Eye
region

Carapace

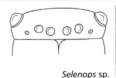

Scytodes sp.

Family Selenopidae   p. 357

Medium-sized to large; two-clawed; eight
eyes, eye pattern distinct, consisting of two
rows (6:2); legs laterigrade; body flattened.
Cryptic, creamish brown or grey, mottled with
black, brown and grey; legs sometimes banded.

Eye
region

Selenops sp.

Family Sicariidae   p. 360

Medium-sized; two-clawed; six eyes in three
diads; legs clothed in sickle-shaped setae; legs
long and slender in *Loxosceles*, stouter and
shorter in *Hexophthalma*; abdomen markedly
depressed, clothed in sickle-shaped setae
(*Hexophthalma*) or barbed, spine-like setae
(*Loxosceles*). Coloration yellowish or reddish
brown with contrasting darker markings.

Hexophthalma sp.   *Loxosceles* sp.

Quick Key: Ground-dwelling families   **275**

Family Stasimopidae   p. 362

Medium-sized to very large mygalomorph spiders; three-clawed; eight eyes; with strong rastellum; distal segments of front legs with lateral bands of short, thorn-like spines in female ①; carapace with strongly procurved fovea ②.

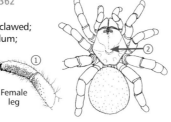

Female leg

Stasimopus sp.

Family Theraphosidae   p. 364

Medium-sized to very large mygalomorph spiders; two-clawed; eight eyes closely grouped ①; body hairy; well-developed scopulae and claw tufts ②; tarsi with clavate trichobothria along length; labium and endites with dense cuspules. Coloration various hues of brown, from pale to dark; abdomen with variegated pattern.

Eye region

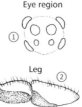

Leg

Ceratogyrus sp.

Family Trachelidae   p. 370

Small to medium-sized; two-clawed; with distinct claw tufts; eight eyes; leg spines usually absent, front legs frequently with ventral cusps ①, especially in males,

Leg I

Orthobula sp.

Afroceto sp.

varying in arrangement between genera; abdomen with a strong tendency towards sclerotisation; males often with abdominal scuta. Carapace shiny red to red-brown; abdomen pale.

Family Zodariidae   p. 373

Morphologically diverse family; small to large; two- or three-clawed; six or eight eyes; cheliceral fangs very short ①; anterior spinnerets on common base, median and posterior spinnerets reduced ②; carapace variable in

Capheris sp.

Chariobas sp.

shape; in general oval, narrowed anteriorly (more so in males); integument varies from entirely smooth to densely granulate or with tiny perforations; digging species usually with numerous strong spines on posterior legs. Coloration variable; pale to dark brown; abdomen usually decorated with simple pattern.

Chelicerae   Abdomen

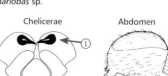

Family Zoropsidae   p. 382

Medium-sized; three-clawed; reduction of unpaired claw in legs III and IV (*Phanotea*); claw tufts weak; eight eyes in two rows; posterior spinnerets with apical segment shorter. Cryptic dark brown or grey.

Phanotea sp.

Griswoldia sp.

276   Ground dwellers

FAMILY ANYPHAENIDAE
Ghost spiders
Spookspinnekoppe

A large, diverse family. It is not well represented in Africa and only one genus, containing a single littoral species, is known.

Amaurobioides
Sea-shore spiders

Medium-sized to large. Carapace longer than wide; fovea longitudinal; eight eyes situated close together in two recurved rows; chelicerae long and slender, slightly porrect. Abdomen oval, with light covering of short setae as well as scattered, longer dark setae. Two tarsal claws with dense scopulae consisting of 3–8 rows of lamelliform setae; trochanters notched. **NOTES:** Free-running intertidal spiders found in the zone between high-water neaps and high-water springs along rocky coasts, an area infrequently flooded by salt water. One species is known from South Africa. (Seekusspinnekoppe)

Amaurobioides africana hiding under limpet shells. The smaller specimen is a juvenile.

Amaurobioides africana
African Sea-shore Spider

Carapace dark reddish brown, darker around eyes. Abdomen bears distinct chevron patterns; venter unpigmented. Legs same colour as carapace; faintly banded. **NOTES:** In areas where the wave action is weak, this spider takes refuge under rocks, rarely building a nest. In areas with strong wave action, it lines the interior of empty shells with silk to make them waterproof. Enough air is retained to enable the spider to survive prolonged immersion. **STATUS:** LC; southern African endemic. (Afrika-seekusspinnekop)

FAMILY ARCHAEIDAE
Long-necked spiders   Pelikaanspinnekoppe

Small, shy spiders recognised by their
elevated cephalic region and enlarged
chelicerae. **NOTES:** Free-living wanderers
commonly found in leaf litter and humus.
They prey mainly on other spiders. The
female attaches the egg sac to leg IV.
One genus is known from South Africa.

Afrarchaea   African assassin spiders

Very small to small. Cephalic region rounded, greatly elevated above thoracic region,
ornamented with small, flattened, granulate tubercles, each with a short, thick seta; anterior
margin of carapace slopes steeply; eight eyes in two rows, almost equal in size; chelicerae
enlarged; fangs short. Abdomen subglobular, soft, with sclerotised patches. Legs long,
slender; three tarsal claws on short, distinct, sclerotised onychium; leg I the longest, leg III
the shortest. **NOTES:** Slow-moving litter dwellers found in shady, humid, dense bush. This
genus is endemic to South Africa and represented by 14 species. (Afrika- moordspinnekoppe)

Afrarchaea cornuta   Long-necked Assassin Spider

Carapace reddish brown;
cephalic edge with small
granulate tubercles; integument with
scattered pale setae. Abdomen round,
triangular, yellowish brown. Legs long, thin,
brown, with darker bands. **NOTES:** Litter
dweller sampled from coastal forest in the
IOCB biome. **STATUS:** Vulnerable; South
African endemic. (Langnek-moordspinnekop)

Afrarchaea woodae   Wood's Assassin Spider

Body and legs dark, with
numerous white setae.
Abdomen round. **NOTES:** Sampled in
the IOCB biome. Specimens were found
under dry *Strelitzia nicolai* leaves on
the forest floor in coastal dune forest,
and in grassy areas behind dunes.
STATUS: Endangered; South African
endemic. (Wood se Moordspinnekop)

FAMILY ATYPIDAE
Purse-web spiders
Beurswebspinnekoppe

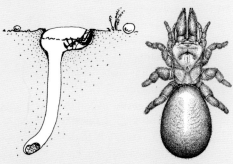

Mygalomorph spiders. Carapace glabrous; cephalic region more strongly arched than thoracic region; sternum with four pairs of sigilla; eyes on compact transverse tubercle; chelicerae dorsally expanded; rastellum absent; labium fused to sternum, junction a narrow groove. Abdomen suboval with single large tergite; irregularly shaped dorsal scutum in males. Legs three-clawed. NOTES: Some species permanently inhabit silk-lined burrows with a tough, tubular, aerial section. An insect walking over this upper part generates vibrations, which are transmitted to the spider inside. The spider strikes through the silk with its long fangs to impale the prey. It then cuts the silk with one fang and drags the prey through the hole. One genus is known from South Africa.

Calommata
African purse-web spiders

Medium-sized to large. Sexes differ in shape, colour and size, males being much smaller. Fovea deep bipartite. Leg formula 4-2-3-1; leg I, especially femur, greatly reduced in females; legs longer and more slender in males; spines absent in both sexes, but small spinules present; tibiae and tarsi of female palp slightly flattened. NOTES: The silk-lined burrow is 25–30cm deep. The upper part consists of a small excavated surface chamber, crater-like in shape. The burrow lid is slightly raised, and gradually slopes outwards and downwards to the level of the ground. The outer surface is covered by earth, blending with the surroundings. Two species are known from South Africa. (Afrika-beurswebspinnekoppe)

Calommata transvaalica
Transvaal's Purse-web Spider

Female Robustly built. Carapace pale creamy brown; single median line runs from front of median ocular tubercle to middle of chilum; chelicerae orange, darker laterally. Abdomen globose, pale grey, with indistinct heart mark. Legs short and stout. **Male** Carapace and chelicerae dark brown; median ocular tubercle raised, darker. Legs weakly covered with bristles. NOTES: Males collected from Grassland and Savanna. STATUS: Vulnerable; South African endemic. (Transvaalse Beurswebspinnekop)

FAMILY BARYCHELIDAE
Brush-footed trapdoor spiders · Borselpootvaldeurspinnekoppe

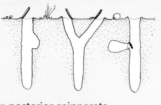

Mygalomorph spiders. Carapace longer than wide; eight eyes arranged in a group; anterior lobes of endites not well developed; rastellum absent. Abdomen oval, hairy; posterior spinnerets short, with dome-shaped apical segment. Legs two-clawed with claw tufts and thick iridescent scopulae arranged in well-developed pads on metatarsi and tarsi I and II; tarsi I have few clavate trichobothria basally. Apical segment of spinnerets short and domed. **NOTES:** Burrows vary from temporary silk retreats to complex silk-lined burrows with concealed doors. Two genera are known from South Africa.

Pisenor · Pisenor baboon trapdoor spiders

Medium-sized to large. Eye grouping wider behind than in front, on distinct eye tubercle; anterior lateral eyes close to clypeal edge. Females have one row of teeth on paired tarsal claws; males have two rows and tibial spur on leg I. Scopulae on metatarsi and tarsi I and II long, thin and divided by setae. **NOTES:** Burrow dwellers. Some specimens were sampled from burrows closed by trapdoors; lids were camouflaged with bits of leaves. Two species have been recorded in South Africa. (Pisenor-bobbejaanvaldeurspinnekoppe)

Pisenor arcturus · Zimbabwean Baboon Trapdoor Spider

Carapace with dense golden-yellow setae; fovea slightly procurved with distinct striae; labium and endites with cuspules. Abdomen hairy with golden-yellow setae, faintly spotted; only two spinnerets. Legs same colour as carapace. **NOTES:** Burrow dweller sampled from the Savanna biome. **STATUS:** LC; southern African endemic. (Zimbabwiese Bobbejaanvaldeurspinnekop)

Pisenor notius   Notius Baboon Trapdoor Spider

Carapace greyish brown. Abdomen bears dense setae with golden sheen. Legs same colour as carapace; claw tufts present on female palp. NOTES: Sampled from the Savanna biome. STATUS: LC; African endemic. (Notius-bobbejaanvaldeurspinnekop)

Sipalolasma   Sipalolasma baboon trapdoor spiders

Medium-sized to large. Carapace longer than wide; endites with six cuspules at lower edge; eyes closely grouped, close to clypeal edge; posterior eye row slightly procurved; anterior lateral eyes largest; fovea a circular pit. Abdomen hairy, with four spinnerets; terminal segment of posterior spinnerets shorter than penultimate. Legs two-clawed. NOTES: Burrow dwellers. Little is known about their natural history. One species has been recorded in South Africa. (Sipalolasma-bobbejaanvaldeurspinnekoppe)

Sipalolasma humicola   Humicola Baboon Trapdoor Spider

Carapace blackish grey; fovea and striae distinct. Abdomen hairy, with faint spots and golden sheen. Legs brownish grey with dense setae. NOTES: Collected in Grassland and Savanna. STATUS: LC; African endemic. (Humicola-bobbejaanvaldeurspinnekop)

FAMILY BEMMERIDAE
Afrasian wishbone spiders   Afrasiese wensbeenspinnekoppe

Mygalomorph spiders. Carapace lightly hirsute; cephalic region strongly arched; fovea broad, procurved; eye tubercle distinct, raised, about twice as wide as long; chelicerae broad, with two rows of strong teeth; rastellum consists of short blunt spines on low mound on inner distal surface, labium wider than long, with few cuspules; sternum broad posteriorly; posterior sigilla large, oval. Abdomen oval; dorsum patterned; in some species posterior lateral spinnerets short with domed apical segment. Scopulae entire on tarsi I and II, distal on metatarsi I and II. NOTES: Ground dwellers that construct burrows of various shapes, some resembling a wishbone, hence the common name. Two genera occur in South Africa.

Homostola   Homostola wishbone spiders

Medium-sized. Carapace with few hairs to glabrous; cephalic region usually strongly arched; fovea broad, transverse to procurved; clypeus narrow to absent; eye group rectangular, twice as wide as long, on distinct eye tubercle; rastellum several short, blunt spines; sternum with six sigilla variable in shape. Abdomen sometimes sports bands or spots. Legs strong, same colour as carapace; legs III and IV longer and stronger than rest. NOTES: Females live in fairly shallow burrows (16–20cm deep) made under leaf litter and covered with a loose-fitting lid. Known from five African species. All occur in South Africa. (Homostola-wensbeenspinnekoppe)

Homostola vulpecula   Vulpecula Wishbone Spider

Carapace dark brown to olive-brown; darker marginally and in eye region; chelicerae dark, with dark setae around edge; fovea straight; labium bears 13–15 cuspules. Abdomen purplish with numerous dark setae and irregular markings; ventrum pale. Legs olive-brown with dark setae; mating spur with three spines. NOTES: Collected in Grassland, IOCB and Savanna. Commonly found in leaf litter and sampled with pitfall traps. STATUS: LC; South African endemic. (Vulpecula-wensbeenspinnekop)

Spiroctenus
Spiroctenus wishbone spiders

Medium-sized. Fovea short, more or less straight; eye tubercle low; rastellum of stout setae on low mound; labium and endites with numerous cuspules; endites rectangular, without heel. Abdomen sometimes with bands or spots; apical segment of posterior lateral spinnerets domed. In males, legs have one S-shaped row of teeth on the paired claws; females have two rows. NOTES: These spiders construct a variety of burrow shapes. The entrances of the burrows are either closed with a trapdoor or decorated with a turret. Males are frequently found under stones or in shallow burrows. Represented by 28 species in South Africa. (Spiroctenus-wensbeenspinnekoppe)

Spiroctenus pectiniger
Cape Wishbone Spider

Carapace and legs dark brown, shiny. Abdomen and legs dark brown with dense layer of long hair-like setae. NOTES: Sampled from Fynbos and Thicket. STATUS: DD; South African endemic. (Kaapse Wensbeenspinnekop)

FAMILY CAPONIIDAE
Orange lungless spiders　　　　　　Oranje longlose spinnekoppe

Carapace oval, narrower anteriorly, lacking a distinct fovea and striation; integument smooth and shiny; two eyes (*Diploglena*) or eight (*Caponia*). Abdomen elongated, oval, with light covering of dark setae; booklungs replaced by two pairs of tracheae; epigastric region and tracheae often have chitinous strip; spinnerets modified, with median spinnerets situated between anterior spinnerets. Legs three-clawed, short, sturdy, without spines; legs fold over the body when at rest. NOTES: Swift runners that pursue their prey across the ground. Nocturnal. During the day, they are usually found under stones or in leaf litter. Two genera are known from South Africa.

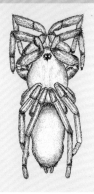

Caponia
Caponia orange lungless spiders

Medium-sized. Carapace oval, clypeus broad and sloping, sometimes porrect; eight eyes, arranged in compact group around anterior median eyes. Abdomen oval, with sparse covering of dark setae. Legs short and sturdy. NOTES: Usually found under stones or in leaf litter. Their small oval retreats of transparent silk are attached to stones and debris. Represented by nine species in South Africa. (Caponia- oranje longlose spinnekoppe)

Caponia capensis

Cape Orange Spider

Carapace orange-yellow; dark spot over eye region. Abdomen silky grey to pale orange. Legs same colour as carapace. NOTES: Wanders the ground surface. Frequently sampled from pitfall traps in Fynbos and Grassland. STATUS: LC; southern African endemic. (Kaapse Oranjespinnekop)

Caponia chelifera

Mozambique Orange Spider

Carapace deep orange-yellow; area around median eyes and base of each lateral eye black. Abdomen pale yellow to grey. Legs deep orange-yellow; tarsal claws very dark. NOTES: Sometimes sampled from pitfall traps. Known from Grassland and Savanna. STATUS: LC; southern African endemic. (Mosambiekse Oranjespinnekop)

Caponia hastifera

Hastifera Orange Spider

Carapace orange-yellow, paler medially. Abdomen silky grey. Legs same colour as carapace. NOTES: Free-living ground dweller frequently collected from pitfall traps. Sampled from Fynbos, Grassland and Thicket. STATUS: LC; South African endemic. (Hastifera-oranjespinnekop)

Caponia spiralifera

Spiralifera Orange Spider

Carapace deep yellow or orange-yellow; area encompassing median eyes black. Abdomen pale yellow, female often with ventral blackish mark posteriorly. Legs same colour as carapace. NOTES: Free-living ground dweller. Sampled from Desert, Grassland, Nama-Karoo, Savanna, Succulent Karoo and Thicket. STATUS: LC; South African endemic. (Spiralifera-oranjespinnekop)

Diploglena
African two-eyed spiders

Small to medium-sized. Carapace oval, narrowed anteriorly, lacking distinct fovea and striation; clypeus broad, sloping, sometimes porrect; only two eyes. Abdomen oval, with sparse covering of dark setae; epigastric region and tracheae often with chitinous strip. Legs short, sturdy, three-clawed; coxae and often patellae of leg I much longer than in other legs. NOTES: Rare nocturnal ground dwellers found mainly in the Northern and Western Cape provinces. Known from six species, all of which occur in southern Africa. (Afrika-tweeoogspinnekoppe)

Diploglena arida
Arida Two-eyed Spider

Carapace and chelicerae bright orange; sternum and mouthparts orange, darker around margins. Abdomen uniformly silky grey. Leg I yellow-orange; legs II–IV creamy yellow; metatarsi and tarsi slightly darker. NOTES: Free-living ground dweller sometimes sampled from pitfall traps in Desert and Succulent Karoo. Two specimens were sampled from scorpion burrows. STATUS: LC; southern African endemic. (Arida- tweeoogspinnekop)

Diploglena capensis
Cape Two-eyed Spider

Carapace and chelicerae yellow-brown; sternum and mouthparts yellow, darker around margins. Abdomen creamy. Leg I yellow; metatarsi and tarsi slightly darker; legs II–IV creamy yellow. NOTES: Free-living ground dweller sampled from humus in the Fynbos biome. STATUS: LC; South African endemic. (Kaapse Tweeoogspinnekop)

FAMILY CITHAERONIDAE
Swift ground spiders   Vinnige grondspinnekoppe

Carapace rounded; eight eyes, relatively large, in two rows (4:4); chelicerae short, vertical; cheliceral furrow without teeth, promargin bears cluster of stiff setae; endites rectangular, obliquely depressed; labium as wide as long or wider. Abdomen elongated, oval. Tarsi long, with two strong dentate claws, pseudo-segmented, curled up in preserved specimens. NOTES: Extremely fast-moving ground spiders. Found in silk retreats under stones during the day. This small family is represented by two genera. Only one genus is known from South Africa.

Cithaeron Cithaeron ground spiders

Medium-sized. Carapace narrowed in eye region; clypeus high; eyes relatively large; both eye rows are slightly procurved; posterior median eyes the largest. Abdomen with setae on the surface; male with long scuta, half the length of the abdomen; anterior spinnerets conical and narrowly separated, bearing a subdistal sclerotised ring and unmodified piriform gland spigots. NOTES: One species is known from South Africa. (Cithaeron-grondspinnekoppe)

Cithaeron contentum Contentum Ground Spider

Carapace pale yellow. Abdomen with faint dark markings; scattered brown setae on surface. Legs very long, pale yellow. NOTES: Sampled from the Savanna biome. STATUS: DD; South African endemic. (Contentum-grondspinnekop)

FAMILY CORINNIDAE
Dark sac spiders Donkersakspinnekoppe

Small to medium-sized spiders that are sometimes ant-like in appearance. Carapace ovoid in dorsal view, sometimes elongated and heavily sclerotised in ant mimics; eight eyes in two rows (4:4), widely spaced or closely grouped. Abdomen ovoid or elongated in ant mimics and sometimes with scuta or transverse bands or patches of white setae; usually with recumbent plumose setae, latter frequently form lines or patterns. Legs sturdy, or long and thin in ant mimics, two-clawed, with varied setae on leg I consisting of clusters, rows or scattered erect setae. NOTES: Free-living ground or plant dwellers. They construct silk retreats in rolled leaves and plant debris. Commonly found in shady, deciduous forest in woody debris, litter or humus on the forest floor. Some of the ant-like species are more common in Grassland and Savanna. A fairly large, cosmopolitan family, with 25 genera known from South Africa.

Apochinomma

Apochinomma ant-like sac spiders

Medium-sized. Carapace elongated, usually more than twice as long as wide, sometimes with median constriction; eyes small, widely spaced; posterior eyes in recurved row; surface finely to coarsely granulate, covered in short straight and plumose setae, with several long, curved setae on clypeus and eye region. Abdomen pear-shaped, or elongated with median constriction. Leg formula 4-1-2-3. NOTES: Displays various morphological adaptations to ant mimicry: a median depression on carapace, elongated pedicel and variable abdominal shape that resembles the abdomen of ants. Three species are known from South Africa. (Apochinomma-miersakspinnekoppe)

Apochinomma decepta — Maputaland Ant-like Sac Spider

Carapace dark brown with black mottling and distinct striae. Abdomen elongated, broadened posteriorly, with distinct median constriction and long pedicel; dorsal scutum narrow, black; dorsum dark mottled grey behind scutum; dorsum with three transverse black bands. Legs dark. NOTES: Mimics large Ponerinae ants. Sampled from the Savanna biome. STATUS: LC; southern African endemic. (Maputalandse Miersakspinnekop)

Apochinomma elongata — Long Ant-like Sac Spider

Carapace narrowed in eye region, silvery grey. Abdomen elongated, broadened posteriorly, silvery grey dorsally, with broad black band just posterior to midpoint. Legs long and thin. NOTES: Mimic of large ground-dwelling Ponerinae ants. Sampled from ground surface in Grassland and Savanna. STATUS: LC; African endemic. (Lang Miersakspinnekop)

Apochinomma formicaeforme — African Ant-like Sac Spider

Carapace elongated, oval. Abdomen covered in white plumose setae, with broad black bands; dorsal scutum black in male, covering entire dorsum. Legs dark with paler distal segment. NOTES: Sampled on ground and from tree canopies in Grassland, IOCB and Savanna. A mimic of silvery ground- and plant-dwelling *Polyrhachis* ants, on which it feeds. STATUS: LC; African endemic. (Afrika-miersakspinnekop)

Austrophaea

Austrophaea zebra sac spiders

Medium-sized. Carapace somewhat flattened. Abdomen oval, tapering posteriorly. Recognised by very robust anterior legs, particularly the tibiae and metatarsi, which are enlarged and broad and very strongly spined ventrally. NOTES: Probably exclusively ground dwelling. Known from one species that is endemic to South Africa. (Austrophaea-sebrasakspinnekoppe)

Austrophaea zebra
Zebra Sac Spider

Carapace cream to deep yellow-orange with broad dark median band and interrupted narrow marginal band. Abdomen with black median band and 5–7 posterior transverse bands. Leg I yellow-orange, enlarged tibiae and metatarsi dark; remaining legs with narrow black bands. Male has narrow dorsal scutum. NOTES: Sampled from moist habitats in dense layer of leaf litter, such as forests in IOCB, Savanna and Thicket. STATUS: LC; South African endemic. (Sebrasakspinnekop)

Cambalida

Cambalida dark sac spiders

Small to medium-sized. Carapace relatively broad; anterior lateral eyes usually larger than anterior median eyes; posterior eyes larger than those of anterior eye row. Abdomen oval; scutum present in male. Legs with fine granulation; males with two or three rows of very distinct, long, thickened setae at distal end of dorsal surface of the palpal cymbium. NOTES: Ground dwelling. Two species are known from South Africa. (Cambalida- donkersakspinnekoppe)

Cambalida dippenaarae
Dippenaar's Dark Sac Spider

Carapace deep red-brown with black mottling; surface granulate, sparsely covered in white plumose setae; eye region nearly black. Abdomen dark with fine cream chevrons laterally and small white spot of dense plumose setae just above spinnerets; large dark red-brown dorsal scutum present in male. Legs with fine granulation; femora I–IV dark brown. NOTES: Fairly common and collected with litter sifting and pitfall traps in Fynbos and Savanna, and occasionally in Grassland, IOCB and Nama-Karoo. Also sampled from citrus and grapefruit orchards and cotton and maize fields. STATUS: LC; African endemic. (Dippenaar se Donkersakspinnekop)

Coenoptychus
Velvet ant dark sac spiders

Small to medium-sized. Carapace longer than wide; eye region narrowed; eight eyes in two rows (4:4); posterior row recurved. Abdomen oval, with plumose dorsal abdominal setae; male with large dorsal scutum. Legs slender, bearing plumose setae. NOTES: Most similar to *Graptartia* in their shared resemblance of velvet ants. Free-running ground spiders found in a variety of habitats. Represented by two species in South Africa. (Fluweelmier-donkersakspinnekoppe)

Coenoptychus eye pattern

Coenoptychus mutillica
Mutillica Dark Sac Spider

Carapace deep orange to reddish brown; eye region darker; surface granulate. Abdomen oval; dorsum covered with short, black plumose setae, with large white triangular marking of dense, white setae medially. Legs brown, with scattered plumose setae; femora darker. NOTES: Usually collected in pitfall traps or under objects such as stones, dry cattle dung pats and logs in Grassland and Savanna. Also found in abandoned nest mounds of *Trinervitermes* snouted harvester termites. STATUS: LC; African endemic. (Mutillica-donkersakspinnekop)

Coenoptychus tropicalis
Tropical Dark Sac Spider

Carapace coloration very variable, from red to dark wine-red; darker around border with thin white marginal band; dark brown rings around eyes. Abdomen oval, broadening posteriorly; dorsal scutum large; dorsum with black undertone, covered with short, straight and plumose black setae; white, plumose setae scattered throughout, forming patterns. Some legs banded. NOTES: Inhabits grasslands and leaf litter and has been collected from Forest, Fynbos, Grassland, IOCB and Savanna. STATUS: LC; African endemic. (Tropiese Donkersakspinnekop)

Copa
Copa dark sac spiders

Medium-sized. Carapace oval; eye region narrower; surface smooth, with markings. Abdomen oval, with black markings or black with white markings; dorsal scutum small, strongly sclerotised, extending less than an eighth of abdomen length in females and slightly more than half of abdomen length in males. NOTES: Common spiders found in the leaf litter of various habitats. Predominantly ground living, occurring widely in Savanna woodlands but also occasionally in forests, where they are well camouflaged. Two species are known from South Africa. (Copa-donkersakspinnekoppe)

Copa flavoplumosa

Flavoplumosa Dark Sac Spider

Carapace bright yellow-orange with broad lateral bands. Abdomen yellow-orange with very small orange-brown anterior dorsal scutum; dorsum cream, densely covered in straight and plumose black setae, small spots in anterior two-thirds and fine transverse chevrons posteriorly. Legs yellow-brown, banded. NOTES: Free-living ground dweller mainly collected from the leaf litter in most biomes except for true deserts and Karoo habitats. Also sampled from crops. STATUS: LC; African endemic. (Flavoplumosa-donkersakspinnekop)

Copa kei

Kei Dark Sac Spider

Carapace yellow-orange, eye region darker; lateral bands of black plumose setae from posterior eye row to posterior slope of carapace; broad dark marginal band. Abdomen has very small red-brown anterior dorsal scutum; dorsum mottled grey; large black spot present anteriorly. Legs yellow-brown, faintly mottled. Male more slender than female. NOTES: Free-living ground dweller mainly collected from the leaf litter layer in forests in Savanna and Thicket. STATUS: LC; South African endemic. (Kei-donkersakspinnekop)

Copuetta

Copuetta dark sac spiders

Medium-sized. Carapace longer than wide, narrower in eye region; integument with plumose setae that form different markings; clypeus with several long, curved setae; posterior eye row slightly procurved. Abdomen oval, with scutum. Legs bear two pairs of ventral setae on anterior tibiae. NOTES: Free-living ground dweller. Sampled from a variety of habitats and found from ground level to tree tops. Five species occur in South Africa. (Copuetta-donkersakspinnekoppe)

Copuetta erecta
Erecta Dark Sac Spider

Carapace creamy yellow with dark lateral bands. Abdomen creamy yellow, densely covered with plumose setae; dorsum has broad creamy oval marking bordered by darker areas. Legs banded. Male resembles female, but abdominal pattern differs. NOTES: Sampled in leaf litter in close-canopied coastal dune forests in Grassland, IOCB and Savanna. STATUS: LC; southern African endemic. (Erecta-donkersakspinnekop)

Copuetta lacustris
Lacustris Dark Sac Spider

Female More robustly built than male. Carapace fawn; with dark irregular lateral bands; eyes rimmed with black. Abdomen fawn with scattered dark markings. Legs banded. **Male** Carapace bright yellow-orange. NOTES: Sampled from a wide range of habitats in Fynbos, Grassland, IOCB, Nama-Karoo, Savanna and Succulent. Also collected from agroecosystems. STATUS: LC; African endemic. (Lacustris-donkersakspinnekop)

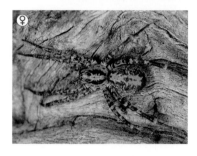

Corinnomma
Corinnomma dark sac spiders

Medium-sized. Carapace oval, elongated; narrower in eye region; eyes small, arranged in slightly recurved posterior eye row. Abdomen oval, widest in posterior third; dorsal scutum entire in males, extending to two-thirds of abdomen length in females; markings distinct and resemble markings found on ant bodies. Leg formula 4-1-2-3; legs bear several short stout spines and straight setae. NOTES: Ground-dwelling ant mimics. Two species are known from South Africa. (Corinnomma-donkersakspinnekoppe)

Corinnomma lawrencei
Lawrence's Dark Sac Spider

Carapace dark brown to nearly black, clothed in very short white setae. Abdomen oval, slightly globose, integument grey; dorsal scutum present, dark red brown, narrow, densely covered with short white setae. Legs dark with white longitudinal bands of setae. NOTES: Ant-mimicking species often found near nests of *Camponotus cinctellus* and *Anoplolepis custodiens* ants in the Savanna biome. STATUS: LC; African endemic. (Lawrence se Donkersakspinnekop)

Corinnomma semiglabrum   Semiglabrum Dark Sac Spider

Carapace dark brown, finely wrinkled, clothed in very short white setae; chelicerae dark brown. Abdomen dark brown, dorsum with four transverse white bands comprising plumose setae. Femora I–IV dark brown with white bands; rest of leg segments brownish. Male less robust than female. NOTES: Ant-mimicking species mainly collected in pitfall traps or leaf litter. Sampled from Grassland, IOCB and Savanna. Also sampled from citrus orchards. STATUS: LC; African endemic. (Semiglabrum-donkersakspinnekop)

Echinax   Echinax dark sac spiders

Small. Carapace oval, narrower in eye region; integument smooth, with brown markings; anterior median eyes two to three times the size of anterior lateral eyes. Abdomen oval. Legs with very long spines present distally on all patellae; long spines present on anterior metatarsi. NOTES: Resembles *Copa* in general body shape and heavily spined legs. Found in the foliage of shrubs and trees. Two species are known from South Africa. (Echinax-donkersakspinnekoppe)

Echinax natalensis   Natal Dark Sac Spider

Carapace fawn with dark brown lateral bands and thin dark marginal band. Abdomen mottled with faint lateral bands. Legs with paired spines, same colour as carapace; seta bases with distinct black markings. NOTES: Sampled in IOCB and Savanna. Collected from tsetse fly traps set up in coastal forest, by canopy fogging and by beating trees in riparian forest and savanna habitats. STATUS: LC; South African endemic. (Natalse Donkersakspinnekop)

Graptartia   Graptartia dark sac spiders

This genus appears most similar to *Coenoptychus*, as both resemble Mutillidae velvet ants. Carapace longer than wide, narrower in eye region, with long erect setae; eyes in circular arrangement; posterior eye row procurved. Abdomen oval; covered with plumose and clavate setae. NOTES: Found in a variety of habitats. One species is known from South Africa. (Graptartia-donkersakspinnekoppe)

Graptartia granulosa — Spotted Graptartia Dark Sac Spider

Carapace uniformly deep orange-brown, slightly elevated towards rear; integument granulate; short and long white setae scattered across surface. Abdomen oval; large dorsal scutum present; dorsum pitted, with black undertone; two pairs of large, white spots present dorsally, composed of white clavate setae. Legs with scattered plumose setae. NOTES: Known from a variety of habitats in the Savanna biome, where it is usually collected in pitfall traps and leaf litter. STATUS: LC; African endemic. (Gekolde Graptartia-donkersakspinnekop)

Hortipes — Hortipes basket-legged spiders

A large genus of small spiders. Carapace evenly domed, highest at fovea; anterior eye row slightly procurved to straight; posterior eye row strongly procurved; anterior median eyes circular. Abdomen covered with thin, light grey setae. Leg formula 4-2-1-3; legs with half-circle array of setae on dorsal side of metatarsi I and II, hence the common name. NOTES: Most species inhabit the litter layer or canopy of Afrotropical mountain forests. Known from 14 species in South Africa. (Hortipes-mandjiepootspinnekoppe)

Hortipes atalanta — Umgeni Basket-legged Spider

Carapace, sternum and chelicerae orange-yellow. Abdomen pale pink, sparsely covered with grey setae. Legs orange-yellow. NOTES: Collected from under bushes along riverbanks in the Savanna biome. STATUS: Vulnerable; South African endemic. (Umgeni-mandjiepootspinnekop)

Hortipes schoemanae — Schoeman's Basket-legged Spider

Carapace, sternum and chelicerae orange-yellow. Abdomen pale pink, sparsely covered with grey setae. Legs orange-yellow. NOTES: Collected from leaf litter and pitfall traps in natural forest and woodlands in Grassland and Savanna. Also sampled from commercial pine plantations. STATUS: LC; South African endemic. (Schoeman se Mandjiepootspinnekop)

Medmassa
Medmassa dark sac spiders

Medium-sized. Carapace broad, oval; eyes large; posterior eye row strongly procurved. Abdomen oval, uniformly dark in colour; with three or four pairs of short spines along anterior margin behind pedicel; anterior tibiae bear 7–10 pairs of ventral spines. NOTES: Active hunting spiders collected from tree bark. One species is known from South Africa. (Medmassa-donkersakspinnekoppe)

Medmassa semiaurantiaca
Semiaurantiaca Dark Sac Spider

Carapace deep orange-brown, eye region slightly darker. Abdomen uniformly dark grey dorsally, slightly paler grey laterally and ventrally. Legs I to IV with orange-brown femora, much darker in distal third. NOTES: Regularly collected during canopy fogging surveys in forests. Sampled from IOCB. STATUS: LC; African endemic. (Semiaurantiaca-donkersakspinnekop)

Merenius
Merenius dark sac spiders

Small to medium-sized. Carapace elongated, oval; eyes small, posterior eye row slightly recurved. Abdomen oval; distinct white markings on dark background. Legs slender. NOTES: Ground dwellers that mimic ants. Two species are known from South Africa. (Merenius-donkersakspinnekoppe)

Merenius alberti
Albert's Dark Sac Spider

Carapace greyish black with broad pale grey median band. Abdomen oval, greyish black with bell-shaped marking anteriorly and broad band posteriorly. Legs same colour as carapace. NOTES: Sampled from Forest, Grassland, IOCB, Savanna and Thicket. STATUS: LC; southern African endemic. (Albert se Donkersakspinnekop)

Messapus
Messapus dark sac spiders

Medium-sized to large. Carapace oval with distinct markings resembling that of wolf spiders (Lycosidae); eyes large, posterior eye row slightly procurved. Abdomen oval with mottled markings. Femora, tibiae and metatarsi usually armed with relatively narrow, elongated spines. Females more robustly built than males. NOTES: Ground dwellers known from three species in South Africa. (Messapus-donkersakspinnekoppe)

Messapus martini   Martin's Dark Sac Spider

Carapace creamy grey, covered with plumose silvery-grey setae and straight
black setae, with two dark irregular lateral bands; integument finely wrinkled;
eye region dark in male. Abdomen oval, widest in posterior third; dorsal scutum entire in
male; dorsum cream, decorated
with dark chevron pattern. Legs
grey with bands. **NOTES:** Collected
from the soil surface, bark and
tree canopies. Known from
Grassland, IOCB and Savanna,
as well as synanthropic habitats.
STATUS: LC; African endemic.
(Martin se Donkersakspinnekop)

 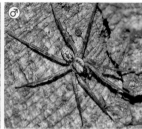

Messapus natalis   Natal Dark Sac Spider

Carapace creamy grey, covered with
plumose silvery grey setae and straight
black setae, with two irregular lateral bands; integument
finely wrinkled; eye region dark. Abdomen oval, cream,
decorated with dark pattern; dorsal scutum entire in male.
Legs banded. **NOTES:** Primarily arboreal; collected from
retreats constructed on tree bark. Sampled from IOCB and
Savanna. **STATUS:** LC; southern African endemic. (Natalse
Donkersakspinnekop)

Vendaphaea   Venda dark sac spiders

Medium-sized. Carapace oval, with finely granulate integument; eye region narrowed.
Abdomen oval, without dorsal or ventral scuta; paired dorsal sigilla present. Legs I and II
strongly built, distal segments of all legs with dense setae. **NOTES:** Free-running ground
dwellers known from one South African species. (Venda-donkersakspinnekoppe)

Vendaphaea lajuma   Lajuma Dark Sac Spider

Carapace deep red, with slightly darker striae
radiating from fovea. Abdomen oval; dorsal
scutum absent; dorsum grey-brown, densely covered with
short straight black and grey setae. Legs stout; distal segment
densely covered in short straight grey setae. **NOTES:** Sampled
from leaf litter of mixed woodland and forest habitats in the
Savanna biome. **STATUS:** DD; South African endemic. (Lajuma-
donkersakspinnekop)

FAMILY CTENIDAE
Tropical wolf spiders — Tropiese wolfspinnekoppe

Medium-sized to very large. Carapace oval, with deep depression or elevation in the region of the fovea; eight eyes usually arranged in three rows (4:2:2 or 2:4:2). Abdomen oval, longer than wide; sometimes with median band, patterns or rows of spots; anterior spinnerets conical, not widely separated. Legs strong and stout, with spines; tarsi two-clawed, with scopulae; tibiae I and II have numerous pairs of ventral spines; trochanters deeply notched. NOTES: Free-living nocturnal ground hunters commonly found under fallen logs. When running, the first pair of legs are usually held off the ground. Abundant in forests and surrounding areas. Regularly collected by hand at night, or by using pitfall traps or sweep-netting low-growing foliage. Females deposit their egg sac on the substrate or carry it between their chelicera and palp. Three genera occur in South Africa.

Africactenus
African tropical wolf spiders

Medium-sized to large. Recognised by the carapace having a deep indentation, the deepest point in front of the fovea; inferior margin of chelicerae armed with four teeth. Abdomen bears well-developed tufts of setae. Legs long; tibiae I and II without terminal pair of spines. NOTES: Free-living ground spiders. Only one species has been recorded in South Africa. (Tropiese Afrika-wolfspinnekoppe)

Africactenus tridentatus
Africactenus Tropical Wolf Spider

Carapace reddish brown with striae radiating from fovea; dark lateral bands present; width of clypeus same as diameter of anterior median eyes. Abdomen reddish brown, suffused with dark dorsal folium. Legs reddish brown with faint bands; tibia I bears five pairs of ventral setae. NOTES: Known from Fynbos and Savanna. STATUS: LC; southern African endemic. (Africactenus- Tropiese Wolfspinnekop)

Ctenus
Ctenus tropical wolf spiders

Medium-sized to large. Carapace highest in region of fovea; eight eyes in three rows (2:4:2); anterior lateral eyes between posterior median and posterior lateral eyes; eyes in anterior row small; posterior row strongly recurved; clypeus high; chelicerae strong, armed with four or five teeth; mouthparts with endites converging slightly. Abdomen bears chevron pattern or rows of spots; usually darker ventrally with double row of sigilla. Tibiae I and II with 3–6 pairs of ventral spines. NOTES: Free-living nocturnal hunters commonly found under fallen logs. Sometimes found in burrows. They hunt their prey on low-growing foliage and on the ground. Six species are known from South Africa. (Ctenus- tropiese wolfspinnekoppe)

Ctenus caligineus　　　　　　　Zaire Tropical Wolf Spider

Body brown to fawn, mottled. Carapace with wide pale median band bordered by darker lateral bands. Abdomen with dark pattern; double row of sigilla present ventrally; tufts of setae arranged in rows on dorsum. Legs mottled, all femora with dark bands. **NOTES:** Sampled from the Savanna biome. **STATUS:** LC; African endemic. (Zaïrese Tropiese Wolfspinnekop)

Ctenus gulosus　　　　　　　Gulosus Tropical Wolf Spider

Carapace fawn, with dense setae, dark brown lateral band and thinner fawn marginal band. Abdomen with pale median band, consisting of triangular shape and bordered by darker lateral bands with tufts of setae in rows. Legs mottled. **NOTES:** Sampled from pitfall traps in Grassland, IOCB and Savanna. **STATUS:** LC; South African endemic. (Gulosus- Tropiese Wolfspinnekop)

Ctenus pulchriventris　　　Pulchriventris Tropical Wolf Spider

Carapace fawn with narrow median band continuing between median eyes; U-shaped marking behind posterior eye row; bordered by two broad brown lateral bands; carapace edge mottled fawn. Abdomen with egg-shaped median band bordered by darker lateral bands. Legs mottled. **NOTES:** Sampled from pitfall traps in Fynbos, Grassland, IOCB, Savanna and Thicket. It has also been collected in crops such as citrus, maize, pine and strawberries. **STATUS:** LC; southern African endemic. (Pulchriventris- Tropiese Wolfspinnekop)

Ctenus transvaalensis　　　Transvaal Tropical Wolf Spider

Carapace fawn with median band extending to median eyes and bordered by broad brown lateral bands; edge mottled fawn. Abdomen with greyish chevrons. Legs banded. **NOTES:** Lives in burrows without trapdoors in Grassland and Savanna. **STATUS:** LC; South African endemic. (Transvaalse Tropiese Wolfspinnekop)

FAMILY CYRTAUCHENIIDAE
Wafer-lid trapdoor spiders
Sagtevaldeurspinnekoppe

Mygalomorph trapdoor spiders. Distinct sexual dimorphism occurs in size, shape and colour. Males more slender and slightly smaller than females. NOTES: They live in silk-lined burrows that are usually closed with a wafer-lid trapdoor. One genus is known from South Africa.

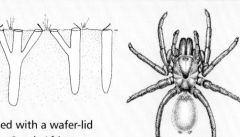

Ancylotrypa
Ancylotrypa wafer-lid trapdoor spiders

Medium-sized to large. Carapace smooth; cephalic region strongly elevated in females; fovea broad, transverse to procurved; eight eyes in two rows (4:4), forming a rectangular group that is wider behind than in front; eye tubercle usually distinctly raised; rastellum present. Abdomen long, oval. Legs with three tarsal claws. NOTES: Free-living ground dwellers that inhabit silk-lined burrows. The depth of the silk-lined burrow varies between species, the main portion being as deep as 32cm. The burrows are closed with

Burrow entrance with a grass turret

soft lids. Some species construct side chambers, which may or may not have lids. By day, the spiders typically reside in the lower portion of the burrow. Males wander in search of females and sometimes land in swimming pools. This genus is represented by 29 species in South Africa. (Ancylotrypa-sagtevaldeurspinnekoppe)

Ancylotrypa barbertoni
Barberton Wafer-lid Trapdoor Spider

Female Carapace chestnut-brown; pale posteriorly. Abdomen dull brown with pale marginal area. Coxa III bears patch of stiff setae. **Male** Carapace dull reddish brown; chelicerae darker. Abdomen fuscous dorsally, pale ventrally, clothed with silky setae. Legs brown. NOTES: Sampled from the Savanna biome. STATUS: DD; South African endemic. (Barbertonse Sagte-valdeurspinnekop)

Ancylotrypa brevipalpis   Short-palp Wafer-lid Trapdoor Spider

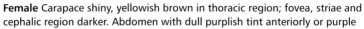

Female Carapace shiny, yellowish brown in thoracic region; fovea, striae and cephalic region darker. Abdomen with dull purplish tint anteriorly or purple band medially. Legs yellowish brown. **Male** Body dark; carapace integument wrinkled; legs long and slender. NOTES: Lives in silk-lined burrows that are usually made underneath large rocks. Sampled from Grassland, IOCB and Savanna. STATUS: LC; South African endemic. (Kortpalp-sagtevaldeurspinnekop)

Ancylotrypa cornuta   Cornuta Wafer-lid Trapdoor Spider

Carapace and chelicerae reddish brown, paler posteriorly. Abdomen dark dorsally and laterally; pallid ventrally; lung area and spinnerets pale yellow. Legs yellowish brown, paler distally. NOTES: Sampled from the Thicket biome. STATUS: DD; South African endemic. (Cornuta-sagtevaldeurspinnekop)

Ancylotrypa dreyeri   Dreyer's Wafer-lid Trapdoor Spider

Carapace brownish dorsally, chelicerae darker; thoracic region pallid. Abdomen with a few strong bristles near anterior edge. Patellae I and II, distal leg segments and palps pale brown. NOTES: Sampled from the Grassland biome. STATUS: DD; South African endemic. (Dreyer se Sagtevaldeurspinnekop)

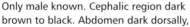

Ancylotrypa nigriceps

Dark Wafer-Lid Trapdoor Spider

Only male known. Cephalic region dark brown to black. Abdomen dark dorsally, yellow ventrally. Legs same colour as thoracic region, with numerous long dark setae. NOTES: Sampled from Grassland and Savanna. STATUS: LC; South African endemic. (Donker Sagtevaldeurspinnekop)

Ancylotrypa pretoriae

Pretoria Wafer-lid Trapdoor Spider

Carapace chestnut-brown, darker in cephalic region; chelicerae dark; cephalic region elevated with procurved fovea; thoracic region narrowed posteriorly; sternum with large posterior sigilla. Abdomen grey. Legs same colour as carapace; coxae III without stiff setae. NOTES: Burrow dweller sampled from Grassland, Nama-Karoo and Savanna. STATUS: LC; South African endemic. (Pretoriase Sagtevaldeurspinnekop)

Ancylotrypa pusilla

Pusilla Wafer-lid Trapdoor Spider

Carapace pale brown with line of long setae down centre; thoracic region darker, especially posterior to fovea; latter procurved; carapace considerably narrower opposite leg III. Abdomen elongated, olive-brown. NOTES: Sampled from Grassland, Nama-Karoo and Savanna. Also sampled from pistachio orchards. STATUS: DD; South African endemic. (Pusilla-sagtevaldeurspinnekop)

Ancylotrypa zebra

Zebra Wafer-lid Trapdoor Spider

Carapace pale yellow-brown. Recognised by distinct dark bands on abdomen, resembling zebra stripes. NOTES: Males commonly found in pitfall traps in Fynbos, Grassland, IOCB and Savanna. STATUS: LC; South African endemic. (Sebra-sagtevaldeurspinnekop)

FAMILY DESIDAE
Intertidal spiders · Tussengetyspinnekoppe

Carapace longer than wide; fovea distinct; eight eyes in two more or less straight rows (4:4), occupying little more than half of head width. Abdomen ovoid; spinnerets stout and broad; anterior pair of spinnerets contiguous, two-segmented; colulus prominent, bearing numerous setae. Legs three-clawed. NOTES: For years only a single species, *Desis formidabilis*, was known from South Africa. A second species, *Badumna longinqua*, known to be invasive, was recently recorded.

Badumna · Badumna grey house spiders

Medium-sized, stout spiders. Carapace broad; cephalic region rounded, partially elevated above thoracic region, covered with dense layer of short and long setae. Abdomen oval, with small, symmetrically placed black markings. Legs strong, usually banded. NOTES: These spiders make cribellate webs between leaves and in hollows. They are commonly found around houses. One species is known from South Africa. (Badumna- grys huisspinnekoppe)

Badumna longinqua female

Badumna longinqua · Longinqua Grey House Spider

Carapace mostly dark brown, clothed with dense white setae. Abdomen charcoal-grey with symmetrical white markings. Legs grey-brown, banded. NOTES: Recently introduced into South Africa. Its scrappy cribellate webs reveal its presence. The female does not leave her web unless forced, and keeps repairing it – old webs look grey and woolly from the constant additions of silk. STATUS: LC; cosmopolitan. (Longinqua- Grys Huisspinnekop)

Desis — Long-jawed intertidal spiders

Large spiders. Chelicerae very large, almost as long as carapace, directed to the front. Abdomen ovoid, clothed with short setae. Legs of moderate length; leg II with some spines. **NOTES:** Intertidal hunters found on rocky shores. These spiders live between the low-water and high-water neap tide levels. Twice a day, they are submerged for several hours. If the wave action is weak, the spiders simply hide beneath rocks, the water-repellent setae

Desis formidabilis female

on their body trapping a film of air, which acts as an external 'lung'. If the wave action is strong, the spiders shelter in empty shells made waterproof with silk, enclosing enough air for gas exchange during immersion. One species is known from South Africa. (Langkaak-tussengetyspinnekoppe)

Desis formidabilis — African Long-jawed Intertidal Spider

Carapace orange-brown to dark brown; fovea distinct; chelicerae darker than carapace; integument with short dense setae. Abdomen ovoid, dark grey, without markings. Legs same colour as carapace. **NOTES:** Found in intertidal zones of rocky coasts in the Eastern and Western Cape. **STATUS:** LC; southern African endemic. (Afrika-langkaak-tussengetyspinnekop)

FAMILY DYSDERIDAE
Woodlice-hunting spiders — Houtluis-jagspinnekoppe

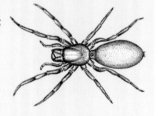

Carapace longer than wide; clypeus narrow; fovea absent; integument sclerotised, with fine granulation; sternum joined to carapace by intercoxal sclerites; six eyes. Abdomen ovoid, with sparse cover of short setae; anterior spinnerets three-segmented; apical segment longest; two booklungs and two pairs of distinct tracheal spiracles. Legs two-clawed, with claw tufts; metatarsi and tarsi bear ventral scopulae distally; tibiae and metatarsi with setae. **NOTES:** Free-living, nocturnal ground dwellers. Only one genus is known from South Africa.

Dysdera — Long-jawed six-eyed spiders

Medium-sized. Six eyes arranged in a compact group close to clypeal edge; chelicerae well developed, extending to the front; fangs long, well developed. Abdomen elongated. **NOTES:** Only one cosmopolitan species is known from South Africa. (Langkaak-sesoogspinnekoppe)

Dysdera crocata   Crocata Long-Jawed Six-Eyed Spider

Carapace and mouthparts deep red to orange. Abdomen pale pinkish grey, without markings. Legs of moderate length, without strong setae, slightly paler orange-red than carapace. **NOTES:** Free-living, nocturnal ground dweller. This solitary spider uses its long chelicerae and fangs to catch prey. During non-active periods it shelters in a sac-like retreat below stones. **STATUS:** LC; cosmopolitan. (Crocata-langkaak-sesoogspinnekop)

FAMILY ENTYPESIDAE
African open burrow spiders   Afrika-ooptonnelspinnekoppe

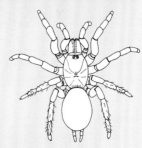

Mygalomorph trapdoor spiders. Carapace longer than wide; eight eyes closely grouped (4:4); endites with cuspules; labium without cuspules; rastellum usually absent, if present it consists of only a few strong setae; sternum has small marginal posterior sigilla. Abdomen ovoid; spinnerets long; median spinnerets situated close together; apical segment of posterior spinnerets digitiform. Legs three-clawed; scopula entire on tarsi II of females and present on tarsi I–III of males; tibia I of males bears mating spur consisting of a strong spine or cuticular spur. **NOTES:** Most species appear to live in silk-lined burrows that vary in shape: a simple, deep burrow; a Y-shaped burrow; or a burrow with side passages or chambers made under rocks or in silk webbing. The entrances are without lids and flush with the soil surface, or rimmed with sticks and grass to form a turret. Five genera are known from South Africa.

Afropesa   Afropesa open burrow spiders

Medium-sized. Clypeus narrow; ocular tubercle raised, darkened, well defined, wider than long; fovea short, procurved; rastellum absent (unlike in some *Hermacha* species); endites with numerous cuspules on posterior inner surface; sternum longer than wide, covered with sparse black setae; posterior sigilla marginal and well defined. Abdomen oval. Legs three-clawed, sparsely covered with setae; leg formula 4-1-3-2; tibia I of male may be either unmodified or swollen, armed with distal megaspine. Mating spur present in male. **NOTES:** These spiders construct sheet-like burrows under stones, with several entrances radiating from a central part. Known from three endemic species. (Afropesa-ooptonnelspinnekoppe)

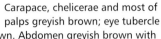

Afropesa gauteng Gauteng Open Burrow Spider

Carapace, chelicerae and most of palps greyish brown; eye tubercle blackish brown. Abdomen greyish brown with a few irregular brownish marks. Femora darker brown dorsally; patella to metatarsus I darker brown; mating spur present. NOTES: Sampled from the Grassland biome. STATUS: DD; South African endemic. (Gautengse Ooptonnelspinnekop)

Afropesa schoutedeni Schouteden's Open Burrow Spider

Carapace, chelicerae and most of palps and legs yellow-brown; tibiae and proximal half of metatarsi I slightly darker; eye tubercle blackish brown. Abdomen yellowish brown, dorsally and laterally with darker brown chevron-like pattern, mottled posteriorly; spinnerets uniformly pale yellowish brown; mating spur present. NOTES: Sampled from the Savanna biome. STATUS: LC; South African endemic. (Schouteden se Ooptonnelspinnekop)

Hermacha Hermacha open burrow spiders

Medium-sized to large. Fovea short, straight; eye tubercle raised, well defined; clypeus narrow; endites rectangular, anterior lobe rounded with numerous cuspules on inner corner; labium without cuspules; rastellum, if present, usually consists of stout setiform spines. Abdomen oval; posterior spinnerets very long, digitiform or triangular. Strong scopulae on tarsi I–III; male mating spur a moderately stout spine on a low mound; NOTES: They make vertical burrows in the ground. The burrows are well lined with silk. The opening is flush with the surface, with no lid. In some species the rim of the burrow is decorated with sticks. This genus is represented by 13 species in South Africa. (Hermacha-ooptonnelspinnekoppe)

Hermacha septemtrionalis Limpopo Open Burrow Spider

Carapace brown to greyish brown with dense layer of fine setae. Abdomen slightly longer than wide, with darker tree pattern. Legs banded. NOTES: Sampled from Grassland and Savanna. STATUS: LC; southern African endemic. (Limpopo-ooptonnelspinnekop)

Lepthercus Lepthercus open burrow spiders

Medium-sized to large. Fovea short, straight; eye region twice as wide as long; eye tubercle elevated and well defined; clypeus narrow; endites rectangular, anterior lobe rounded, numerous cuspules on inner corner; labium without cuspules; rastellum absent or with slender, moderately stout setae. Male mating spur long, with apical tubercle. NOTES: These spiders make silk burrows running along the underside of rocks, with transparent webbing. Males, which are more active than females, are collected with pitfall traps or frequently trapped in swimming pools. Represented by 11 species in South Africa. (Lepthercus-ooptonnelspinnekoppe)

Lepthercus kwazuluensis KwaZulu Open Burrow Spider

Male Carapace rounded, orange-brown, with setae on lateral margin and little pubescence; fovea short, straight, with faint striae; strong mating spur and palp. Abdomen ovoid, covered by dense brown setae and spots; spinnerets dark ventrally. Legs same colour as carapace; metatarsus swollen. **Female** Red-brown overall. NOTES: Sampled from Grassland, IOCB and Savanna. **STATUS:** LC; southern African endemic. (KwaZulu-ooptonnelspinnekop)

FAMILY GALLIENIELLIDAE
Gallieniellid ground spiders Gallieniellid-grondspinnekoppe

Carapace longer than wide; chelicerae moderately to greatly elongated; eight eyes in two rows (4:4); posterior median eyes flattened and irregular in shape. Abdomen elongated, oval; anterior spinnerets widely spaced. Legs two-clawed; slender; leg I longest. NOTES: Free-living, agile ground dwellers frequently found in association with ants. Sampled with pitfall traps and leaf litter sifting. Two genera occur in South Africa.

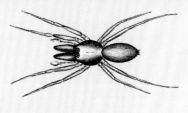

Austrachelas Austrachelas long-jawed ground spiders

Medium-sized. Carapace evenly elevated along midline, sloping sharply posteriorly; eyes closely grouped; anterior eye row procurved; posterior eye row straight or very slightly recurved; chelicerae do not protrude far beyond anterior margin of carapace; fangs long, directed obliquely. Abdomen elongated; short dorsal scutum present in some species; anterior lateral spinnerets conical, nearly cylindrical, not widely spaced. Metatarsi and tarsi I and II densely scopulate ventrally; legs III and IV strongly spined. NOTES: Free-running ground dwellers. Ten species endemic to South Africa. (Austrachelas-grootkaakgrondspinnekoppe)

Austrachelas incertus Incertus Long-Jawed Ground Spider

Carapace and chelicerae deep red-brown, dark orange-red along midline. Abdomen dark grey dorsally, with cream chevron markings, cream laterally and ventrally. Legs yellow-orange. Scutum absent. NOTES: Collected in Fynbos, Grassland and Savanna. STATUS: Vulnerable; South African endemic. (Incertus-grootkaakgrondspinnekop)

Drassodella Drassodella long-jawed ground spiders

Small to medium-sized. Carapace broad, oval; lateral eyes set on low tubercles; posterior median eyes flattened, transversely oval; integument smooth, sparsely covered in short erect and plumose setae; fovea short to elongated, narrow; chelicerae usually moderately protruding in males, vertically orientated in females. Abdomen elongated, oval; dorsum covered in short erect and plumose setae, markings comprise dense plumose setae. Legs long, moderately thin; leg formula 4-1-2-3. NOTES: Fast-moving ground dwellers frequently collected under small rocks and stones, as well as in leaf litter. Sometimes encountered in close association with ants. Represented by 19 species, all endemic to South Africa. (Drassodella-grootkaakgrondspinnekoppe)

Drassodella melana Dark Long-jawed Ground Spider

Carapace and abdomen almost black; carapace with thin white marginal band. Legs reddish brown. NOTES: Sampled mainly from Grassland, IOCB and Savanna, but also from indigenous forests and pine plantations. STATUS: LC; South African endemic. (Donker Grootkaakgrondspinnekop)

Drassodella montana Spotted Long-jawed Ground Spider

Carapace dark brown to black with sparse band of white setae down the centre; white marginal band present. Abdomen brownish black with paired white dorsal spots. Legs same colour as carapace. NOTES: Sampled from Grassland and Savanna. STATUS: LC; South African endemic. (Gekolde Grootkaakgrondspinnekop)

Drassodella quinquelabecula Western Cape Long-jawed Ground Spider

Carapace mahogany-brown, covered with white setae, with narrow white marginal band. Abdomen dark dorsally with three pairs of white spots and single spot above spinnerets. Legs same colour as carapace, banded; leg I with dense white band of setae on tibiae; femora and patellae darker than rest of legs. NOTES: Sampled from Fynbos and Nama-Karoo. STATUS: LC; South African endemic. (Wes-Kaapse Grootkaak-grondspinnekop)

FAMILY GNAPHOSIDAE
Flat-bellied ground spiders Platmaag-grondspinnekoppe

A large family of spiders. Carapace ovoid, smoothly convex, usually with distinct fovea; eight small eyes arranged in two rows (4:4); anterior eyes round; posterior median eyes flattened, oval or irregularly shaped; endites obliquely depressed ventrally. Abdomen elongated to oval, hairy, usually with cluster of erect curved setae on anterior edge; in male anterior scuta sometimes present; spinnerets distinct; anterior spinnerets parallel, large, cylindrical and usually well separated. Legs usually short and stout, two-clawed, with claw tufts; tarsi I and II often with dense scopulae. NOTES: Most are free-living ground dwellers, with only a few species found on plants. Represented by 30 genera in South Africa.

Ammoxenus　　　　Ammoxenus termite-feeding spiders

Small to medium-sized. Carapace slightly longer than wide, narrowed in eye region, extending to form horizontal clypeus; chelicerae modified, with main portion curving downwards, numerous obtuse spines present; eyes in compact group on small protuberance. Abdomen oval, covered with dense, plumose setae. Legs two-clawed; leg formula 4-3-2-1; tarsi long, flexible, pseudo-segmented. Males resemble females, but legs, especially leg IV, longer. NOTES: Well-studied specialist predators of harvester termites. Extremely fast, these spiders move rapidly between foraging termites and even enter termite nest tunnels. They select a termite, kill it, and then drag it into loose sand, submerging themselves before eating their prey. When disturbed, they dive head-first into the sand. They also bury their cup-like egg sacs. Six species are known from southern Africa. (Ammoxenus-termietvreterspinnekoppe)

Ammoxenus amphalodes　　Amphalodes Termite-feeding Spider

Carapace and abdomen clothed in dense creamy setae; paired dark lateral bands present in females; males covered with shiny reddish-brown setae. Legs greyish, with numerous erect setae. NOTES: Ground dweller sampled from Grassland and Savanna. STATUS: LC; South African endemic. (Amphalodes-termietvreterspinnekop)

Ammoxenus coccineus　　　Desert Termite-feeding Spider

Carapace and abdomen clothed in dense creamy setae; paired dark lateral bands present; in some specimens lateral bands have grey chevrons. Legs greyish, with numerous erect setae. NOTES: Sampled from Desert, Grassland, Nama- and Succulent Karoo and Savanna. STATUS: LC; African endemic. (Woestyn-termietvreterspinnekop)

Ammoxenus kalaharicus　　Kalahari Termite-feeding Spider

Slightly larger than other species in genus. Carapace and abdomen clothed with dense creamy setae; paired dark lateral bands. Legs greyish, with erect setae. NOTES: Sampled from Fynbos and Succulent Karoo. Very abundant in the Cederberg Wilderness Area. STATUS: LC; southern African endemic. (Kalahari-termietvreterspinnekop)

Ammoxenus psammodromus Sand-loving Termite-feeding Spider

Two abdominal colour patterns recorded: a glossy pattern appears to be dominant in the Free State, whereas a dull pattern is dominant in Limpopo. **NOTES:** Sampled from Fynbos, Grassland, Nama-Karoo and Savanna. **STATUS:** LC; southern African endemic. (Sandlewende Termietvreterspinnekop)

Aphantaulax

Aphantaulax ground spiders

Small. Carapace oval, longer than wide; blackish, broad median band of whitish setae present; posterior eye row nearly straight in dorsal view; eyes small; median eyes wide apart; clypeus wider than anterior eyes. Abdomen oblong, with white transverse bands and spots; spinnerets long; male with abdominal scutum. **NOTES:** Free-living plant dwellers sampled from vegetation where they make their retreats in folded leaves. Four species are known from South Africa. (Aphantaulax-grondspinnekoppe)

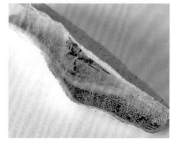

Aphantaulax sp. in rolled leaf

Aphantaulax inornata

Common Aphantaulax Ground Spider

Carapace dark, covered with dense setae. Abdomen black, with faint anterior lateral patches and more conspicuous light median patches covered with white setae. Legs with distal portion, especially tarsi, paler. **NOTES:** Plant dweller sampled from Fynbos, Grassland, Nama-Karoo and Savanna. **STATUS:** LC; southern African endemic. (Gewone Aphantaulax-grondspinnekop)

Aphantaulax signicollis

Banded Ground Spider

Carapace very dark, almost black. Abdomen brownish black, with two small, oblique, reddish-brown spots anteriorly and two long, narrow, oblique spots medially, latter extending almost to ventral surface. Legs same colour as carapace. **NOTES:** Sampled from Forest, Grassland, IOCB, Nama-Karoo, Savanna and Thicket. **STATUS:** LC; southern African endemic. (Gebande Grondspinnekop)

Asemesthes

Small to medium-sized spiders that resemble the Lycosidae (wolf spiders) in being yellowish brown with darker lateral bands on the carapace and sometimes on the abdomen. Carapace slightly longer than wide; eyes distinct; posterior eye row strongly recurved, narrower than anterior row; lateral eyes larger than median eyes. Abdomen elongated, oval, hairy; spinnerets with two or three tubules. Legs strong, well spined. NOTES: A very abundant group of free-living ground dwellers, commonly found in pitfall traps and sampled from all biomes. Represented by 26 species in South Africa. (Asemesthes-grondspinnekoppe)

Asemesthes female

Asemesthes ceresicola

Ceresicola Ground Spider

Carapace light yellowish brown with two dark lateral bands and a dark marginal band. Abdomen reddish brown, with dark serrated median band; latter broken and constricted towards centre, not extending to spinnerets. Legs slightly darker. NOTES: Ground dwellers sampled from all biomes except Desert. Also found in cotton and tomato fields. STATUS: LC; South African endemic. (Ceresicola-grondspinnekop)

Asemesthes flavipes

Flavipes Ground Spider

Carapace fawn with dark lateral bands, bordered by narrow black marginal band. Abdomen dull reddish brown. Legs faintly banded. NOTES: Sampled from the Savanna biome. STATUS: LC; southern African endemic. (Flavipes-grondspinnekop)

Asemesthes lineatus

Striped Ground Spider

Carapace fawn with irregular brown lateral bands. Abdomen dull reddish brown with irregular dark median band and chevrons. Legs banded. NOTES: Sampled from Desert, Fynbos, Grassland, Nama-Karoo and Savanna. Also sampled from pistachio orchards. STATUS: LC; African endemic. (Gestreepte Grondspinnekop)

Asemesthes subnubilus   Kalahari Ground Spider

Carapace dark, clothed with dense layer of short grey setae. Abdomen dark with broad fawn band of short setae; legs dark with layer of grey setae on patellae and tibiae.

NOTES: Ground dweller that makes tube-like burrows between small stones. Sampled from Desert and Succulent Karoo. STATUS: LC; southern African endemic. (Kalahari-grondspinnekop)

Camillina   Pearly-eyed ground spiders

Medium-sized. Carapace longer than wide; posterior median eyes large, almost touching; anterior row of eyes procurved when seen from front; posterior row distinctly procurved when seen from above; lateral eyes larger than median eyes. Abdomen long, oval. Legs with preening comb on metatarsi III and IV. NOTES: Common ground dwellers often sampled from pitfall traps. Represented by eight species in South Africa. (Pêreloog-grondspinnekoppe)

Camillina aldabrae   African Pearly-eyed Ground Spider

Carapace brown; eye region slightly darker. Abdomen pallid, darkened with brownish tint; dorsally clothed with dark setae. Legs light brown. NOTES: Sampled from Fynbos, IOCB and Savanna. Also sampled from maize fields. STATUS: LC; African endemic (Afrikapêrelooggrondspinnekop)

Camillina biplagia   Biplagia Pearly-eyed Ground Spider

Carapace pale brown, mottled and darkened anteriorly and laterally. Abdomen dull reddish brown, uniformly darkened on dorsal surface. Legs same colour as carapace distally, but slightly paler proximally. NOTES: Sampled from Fynbos, Nama-Karoo, Savanna and Thicket. STATUS: LC; South African endemic. (Biplagia-pêrelooggrondspinnekop)

Camillina cordifera
Cordifera Pearly-eyed Ground Spider

Carapace brown; eye region darker.
Abdomen reddish brown. Legs brown;
leg I with patella and tibia darker. **NOTES:** Sampled
from all biomes except Desert and Succulent Karoo.
Also sampled from citrus, cotton, maize, pistachio
and sunflower fields. **STATUS:** LC; African endemic.
(Cordifera-pêrelooggrondspinnekop)

Drassodes
Drassodes ground spiders

Medium-sized. Carapace longer than wide, narrowed anteriorly; clypeus and front of
chelicerae dark; two eye rows well separated. Abdomen greyish, clothed with dense setae,
in some species marked with small spots. Legs strong, same colour as carapace. Males
darker than females. **NOTES:** Free-living ground dwellers. Represented by 16 species in
South Africa. (Drassodes-grondspinnekoppe)

Drassodes bechuanicus
Botswana Ground Spider

Carapace pale brown, becoming darker
and redder in eye region; chelicerae
dark red. Abdomen reddish brown, dorsal surface
bearing faint dark spots or chevrons. Legs same colour
as carapace. **NOTES:** Ground dweller sometimes
associated with termites. Sampled from Grassland
and Savanna. **STATUS:** LC; southern African endemic.
(Botswana- grondspinnekop)

Drassodes splendens
Splendens Ground Spider

Carapace yellowish brown, darker anteriorly; chelicerae brown. Abdomen dull
reddish brown; dorsum with dark median band anteriorly, which extends over
one third of abdomen length; remainder of dorsal surface marked with numerous distinct dark
spots; integument clothed
with dense dark setae.
Legs pale reddish brown,
slighty darker distally.
NOTES: Sampled from
all biomes except Desert
and Thicket. **STATUS:** LC;
southern African endemic.
(Splendens-grondspinnekop)

Drassodes stationis — Stationis Ground Spider

Carapace reddish brown, becoming darker in eye region; chelicerae blackish brown. Abdomen pale; dorsum with dark chevron markings. Legs yellowish brown. **NOTES:** Sampled from Fynbos, Grassland, IOCB, Nama-Karoo and Savanna. Also found in cabbage fields. **STATUS:** LC; South African endemic. (Stationis-grondspinnekop)

Ibala — Ibala ground spiders

Small to medium-sized. Distinguished by the dark abdomen with white spots. Carapace longer than wide; covered in fine setae; anterior lateral eyes largest; posterior median eyes oval; anterior eye row slightly recurved; posterior eye row straight; fovea short. Abdomen covered in fine setae, with some strong, curved setae anterodorsally. Preening comb present on metatarsi III and IV. **NOTES:** Free-living ground dwellers that mimic velvet ants (Mutillidae) and are often caught alongside these insects in pitfall traps. Represented by five species in South Africa. (Ibala-grondspinnekoppe)

Ibala arcus — Arcus Ground Spider

Carapace reddish brown, clothed with white setae. Abdomen brownish black, with two small anterior and two larger median white spots on dorsum. Legs brown, slightly paler distally; femora, patellae and tibiae of leg I slightly darkened. **NOTES:** Sampled from Grassland, Nama-Karoo, Savanna and Succulent Karoo. Also recorded in maize fields. **STATUS:** LC; southern African endemic. (Arcus-grondspinnekop)

Ibala bilinearis — Bilinearis Ground Spider

Carapace reddish brown. Abdomen brownish black, with two small anterior and two larger median white spots on dorsum; median spots extend laterally, merging with large ventrolateral white spot. Legs brown, slightly paler distally, coxae and trochanters of all legs with white setae. **NOTES:** Sampled from Fynbos, Nama-Karoo, Savanna and Thicket as well as in agroecosystems. **STATUS:** LC; southern African endemic. (Bilinearis-grondspinnekop)

Ibala lapidaria　　　　　　　　　Lapidaria Ground Spider

Carapace dark brown. Abdomen dark with two broad white longitudinal spots. Legs same colour as carapace; femora dark. NOTES: Ground dweller recorded in Grassland and Savanna. STATUS: LC; southern African endemic. (Lapidaria-grondspinnekop)

Megamyrmaekion　　　　　　Curly-legged ground spiders

Medium-sized spiders with elongated bodies and long spinnerets. Carapace longer than wide; anterior median eyes largest, close to anterior lateral eyes; posterior eye row recurved; fovea present. Abdomen longer than wide, with markings; ventral spinnerets longer than dorsal spinnerets. Legs long, slender; tarsi flexible, heavily scopulated at base. When these spiders die, their legs curl up, hence the common name. NOTES: Swift ground runners. Three species are known from South Africa. (Krulpootgrondspinnekoppe)

Megamyrmaekion transvaalense　　Transvaal Curly-legged Ground Spider

Carapace pale brown with faint median and lateral band and dark marginal band. Abdomen silky grey; integument covered with dense setae. Legs uniformly pale brown, armed with black spines. NOTES: Ground dweller sampled from Fynbos, Grassland, Nama-Karoo and Savanna. Also sampled from citrus, cotton and pistachio. STATUS: LC; South African endemic. (Transvaalse Krulpootgrondspinnekop)

Micaria　　　　　　　Micaria ant-like ground spiders

Small spiders that resemble ants. Carapace longer than wide, with squamose setae. Abdomen cylindrical in shape, sometimes constricted, most prominently in males; with squamose setae; iridescent coloration owing to the unique structure of the squamose setae; anterior lateral spinnerets shorter than in other gnaphosids. Legs thin, with dense setae; tarsi pseudo-segmented, with two or four rows of scopulate setae ventrally. NOTES: Ant-like, free-living ground dwellers. Smaller species prefer leaf litter microhabitats. Represented by 14 species in South Africa. (Micaria-miergrondspinnekoppe)

Micaria basaliducta
Cape Ant-like Ground Spider

Carapace dark brown; chelicerae with plumose setae. Abdomen dark brown, cylindrical in shape, with squamose setae. Femora darker than rest of leg segments. NOTES: Ground dweller collected from pitfall traps in Fynbos and Succulent Karoo. STATUS: DD; South African endemic. (Kaapse Miergrondspinnekop)

Micaria beaufortia
Common Ant-like Ground Spider

Carapace dark brown, smooth, with squamose setae; indistinct dark pattern radiating from middle; two white lines present on posterior quarter; posterior margin with indentation in middle. Abdomen dark brown, cylindrical in shape, with squamose setae; white setae form transverse dorsal stripe medially and longitudinally from midpoint of abdomen to spinnerets. Femora slightly darkened. NOTES: Ground dweller sampled from all biomes. STATUS: LC; African endemic. (Gewone Miergrondspinnekop)

Nomisia
Nomisia ground spiders

Medium-sized. Carapace longer than wide, highest in foveal region; fovea present, with striae; eyes in anterior row small; eyes in posterior eye row larger, in wider row. Abdomen oval. Legs robust, especially hind legs. NOTES: Free-living ground spiders that make silken sacs under stones and surface debris. Six species are known from South Africa. (Nomisia-grondspinnekoppe)

Nomisia transvaalica
Transvaal Ground Spider

Carapace fawn with irregular dark lateral bands. Abdomen fawn with numerous pale spots and chevron markings. Legs fawn. NOTES: Sampled from Grassland and Savanna. STATUS: LC; South African endemic. (Transvaalse Grondspinnekop)

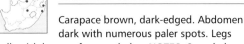

Nomisia tubula — Spotted Ground Spider

Carapace brown, dark-edged. Abdomen dark with numerous paler spots. Legs yellowish brown, femora darker. **NOTES:** Sampled from Grassland, IOCB and Savanna. **STATUS:** LC; southern African endemic. (Gekolde Grondspinnekop)

Nomisia varia — Varia Ground Spider

Carapace brown, paler in eye region, dark-edged, with slight radial striae, especially to base of eye region. Abdomen dark, with numerous paler spots. Legs yellowish brown, banded. **NOTES:** Sampled from Fynbos, Grassland, Savanna and Thicket. Also sampled from cotton fields and pistachio orchards. **STATUS:** LC; southern African endemic. (Varia-grondspinnekop)

Rastellus — Rastellus termite-feeding spiders

Small. Carapace oval, convex in cephalic region; eyes in circular arrangement; posterior median eyes large; chelicerae bear complex cluster of modified setae distally, known as a 'digging scoop'. Abdomen and legs same colour as carapace. Legs of medium length. **NOTES:** Ground-living spiders adapted to life in sandy habitats, the 'digging scoops' on their chelicerae enabling them to delve into the soil. They presumably spend most of their time buried under the sand surface. Seven species are endemic to southern Africa, three of which are known from South Africa. (Rastellus-termietvreterspinnekoppe)

Rastellus deserticola — Desert Lesser Termite-feeding Spider

Carapace pale yellow; eye region and tip of chelicerae darker; cephalic region convex. Abdomen and legs same colour as carapace. **NOTES:** Sampled from Desert and Succulent Karoo in the Northern Cape and Namibia. **STATUS:** LC; southern African endemic. (Klein Woestyn-termietvreterspinnekop)

Rastellus florisbad   Florisbad Lesser Termite-feeding Spider

Carapace pale yellow; digging scoop and eye region darker. Abdomen and legs same colour as carapace. **NOTES:** Sampled from pitfall traps in Grassland and Savanna. **STATUS:** DD; South African endemic. (Klein Florisbad-termietvreterspinnekop)

Rastellus kariba   Kariba Lesser Termite-feeding Spider

Carapace pale yellow; digging scoop and eye region darker. Abdomen and legs same colour as carapace. **NOTES:** Some specimens were sampled with small termites in dead wood in the Savanna biome. **STATUS:** LC; southern African endemic. (Klein Kariba-termietvreterspinnekop)

Scotophaeus   Golden ground spiders

Medium-sized. Recognised by the shiny, golden body setae. Carapace longer than wide, with dense setae; eyes in two rows; anterior median eyes large; posterior eye row procurved. Abdomen ovoid, with dense setae, similar to carapace. Legs strong. **NOTES:** Some sampled specimens were free living on the ground, while others were found on the trunks of trees or under their bark. Four species are known from South Africa. (Goue Grondspinnekoppe)

Scotophaeus marleyi   Marley's Golden Ground Spider

Carapace golden-brown, slightly darker anteriorly. Abdomen with brown pubescence dorsally. Legs slightly paler than carapace, darker distally. **NOTES:** Sampled from Grassland and Savanna. **STATUS:** LC; South African endemic. (Marley se Goue Grondspinnekop)

Scotophaeus natalensis   Natal Golden Ground Spider

Carapace brown. Abdomen dull reddish brown, slightly darker posteriorly, sparsely clothed with dense dark setae. Legs brown, slightly darker distally. **NOTES:** Sampled from IOCB and Savanna. **STATUS:** LC; southern African endemic. (Natalse Goue Grondspinnekop)

Setaphis

Setaphis ground spiders

Small. Carapace oval; fovea short; anterior eye row recurved; posterior row procurved; posterior median eyes irregular. Abdomen ovoid. Leg formula 4-1-2-3; preening comb on metatarsi I. NOTES: Free-living ground dwellers. Four species are known from South Africa. (Setaphis-grondspinnekoppe)

Setaphis browni

Brown's Ground Spider

Carapace uniformly light brown. Abdomen greyish red. Legs uniformly light brown. NOTES: Sampled in all biomes except Thicket. Also sampled from cotton fields and pistachio orchards. STATUS: LC; African endemic. (Brown se Grondspinnekop)

Setaphis subtilis

Common Ground Spider

Carapace golden-yellow. Abdomen slightly darker on dorsal surface. Legs uniformly light brown. NOTES: Sampled from all biomes except Desert and Succulent Karoo. Also sampled from cabbage, citrus, cotton, maize, pistachio and tomato fields. STATUS: LC; African endemic. (Gewone Grondspinnekop)

Smionia

Smionia ground spiders

Small to medium-sized. Posterior eye row wider than anterior row; posterior row straight to slightly recurved; anterior lateral eyes larger than median eyes. Abdomen ovoid. Legs slender. NOTES: Free-running ground dwellers. Represented by two species, both known from South Africa. (Smionia-grondspinnekoppe)

Smionia lineatipes

Smionia Ground Spider

Carapace light to medium brown, tinged with red anteriorly; lateral margins slightly darkened; surface clothed with sparse setae. Abdomen dull reddish brown, slightly darkened, with indistinct chevron-like markings. Legs same colour as carapace. NOTES: Sampled from Fynbos, Grassland and Nama-Karoo. STATUS: LC; southern African endemic. (Smionia-grondspinnekop)

Trephopoda
Trephopoda ground spiders

Small to medium-sized. Carapace short, oval, narrowed anteriorly, slightly flattened; thoracic striae short, inconspicuous; posterior eye row wider than anterior row, straight to slightly procurved. Abdomen oblong. Legs short, stout, especially tarsal and metatarsal joints; anterior tarsi slightly swollen centrally; legs with numerous setae; tarsi I and II scopulate. NOTES: Free-living ground dwellers. Represented by five species in South Africa. (Trephopoda-grondspinnekoppe)

Trephopoda kannemeyeri
Kannemeyer's Ground Spider

Carapace medium to dark brown, redder anteriorly, mottled posteriorly and laterally. Abdomen dull grey, with indistinct chevron-like markings posteriorly on dorsal surface. Legs slightly paler than carapace; tarsi and metatarsi tinged with red. NOTES: Sampled from Fynbos, Grassland, Nama-Karoo and Savanna. STATUS: LC; South African endemic. (Kannemeyer se Grondspinnekop)

Trephopoda parvipalpa
Parvipalpa Ground Spider

Carapace reddish brown, becoming darker anteriorly and laterally. Abdomen dull reddish brown, slightly darkened dorsally. Legs brown. NOTES: Sampled from Fynbos, Grassland, IOCB, Nama-Karoo and Savanna. Also sampled from cotton fields. STATUS: LC; southern African endemic. (Parvipalpa-grondspinnekop)

Trichothyse
Trichothyse ground spiders

Small to medium-sized. Carapace oval, convex, narrowed anteriorly; thoracic striae faint; anterior row of eyes close together; median eyes large and round, narrowly separated, touching the lateral eyes, which are much smaller and oval; clypeus narrow, equal to short diameter of lateral eye; posterior eye row procurved, median eyes subtund, about a diameter apart. Abdomen ovoid. Legs short and stout. NOTES: Free-living ground dwellers. Represented by two species in South Africa. (Trichothyse-grondspinnekoppe)

Trichothyse africana
African Trichothyse Ground Spider

Carapace fawn, clothed with sparse dark setae. Abdomen uniformly dull reddish brown. Legs slightly paler than carapace. NOTES: Ground dwellers, also collected with canopy fogging. Sampled from Fynbos, Grassland and Savanna. STATUS: LC; southern African endemic. (Afrika- Trichothyse-grondspinnekop)

Xerophaeus — Xerophaeus mouse ground spiders

Small to medium-sized. Carapace moderately convex, narrowed anteriorly, with thoracic striae; anterior row of eyes strongly procurved; anterior median eyes large; posterior row of eyes wider, moderately or strongly procurved; posterior median eyes generally large, obliquely oval or angular and rather close together. Abdomen without distinct patterns; male with small scutum. Legs generally rather short, robust; metatarsi and tarsi I and II with paired spines. NOTES: Ground dwellers commonly found under stones. At present 32 species have been recorded from South Africa. (Xerophaeus-muisgrondspinnekoppe)

Xerophaeus appendiculatus — Appendiculatus Mouse Ground Spider

Carapace pale reddish brown, clothed with dense setae. Abdomen slightly paler, clothed with dark setae; male with small brown scutum. Legs pale reddish brown. NOTES: Sampled from Fynbos, Grassland, IOCB, Nama-Karoo and Savanna. STATUS: LC; South African endemic. (Appendiculatus-muisgrondspinnekop)

Xerophaeus aurariarum — Aurariarum Mouse Ground Spider

Carapace dark reddish brown, clothed with dense setae. Abdomen slightly darker, clothed with dark setae; male with small brown scutum. Legs dark reddish brown, clothed with adpressed setae. NOTES: Sampled from Fynbos, Grassland, Nama-Karoo and Savanna. STATUS: LC; southern African endemic. (Aurariarum-muisgrondspinnekop)

Xerophaeus patricki — Patrick's Mouse Ground Spider

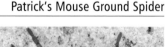

Carapace dull reddish brown, clothed with dense setae. Abdomen slightly darker, also clothed with dark setae; male with small brown scutum. Legs dark reddish brown, clothed with adpressed setae. NOTES: Sampled from Grassland and Savanna. STATUS: LC; southern African endemic. (Patrick se Muisgrondspinnekop)

Zelotes

Zelotes dark ground spiders

Small to medium-sized. Carapace ovoid, narrowed in front, with median fovea; anterior median eyes circular, dark; posterior median eyes irregular, light; lateral eyes oval, light. Abdomen ovoid. Legs of medium length; femur I frequently with paler patch on inside of leg; preening comb present on metatarsi III and/or IV. NOTES: Very common ground dwellers, sampled from all biomes, mainly with pitfall traps. Known from 43 species in South Africa. (Zelotes-donkergrondspinnekoppe)

Zelotes corrugatus — Corrugatus Dark Ground Spider

Carapace golden-brown. Abdomen deep reddish brown, darker in male. Legs same colour as carapace. NOTES: Sampled from all biomes except Desert. STATUS: LC; African endemic. (Corrugatus-donkergrondspinnekop)

Zelotes frenchi — French's Dark Ground Spider

Carapace dark brown with dark mottling. Abdomen brown, darker on dorsal surface. Legs dark olive-brown; metatarsi and tarsi redder; light patch on anterior femora. NOTES: Sampled from Fynbos, Grassland and Savanna. STATUS: LC; southern African endemic. (French se Donkergrondspinnekop)

Zelotes fuligineus — Fuligineus Dark Ground Spider

Carapace dark brown. Abdomen brown, darker on dorsal surface. Legs dark olive-brown, metatarsi and tarsi reddish, light patch on anterior femora. NOTES: Sampled from all biomes. Also collected from citrus and pistachio orchards. STATUS: LC; African endemic. (Fuligineus-donkergrondspinnekop)

Zelotes natalensis — Natal Dark Ground Spider

Carapace dark brown, almost black. Abdomen dull reddish brown, darker on dorsal surface. Legs dark; with conspicuous light patch on femur I. NOTES: Sampled from all biomes except Desert and Succulent Karoo. Also sampled from avocado, citrus, cotton and sunflowers. STATUS: LC; southern African endemic. (Natalse Donkergrondspinnekop)

FAMILY IDIOPIDAE
Armoured trapdoor spiders
Pantservaldeurspinnekoppe

Mygalomorph trapdoor spiders. Carapace smooth in females and granulate in males; cephalic region arched; fovea strongly procurved; rastellum consists of distinct process with strong setae; anterior lateral eyes usually on tubercles, large, near clypeal edge; posterior eye row procurved; posterior lateral eyes usually large and kidney- or pear-shaped. Abdomen oval, except in *Galeosoma*, where abdominal shield is present. Legs three-clawed; legs I and II with strong setae; tibia I of male with single mating spur bearing two apophyses distally. NOTES: These spiders close their burrows with a trapdoor hinged with silk at one side. The thickness of the lids varies from wafer-thin to thick and cork-like. The males do not live permanently in burrows, but move around in search of females and frequently land in pitfall traps and swimming pools. Six genera are known from South Africa.

Ctenolophus
Ctenolophus trapdoor spiders

Large. Carapace glabrous; cephalic region arched; chelicerae with rastellum on distinct mound; cheliceral furrow armed with teeth, inner row of teeth large, outer row of teeth reduced or consists of only a few small denticles posteriorly; sternum with two pairs of small marginal sigilla. Abdomen oval. Strips of slender setae on posteroventral border of coxae III. NOTES: The burrows of these spiders are not very deep, measuring about 7.5cm. The silk lining extends above the soil surface. The lid is flat, not thickened and closes against a rim decorated with bits of grass. This African genus is known from six species endemic to South Africa. (Ctenolophus-valdeurspinnekoppe)

Ctenolophus fenoulheti
Fenoulhet's Trapdoor Spider

Only female known. Legs and carapace light brown, shiny. Abdomen pale, darker in middle dorsal region. Legs shiny, same colour as carapace. NOTES: Found in Grassland and Savanna. Also recorded in cotton fields. STATUS: LC; South African endemic. (Fenoulhet se Valdeurspinnekop)

Ctenolophus oomi   Oom's Trapdoor Spider

Only female known. Carapace
and legs dark brown. Abdomen
pale brown, dark medially, paler ventrally. Legs
very dark, almost black. **NOTES:** Burrows were
found in Grassland and Savanna. **STATUS:** LC;
South African endemic. (Oom se Valdeurspinnekop)

Galeosoma   Shield-bum trapdoor spiders

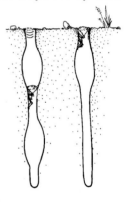

Large. **Female** Carapace smooth; cephalic region high. Posterior
half of abdomen very thick, hard and inflexible, forming
symmetrical oval shield of armour, which encases dorsal and
upper surface and completely covers the spinnerets from above;
shield shape varies between species, and may vary according
to the maturity of the individual; underside of abdomen soft-
skinned. **Male** Abdomen small, without well-developed shield.
NOTES: These spiders dig burrows that descend straight down
and expand into one or two chambers. The spider uses the
wider portion of the burrow as a turning chamber. The shield
on the female's abdomen closely fits within the narrow passage
and is used as a false bottom to close and protect the lower
part of the burrow. The upper part of the burrow is topped
with a thin wafer-like lid, positioned slightly above the ground.
Known from 10 species in South Africa. (Platboudvaldeurspinnekoppe)

Galeosoma coronatum   Coronatum Shield-bum Trapdoor Spider

Only female known. Carapace pale brown;
cephalic region and mouthparts darker.
Abdominal shield dark brown; upper surface of shield
strongly convex, curving gradually without interruption,
except in posterior half, where there is a distinct but
not prominent ridge; shield covered with setae; lines of
setae present adjacent to shield on upper
and lateral surface of abdomen.
Legs same colour as carapace.
NOTES: Burrow dweller sampled from
Grassland and Savanna. **STATUS:** DD;
South African endemic. (Coronatum-
platboudvaldeurspinnekop)

Abdomen

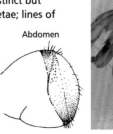

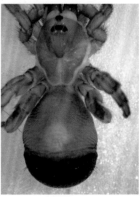

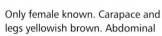

Galeosoma hirsutum
Hairy Shield-bum Trapdoor Spider

Only female known. Carapace and legs yellowish brown. Abdominal shield dark brown, oval; dorsal surface of shield convex, rough, corrugate, with numerous stiff setae giving it a bearded appearance; ridge of shield partly defined anteriorly; upper edge well defined posteriorly. **NOTES:** Sampled from Grassland and Savanna. Burrows are made on level ground where there are bare patches interspersed with tufts of grass and small shrubs. Numerous burrows were observed in a small area, distinguished by the raised entrances that are well above the ground level (height 2mm). Entrances as well as lids were decorated with bits of grass or small pebbles. **STATUS:** Endangered; South African endemic. (Harige Platboudvaldeurspinnekop)

Abdomen

Galeosoma planiscutatum
Planiscutatum Shield-bum Trapdoor Spider

Only female known. Carapace pale brown; cephalic region reddish brown; mouthparts dark brown. Upper surface of abdominal shield almost flat, dark brown, pitted, with very few setae; ridge of shield well defined, upturned all around. Legs same colour as carapace, distal segment with reddish tint. **NOTES:** Sampled from Grassland and Savanna. **STATUS:** LC; South African endemic. (Planiscutatum-platboudvaldeurspinnekop)

Abdomen

Galeosoma robertsi
Robert's Shield-bum Trapdoor Spider

Only female known. Carapace pale. Abdominal shield a rich dark brown; upper surface of shield very strongly convex, but less curved in longitudinal line; on transverse vertical section the upper surface shows an almost semicircular outline; shield finely pitted to smooth and glossy, devoid of long stiff setae. Legs same colour as carapace. **NOTES:** Sampled from the Grassland biome. **STATUS:** Vulnerable; South African endemic. (Robert se Platboudvaldeurspinnekop)

Galeosoma vandami   Van Dam's Shield-bum Trapdoor Spider

Carapace reddish brown; chelicerae

Abdomen

brown. Abdominal shield black; upper surface of shield almost regularly oval in outline; slightly convex behind, more strongly so anteriorly, with distinct ridge that is sharp and slightly upturned in at least the posterior third, but less prominent in the anterior half. Legs reddish brown. Male smaller than female, with faint shield outline. **NOTES:** Sampled from the Savanna biome. **STATUS:** LC; South African endemic. (Van Dam se Platboudvaldeurspinnekop)

Gorgyrella   Gorgyrella trapdoor spiders

Large. Only females known. Carapace narrowed in posterior third; posterior median eyes widely spaced, close to posterior lateral eyes; cheliceral furrow has two rows of teeth; chelicerae anteriorly narrowed; sternum with three pairs of sternal sigilla, posterior pair enlarged; lateral margin of carapace lightly narrowed above base of leg III. Abdomen ovoid. Coxae II–III have large areas densely studded with spinules. **NOTES:** Burrows more slanting and, although cylindrical, widen funnel-like towards entrance. Three species are known from South Africa. (Gorgyrella-valdeurspinnekoppe)

Gorgyrella inermis   Inermis Trapdoor Spider

Carapace dull yellow with brownish tinge; chelicerae

yellowish brown; coxae of pedipalps and labium reddish. Abdomen dirty pale yellow, soft-skinned, evenly rounded. Legs dull yellow. **NOTES:** Burrow dwellers sampled from Fynbos and Nama-Karoo. **STATUS:** DD; South African endemic. (Inermis-valdeurspinnekop)

Gorgyrella namaquensis   Namaqua Trapdoor Spider

Carapace with brownish tinge. Abdomen pale yellow to dirty yellow-

brown; dorsal surface sometimes darkened with purplish brown, soft-skinned, evenly rounded. Legs dull yellow with brownish tinge. **NOTES:** Sampled from Fynbos and Succulent Karoo. **STATUS:** DD; South African endemic. (Namakwa-valdeurspinnekop)

Idiops Idiops trapdoor spiders

Large to very large. Carapace narrowed posteriorly; median eye region widest posteriorly; posterior eye row recurved; cheliceral fang furrows with equal rows of teeth along inner and outer margins; chelicerae narrow, especially in males; sternum with only two pairs of sigilla marginally. Coxae without spinules, unlike in related genera. NOTES: These spiders frequently make burrows with a gentle slope in open grassy plains with low shrubs. The trapdoor varies from cork-like to flat. The outer surface is well camouflaged with, for instance, sand grains, grass tufts or even dry black lichen. A large genus, with 23 species and one subspecies known from South Africa. (Idiops-valdeurspinnekoppe)

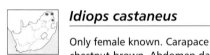

Idiops castaneus Castaneus Trapdoor Spider

Only female known. Carapace chestnut-brown. Abdomen dark brownish grey. Legs chestnut-brown, legs I and II almost black; femur IV dark above; lower surface and more distal parts of legs pale brown. NOTES: Sampled from the Savanna biome. STATUS: LC; South African endemic. (Castaneus-valdeurspinnekop)

Idiops grandis Grandis Trapdoor Spider

Only female known. Carapace chestnut-brown, ventral surfaces paler; sternum yellowish brown. Abdomen grey. Legs with reddish tinge; coxae III–IV yellowish brown; coxae clothed inferiorly with stout spines. NOTES: Sampled from IOCB and Savanna. STATUS: DD; South African endemic. (Grandis-Valdeurspinnekop)

Idiops gunning Gunning's Trapdoor Spider

Only female known. Carapace dark brown, almost black. Abdomen pale brown. Legs almost black. NOTES: Burrow lids covered with pieces of dry grass. Sampled from Grassland and Savanna. STATUS: DD; South African endemic. (Gunning se Valdeurspinnekop)

Idiops pretoriae Pretoria Trapdoor Spider

Carapace orange-brown; eyes greyish brown; eye region wider than long. Legs same as carapace with leg I and II darker. Male body earthy red. **NOTES:** Sampled from the Grassland biome. **STATUS:** Vulnerable; South African endemic. (Pretoriase Valdeurspinnekop)

Idiops sylvestris Sylvestris Trapdoor Spider

Male carapace brown dorsally; sternum, genital region, lung opercula, and spinnerets yellowish. Abdomen blackish brown. Legs same colour as carapace; female unknown. **NOTES:** Burrow dwellers sampled from Grassland and Savanna. **STATUS:** DD; South African endemic. (Sylvestris-valdeurspinnekop)

Segregara Segregara trapdoor spiders

Large. Carapace longer than wide; posterior eye row procurved; posterior median eyes widely spaced; sternum with three pairs of small marginal sigilla. Abdomen ovoid. Coxae III with spinules; tibiae III cylindrical. **NOTES:** They make burrows in steeply sloping hillsides, in sloping ground under stones or in areas protected by vegetation. The trapdoor lid hangs almost vertically, and may be heavy, thick and D-shaped, with strongly bevelled edges, or are very thin, wafer-like and almost circular. Represented by three species endemic to South Africa. (Segregara-valdeurspinnekoppe)

Segregara transvaalensis Transvaal Trapdoor Spider

Carapace yellowish brown; inner row of teeth on underside of chelicerae, including four strong teeth. Abdomen fawn with dark setae. Legs yellowish brown. **NOTES:** Sampled from Grassland and Savanna. **STATUS:** LC; South African endemic. (Transvaalse Valdeurspinnekop)

FAMILY LIOCRANIDAE
Spiny-legged sac spiders   Stekelpootsakspinnekoppe

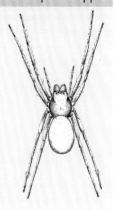

Small to medium-sized. Carapace as wide as long, or longer than wide, and narrowed in eye region; eight eyes in two rows (4:4), sometimes reduced to four. Abdomen oval; dorsal scutum sometimes present; in female, median spinnerets flattened, posterior and median spinnerets have cylindrical gland spigots. Leg two-clawed; tibiae and metatarsi I and II armed with biseriate row of long spines ventrally. **NOTES:** Free-living, ground-dwelling spiders. Several genera commonly found in dense litter. Although some species are found only in forest litter, others occur in Grassland, Savanna and even in Desert regions. Three genera are known from South Africa.

Andromma   Andromma sac spiders

Small. Carapace longer than wide, narrowed in eye region, darker in male; anterior median eyes dark and larger than rest; posterior eye row procurved; posterior median eyes very small, wide apart. Abdomen covered with stiff short setae. Legs darker in male. **NOTES:** Ground dwellers. Only one species has been recorded from South Africa. (Andromma-sakspinnekoppe)

Andromma raffrayi   Raffray's Sac Spider

Carapace and chelicerae pale golden-yellow; sternum paler; carapace with dark edge; anterior median eyes larger than rest, black; posterior eye row procurved; posterior median eyes small, wide apart. Abdomen pale reddish brown; body covered with distinct stiff short setae. Legs pale. **NOTES:** Ground-dwelling spiders collected from nests of *Plagiolepis custodiens* ants in Fynbos, Savanna and Thicket. **STATUS:** DD; South African endemic. (Raffray se Sakspinnekop)

Coryssiphus   Coryssiphus sac spiders

Small to medium-sized. Carapace oval, slightly convex, integument smooth, shiny; anterior eye row recurved; anterior median eyes slightly larger than lateral eyes; posterior eye row slightly procurved. Abdomen oval. Legs long; leg formula 1-4-2-3; tibiae and metatarsi I and II with paired setae. **NOTES:** Known from only three South African species. (Coryssiphus-sakspinnekoppe)

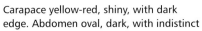

Coryssiphus praeustus　　　　Table Mountain Sac Spider

Carapace yellow-red, shiny, with dark edge. Abdomen oval, dark, with indistinct spots. Legs yellow. **NOTES:** Free-living ground dweller sampled from the Fynbos biome. **STATUS:** DD; South African endemic. (Tafelbergse Sakspinnekop)

Rhaeboctesis　　　　Rhaeboctesis sac spiders

Medium-sized. Carapace oblong, slightly convex; posterior median eyes oblique and subungular; clypeus wide. Abdomen covered with shiny and partly plumose setae. Leg tibiae I and II armed with paired setae. **NOTES:** Rare free-running ground spiders. Little is known about their behaviour. Seven southern African species have been recorded. (Rhaeboctesis-sakspinnekoppe)

Rhaeboctesis denotatus　　　　Namibian Sac Spider

Carapace reddish brown. Abdomen pale brown, paler ventrally. Legs similar to carapace, but darker distally. **NOTES:** Sampled from the Nama-Karoo biome. Also sampled from pistachio orchards. **STATUS:** LC; southern African endemic. (Namibiese Sakspinnekop)

Rhaeboctesis transvaalensis　　　　Transvaal Sac Spider

Carapace brown, redder and darker anteriorly; fovea with radiating striae. Abdomen pale brown, paler ventrally, without any markings. Legs similar to carapace, but darker distally. **NOTES:** Sampled from Grassland and Savanna. **STATUS:** LC; South African endemic. (Transvaalse Sakspinnekop)

FAMILY LYCOSIDAE
Wolf spiders   Wolfspinnekoppe

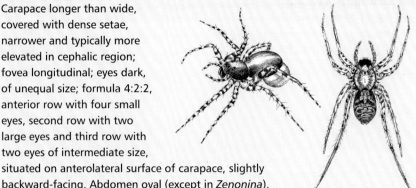

Carapace longer than wide, covered with dense setae, narrower and typically more elevated in cephalic region; fovea longitudinal; eyes dark, of unequal size; formula 4:2:2, anterior row with four small eyes, second row with two large eyes and third row with two eyes of intermediate size, situated on anterolateral surface of carapace, slightly backward-facing. Abdomen oval (except in *Zenonina*), covered with dense setae. Legs three-clawed, longer in males, usually with scopula and spines. **NOTES:** These ground dwellers are often observed running on the soil surface or hiding under dry leaves. They are only occasionally collected on the leaves and flowers of short herbaceous plants and grasses. The females carry the egg sac attached to the spinnerets. After hatching, the young swarm onto the mother's back. Only a few genera live in burrows, which may or may not have trapdoors, or construct funnel-webs. A large family, with 24 genera known from South Africa.

Allocosa   Allocosa wolf spiders

Medium-sized. Carapace with dark lateral bands and paler median band; anterior eye row slightly procurved, equal in length to middle row or somewhat shorter; anterior median eyes larger than anterior lateral eyes and situated slightly closer to anterior lateral eyes than to each other. Abdomen oval, patterned with yellow, sports darker spots or bands. **NOTES:** Free-running ground dwellers. A large genus, with 13 species known from South Africa. (Allocosa-wolfspinnekoppe)

Allocosa aurata   Aurata Wolf Spider

Carapace with broad brown lateral bands and narrow yellow submarginal bands. Abdomen bears mottled yellow and golden setae, anterior half with pair of golden-yellow bands merging anteriorly and diverging posteriorly; lateral bands with white spots. Legs brownish yellow. **NOTES:** Sampled from Grassland and Savanna. **STATUS:** LC; South African endemic. (Aurata-wolfspinnekop)

Allocosa exserta
Gauteng Wolf Spider

Carapace fawn with broad brown lateral bands and narrow yellow submarginal bands. Abdomen with dark triangular patterns centrally and paler submarginal bands. Legs pale brown; femora spotted. **NOTES:** Sampled from Grassland and Savanna. **STATUS:** LC; southern African endemic. (Gautengse Wolfspinnekop)

Allocosa lawrencei
Lawrence's Wolf Spider

Carapace fawn with broad dark brown lateral bands and narrow yellow submarginal bands; lateral bands very dark in male, almost black. Abdomen with lined heart mark; broad pale median band bordered by two dark lateral bands. Legs fawn; distal segments of legs I and II darker. Legs with longitudinal bands. **NOTES:** Sampled from Grassland, IOCB and Savanna. **STATUS:** LC; southern African endemic. (Lawrence se Wolfspinnekop)

Amblyothele
Amblyothele wolf spiders

Small to medium-sized. Recognised by the anterior lateral spinneret being twice the length of the anterior median spinneret and clearly three-segmented. Carapace without distinct pattern, sometimes with pale median band and darker striae radiating from fovea; anterior eye row either straight or more often recurved; anterior median eyes twice the diameter of anterior lateral eyes. Sternum shield-shaped, somewhat narrowed between hind coxae. Abdomen with paired spots in some species. Legs clothed with short dense setae; all leg spines long, thin and pale; tibia and metatarsus I with paired setae; leg IV longer than leg I. **NOTES:** Free-running ground dwellers frequently sampled from pitfall traps. Three species are known from South Africa. (Amblyothele-wolfspinnekoppe)

Amblyothele latedissipata
Latedissipata Wolf Spider

Carapace pale chestnut-brown, grey striae radiate from fovea; Abdomen chestnut-brown dorsally, suffused with grey, five pairs of lighter spots along length; pale cream ventrally. Legs banded. **NOTES:** Sampled from Fynbos, Grassland, IOCB, Savanna and Thicket. **STATUS:** LC; African endemic. (Latedissipata-wolfspinnekop)

Arctosa
Arctosa wolf spiders

Medium-sized. Carapace broad, rather low, usually smooth. Abdomen oval, spotted. Legs robust, lightly scopulate. **NOTES:** Swift runners, found in sandy places, such as seashores or the banks of rivers and lakes, though some occupy heath or lichen habitats in high mountains. Ten species have been recorded in South Africa. (Arctosa-wolfspinnekoppe)

Arctosa promontorii
Promontorii Wolf Spider

Body dark, carapace with dark lateral bands and narrow fawn submarginal stripe; chelicerae thinly clothed with yellow setae. Abdomen dark reddish grey dorsally, mottled black and marked with short paler median stripe anteriorly, entirely black ventrally. Legs mottled with dark and paler spots. **NOTES:** Sampled from Fynbos, Grassland and Thicket, as well as from vineyards. **STATUS:** LC; South African endemic. (Promontorii-wolfspinnekop)

Arctosa transvaalana
Transvaal Wolf Spider

Carapace brown with broad pale irregular median band. Abdomen greyish brown with paler median longitudinal band and paired row of faint white spots. Legs mottled brown. **NOTES:** Sampled from the Savanna biome. **STATUS:** DD; South African endemic. (Transvaalse Wolfspinnekop)

Evippomma
Evippomma wolf spiders

Small to medium-sized. Body densely covered with flat leaf-shaped setae. Carapace has typical transverse depression behind eye region. Abdomen oval. Tibia I with four or five ventral paired setae; in some species males have striking fringe of black setae on tibia I. **NOTES:** Free-running ground dwellers. Known from two species in South Africa. (Evippomma-wolfspinnekoppe)

Evippomma plumipes
White-leg Wolf Spider

Male Carapace brown, with broad pale median band; depression behind eyes very distinct. Abdomen pale brown dorsally with two rows of spots becoming smaller towards end. Legs brown; metatarsi and tarsi I covered with striking fringe of white setae; fringe absent in subadults and female. **NOTES:** Sampled from Grassland, IOCB and Savanna. **STATUS:** LC; African endemic. (Witpoot-wolfspinnekop)

Evippomma squamulatum
Squamulatum Wolf Spider

Female Carapace dark brown, with orange-brown median band and brown lateral bands; depression behind eyes very distinct. Abdomen brown dorsally with pale median band. Legs uniformly brown, without setae. **Male** Slightly smaller and darker; tibia I covered with striking fringe of black setae; fringe absent in subadults. **NOTES:** Sampled from all biomes except Desert. Also sampled from pistachio orchards. **STATUS:** LC; southern African endemic. (Squamulatum-wolfspinnekop)

Foveosa
Foveosa wolf spiders

Small. Unlike most related genera, males often lack median or lateral bands on carapace. Carapace narrowed in cephalic region; cephalic region moderately elevated; anterior row of eyes slightly procuved; median eyes paler than lateral eyes and much nearer to these than to each other. Legs with long spines. **NOTES:** Free-running ground dwellers commonly found in pitfall traps. Known from two species in South Africa. (Foveosa-wolfspinnekoppe)

Foveosa adunca
Adunca Wolf Spider

Carapace dark chestnut-brown with broad orange-brown median band extending from just behind posterior eyes to hind margin of carapace. Abdomen greyish black dorsally, with central longitudinal orange-brown band extending half its length. Legs dark. **NOTES:** Sampled from Grassland and Savanna. **STATUS:** LC; South African endemic. (Adunca-wolfspinnekop)

Foveosa foveolata
Foveolata Wolf Spider

Carapace dark chestnut-brown to black. Abdomen very dark grey to black. Legs distinct: coxae and femora dark, other leg segments orange-yellow. **NOTES:** Ground dweller sampled from Fynbos, Grassland, IOCB, Nama-Karoo, Savanna and Thicket. Also sampled from crops such as citrus and pistachio. **STATUS:** LC; African endemic. (Foveolata-wolfspinnekop)

Geolycosa
Geolycosa wolf spiders

Medium-sized. Cephalic region elevated anteriorly, sloping posteriorly. Abdomen oval, with median band. Legs I and II sturdy and strong. NOTES: Burrow dwellers. Some build low turrets and place sticks around the opening. Four species are known from South Africa. (Geolycosa-wolfspinnekoppe)

Geolycosa nolotthensis
Port Nolloth Wolf Spider

Carapace cream, with longitudinal pale brown median band; faint striae radiate from fovea. Abdomen same colour as carapace, with dark median band and markings. Legs same colour as carapace, bearing strong setae. NOTES: Sampled from the Succulent Karoo biome. Collected from silk-lined burrows without a trapdoor but with a turret made of silk and soil. STATUS: LC; southern African endemic. (Port Nolloth-wolfspinnekop)

Hippasa
Hippasa funnel-web wolf spiders

Medium-sized. Recognised by the two-segmented posterior pair of spinnerets, with an elongated basal segment, and by the white spots on their abdomen. Body covered with long setae. Fovea with radiating striae. Legs relatively long. NOTES: They construct funnel-webs in low vegetation or among roots at ground level. The web consists of a densely woven sheet with a funnel retreat leading into dense vegetation. Dew-soaked webs are especially visible early in the morning. Juveniles often occur in high numbers, covering the grass with their webs. Three species are known from South Africa. (Hippasa-tregterwebwolfspinnekoppe)

Hippasa australis
African Funnel-web Wolf spider

Carapace brown with dark lateral margins and pale lateral bands; striae radiate from fovea. Abdomen brown with pale median band and markings. Legs yellow with irregular bands. NOTES: Commonly found in Grassland, IOCB and Savanna. STATUS: LC; African endemic. (Afrika-tregterwebwolfspinnekop)

Hippasa funerea
Funerea Funnel-web Wolf Spider

Carapace brown with faint lateral bands and spots. Abdomen brown with rows of pale spots. Legs yellow with darker patches. NOTES: Sampled from Fynbos, Grassland, IOBC, Savanna and Thicket. STATUS: LC; southern African endemic. (Funerea-tregterwebwolfspinnekop)

Hippasosa
Hippasosa burrowing wolf spiders

Large. Carapace broad, eye region narrowed; cephalic region elevated; anterior eye row slightly recurved; anterior lateral eyes smaller than anterior median eyes; eyes of posterior two rows of similar size. Abdomen more globular than in most wolf spiders; anterior spinnerets longer than posterior spinnerets, apical segment short and round. Legs strong; leg III longer than leg I. NOTES: These spiders live in burrows. Their spotted appearance makes them well camouflaged. Two species are known from South Africa. (Hippasosa-tonnelwolfspinnekoppe)

Hippasosa guttata
Guttata Burrowing Wolf Spider

Carapace pale brown with irregular darker pattern. Abdomen grey dorsally, usually with two large pale spots on anterior half. Legs similar to body, spotted, with bands. NOTES: Free-running ground spider. Hides in a silk-lined burrow that closes with a soft floppy silk lid. Sampled from Fynbos, Grassland, IOCB and Savanna. Also sampled from tomato fields. STATUS: LC; African endemic. (Guttata-tonnelwolfspinnekop)

Hogna
Hogna burrow wolf spiders

Medium-sized. Carapace broad, uniform in height, with distinct longitudinal bands; chelicerae frequently bear a patch of red setae that the spider flashes if disturbed. Abdomen has distinct patterns dorsally, usually black ventrally, sometimes marked with white spots that differ between species. Legs of medium length. NOTES: These spiders live in open burrows that are not closed with a trapdoor. Twelve species have been recorded in South Africa. (Hogna-tonnelwolfspinnekoppe)

Hogna spenceri
Spencer's Burrow Wolf Spider

Carapace with broad cream median band bordered by brown lateral bands with radiating stripes; narrow pale marginal band; chelicerae pale, with patch of red, which the spider flashes if disturbed. Abdomen with distinct dark dorsal pattern; ventrally black without white spots, unlike related species. NOTES: Sampled from Grassland, IOCB and Savanna. Also sampled from cotton, maize and strawberry fields. STATUS: LC; African endemic. (Spencer se Tonnelwolfspinnekop)

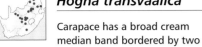

Hogna transvaalica
Six-spotted Burrow Wolf Spider

Carapace has a broad cream median band bordered by two brown bands with radiating stripes; narrow pale marginal band; chelicerae fawn, with patch of red, which the spider flashes if disturbed. Abdomen with distinct dark dorsal pattern, ventrally black with six white spots. Legs cream, femora darker. **NOTES:** Sampled from Grassland and Savanna. **STATUS:** LC; southern African endemic. (Seskol-tonnelwolfspinnekop)

Hogna zuluana
Zululand Burrow Wolf Spider

Carapace with narrow cream median band; bordered by brown lateral bands with radiating stripes; narrow pale mottled marginal band; chelicerae with pale setae. Abdomen with distinct dark dorsal pattern, ventrally black with dark central band bordered by paler bands. Legs with numerous spots. **NOTES:** Sampled from Grassland, IOCB and Savanna. **STATUS:** LC; South African endemic. (Zululandse Tonnelwolfspinnekop)

Lycosa
Lycosa wolf spiders

Large. Carapace long, facial area vertical with slanting sides; four large posterior eyes arranged in a quadrangle that is slightly wider behind than in front; eyes in second row larger than those in third row; labium always longer than wide; clypeus not vertical. Tibiae I and II armed with three pairs of ventral spines. **NOTES:** Burrow dwellers. A diverse genus with eight species known from South African. (Lycosa-wolfspinnekoppe)

Lycosa inviolata
Kimberley Wolf Spider

Carapace blackish brown with fawn median band bordered by two dark lateral bands and a thin white marginal band. Abdomen blackish brown dorsally, with black chevron pattern posteriorly. Legs banded. **NOTES:** Lives in open burrows sampled from the Nama-Karoo biome. **STATUS:** DD; South African endemic. (Kimberleyse Wolfspinnekop)

Lycosa pachana

East African Wolf Spider

Carapace greyish brown with fawn median band bordered by darker lateral bands and thin white marginal band. Abdomen greyish brown with fawn lateral bands bordered by small black spots; chevrons present posteriorly. **NOTES:** Ground dweller that lives in open burrows. Sampled from Grassland and Savanna. **STATUS:** LC; African endemic. (Oos-Afrika-wolfspinnekop)

Minicosa

Mini wolf spiders

Very small (<2.5mm). Eye region occupies almost half of carapace, eye pattern characteristic: anterior eyes very large; posterior eyes situated almost halfway down carapace. In female, abdomen ventro-apically concave to accommodate proportionally very large egg cocoon. Legs mainly pale yellow, with only few dark spots. **NOTES:** Agile ground runners often found in leaf litter. Monotypic. (Kleinwolfspinnekoppe)

Minicosa eye arrangement

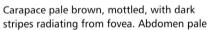

Minicosa neptuna

Neptuna Mini Wolf Spider

Carapace pale brown, mottled, with dark stripes radiating from fovea. Abdomen pale yellow dorsally with series of dark spots and stripes. Legs mainly yellow with few spots. **NOTES:** Sampled from Fynbos, IOCB and Savanna. **STATUS:** LC; southern African endemic. (Neptuna-kleinwolfspinnekop)

Pardosa

Pardosa wolf spiders

Small. Cephalic region elevated; clear median and lateral bands on carapace; clypeus vertical; chelicerae much smaller than in most related genera, their height being less than that of the head; cephalic region almost entirely occupied by posterior two rows of eyes; anterior row of eyes shorter than the second row; labium usually wider than long, with basal articular notches. Legs relatively long and thin, with long spines; metatarsus IV at least as long as patella plus tibia together; tibia I provided with three pairs of ventral spines. In some species males have dense dark setae on the palp. **NOTES:** Generally found in dry open woods, as well as on wet ground near ponds and streams. The egg sac is lenticular, usually greenish when fresh, changing to dirty grey with time. Ten species are known from South Africa. (Pardosa-wolfspinnekoppe)

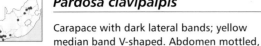

Pardosa clavipalpis — Cape Town Wolf Spider

Carapace with dark lateral bands; yellow median band V-shaped. Abdomen mottled, dark laterally. Legs banded. NOTES: Sampled from Fynbos, Grassland, Nama-Karoo and Savanna. Also sampled from crops such as maize. STATUS: LC; African endemic. (Kaapstadse Wolfspinnekop)

Pardosa crassipalpis — Black-palp Wolf Spider

Carapace with dark lateral bands; broad yellow median band dilated behind eyes; broad yellow submarginal band with row of black spots. Abdominal median pattern fused to single broad yellow area. Legs pale, spotted, banded. Male more slender than female, with very distinct dark hairy palps.

NOTES: Ground dweller sampled from all biomes other than Desert. An agrobiont species commonly found in crops. STATUS: LC; southern African endemic. (Swartpalpwolfspinnekop)

Pardosa manubriata — Starburst Wolf Spider

Carapace has broad scalloped median yellow band; broad dark submarginal bands with narrow band around edge. Abdomen dark laterally; median pattern fused to single broad yellow area. Legs pale, banded. Male more slender than female, with very distinct dark hairy palps. NOTES: Sampled from Fynbos, Grassland, IOCB, Savanna, Succulent Karoo and Thicket. STATUS: LC; southern African endemic. (Ster-wolfspinnekop)

Passiena — Passiena wolf spiders

Small. Carapace and abdomen with wide, longitudinal light median band; fovea on carapace very distinct and dark in colour; anterior eye row slightly procurved, anterior median eyes and anterior lateral eyes subequal in size; posterior median eye row narrower than that of posterior lateral eyes. Abdomen of males with short modified setae ventrally. Femora with oblique or irregular bands in females, males with different colour pattern on femora I, distal segments of legs uniform in colour, sometimes with a pattern on tibiae I. NOTES: Free-running ground spiders. Only one species is known from South Africa. (Passiena-wolfspinnekoppe)

Passiena auberti   Aubert's Wolf Spider

Carapace fawn with two broad brown
lateral bands. Abdomen with a broad
creamy median band; darker mottled area laterally. Legs
fawn. **NOTES:** Sampled from Savanna. **STATUS:** DD;
South African endemic. (Aubert se Wolfspinnekop)

Pirata   Pirata water wolf spiders

Medium-sized. Cephalic region slightly flattened, with dark V-shaped mark within the
central pale region; anterior eye row not procurved; narrow white marginal band.
Abdomen dark brown with two distinct rows
of white spots. Legs long, same colour as body,
strongly mottled. **NOTES:** These spiders typically
live on plants close to dams and rivers, running
across the water with ease. When diving, an air
bubble is trapped around the body, enabling the
spider to breathe underwater. Water wolf spiders
tend to be social and several individuals can be
found living together. One species occurs in South
Africa. (Pirata-waterwolfspinnekoppe)

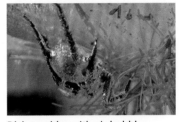

Diving spider with air bubbles

Pirata africana   African Water Wolf Spider

Carapace pale brown to dark grey,
mottled, narrow white marginal band.
Abdomen dark brown with two distinct rows of white
spots. Legs long, same colour as body, strongly mottled.
NOTES: Free-running ground spider associated with fresh
water. Sampled from IOCB and Savanna. **STATUS:** LC;
southern African endemic. (Afrika-waterwolfspinnekop)

Proevippa   Proevippa wolf spiders

Medium-sized. Sexes similar in body shape, but some differences can be seen in
abdominal pattern. Carapace variable in shape, ranging from long and narrow to broad
and oval; cephalic region sometimes elevated, usually clothed with minute plumose setae
not visible to naked eye; broad pale median band; fovea long; anterior eye row procurved.
Abdomen typical lycosid shape, in many species with broad pale longitudinal band
dorsally. Legs of moderate length; spines numerous, typically with three ventral pairs on
metatarsus I. **NOTES:** Free-living ground dwellers commonly found in pitfall traps. Nine
species are known from South Africa. (Proevippa-wolfspinnekoppe)

Proevippa albiventris
Mottled Wolf Spider

Carapace relatively long and narrow; cephalic region slightly elevated; carapace chestnut-brown with faint bands of darker brown radiating from fovea, clothed with plumose setae. Abdomen with longitudinal dark median band on paler background and few faint chevrons posteriorly. Legs moderately robust, pale brown, other than tibiae and tarsi I and II, which are slightly darker. **NOTES:** Sampled from Fynbos, Grassland, Nama-Karoo, Savanna and Thicket. **STATUS:** LC; southern African endemic. (Bont Wolfspinnekop)

Proevippa biampliata
Biampliata Wolf Spider

Female Carapace dark, dense setae forming pale median band bordered by darker lateral bands. Abdomen integument dark, but clothed with dense setae with series of transverse black markings medially; sides of abdomen mottled with black and white. Leg segments from femur to metatarsus strongly banded with black. **Male** Abdomen with anterior pair of yellow lines that often diverge strongly; legs longer and more slender. **NOTES:** Sampled from Fynbos, Grassland, Savanna and Thicket. **STATUS:** LC; southern African endemic. (Biampliata-wolfspinnekop)

Proevippa fascicularis
Pale-banded Wolf Spider

Carapace very long, narrow; cephalic region raised; carapace with broad creamy median band bordered by brown lateral bands. Abdomen with yellowish-white median band. Legs long, same colour as body; tibia I fringed ventrally with long fine dark setae. **NOTES:** Sampled from Fynbos, Grassland and Savanna. **STATUS:** LC; southern African endemic. (Roomband-wolfspinnekop)

Proevippa lightfooti — Light-foot Wolf Spider

Carapace long and narrow, pale brown, mottled; cephalic region raised; abdomen yellowish, mottled. Legs long, same colour as body; tibia I and metatarsi fringed with fine white setae. **NOTES:** A free-running ground dweller found in the Fynbos biome. **STATUS:** LC; South African endemic. (Witpoot-wolfspinnekop)

Pterartoria — Pterartoria wolf spiders

Medium-sized. Cephalic region usually elevated; clothed with translucent white, adpressed, plumose setae, often with erect black setae in cephalic region. Abdomen integument covered in translucent white, dense, plumose setae and often with longer, erect black setae; ventrum pale. Leg spines normally long, thin and tapering; clothed in translucent white, dense, plumose setae as well as longer erect setae. **NOTES:** Free-running ground dwellers represented by 10 species endemic to South Africa and Lesotho. (Pterartoria-wolfspinnekoppe)

Pterartoria confusa — Confusa Cape Wolf Spider

Carapace fawn with two dark lateral bands. Abdomen dark brown or grey with more or less broad yellow median band; paler lanceolate area sometimes outlined in black within anterior portion of median band. **NOTES:** Sampled from Fynbos and Succulent Karoo. Also collected in vineyards. **STATUS:** LC; South African endemic. (Kaapse Wolfspinnekop)

Trabea — Trabea wolf spiders

Small. Carapace typically elevated with markedly square-fronted appearance owing to enlargement of second eye row; anterior eye row strongly procurved; eyes either equidistant or lateral eyes further from median eyes than distance between median eyes; entire eye region blackened. Abdomen oval. Legs slender. **NOTES:** Free-running ground dwellers frequently found on marshy ground as well as in dry sandy areas. Often sampled from pitfall traps. Eight species are known from South Africa. (Trabea-wolfspinnekoppe)

Trabea heteroculata

Heteroculata Wolf Spider

Pale yellow-brown with two broad brown stripes. Abdomen pale yellow, with two broad brown lateral bands extending length of the dorsal surface and a paler V-shaped patch between them. Legs pale orange-yellow; spines long, stout, tapered. **NOTES:** Free-running ground dweller sampled from the Savanna biome. **STATUS:** LC; African endemic. (Heteroculata-wolfspinnekop)

Trabea purcelli

Purcell's Wolf Spider

Carapace with two broad brown lateral bands; eye region black. Abdomen relatively narrow, pointed posteriorly, orange-yellow with two broad dark lateral bands with small spots in between. Legs cream, becoming darker distally. **NOTES:** Sampled from Fynbos, Grassland, Nama-Karoo, Savanna and Thicket. Also sampled from pistachio orchards. **STATUS:** LC; southern African endemic. (Purcell se Wolfspinnekop)

Trabea rubriceps

Rubriceps Wolf Spider

Female Carapace uniformly fawn to grey; eye region with many forward-pointing black bristles. Abdomen mottled orange-grey, posterior portion uniformly and densely clothed with erect black setae. Legs same colour as carapace.
Male Dark grey.
NOTES: Free-running ground dweller. Sampled from Fynbos, Grassland, Nama-Karoo and Savanna. **STATUS:** LC; southern African endemic. (Rubriceps-wolfspinnekop)

Zenonina

Zenonina wolf spiders

Medium-sized. Recognised by the round carapace and triangular abdomen. They lack the typical lycosid bands on the carapace and abdomen. Carapace round; eye region narrowed and bearing strong setae; thoracic region with strong indentation where abdomen fits. Legs strong; tibiae and metatarsi I and II with paired setae. **NOTES:** Free-running ground dwellers. Two species have been recorded in South Africa. (Zenonina-wolfspinnekoppe)

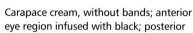

Zenonina albocaudata — White-tailed Wolf Spider

Carapace cream, without bands; anterior eye region infused with black; posterior declivity of carapace dark; narrow marginal line. Abdomen dark grey with creamy white spot above spinnerets. Legs cream, without markings. **NOTES:** Sampled from Fynbos, Grassland and Savanna. **STATUS:** LC; South African endemic. (Witstert-wolfspinnekop)

Zenonina mystacina — Mystacina Wolf Spider

Carapace fawn, without bands; anterior eye region infused with black; posterior declivity of carapace brown. Abdomen dark grey to black. Legs cream, without markings. **NOTES:** Sampled from Grassland, Nama-Karoo and Savanna. **STATUS:** LC; southern African endemic. (Mystacina-wolfspinnekop)

FAMILY MICROSTIGMATIDAE
Microstigmatid spiders — Microstigmatid-spinnekoppe

Free-living mygalomorph spiders recognised by their small size, the abdomen being covered with erect, blunt-tipped clavate setae, and the presence of four oval booklung openings. Legs three-clawed. **NOTES:** These spiders are usually encrusted with earth and often found in the undergrowth of humid forests. One genus is known from South Africa.

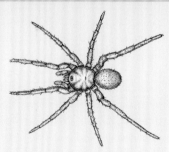

Microstigmata — Microstigmatid spiders

Medium-sized. Carapace smooth, covered with blunt-tipped or clavate setae; thoracic region as elevated as cephalic region; fovea straight to slightly recurved, depressed; sternum sigilla small, marginal; eight eyes closely grouped in two rows on a tubercle; rastellum absent. Abdomen oval, covered with setae; four spinnerets. Legs three-clawed. Tibiae I in male with prolateral mating spur. **NOTES:** Free-living ground dwellers found in humid areas, usually in the undergrowth of forests, under stones or damp, decaying logs. Represented by six species in South Africa. (Mikrostigmataspinnekoppe)

Microstigmata longipes

Longipes Microstigmatid Spider

Carapace light, darker on thoracic striae. Abdomen yellow-brown, grey or dark brown; dorsum with series of dark grey chevrons, mottled with grey or unmarked; venter unmarked or with faint, transverse grey stripe. Legs light brown. **NOTES:** Ground dweller sampled from IOCB and Savanna. **STATUS:** LC; South African endemic. (Longipesmikrostigmataspinnekop)

Microstigmata zuluensis

Zululand Microstigmatid Spider

Carapace grey; abdomen considerably darker; both covered with fine grains of sand and fine soil; all spines and setae blackish brown. **NOTES:** Found in the understorey and litter layer of IOCB and Savanna. **STATUS:** LC; South African endemic. (Zululandse Mikrostigmataspinnekop)

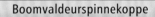

FAMILY MIGIDAE
Tree trapdoor spiders

Boomvaldeurspinnekoppe

Mygalomorph spiders. Fovea recurved, straight or T-shaped; cephalic region smooth; thoracic region arched or lower than fovea; eight eyes in two rows (4:4), occupying almost half of head width; chelicerae short; fangs directed obliquely; outer surface of cheliceral fang with two distinct keels; cheliceral furrow usually armed with two rows of teeth; rastellum absent. Abdomen oval; apical segment of posterior spinnerets domed; four booklungs. Legs three-clawed, metatarsi I and II with four or more pairs of strong setae. **NOTES:** These are trapdoor spiders that live in burrows or sac-like nests made in trees or in the soil. Burrows are closed with hinged trapdoors. The spiders occur in a wide variety of habitats, from Grassland and Savanna to tropical wet forests. Two genera with 22 species are known from South Africa.

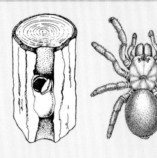

Moggridgea Bag-nest trapdoor spiders

Large. Carapace smooth in females, wrinkled to striate in males; fovea almost straight to recurved; pair of setae present anterior to fovea in some species; sternal sigilla narrowly oval to almost round. Abdomen pattern variable: may have chevron pattern breaking up into spots posteriorly and laterally; or be uniformly dark; or have faint, pale chevrons on a dark background. Group of erect, lamellate setae present on underside of patellae I, II and IV (rarely on III); group of stout, elongated setae present on underside of femur II; preening comb present on metatarsus IV. **NOTES:** These spiders are more likely to construct bag-like retreats in trees than dig burrows in the soil. The lid of the retreat varies from thin and wafer-like to thick and cork-like. The retreat is closed with a single door. Twenty species are known from South Africa. (Saknes-valdeurspinnekoppe)

Moggridgea microps Microps Trapdoor Spider

Carapace and appendages chestnut-brown; carapace longer than wide; fovea recurved, with distinct but rather superficial narrow median furrow posteriorly; lateral eyes of anterior row not quite as large as median eyes. Abdomen dark purplish dorsally and laterally, paler ventrally, yellow-grey over booklungs and anterior to epigastric furrow. **NOTES:** An arboreal trapdoor spider sampled from Grassland, IOCB and Savanna. **STATUS:** LC; southern African endemic. (Microps-valdeurspinnekop)

Moggridgea peringueyi Peringuey's Tree Trapdoor Spider

Carapace brown, darker around fovea and along carapace; eye region dusky. Abdomen dark grey. Legs yellow-brown. In male carapace, chelicerae and legs dark red-brown. **NOTES:** A terrestrial trapdoor species. It makes a cylindrical burrow closed with thick, D-shaped lids that overlap the mouth. Burrows are found in the open veld, but spiders have also been collected under the bark of *Eucalyptus* trees. **STATUS:** LC; South African endemic. (Peringuey se Boomvaldeurspinnekop)

Moggridgea quercina Cape Town Tree Trapdoor Spider

Carapace red-brown, slightly darker bands radiate from fovea; eye region with black pigment. Abdomen dark grey dorsally and laterally. Legs red-brown. **NOTES:** A trapdoor spider sampled from both ground burrows and trees. Common on oak tree bark. Some specimens were taken from oval nests beneath stones. **STATUS:** Owing to habitat loss to urban development and agriculture the species is listed as Endangered under criterion B. (Kaapstadse Boomvaldeurspinnekop)

Poecilomigas   Banded-legged trapdoor spiders

Medium to large. Recognised by the dark dorsal and lateral bands on the legs. Carapace with few setae in males and smooth in females; both eye rows recurved; fangs bear basal teeth. Abdomen with broad, dark bands dorsally, or pale with anteromedian dark diamond and chevron pattern. Tibiae II cylindrical; dorsal spines on femora short, stout or absent; dense scopula present beneath tarsi and metatarsi III and IV in males, without clasping spines. Males more slender than females, but with longer legs.

NOTES: Exclusively arboreal, living in sac-like nests made in a great variety of large shady indigenous trees. The retreat is made in a depression or crevice on the trunk with soft, irregular bark. The nests are usually open at each end and the openings are furnished with an oval wafer-type lid. The bottom opening is used as an escape. Two species are known from South Africa. (Streeppootvaldeurspinnekoppe)

Poecilomigas abrahami   Abraham's Tree Trapdoor Spider

Recognised by the broad dark median band on the abdomen, which has paler sides. Carapace reddish brown, with paired dark band stretching from posterior median eyes to fovea. Legs reddish brown, banded.

NOTES: Trapdoor spider, exclusively arboreal. Lives in sac-like nests made in large shady trees. Found in wide habitat range in Forest, Grassland, IOCB, Nama-Karoo, Savanna, Succulent Karoo and Thicket.

STATUS: LC; South African endemic. (Abraham se Boomvaldeurspinnekop)

FAMILY OONOPIDAE
Goblin spiders   Kabouterspinnekoppe

Carapace convex to flat with no fovea or depressions, markedly narrowed anteriorly; integument often smooth and shiny; six eyes in compact group; median eyes large, contiguous with anterior lateral eyes. Abdomen oval, either enclosed in dorsal and ventral shield or soft-bodied. Legs short, with two biserially dentate claws and an onychium.

NOTES: Nocturnal ground-living hunters that actively run or move about in a series of jumps in search of prey. During the day they hide under stones and amongst dry plant debris, humus and leaf litter. Eight genera are known from South Africa.

Gamasomorpha   Shield-bodied goblin spiders

Small. Carapace integument with variable texture, often smooth and shiny, sometimes granulate, with fine striation or punctate. Abdomen oval, enclosed in dorsal and ventral shield. Legs short, devoid of scopulae. NOTES: Free-living ground dwellers, occurring largely among humus, especially in indigenous forests. Three species are known from South Africa. (Pantserlyf-kabouterspinnekoppe)

Gamasomorpha australis   Australis Goblin Spider

Carapace bright reddish brown, with fine striation laterally; broad smooth area medially bordered by 4–6 setae with conspicuous bases. Abdomen oval, enclosed in dorsal and ventral shield; ventral plate large, covering most of surface; dorsal plate punctuated, bearing numerous short setae. Legs same colour as carapace. NOTES: Sampled from Grassland, Savanna and Thicket. STATUS: LC; South African endemic. (Australis-kabouterspinnekop)

Gamasomorpha humicola   Humicola Goblin Spider

Carapace and scutum of abdomen orange-brown; carapace slightly rounded anteriorly, its posterior margin slightly concave with narrow raised chitinous rim along its margins; carapace with fine longitudinal striations laterally, smooth in the middle. Legs without spines but with numerous fairly short setae, especially at sides; femora laterally compressed and deep. NOTES: Free-living ground dweller sampled from Fynbos, Grassland and Savanna. STATUS: LC; South African endemic. (Humicola-kabouterspinnekop)

Gamasomorpha longisetosa   Hairy Goblin Spider

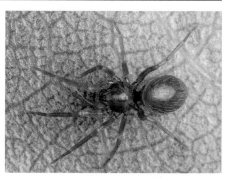

Carapace orange-brown. Abdomen has dorsal and ventral scutum with fairly numerous long spiniform setae; similar setae present on cuticle of scutum; abdomen completely covered by dorsal scute, ventral scute and epigastric region. Legs evenly and thickly covered with long setiform setae, but no spines. NOTES: Free-living ground dweller sampled from Forest, IOCB and Savanna. STATUS: DD; South African endemic. (Harige Kabouterspinnekop)

Opopaea
Opopaea goblin spiders

Resembles *Gamasomorpha*: dorsal and ventral surfaces of the abdomen are both covered with shields; dorsal scutum of female is entire. Posterior eye row recurved; anterior lateral eyes well separated. Legs short, thick and spineless. **NOTES:** Members of this genus are free-living ground dwellers. Specimens have been collected from a thatch roof, where they were found in high numbers. Two species are known from South Africa. (Opopaea-kabouterspinnekoppe)

Opopaea mattica
Cape Town Goblin Spider

Carapace yellow, narrower in eye region. Abdomen oval; enclosed in dorsal and ventral shield; ventral plate large, covering most of surface. Legs same colour as carapace. **NOTES:** Free-living ground dweller. Sampled from Fynbos and Grassland. **STATUS:** LC; South African endemic. (Kaapstadse Kabouterspinnekop)

FAMILY ORSOLOBIDAE
Six-eyed ground spiders
Sesoog-grondspinnekoppe

Carapace broadly oval, narrowed anteriorly; six eyes in two rows (4:2); posterior lateral eyes behind anterior lateral eyes, widely spaced. Abdomen oval; spinnerets slender, subequal in length; anterior spinnerets three-segmented. Legs long and slender, uniformly clothed with ciliate setae; no scopulae; presence of an elevated tarsal organ distinct for spiders in this family; two biserially dentate paired claws, onychium and spatulate claw tufts. **NOTES:** Free-running ground dwellers. They live in humus, leaf litter and moss, usually in Afromontane forests. Three genera and four endemic species are known from South Africa.

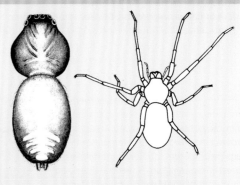

Afrilobus

Afrilobus six-eyed ground spiders

Small. Carapace oval; chelicerae with two promarginal and two retromarginal teeth. Sternum with long, triangular extensions to, and slight elevations opposite, each coxa. Abdomen oval. Legs slender, with two tarsal claws, onychium and spatulate claw tufts. NOTES: Free-running, found in low vegetation, humus, leaf litter and moss. Represented by two species in South Africa. (Afrilobus-sesooggrondspinnekoppe)

Afrilobus australis

Australis Six-eyed Ground Spider

Carapace yellowish brown, black around eyes, with dark reticulations, especially behind eyes and on foveal region, faint reticulations on sides; margins dark. Abdomen white, suffused dorsally and posterolaterally with purple pigment, broken by anteromedian white band and white chevrons. Femora white, pale distally with dorsolateral purple tint, patellae to tarsi yellow-brown. NOTES: Ground dwellers sampled from Forest and Fynbos. STATUS: DD; South African endemic. (Australis-sesoog-grondspinnekop)

Azanialobus

Azanialobus six-eyed ground spiders

Small. Carapace broadly oval. Abdomen elongated, oval, without scuta; abdominal markings uniform to absent; body and legs finely setose. Legs slender, with two tarsal claws, onychium and spatulate claw tufts with spines present on tibiae and metatarsi III and IV, and occasionally on tibiae I and II; claws with outer row of teeth not restricted to lateral flange, with tufts of few spatulate setae. NOTES: Free-running ground dwellers. Represented by a single species in South Africa. (Azanialobus-sesooggrondspinnekoppe)

Azanialobus lawrencei

Lawrence's Six-eyed Ground Spider

Carapace orange-brown; black pigment surrounds eyes and extends between eyes. Abdomen with faint mottling on dorsum, diffuse purple-brown ring surrounds base of spinnerets. Legs pale yellow. NOTES: Sampled from Forest, Grassland and Savanna. STATUS: LC; southern African endemic. (Lawrence se Sesoog-grondspinnekop)

FAMILY PALPIMANIDAE
Palp-footed spiders   Pantservoetspinnekoppe

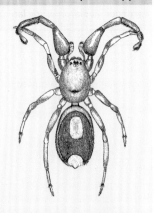

Carapace suboval in outline; cephalic region evenly rounded, sloping gently towards thoracic region; fovea usually distinct; integument hard and granulate; eight eyes in two rows (4:4) that vary in position between genera; lateral eyes either close together or widely separated and posterior median eyes either small or large and irregularly shaped. Abdomen oval; epigastric region heavily sclerotised forming a ring-like scutum which extends dorsally to encircle pedicel while the rest of abdomen is covered with a light cover of short setae. Legs three-clawed; leg I enlarged and much stronger than other three pairs; femur I greatly expanded dorsally, with thick scopula present distally on prolateral surface of tibiae, metatarsi and tarsi.
NOTES: Ground dwellers, found during the day in small irregular sac-like retreats made under stones. These slow-moving spiders walk with their strong front legs held up in the air. Represented by two genera and 15 species in South Africa.

Diaphorocellus   Diaphorocellus palp-footed spiders
Small to medium-sized. Carapace longer than wide; lateral eyes close together; posterior median eyes white and irregularly shaped. Abdomen oval. Leg I enlarged and much stronger than others. Males slightly smaller than females. NOTES: Free-running ground dwellers frequently collected in pitfall traps. A small genus, with six species known from the Afrotropical region. One species is presently known from South Africa.
(Diaphorocellus-pantservoetspinnekoppe)

Diaphorocellus biplagiatus   Two-spotted Palp-footed Spider

Carapace dark red. Abdomen grey with two large oval spots; anterior spot larger than posterior one. Leg I enlarged with dark femur, similar to carapace; other leg segments shiny, paler. NOTES: Sampled from Desert, Fynbos, Grassland, Nama-Karoo and Succulent Karoo. Also sampled from pistachio orchards. STATUS: LC; southern African endemic.
(Tweekol-panservoetspinnekop)

Palpimanus   Palpimanus palp-footed spiders

Medium-sized. Carapace longer than wide, covered in dense setae; posterior eye row straight or recurved; posterior median eyes usually closer to each other than lateral eyes; anterior median eyes the largest of all the eyes. Abdomen oval, clothed with dense setae. Anterior pair of legs enlarged; metatarsi and tarsi I reduced in size; legs with thick scopula; spatulate setae distally on prolateral surface of the tibia, metatarsi and tarsi. NOTES: Free-living ground dwellers found in sac retreats under stones. The female deposits a round white egg sac in a nest constructed of stones, plant material and silk threads. Fourteen species have been recorded from South Africa. (Palpimanus-panservoetspinnekoppe)

 ### *Palpimanus armatus*   Armatus Palp-footed Spider

Carapace, mouthparts and sternum mahogany-brown; posterior eye row straight. Abdomen thickly covered in setae of the same colour. Leg I brown; rest of legs yellowish red. In male, leg I has stout conical processes. NOTES: Free-running ground dweller sampled from pitfall traps in Grassland, IOCB and Savanna. STATUS: LC; South African endemic. (Armatus-panservoetspinnekop)

 ### *Palpimanus aureus*   Aureus Palp-footed Spider

Carapace, sternum and leg I dark orange; rest of legs yellow-brown; anterior median eyes large. Abdomen dull golden, covered with dense grey layer of setae. NOTES: Free-living ground dweller sampled from the Savanna biome. STATUS: DD; southern African endemic. (Aureus-panservoetspinnekop)

Palpimanus paroculus   Paroculus Palp-footed Spider

Carapace dark red with dense layer of white setae. Abdomen reddish brown, covered with grey layer of setae. Legs dark brown. NOTES: Free-living ground dweller. Sampled from the Succulent Karoo biome. The round white egg sac is deposited in a silk nest made of stones and plant material. STATUS: DD; South African endemic. (Paroculus-panservoetspinnekop)

Palpimanus potteri
Potter's Palp-footed Spider

Carapace reddish brown, covered with fine granules, fairly thickly clothed with grey setae, especially in eye region. Abdomen greybrown. Legs same colour as carapace. **NOTES:** Freeliving ground dweller. Sometimes found in rocky areas. Sampled from IOCB and Savanna. **STATUS:** LC; South African endemic. (Potter se Panservoetspinnekop)

Palpimanus transvaalicus
Transvaal Palp-footed Spider

Carapace dark brown covered in layer of white setae; marginal band of white setae; posterior eye row straight. Abdomen reddish brown, covered in ashy white layer of setae. Leg I darker than other legs. **NOTES:** Sampled from Grassland, Savanna and Thicket as well as crops such as citrus and cotton. **STATUS:** LC; South African endemic. (Transvaalse Panservoetspinnekop)

FAMILY PRODIDOMIDAE
Long-spinneret ground spiders   Langspintepel-grondspinnekoppe

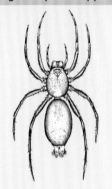

A morphologically diverse family. Carapace oval, smoothly convex, rather flat; fovea absent in most genera; eight eyes in two rows (4:4), or in semicircular arrangement. Abdomen hairy, narrow-oblong, large in proportion to carapace, usually with dark setae; anterior spinnerets well developed, spigots bear long plumose setae. Legs moderately long, bearing setae and spines. **NOTES:** Ground dwellers that prey on small invertebrates and insects such as ants and termites. During the day they are found hiding beneath stones or other ground debris. Five genera and 28 species are known from South Africa.

Austrodomus
Austrodomus ground spiders

Small. Carapace longer than wide, oval, fairly flat, without thoracic striae, clypeus narrowed with dense long setae on edge; eight eyes in semicircular arrangement; posterior eye row strongly procurved; anterior median eyes dark; anterior eye row straight; chelicerae large, generally projected forward. Sternum longer than wide; anterior margin rounded. Abdomen elongated, oval, without scales. Legs long and slender; formula 4-1-2-3. **NOTES:** Free-running ground dwellers. Two species are known from South Africa. (Austrodomus-grondspinnekoppe)

Austrodomus scaber — Scaber Ground Spider

Carapace orange-brown, shiny. Abdomen orange-brown with thin layer of setae; inferior spinnerets same length as superior spinnerets. Legs long, slender; leg I stronger than others; same colour as carapace, with only coxae and trochanters paler. **NOTES:** Ground dweller sampled from Grassland, Savanna and Nama-Karoo. **STATUS:** LC; southern African endemic. (Scaber-grondspinnekop)

Austrodomus zuluensis — Zululand Ground Spider

Carapace orange-brown with scattered dark setae. Abdomen yellowish brown with layer of setae. Legs same colour as carapace; leg I darker. **NOTES:** Free-running ground dwellers sampled from Desert, Grassland, Nama-Karoo and Savanna. **STATUS:** LC; southern African endemic. (Zululandse Grondspinnekop)

Eleleis — Eleleis pale ground spiders

Small. Carapace longer than wide, slightly narrow at cephalic region, almost oval; fovea absent to very long and oblique; clavate setae present on thoracic region; eye arrangement semicircular; posterior eye row strongly procurved; anterior eye row approximately straight. Abdomen oval, longer than wide; clavate setae on posterior region of abdomen; dorsum of abdomen without posteriorly curved setae. Legs with clavate setae resembling spines; leg formula 4-1-2-3. **NOTES:** Free-living ground dwellers found in association with ants under rocks. Four species have been recorded in South Africa. (Eleleis-vaalgrondspinnekoppe)

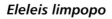

Eleleis limpopo — Limpopo Pale Ground Spider

Carapace fawn to orange-brown; chelicerae slightly darker. Abdomen fawn with rows of dark setae. Legs same colour as carapace; leg I darker in male. **NOTES:** Ground dwellers sampled from Grassland and Savanna. Commonly found under rocks, always associated with red ants. **STATUS:** LC; African endemic. (Limpopo-vaalgrondspinnekop)

Theuma
Theuma ground spiders

Medium-sized. Carapace oval, rather flat; eyes in two rows (4:4); posterior eye row recurved; anterior median eyes equal or smaller than lateral eyes; chelicerae well developed. Abdomen narrowly oblong, large relative to carapace, with dense, dark setae; inferior spinnerets twice as long and stout as superior spinnerets, well separated. Legs moderately long, bearing setae and spines; tarsi and metatarsi I and II scopulate. NOTES: Free-living, nocturnal ground dwellers. These spiders hide under stones or debris on the ground during the day. Commonly found in the warm, dry regions. Known from 16 species in South Africa. (Theuma-grondspinnekoppe)

Theuma cedri
Cederberg Ground Spider

Carapace uniform, fawn to yellow-brown. Abdomen grey; with dense, dark setae. Legs same colour as carapace, with setae and spines. NOTES: Ground dwellers sampled from Desert, Fynbos, Grassland, Savanna and Succulent Karoo. STATUS: LC; South African endemic. (Cederbergse Grondspinnekop)

Theuma fusca
Fusca Ground Spider

Carapace fawn. Abdomen pale yellowish, densely clothed with grey setae. Legs same colour as carapace. NOTES: Ground dwellers sampled from all biomes except Desert and Thicket. Also sampled from pistachio orchards. STATUS: LC; southern African endemic. (Fusca-grondspinnekop)

FAMILY SCYTODIDAE
Spitting spiders
Spoegspinnekoppe

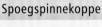

Carapace domed towards thoracic region to accommodate large glue-producing glands; six eyes arranged in three well-separated groups, each pair contiguous. Abdomen broad, oval, with light covering of dark setae; venter with chitinous depressions behind genital groove. Legs long, slender with light covering of short dark setae; tarsi with three claws and onychium.

Scytodes

Scytodes spitting spiders

Small to medium-sized. Description as for family. **NOTES:** Nocturnal cursorial spiders with a specialised way of catching prey. They are the only spiders known to possess special glands in their carapace that produce silky glue. Rapid contraction of the carapace muscles squirts a mixture of venom and gluey silk from the chelicerae over a distance of 1.5–2cm. The prey is stuck to the substrate and becomes paralysed. The eggs are simply held together by a few silk threads and carried in the chelicerae. From South Africa 30 species are known. (Scytodes-spoegspinnekoppe)

Scytodes arenacea
Arenacea Spitting Spider

Carapace with three black dorsal bands that pass over eye region; two dark wavy bands laterally. Abdomen has some small black spots dorsally. Legs banded. **NOTES:** Wandering ground dwellers collected from under stones and dark places on the soil surface. Sampled from Desert, Nama-Karoo, Savanna and Succulent Karoo. Common in the true deserts and Karoo habitats of the Northern Cape. **STATUS:** LC; southern African endemic. (Arenacea-spoegspinnekop)

Scytodes caffra
Dark Spitting Spider

Carapace dark, anterior two-thirds with yellow median band containing a narrow black median line that almost reaches to middle of carapace; upper anterior surface of carapace fairly thickly covered with short, curved spines. Abdomen transversely striped. Legs dark. **NOTES:** Free-living ground dweller sampled from Forest, Fynbos, Grassland, IOCB and Savanna as well as from commercial pine plantations. **STATUS:** LC; African endemic. (Donker Spoegspinnekop)

Scytodes constellata
Constellata Spitting Spider

Carapace fawn with thin dark stripes, some short and covering only part of the surface while others stretch from posterior eyes to posterior edge. Abdomen fawn with dark wavy transverse bands. Legs spotted. **NOTES:** Sampled from IOCB, Savanna and Thicket. **STATUS:** DD; South African endemic (known only from juveniles). (Constellata-spoegspinnekop)

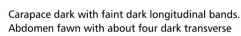

Scytodes fusca

Fusca Spitting Spider

Carapace dark with faint dark longitudinal bands. Abdomen fawn with about four dark transverse bands. Legs dark, without bands. **NOTES:** Frequently found in houses. Sampled from Fynbos, Grassland, Nama-Karoo, Savanna and Thicket. **STATUS:** LC; cosmopolitan species introduced to Europe and Africa. (Fusca-spoegspinnekop)

Scytodes maritima

Maritima Spitting Spider

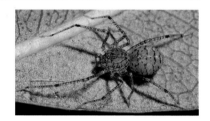

Carapace pale yellow with brown lines and spots. Abdomen pale with thin wavy transverse bands and spots. Legs spotted. **NOTES:** Sampled from Forest, Grassland, IOCB and Savanna as well as from commercial pine plantations. **STATUS:** LC; South African endemic. (Maritima-spoegspinnekop)

Scytodes schultzei

Schultz's Spitting Spider

Carapace pale yellowish with darker irregular lateral bands on both sides of carapace; marginal band irregular. Abdomen with dark transverse bands and rows of spots. Legs faintly banded. **NOTES:** Collected in Desert and Succulent Karoo. **STATUS:** DD; South African endemic. (Schultz se Spoegspinnekop)

Scytodes thoracica

Yellow House Spitting Spider

Carapace fawn to yellow-brown with irregular dark lateral bands. Abdomen same colour as carapace, with dark markings arranged in indistinct transverse bands. Legs same colour as carapace, with dark bands. **NOTES:** Sampled from Grassland and Savanna. This wandering spider is commonly collected from under stones and dark places on the soil surface. Frequently found in houses. **STATUS:** LC; cosmopolitan. (Geel Huisspoegspinnekop)

FAMILY SELENOPIDAE
Flatties or wall spiders
Plat muurspinnekoppe

Carapace flattened, subcircular; eye pattern distinct; anterior row contains six eyes, wide near the edge of the carapace; posterior row has two eyes, one on each side (6:2). Abdomen flattened, round to oval, densely clothed with setae. Legs laterigrade, two-clawed, with claw tufts and scopula; anterior legs with strong, paired setae on tibiae and metatarsi I and II. **NOTES:** Cryptozoic, nocturnal spiders found on or under rocks, on tree trunks and inside houses where their flattened bodies enable them to disappear into narrow crevices. They are commonly found in agroecosystems, especially in orchards such as avocado and macadamia. Flatties are among the most common spiders encountered in houses in southern Africa, often living on the walls. From South Africa two genera are known.

Anyphops
Anyphops flat spiders

Medium-sized. Carapace flattened; fovea and thoracic region with striae; anterior median eyes and posterior median eyes in strongly recurved line; posterior median eyes larger than anterior median eyes; posterior lateral eyes the largest, anterior lateral eyes the smallest. Abdomen round to oval. Anterior legs with 4–7 strong pairs of ventral spines on tibiae and metatarsi I and II; tarsal claws smooth; leg formula typically 4-3-2-1; all femora with scattered long setae. **NOTES:** Free-living, agile spiders found on rocks, walls and tree trunks. With their very flattened bodies they are able to move into narrow crevices. Different species frequently occur sympatrically but occupy different microhabitats. The egg sac is round, flat and papery and is attached to stones or bark. From South Africa 58 species are known. (Anyphops-platspinnekoppe)

Anyphops barbertonensis
Barberton Flat Spider

Carapace light brown with spots and dashes of brown; with two dark lateral bands and pale marginal band; eye region darker. Abdomen light brown, finely speckled with some larger indistinct bars and spots. Legs usually with irregular bands. **NOTES:** Sampled from Fynbos, Grassland, IOCB and Savanna. **STATUS:** LC; southern African endemic. (Barbertonse Platspinnekop)

Anyphops braunsi

Braun's Flat Spider

Carapace light reddish brown, thoracic stria well defined, with some fine bands radiating from it. Abdomen yellow dorsally with some darker spots and blotches above the spinnerets. Legs banded. **NOTES:** Sampled from Forest, Fynbos, Savanna and Thicket. Also sampled on the ground in a pine plantation at Sabie, South Africa. **STATUS:** LC; South African endemic. (Braun se Platspinnekop)

Anyphops broomi

Broom's Flat Spider

Carapace fawn with markings; fovea and thoracic striae dark, strongly defined, continued onto the cephalic portion; dark marginal band. Abdomen light brown with some short dark bars and spots, a wavy transverse blackish band above spinnerets. Legs banded. Male paler than female; legs yellow without markings. **NOTES:** Sampled from Fynbos, Desert, Grassland, Savanna and Succulent Karoo. **STATUS:** LC; South African endemic. (Broom se Platspinnekop)

Anyphops civicus

Burgersdorp Flat Spider

Carapace fawn with fairly well-defined fovea and two darker lateral bands, sides with narrow marginal band; thoracic striae indistinct. Abdomen fawn above with some indistinct brown markings on posterior half. Legs banded. **NOTES:** Sampled from Grassland, Nama-Karoo and Savanna. **STATUS:** LC; South African endemic. (Burgersdorpse Platspinnekop)

Anyphops lawrencei

Lawrence's Flat Spider

Carapace orange-brown with irregular lateral bands and narrow marginal band; chelicerae orange-brown. Abdomen dark brown with yellowish spots and reddish ones; darker irregular median band. Legs banded. **NOTES:** Sampled from Forest, Grassland, IOCB and Savanna. **STATUS:** LC; southern African endemic. (Lawrence se Platspinnekop)

Selenops

Selenops flat spiders

Medium-sized. *Selenops* differs from *Anyphops* in the arrangement of the eyes: the anterior median eyes, posterior median eyes and anterior lateral eyes align or are slightly recurved. Leg II longer than leg IV; tibiae I and II with three pairs of ventral spines; metatarsi I and II with two pairs of spines. Abdomen oval. **NOTES:** Free-living, agile spiders found on rocks, walls and tree trunks. With their very flattened bodies they are able to move into narrow crevices. From South Africa 13 species are known. (Selenops-platspinnekoppe)

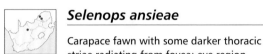

Selenops ansieae

Ansie's Flat Spider

Carapace fawn with some darker thoracic striae radiating from fovea; eye region dark. Abdomen dark, mottled brown dorsally, with predominately brown spots and some pale ones. Legs banded. **NOTES:** Sampled from Savanna. **STATUS:** DD; South African endemic. (Ansie se Platspinnekop)

Selenops brachycephalus

Brachycephalus Flat Spider

Carapace fawn with some darker thoracic striae radiating forwards and sideways from fovea, those in cephalic portion more strongly defined. Abdomen mottled brown above, with faint chevron markings and a few white speckles on posterior border. Legs banded. **NOTES:** Sampled from the Savanna biome. **STATUS:** LC; southern African endemic. (Brachycephalus-platspinnekop)

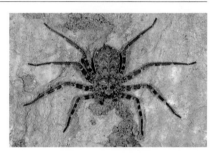

Selenops radiatus

House Wall Spider

Carapace fawn with dark thoracic striae radiating forwards and sideways from fovea; thin dark marginal band. Abdomen grey with dark median band; dark mottling on sides, a few white speckles among the predominating brown ones. Legs grey with distinct fawn bands. **NOTES:** Sampled from Grassland, Savanna and Thicket. Commonly found in houses and outbuildings as well as in a wide range of other habitats. **STATUS:** LC; cosmopolitan. (Huisplatmuurspinnekop)

FAMILY SICARIIDAE

Violin spiders and six-eyed sand spiders

Vioolspinnekoppe en sesoogsandspinnekoppe

Medium-sized. Family comprises two diverse genera that vary in shape and colour. Six eyes arranged in three diads in a recurved row. Legs two-clawed. NOTES: Ground dwellers. Two genera represented by 14 species are known from South Africa.

Hexophthalma

Six-eyed sand spiders

Robust, medium-sized spiders. Carapace relatively flat, as wide as long; integument hard and covered with numerous short thick setae; sternum wider than long. Abdomen round, relatively flat, with sickle-shaped setae arranged in rows. Legs stout, clothed with numerous sickle-shaped setae; femora bear distinct setae dorsally that differ between species. Males have longer legs than females. NOTES: Free-living ground spiders that have the ability to stay beneath the soil surface for long periods. Using their legs, they rapidly throw sand over their bodies and completely disappear beneath the surface. The tufts of sickle-shaped setae on their abdomen aid in holding the sand covering in place. Their egg sac is cup-like in shape and buried in the sand. This genus is known from four species in South Africa. (Sesoogsandspinnekoppe)

Hexophthalma hahni

Hahn's Six-eyed Sand Spider

Carapace reddish brown. Abdomen dark brownish grey. Legs greyish brown; femora have 8–12 long pale brown plumiform setae interspersed among regular brown setae of posterior margin; leg formula 2-1-3-4. NOTES: Sampled from all biomes except Thicket. STATUS: LC; southern African endemic. (Hahn se Sesoogsandspinnekop)

Hexophthalma spatulata

Spatulata Six-eyed Sand Spider

Body and legs dark grey; whole body covered with sand particles or mud. Femora bear enlarged setae dorsally, latter raised on slight mound and scoop-shaped. NOTES: Sampled from Fynbos and Thicket. STATUS: LC; South African endemic. (Spatulata-sesoogsandspinnekop)

Loxosceles
Violin spiders

Medium-sized, slender spiders. Carapace longer than wide; usually with violin-shaped darker marking on the anterior part of the carapace; six small eyes arranged in three diads forming a recurved row. Abdomen oval. Legs long and slender. Males smaller than females, with more slender bodies and longer legs. NOTES: Members of *Loxosceles* can be divided into two groups: the Savanna or Grassland species and the cave dwellers. Ten species are known from South Africa. (Vioolspinnekoppe)

❗ Spiders in this genus have venom of medical importance. See p. 19.

Loxosceles parramae
Parram's Violin Spider

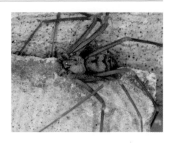

Carapace dull brown; violin marking indistinct, only two triangular markings. Abdomen with transverse bands of dark setae. Legs unicolour, very long, especially in male. NOTES: Introduced to South Africa. Sampled from the Grassland biome, often under rocks and in caves and buildings. Also found in cracks and crevices in houses where it takes refuge in dark corners of cupboards and drawers. STATUS: LC; South African endemic. (Parram se Vioolspinnekop)

Loxosceles simillima
Simillima Violin Spider

Body ranges from dull reddish brown with dark grey markings in the western populations to brown with black markings in the eastern populations. Carapace bears thoracic striae and dark violin-shaped marking; thin pale marginal band. Abdomen dark with yellowish chevron pattern, yellowish ventrally. Legs reddish brown. NOTES: Collected from under rocks, logs and bark and from inside termite mounds, leaf litter, caves and buildings. Sampled from Grassland, Nama-Karoo and Savanna. STATUS: LC; African endemic. (Simillima-vioolspinnekop)

Loxosceles speluncarum
Cave Violin Spider

Carapace brown with darker violin-shaped marking on cephalic region. Abdomen brown, sometimes with series of dark markings down dorsal length of abdomen. NOTES: Known only from three cave complexes in the Pretoria area. A troglobite cave species that is more abundant in totally dark areas where it has been recorded in crevices or wandering around on cave walls. STATUS: Vulnerable; South African endemic. (Grot-vioolspinnekop)

FAMILY STASIMOPIDAE

Cork-lid trapdoor spiders   Kurkpropvaldeurspinnekoppe

Mygalomorph spiders. The family Stasimopidae is known from only a single genus, *Stasimopus*, and their morphology is discussed below.

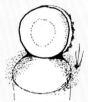

Stasimopus   Stasimopus cork-lid trapdoor spiders

Large to very large spiders. Carapace domed, narrowed posteriorly, smooth, without setae; fovea procurved; eight eyes in two rows (4:4), anterior row usually procurved; rastellum consists of thick spines. Abdomen oval, covered with thin layer of short setae, usually a pallid dull colour. Legs short, strong, thickly spined; tibiae III cylindrical without a dorsal saddle-shaped depression; in the female distal segments of legs I and II with lateral bands of short thorn-like spines. Males smaller than females, more slender,

Stasimopus female in entrance of burrow

with long legs, darker in colour; carapace with three keels that can reach as far back as the fovea; integument lightly sculptured or roughened throughout. NOTES: These spiders live in silk-lined burrows of various shapes and depths that are closed off with well-fitting, hinged trapdoors of variable thickness. Represented by 45 species in South Africa. (Stasimopus-kurkpropvaldeurspinnekoppe)

Stasimopus artifex   Grahamstown Cork-lid Trapdoor Spider

Only female known. Carapace dark brown; cephalic region elevated, very dark brown; thoracic region narrower, paler brown. Abdomen pale greyish brown dorsally, with darker central area. Legs dark brown. NOTES: Sampled from Savanna and Thicket. STATUS: DD; South African endemic. (Grahamstadse Kurkpropvaldeurspinnekop)

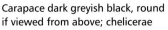

Stasimopus coronatus — Kroonstad Cork-lid Trapdoor Spider

Carapace dark greyish black, round if viewed from above; chelicerae with red setae distally. Abdomen pale above, with darker central area. Legs dark greyish black. Male unknown. **NOTES:** Ground dweller living in a silk-lined burrow closed with a round cork-lid trapdoor. Sampled from Grassland and Savanna. **STATUS:** DD; South African endemic. (Kroonstadse Kurkpropvaldeurspinnekop)

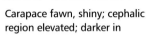

Stasimopus filmeri — Horned Cork-lid Trapdoor Spider

Carapace fawn, shiny; cephalic region elevated; darker in very large specimens; fovea has prominent, posteriorly inclined horn-like protuberance. Abdomen dorsum greyish with scattered setae. Legs same colour as carapace. Male smaller, with slender legs; horn-like protuberance smaller. **NOTES:** Sampled from the Grassland biome. **STATUS:** Endangered; South African endemic. (Horing-kurkpropvaldeurspinnekop)

Stasimopus longipalpis — Long-palp Cork-lid Trapdoor Spider

Only male known. Carapace dark brown, almost black; fovea procurved; three prominent keels in cephalic region. Abdomen dark with scattered dark setae. Legs long and slender; I and II same colour as carapace, dark brown; legs III and IV pale brown. **NOTES:** Sampled from Grassland and Savanna. **STATUS:** DD; South African endemic. (Langpalp-kurkpropvaldeurspinnekop)

Stasimopus mandelai — Mandela's Cork-lid Trapdoor Spider

Male Carapace reddish brown to nearly black. Abdomen paler. Legs similar to carapace; hind legs slightly paler. **Female** Carapace paler than in male; cephalic region elevated, dark brown; thoracic region paler. **NOTES:** Ground dweller living in silk-lined burrows closed with a cork-lid trapdoor in the Thicket biome. **STATUS:** Critically Rare; South African endemic. (Mandela se Kurkpropvaldeurspinnekop)

Stasimopus minor

Minor Cork-lid Trapdoor Spider

Only male known. Carapace jet-black dorsally; sternum paler. Abdomen jet-black. Legs black; distal portions of all legs and palp reddish brown. **NOTES:** Ground dwellers living in silk-lined burrows closed with a cork-lid trapdoor. **STATUS:** DD; South African endemic. (Minor-kurkpropvaldeurspinnekop)

Stasimopus oculatus

Free State Cork-lid Trapdoor Spider

Only female known. Carapace dark chestnut, shiny, with scattered setae in eye region; chelicerae dark, copper-red setae near extremity. Abdomen greyish with fine dense setae. Legs same colour as carapace; legs I and II slightly darker. **NOTES:** Lives in silk-lined burrows closed with a cork-lid trapdoor. The lid is thick, D-shaped, with a bevelled edge. The upper surface is coated with mud. **STATUS:** LC; South African endemic. (Vrystaatse Kurkpropvaldeurspinnekop)

FAMILY THERAPHOSIDAE
Baboon spiders
Bobbejaanspinnekoppe

Mygalomorph spiders. Carapace with wide clypeus; fovea variable; outer face of chelicerae hirsute or with dense scopulae and/or stridulating organs; rastellum absent or weak; eight eyes in two rows (4:4), on distinct tubercle; labium and endites with dense cuspules. Abdomen oval, hirsute; apical segment of posterior spinnerets long and digitiform. Legs two-clawed, with dense tarsal scopulae and claw tufts; tarsi with clavate trichobothria along its length. **NOTES:** Free-living spiders inhabiting terrestrial, silk-lined burrows, arboreal retreats or retreats made under rocks or in holes under bark or under epiphytes. Represented by eight species in South Africa.

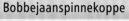

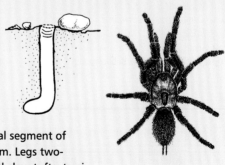

Augacephalus Golden baboon spiders

Very large spiders. Unlike in related genera, plumose setae on inside of chelicerae absent; no stout setae beneath plumose pads; long emergent setae on female chelicerae absent; chelicerae with a velvety appearance; fovea transverse. Abdomen oval. Legs I and II robust; spines present on tibiae and metatarsi III and IV; legs dark; ventral and prolateral palpal surfaces black. Males smaller and more slender than females; tibial spur reduced or absent. **NOTES:** They live in silk-lined burrows without trapdoors. Two species are known from South Africa. (Goue bobbejaanspinnekoppe)

Augacephalus breyeri Breyer's Golden Baboon Spider

Carapace fawn with short dense setae forming dark radiating pattern, with paler setae scattered in between; fovea very narrow and shallow; area in front of fovea elevated; sternum and coxae covered with dense black velvety setae with long emergent setae in between. Abdomen fawn with long red-brown setae scattered in between; underside black but not velvety. Legs hirsute, same colour as carapace. **NOTES:** Lives in silk-lined burrows, about 20cm deep, made in thornveld and grassland in Savanna. **STATUS:** LC; southern African endemic. (Breyer se Goue Bobbejaanspinnekop)

Augacephalus junodi Junod's Golden Baboon Spider

Carapace with dense golden setae; dark setae forming radiating pattern; long dense setae form marginal band; sternum and coxae covered in dense black velvety setae. Abdomen with golden-brown setae, faint median band and scattered dark spots. Legs bear very dense golden layer of setae. Male smaller than female. **NOTES:** Lives in silk-lined burrows and sampled from Grassland and Savanna. **STATUS:** LC; African endemic. (Junod se Goue Bobbejaanspinnekop)

Brachionopus Brachionopus baboon spiders

Large. Clypeus equal to half the length of eye tubercle; cuspules on labium sometimes reduced or absent; chelicerae without plumose pad on the side. Abdomen mottled or marked with median band and chevrons; basal segment of posterior spinnerets as long as other two segments. Legs short and robust; scopulae not broader than leg segment; scopulae on tarsus I entire, tarsi II–IV divided by setae; scopulae on metatarsi III and IV not very dense, extending to middle of segment; male lacks tibial spur. **NOTES:** Frequently found in tubular, silk-lined burrows made under rocks or logs, sometimes with light webbing at the entrance. The males wander around and are often collected in pit traps. Known from four South African species. (Brachionopus-bobbejaanspinnekoppe)

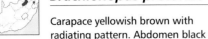

Brachionopus pretoriae

Pretoria Baboon Spider

Carapace yellowish brown with radiating pattern. Abdomen black dorsally, with numerous yellow spots; ventrum yellow. Legs yellowish cream. NOTES: Frequently found in short, shallow, tubular silk-lined burrows, 5–15cm in depth, which are constructed under rocks, logs, in leaf litter or in grass tussocks. Sampled from Grassland and Savanna. STATUS: LC; South African endemic. (Pretoriase Bobbejaanspinnekop)

Brachionopus robustus

Robustus Baboon Spider

Carapace dark brown, covered with short dense setae, faintly tipped with orange. Abdomen dark brown; covered with dense setae with orange tips intermingled with black setae. Legs same colour as carapace. NOTES: They live in silk-lined burrows under rocks. Sampled from Fynbos, Grassland, IOCB, Nama-Karoo and Savanna. STATUS: LC; South African endemic. (Robustus-bobbejaanspinnekop)

Ceratogyrus

Horned baboon spiders

Large to very large spiders recognised by the foveal tubercle forming a low dome or prominent horn. Eyes grouped in a small rectangle on a compact tubercle; rastellum absent; dense scopulae on side of chelicerae; labium and endites with blunt cuspules. Abdomen oval, with a dense layer of setae, fishbone pattern dorsally. All tarsal and metatarsal segments with scopulae ventrally; male with tibial spur on tibia I. NOTES: They live in silk-lined burrows frequently made near grass tufts. Known from three species in South Africa. (Horingbobbejaanspinnekoppe)

Ceratogyrus darlingi

Darling's Horned Baboon Spider

Carapace greyish brown; carapace with foveal protuberance projecting backwards. Abdomen with darker spots. Ventral and prolateral surfaces of palpi and legs I and II darkened. NOTES: Sampled from Grassland, IOCB, Nama-Karoo, Savanna and Succulent Karoo. STATUS: LC; southern African endemic. (Darling se Horingbobbejaanspinnekop)

Ceratogyrus paulseni
Paulsen's Horned Baboon Spider

Recognised by the absence of a foveal horn; fovea transverse with strong radiating pattern. Abdomen fawn with two dark spots and faint chevrons in posterior half. Legs fawn. **NOTES:** Found exclusively in a small part of the Kruger National Park and associated with Mopani-Acacia woodland in Savanna. **STATUS:** Vulnerable; South African endemic. (Paulsen se Horingbobbejaanspinnekop)

Harpactira
Harpactira baboon spiders

Large. Carapace frequently sports radiating bands and pale border; pad of plumose setae present on side of chelicerae (less distinct in juveniles), with row of long, stout setae below and corresponding group of stout, plumose setae on palpal coxa; fovea transverse; clypeus wide. Abdomen frequently with median line and bands, darker ventrally; colour varies from mouse-brown to greenish black to golden-yellow. Males smaller than females; with tibial mating spur, consisting of a single mound with a spine. **NOTES:** These spiders live in silk-lined burrows under stones on hillsides or in the open. Known from 15 species, all endemic to South Africa. (Harpactira-bobbejaanspinnekoppe)

Harpactira atra
Black Baboon Spider

Carapace black to dark brown, with olive-black setae. Abdomen black to brown with fox-red setae; apical segment of spinnerets shorter than eye tubercle. Legs black to dark brown, with olive-black setae; metatarsus I only slightly curved. **NOTES:** Sampled from the Fynbos biome. Common throughout the Cape Peninsula, living in silk-lined burrows under rocks on hillsides. **STATUS:** LC; South African endemic. (Swart Bobbejaanspinnekop)

Harpactira cafreriana
Cape Orange Baboon Spider

Cephalic region densely covered with brilliant orange-red setae; thoracic region also covered with similar setae arranged in radiating, denser stripes of setae alternating with less hairy interspaces. Abdomen with distinct black markings dorsally; bristles of reddish orange; undercoat of short setae on legs and abdomen bright reddish orange. **NOTES:** Sampled from the Fynbos biome. **STATUS:** LC; South African endemic. (Kaapse Oranje Bobbejaanspinnekop)

Harpactira chrysogaster

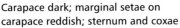

Red-rump Baboon Spider

Carapace dark; marginal setae on carapace reddish; sternum and coxae black. Abdomen clothed with fox-red setae. Legs dark with reddish setae. **NOTES:** Usually found under rocks in the Fynbos biome. **STATUS:** LC; South African endemic. (Rooi Bobbejaanspinnekop)

Harpactira curator

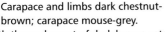

Starbust Baboon Spider

Carapace and legs uniformly mouse-grey to brown; carapace darker with pale radiating lines. Abdomen has mouse-grey to brown median line and bands. Leg joints with pale bands. **NOTES:** Female collected from under stones in a large web-lined chamber with two exit passages. Sampled from the Savanna biome. **STATUS:** DD; South African endemic. (Sterbobbejaanspinnekop)

Harpactira dictator

Ashton Baboon Spider

Carapace and limbs dark chestnut-brown; carapace mouse-grey. Abdomen with the undercoat of dark brown setae thickly speckled all over with mouse-grey spots and furnished with the usual dark pattern above, the middle coat variable, of brown or black, mostly pale-tipped bristles. Carapace and limbs darker in male. **NOTES:** Lives in silk-lined burrows under rocks in Fynbos. **STATUS:** LC; South African endemic. (Ashtonse Bobbejaanspinnekop)

Harpactira hamiltoni

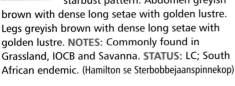

Hamilton's Starbust Baboon Spider

Carapace dark with golden-yellow starbust pattern. Abdomen greyish brown with dense long setae with golden lustre. Legs greyish brown with dense long setae with golden lustre. **NOTES:** Commonly found in Grassland, IOCB and Savanna. **STATUS:** LC; South African endemic. (Hamilton se Sterbobbejaanspinnekop)

Harpactirella
Harpactirella baboon spiders

Large. Carapace without plumose pad on chelicerae; labium with reduced number of cuspules. Tarsal segment of leg IV divided; spines limited to the base of the tibia and metatarsi of all legs; male has a single tibial spur. Males smaller than females. **NOTES:** Burrows range from silk-lined holes under rocks to branched burrows up to 17–18cm deep, widening towards opening, strongly inclined and descending towards hinge-side at an angle of nearly 45°. The lid is flat, oval in outline, but broadly truncated at the hinges. Known from 11 species in South Africa. (Harpactirella-bobbejaanspinnekoppe)

Harpactirella overdijki
Overdijk's Lesser Baboon Spider

Carapace dark brown with radial pattern of yellow-brown striae. Abdomen yellow-brown with dark pattern of bars, spots and reticulation. Legs dark brown. **NOTES:** Sampled from the Savanna biome. **STATUS:** LC; South African endemic. (Overdijk se Klein Bobbejaanspinnekop)

Idiothele
Idiothele baboon spiders

Large. Recognised by the absence of prolateral cheliceral scapulae and the absence of prolateral stridulation strikers on the maxillae. Clypeus wide; fovea transverse; labium with 20 cuspules. Abdomen with chevrons and dark median band; distal segments of posterior spinnerets short. Metatarsi III and IV with prodorsal distal spines. **NOTES:** The burrow has a tubular retreat with a well-developed trapdoor. The door is very large and thin, becoming very delicate at the margin. Known from two southern African species. (Idiothele-bobbejaanspinnekoppe)

Idiothele mira
Blue-footed Baboon Spider

Distinguished by the sky-blue coloration on the tarsi and metatarsi. Carapace elongated, domed, with dark brown distinct metallic brown radiating striae and dark mask around eyes; sternum very dark. Abdomen beige with dark patterns, ventrally dark, paler over booklungs. Legs ventrally dark on coxae and trochanters. **NOTES:** Lives in dense silk-lined cells or burrows made beneath rocks and logs in the IOCB biome. The entrance is a thin wafer-like trapdoor. **STATUS:** Rare; South African endemic. (Blouvoet-bobbejaanspinnekop)

FAMILY TRACHELIDAE
Dark sac spiders

Donkersakspinnekoppe

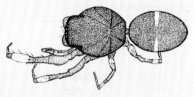

A diverse family. Carapace oval, longer than wide; eyes in two rows (4:4), with anterior median eyes often the largest; fovea distinct. Abdomen with strong tendency towards sclerotisation, especially in the booklung region; some species ant-like. Legs two-clawed; spines often reduced; distal segments of anterior legs often possess ventral cusps, especially in males; anterior spinnerets close together. NOTES: They live in silk retreats spun in rolled leaves or under bark or debris on the soil surface. Represented by 12 genera in South Africa.

Afroceto

Afroceto dark sac spiders

Small to medium-sized. Carapace narrower in eye region; eye region darkened; integument smooth. Abdomen integument smooth; two muscle attachment points distinct. Legs typically pale yellow to light brown, usually banded. NOTES: Free-living wanderers, predominantly captured from the ground surface by pitfall trapping or sifting leaf litter, but they have also been collected from foliage or beneath loose bark of trees, sometimes in high numbers. Represented by 16 species in South Africa. (Afroceto-donkersakspinnekoppe)

Afroceto martini

Martin's Dark Sac Spider

Carapace reddish brown; eye region reddish brown to dark brown, blackish rings around eyes; anterior surface covered in pale, fine setae; surface smooth, with short, distinct, slightly thickened fovea. Abdomen brown, mottling dorsally. Legs banded. NOTES: Free-living ground dwellers collected from pitfall traps in all biomes. Also sampled from macadamia and pistachio orchards. STATUS: LC; southern African endemic. (Martin se Donkersakspinnekop)

Afroceto plana

Tree Dark Sac Spider

Carapace brown to dark brown, slightly paler posterior to fovea; eye region dark brown. Abdomen cream to light brown dorsally, with dark grey ventral line, either branched into a chevron or unbranched. Legs uniformly pale yellow to light brown, with incomplete grey bands on femora to metatarsi. NOTES: Associated with the bark of trees; egg sacs constructed underneath bark and under stones or logs. Also collected from leaf litter. Sampled from Fynbos, Grassland and Savanna. STATUS: LC; African endemic. (Boom-donkersakspinnekop)

Jocquestus
Jocquestus dark sac spiders

Small. Carapace longer than wide. Distinguished by blunt ventral cusps on the tibiae and metatarsi of leg I (only in males), and sometimes also on tarsi I and/or tibiae and metatarsi II. **NOTES:** Ground dwellers. Five species are known from South Africa. (Jocquestus-donkersakspinnekoppe)

Jocquestus schenkeli
Schenkel's Dark Sac Spider

Carapace orange-brown to reddish brown, finely granulate. Abdomen dark grey, with two paired cream markings anteriorly, anterior pair separated by faint grey narrow median line, posterior pair fused medially. Legs brown, anterior legs darker than posterior legs. **NOTES:** Ground dweller sampled from Forest, Grassland, IOCB, Savanna and Thicket. **STATUS:** LC; African endemic. (Schenkel se Donkersakspinnekop)

Orthobula
Orthobula dark sac spiders

Small spiders. Carapace oval, slightly longer than wide, granulate; eyes large, close together, posterior eye row is slightly recurved. Abdomen roundish oval with markings. Legs slender; leg I stronger than rest; tibiae I with paired setae ventrally. **NOTES:** Free-running ground dwellers represented by two species in South Africa. (Orthobula-donkersakspinnekoppe)

Orthobula radiata
Radiata Dark Sac Spider

Carapace dark brown. Abdomen dark with yellow pattern dorsally. Legs paler brown than carapace; all segments same colour other than tibia I which is darker. **NOTES:** Free-running ground dwellers sampled from Forest, Grassland, IOCB and Savanna. **STATUS:** LC; African endemic. (Radiata-donkersakspinnekop)

Patelloceto
Patelloceto dark sac spiders

Medium-sized. Carapace oval, narrower in eye region, without any markings; eyes in two rows, posterior eye row slightly procurved. Abdomen without markings. **NOTES:** Primarily arboreal, collected by beating, bark searching or by canopy fogging. Known from one species in South Africa. (Patelloceto-donkersakspinnekoppe)

Patelloceto secutor
Patelloceto Dark Sac Spider

Carapace very dark brown, almost black, smooth and shiny. Abdomen the same colour. Legs paler brown; only femora dark. **NOTES:** Sampled from IOCB and Savanna. **STATUS:** LC; southern African endemic. (Patelloceto-donkersakspinnekop)

Spinotrachelas

Spinotrachelas dark sac spider

Small. Spiders in this genus superficially resemble *Trachelas* but can be distinguished by the presence of strong prolateral spines on the femora and patellae and paired spines on tibiae I in both males and females. Males have a large number of short, peg-like cusps on the metatarsi and tarsi of legs I and II, while the females lack cusps on all leg segments other than the tarsi of leg I. The abdominal scutum covers the entire abdominal dorsum in males, but is absent in females. **NOTES:** These spiders are found on the ground surface, usually at base of grasses. Represented by four species in South Africa. (Spinotrachelas-donkersakspinnekoppe)

Spinotrachelas montanus

Montanus Dark Sac Spider

Carapace uniformly dark brown, nearly black, shiny. Abdomen elongated, oval; dorsum very dark brown, nearly black. Leg I stronger than rest, dark, with strong prolateral spines on the femora and patellae and paired spines on tibiae I; rest of legs with pale yellow bands. **NOTES:** Plant and ground dwellers sampled from the base of grass tussocks in forest-grassland and riparian forest ecotones in Forest and Grassland. **STATUS:** LC; South African endemic. (Montanus-donkersakspinnekop)

Thysanina

Thysanina dark sac spiders

Small to medium-sized. Carapace slightly flattened, with finely wrinkled integument that appears smooth; fovea present. Abdomen oval with dense setae. **NOTES:** Collected from the ground surface, grass and short shrubs. Known from five species in South Africa. (Thysanina-donkersakspinnekoppe)

Thysanina absolvo

Free State Dark Sac Spider

Carapace chestnut-brown, smooth. Abdomen dorsum creamy white with grey chevron and darkened median band. Legs brown with light grey transverse bands. **NOTES:** Appears to be associated primarily with the lower strata of grassland ecosystems, and was collected from the ground surface, grass and short shrubs in the Grassland biome. **STATUS:** LC; South African endemic. (Vrystaatse Donkersakspinnekop)

FAMILY ZODARIIDAE
Zodariid spiders
Zodariidspinnekoppe

Diverse family. Carapace variable in shape, usually oval, narrowed anteriorly; fovea varies from well-developed and deep to poorly developed or absent; integument varies from entirely smooth to densely granulated or with tiny perforations; eyes arranged in two or three rows (2:4:2 or 2:2:4); eye size and arrangement variable; chelicerae strong; fangs usually short, thick at the base. Abdomen sometimes elongated, oval, sometimes twice as long as wide, or higher in the back than in the front; scuta present in males of some genera. Legs with spines, usually strongly developed; species that dig have numerous strong spines on posterior legs. NOTES: Wandering spiders, the vast majority of which are ground dwelling. Some spend most of their time under the ground in loose sand. Others live in burrows. Only a single species has adapted to a life on vegetation. Represented by 22 genera in South Africa.

Caesetius
Caesetius zodariid spiders

Medium-sized. Carapace smooth, domed, highest point just before fovea, with fine setae and long hairs between fovea and eyes; eyes in two rows, anterior eye row procurved and narrower than posterior row, the latter strongly recurved; field of small spinules on mesial side of chelicerae. Leg IV the longest. Numerous spines on legs III and IV. NOTES: Sand diggers. Known from ten species, all endemic to southern Africa. (Caesetius-zodariidspinnekoppe)

Caesetius globicoxis
Globicoxis Zodariid Spider

Carapace chestnut-brown, cephalic region darker; sparsely covered with fine silvery setae; dense cluster of fine setae on clypeus; chelicerae dark brown. Abdomen mottled with white and grey dorsally and ventrally. Legs same colour as carapace. NOTES: Sampled from Fynbos, IOCB and Savanna. STATUS: LC; South African endemic. (Globicoxis-zodariid-spinnekop)

Capheris

Capheris zodariid spiders

Medium-sized. Carapace oval, narrowed in front; profile domed, the highest point between fovea and posterior median eyes; fovea deep; integument finely to coarsely granulated, often with short silvery setae. Abdomen oval, usually with dense cover of setae. Legs I and II with long slender spines; legs III and IV with shorter, strong spines. NOTES: They live mainly in semi-arid areas and deserts. Six species recorded from South Africa. (Capheris-zodariidspinnekoppe)

Capheris crassimana

Crassimana Zodariid Spider

Carapace dark chestnut-brown with many short silvery setae; chelicerae and sternum reddish brown. Abdomen dark grey, sparsely covered with silvery and fawn setae that form broad chevron pattern. Legs same colour as carapace. In male dorsum of abdomen with dense cover of pale setae. NOTES: Ground-burrowing spiders sampled from Nama-Karoo and Savanna. STATUS: LC; southern African endemic. (Crassimana-zodariidspinnekop)

Capheris langi

Lang's Zodariid Spider

Carapace, abdomen and legs blackish brown with many short silvery setae; pale setae form marginal band. Abdomen sparsely covered with mixed, short, creamy and blackish setae. Legs same colour as carapace; legs III and IV with numerous spines. NOTES: A burrow dweller sampled from the Savanna biome. STATUS: LC; southern African endemic. (Lang se Zodariidspinnekop)

Chariobas

Chariobas grass-stitching spiders

Medium-sized. Carapace elongated; eyes closely grouped. Abdomen elongated, three times longer than wide, not overlapping the carapace; two elongated muscle points present behind pedicels. Leg formula 1-4-2-3. NOTES: Free-living plant dwellers that live in grass, which they stitch together to form a tube. The egg sacs are deposited in these grass-tube nests. Four species are known from South Africa. (Chariobas-grasweefspinnekoppe)

Chariobas lineatus
Striped Grass-stitching Spider

Carapace pale yellow with broad dark medial band and dark marginal band. Abdomen long and narrow, pale grey with broad dark central, median band covering whole dorsal area. Legs similar to carapace but legs I and II darker distally. **NOTES:** Sampled from Fynbos and Grassland. **STATUS:** LC; South African endemic. (Gestreepte Grasweefspinnekop)

Chariobas navigator
Cape Grass-stitching Spider

Carapace, abdomen and legs dark brown, almost black. Abdomen decorated with four pairs of white spots. **NOTES:** Free-living plant dwellers. Type locality in Fynbos. **STATUS:** DD; South African endemic. (Kaapse Grasweefspinnekop)

Cicynethus
Cicynethus zodariid spiders

Medium-sized to large. Carapace with smooth to finely granulate integument, longer than wide, fairly flat, protruding anteriorly, widest at level of coxae II–III, profile highest just behind eyes and with slight dip at level of fovea; eyes in two procurved rows. Abdomen elongated oval or cylindrical, at least twice as long as wide. Legs fairly slender, anterior legs more robust than posterior ones; formula 1-2-4-3 or 1-4-2-3; spination on legs reduced to a few small distal spines on ventral side of metatarsi. **NOTES:** They have a mixed lifestyle and spend part of their life cycle at ground level and part in the shrub layer. Five species are known from South Africa. (Cicynethus-zodariidspinnekoppe)

Cicynethus acer
Mariepskop Zodariid Spider

Carapace dark brown, darker laterally; chelicerae brown with pale distal patch; fovea a deep pit; sternum brown. Abdomen dorsum fawn with broad dark median band that splits posterior third. Legs pale yellow; leg I with distal half of patellae, tibiae, metatarsi and tarsi dark. **NOTES:** Sampled from shrub layer in forest areas in the Savanna biome. **STATUS:** LC; southern African endemic. (Mariepskopse Zodariidspinnekop)

Cicynethus decoratus

Decoratus Zodariid Spider

Carapace fawn, with dark lateral bands; narrow fawn marginal band. Abdomen fawn, dorsum with dark pattern; lateral bands with three ill-defined triangles; median band consists of diamond, stripe, two chevrons and two-segmented spot in front of spinnerets. Legs yellowish orange; leg I with distal half of patellae, tibiae, metatarsi and tarsi dark. NOTES: Found while sifting leaf litter and humus in Fynbos, IOCB and Savanna. STATUS: DD; South African endemic. (Decoratus-zodariidspinnekop)

Cicynethus subtropicalis

Kosibay Zodariid Spider

Carapace reddish brown, with dark median and two lateral bands and narrow fawn marginal band. Abdomen uniformly grey with ill-defined darker median band ending in faint lateral bands. Legs greyish yellow, leg I stronger, with distal half of patellae, tibiae, metatarsi and tarsi dark. NOTES: Sampled from under tree bark and by sweeping grass, bushes and herbs in IOCB and Savanna. STATUS: LC; South African endemic. (Kosibaaise Zodariid-spinnekop)

Cydrela

Cydrela zodariid spiders

Medium-sized. Carapace with raised cephalic region with slight dip near fovea; oval, narrower in eye region; eyes in three rows (2:2:4); fovea deep; sternum has slightly indented anterior margin without procoxal sclerites. Abdomen oval, with two or four muscle points. Legs III and IV with numerous strong setae. NOTES: Ground dwellers. Some species were sampled from burrows in the ground that were closed with a thick circular trapdoor. Five species are known from South Africa. (Cydrela-zodariidspinnekoppe)

Cydrela male showing strong setae on legs

Cydrela schoemanae
Schoeman's Cydrela Spider

Carapace uniformly dark brown, bearing white setae especially in cephalic region. Abdomen dorsum dark brown with white setae forming spots: two in front, two in middle and one longitudinal in front of spinnerets. Femora dark brown; other leg segments paler brown. NOTES: Sampled from pitfall traps in Grassland and Savanna. Also sampled from maize fields and pine plantations. STATUS: LC; South African endemic. (Schoeman se Cydrela-spinnekop)

Diores
Igloo spiders

Small. Carapace oval, slightly narrower anteriorly, widest between coxae II and III; fovea well developed; integument smooth; eyes in two procurved rows; anterior median eyes large and dark in colour; other eyes circular and pale. Abdomen sometimes with pale pattern on a darker background. Legs slender, with spines and spinules. NOTES: Agile, nocturnal, wandering ground dwellers. Some species prey on ants while others prey on termites. In the early morning they construct a small, semi-spherical, igloo-shaped retreat made of small stones and silk. Most species have large glands on the femora. These appear to play a role in capturing prey since merely a touch from the spider results in paralysis of the prey. Represented by 31 species in South Africa. (Igloespinnekoppe)

Igloo retreat

Diores bifurcatus
Cape Igloo Spider

Carapace orange-brown, with some pale setae. Abdomen grey with broad dark lateral bands. Legs same colour as carapace; femora slightly darker. NOTES: Free-living ground dwellers sampled from Fynbos. STATUS: LC; South African endemic. (Kaapse Igloespinnekop)

Diores pauper
Pauper Igloo Spider

Male Carapace yellowish with darker area in front of fovea with faint radiating striae. Abdomen sepia, with darker scutum and three spots in front of spinnerets. Legs similar to carapace. Female Dorsum uniformly sepia with only one small patch in front of spinnerets. NOTES: Sampled from Grassland and Thicket. STATUS: LC; South African endemic. (Pauper-igloespinnekop)

Diores poweri

Power's Igloo Spider

Carapace and chelicerae pale yellow; carapace sparsely haired; sternum markedly orange, yellow along margin. Abdomen with two irregular sepia lateral bands. Legs same colour as carapace. NOTES: Associated with Fynbos, Grassland, Nama-Karoo and Savanna. STATUS: LC; southern African endemic. (Power se Igloespinnekop)

Heradida

Heradida zodariid spiders

Small. Carapace elongated, widest at coxae II; narrowed in front; integument reticulated; eyes in two rows, both procurved. Abdomen elongated; with strongly developed, structural dorsal scutum in both sexes; ventrally with chitinised areas in front of epigastric fold and in front of spinnerets. Legs slender, leg formula 4-1-2-3. NOTES: Small ground dwellers seen running around on the soil surface. Represented by five species in South Africa. (Heradida-zodariidspinnekoppe)

Heradida loricata

Loricata Zodariid Spider

Carapace, chelicerae and sternum chestnut-brown; eyes equal in size. Abdomen cream with brown scutum, darker along margin. Legs yellowish brown. NOTES: Sampled with pitfall traps from the Grassland biome. STATUS: LC; South African endemic. (Loricata-zodariidspinnekop)

Hermippus

Hermippus zodariid spiders

Medium-sized. Carapace elevated, oval, without indication of cervical grooves; fovea evident; eyes in two rows, both procurved. Abdomen oval; male with a small dorsal scutum. Legs almost equal in length; tarsi laterally compressed, with two claws and claw tufts; numerous short spines ventrally on tarsi and metatarsi. NOTES: Free-running ground dwellers. Three species recorded from South Africa. (Hermippus-zodariidspinnekoppe)

Female *Hermippus tenebrosus*

Hermippus tenebrosus — Kruger Park Zodariid Spider

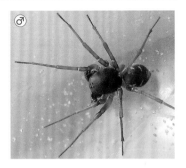

Carapace dark blackish brown, without markings. Abdomen black with few white markings; scutum covering dorsum chestnut-brown with orange-red marking. Legs orange to chestnut-brown, dorsal side of trochanters and coxae has creamy white distal margin. Females and males look very similar, but the abdomen is without scuta in the female and has a different colour pattern. NOTES: Sampled from pitfall traps from IOCB and Savanna. STATUS: LC; South African endemic. (Krugerwildtuin-zodariidspinnekop)

Mallinus — Mallinus zodariid spiders

Small. Carapace broadly oval; thoracic region elevated, reaching highest point just in front of fovea; cephalic region rounded anteriorly, parallel-sided laterally, thoracic region almost circular; broadest at middle of coxa II; eyes in two procurved rows; all eyes circular; anterior median eyes dark; remainder light. Abdomen higher than long. Leg formula 4-1-2-3; two tarsal claws with minute teeth. NOTES: Free-running ground dwellers, behaviour poorly known. Known from a single species endemic to South Africa. (Mallinus-zodariidspinnekoppe)

Mallinus nitidiventris — Round-head Zodariid Spider

Carapace broadly oval; thoracic region raised, carapace and chelicerae dark brown, bear some white setae; sternum paler. Abdomen and legs dark brown. NOTES: Sampled with pitfall traps from Nama-Karoo. STATUS: LC; South African endemic. (Rondekop-zodariidspinnekop)

Palfuria — Palfuria zodariid spiders

Small. Carapace with strongly raised cephalic lobe, slanting back over thoracic region in adults; narrowed in front; eyes in two strongly procurved rows; integument slightly to strongly granulated. Abdomen rounded, slightly longer than wide; slightly sclerotised on dorsum in females, more strongly so in males; anterior part of abdomen strongly sclerotised, forming tube around the petiolus. Leg formula 4-1-2-3; legs more slender in males than in females; two claws on short onychium. NOTES: Very small ground dwellers frequently sampled from pitfall traps. Three species are known from South Africa. (Palfuria-zodariidspinnekoppe)

Palfuria retusa   Retusa Zodariid Spider

Carapace and chelicerae dark brown. Abdomen pale to dark sepia on dorsum, pale on sides and venter. Legs dark brown to pale yellow, sometimes with dark stripes; coxae and trochanters pale yellow; femora slightly darker; other leg segments paler. **NOTES:** Very small rare ground dwellers sampled from Desert, Savanna and Succulent Karoo. **STATUS:** LC; southern African endemic. (Retusa-zodariidspinnekop)

Psammoduon   Psammoduon back-flipping spiders

Medium-sized. Cephalic region domed, with dense layer of setae; dip in dorsal profile posterior to cephalic region; chelicerae have median field of spinules; eyes small, in two rows; anterior row procurved; posterior row strongly recurved. Abdomen globular or oval, colour variable. Legs I and II with two tarsal claws and an extra pair of digging claws. **NOTES:** Like members of the genus *Ammoxenus* they dive head-first into the ground, landing on their back. This behaviour is also called back-flipping. Known from three southern African species. (Psammoduon-sandduikspinnekoppe)

Psammoduon conosum   Namaqualand Back-flipping Spider

Carapace dark, bearing dense median band of white setae, denser towards the eyes. Abdomen dorsum dark, background mottled, with patch of white setae. Legs dark with bands of white setae; legs III and IV with numerous spines. **NOTES:** Rare spiders that dive into loose sand. Sampled from Desert, Fynbos and Succulent Karoo. **STATUS:** LC; southern African endemic. (Namakwalandse Sandduikspinnekop)

Psammoduon deserticola   Desert Back-flipping Spider

Carapace of dark, bearing medial band of dense white setae. Abdomen with dense white setae on dorsum, dark grey on sides. Legs dark, bearing white setae. Sexes look alike, but dorsum sometimes has faint grey pattern in female. Sampled from Savanna and Succulent Karoo. **STATUS:** LC; southern African endemic. (Woestyn-sandduikspinnekop)

Psammorygma

Medium-sized. Carapace smooth; profile strongly raised in cephalic region; fovea a deep depression; cheliceral fang with knob-like extension; eyes in three rows; posterior eye row slightly procurved; only anterior median eyes dark. Abdomen oval. Leg formula 4-3-1-2; double row of dorsal spines on patellae III and IV, sometimes also on tibiae III and IV. **NOTES:** Two species are known from South Africa. (Psammorygma-zodariidspinnekoppe)

Psammorygma aculeatum male

Psammorygma aculeatum

Zululand Zodariid Spider

Carapace dark brown, almost black. Abdomen dark with bright red U-shaped pattern dorsally. Legs dark, becoming paler distally. **NOTES:** Sampled from IOCB and Savanna. Although they are burrowing spiders, they have been found in pitfall traps. **STATUS:** LC; South African endemic. (Zululandse Zodariidspinnekop)

Ranops

Long-legged igloo spiders

Small. Recognised by their small size and very large front eyes. Carapace oval, narrow in eye region; eyes in two rows, posterior row strongly procurved; with dense pale setae; sternum broad; setae along thoracic margin. Abdomen oval with dense setae. Leg formula 4-3-2-1. **NOTES:** Free-running ground dwellers represented by two species from South Africa. (Langbeen-igloespinnekoppe)

Ranops sp. female

Ranops robinae

Robin's Igloo Spider

Carapace brown with fine reticulation and numerous white setae. Abdomen with dense cover of silvery setae. Legs yellow-brown, femora darker.

NOTES: Specimens have been sampled from pitfall traps from Grassland and Savanna. **STATUS:** LC; South African endemic. (Robin se Igloespinnekop)

Systenoplacis

Systenoplacis zodariid spiders

Medium-sized. Carapace short, oval, domed, highest point behind deep fovea; anterior lateral eyes further apart than anterior median eyes; integument coarsely granulated, sometimes with silvery setae; sternum with three concavities in anterior margin. Abdomen dark with some pale spots. NOTES: Sampled mainly in Savanna. It is possible that they also dig burrows. Represented by two species in South Africa. (Systenoplacis-zodariidspinnekoppe)

Systenoplacis vandami

Van Dam's Systenoplacis Spider

Carapace uniformly dark brown to black; sternum orange. Abdomen dorsum dark grey, darker in middle, with white spot on anterior border. Legs brown. NOTES: Sampled during the day from under stones in Fynbos, Grassland and Savanna. STATUS: LC; South African endemic. (Van Dam se Systenoplacis-spinnekop)

FAMILY ZOROPSIDAE

False wolf spiders

Vals wolfspinnekoppe

Carapace broadly oval to pear-shaped; cephalic region distinct; fovea well defined; sternum shield-shaped; eight eyes in two rows (4:4). Abdomen oval, with dense layer of fine setae; cribellum absent or, if present, bipartite. Legs three-clawed, formula 4-1-2-3, fairly long, especially in males. NOTES: Free living, hiding under stones or in ground debris. Known from two genera in South Africa.

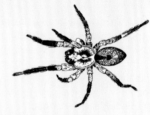

Griswoldia

Griswold's forest ground spiders

Medium-sized. Carapace pear-shaped; distinct longitudinal fovea; posterior eye row recurved, anterior row straight; anterior median eyes the smallest. Abdomen oval, with faint markings. Tibia I with strong paired setae ventrally. Cryptic coloration, resembling wolf spiders. NOTES: Swift-moving ground dwellers that are usually found in forested areas. They are among the commonest cursorial spiders of the cool, moist forests of southern Africa. During the day they are found beneath logs or stones, or within rotting logs. No webs have been observed. Represented by 12 species known from South Africa. (Griswold se woudgrondspinnekoppe)

Griswoldia urbensis — Urbensis Ground Spider

Carapace orange-brown, chelicerae red-brown; eye region yellow-brown with black pigment surrounding each eye, dark between anterior median eyes; with broad dark lateral bands and narrow marginal band. Abdomen mottled with fawn patches, venter fawn, unmarked. Male paler than female. NOTES: Free-living ground dweller sampled from under logs, rocks and in leaf litter from forest areas in Forest, Grassland, IOCB and Savanna. STATUS: LC; South African endemic. (Urbensis-grondspinnekop)

Phanotea — Phanotea ground spiders

Medium-sized. Carapace pear-shaped; eye region very broad; eight eyes in two nearly straight rows, anterior median eyes the smallest. Abdomen oval. Legs long; leg formula 4-1-2-3. Males slightly smaller than females, but with relatively longer legs. NOTES: Found in closed-canopy forests and some species have been collected from caves in South Africa. Represented by 13 South African species. (Phanotea-grondspinnekoppe)

Phanotea digitata — Digitata Ground Spider

Carapace orange-brown with dark radial bands extending from thoracic fovea halfway to lateral margin; eye region with black pigment surrounding each eye. Abdomen orange-brown, mottled with dark markings. Legs dark brown. Female markings as in male, only darker. NOTES: Free-living ground spider found hiding under logs and stones in closed-canopy forest from Forest, Fynbos and Thicket. STATUS: DD; South African endemic. (Digitata-grondspinnekop)

GLOSSARY

abdomen: belly, posterior part of the body

Afromontane: pertaining to subregions of the Afrotropical realm that include species found in the mountains of Africa and the southern Arabian Peninsula

agrobiont: an organism that lives mainly in an agricultural environment

annulation: ring-like formation

anterior: front; nearer head-end

anterodorsal: situated in front and on or toward the upper surface

anterolateral: situated in front and away from the middle line; on the side

anteroventral: situated in front and toward the lower surface

apical: located at the tip

apophysis: special structure, usually found on the male's palp, that differs in shape between species

appressed: pressed close to or lying flat against

arboreal: tree-living

attenuated: tapering to a point

basal: pertaining to or situated near a base

bipartite: consisting of two parts

biserially: arranged in two rows

calamistrum: comb-like organ with modified hairs, situated on metatarsus IV of cribellate spiders and used to comb silk produced by cribellum

camouflage: to blend in with surroundings

carapace: dorsal shield covering cephalothorax

carina: keel-like ridge

caudally: situated or directed toward the posterior part of the body

cephalic region: frontal part of cephalothorax

cephalothorax: anterior part of body, covered by carapace

chelicera (pl. chelicerae): a mouthpart, comprising a basal segment and fang

chitinised/chitinous: hardened by the deposition of chitin

clavate: club-shaped; thicker at apex than at base

clypeus: part of carapace between eyes and anterior margin

colulus: short projection in front of spinnerets

convex: curving outward

coxa (pl. coxae): first leg segment

cribellate: provided with a cribellum

cribellum: sieve-like spinning plate in front of spinnerets

cryptic: camouflaging coloration and/or patterning

cryptozoic: (of small invertebrates) living on the ground but hidden in the leaf litter, under stones or among pieces of wood

cursorial: adapted for running

cuspules: small spiny warts on endites and labium of some spiders

cytotoxic: affecting tissue around bite; toxic to cells

dentate: with teeth

denticulate: having small teeth or tooth-like projections; finely toothed

distal: furthest from middle line

distensible: able to stretch and expand

diurnal: active in the daytime

diverting: drawing apart from common point

dorsal/dorsum: upper surface

ecribellate: without a cribellum

embolus: part of the male palpal bulbus, carrying terminal part of sperm duct

endemic: restricted to a certain region

endites: paired mouthparts

epigastric furrow: transverse slit on anterior part of abdomen where sexual opening is situated

epigyne: chitinous plate on ventral side of female abdomen in which the genital openings are located

epigynum: female genital opening

eye formula: position of eyes expressed by digits separated by colons (e.g. 2:2:2:2)

fang: distal part of chelicera

femur (pl. femora): third leg segment

folium: leaf-shaped pattern on dorsum

fovea: central depression on cephalothorax, often reduced to a dark longitudinal stripe, corresponding with an internal ridge to which muscles are attached

fuscous: of a brownish-grey colour

genital opening: the opening of the uterine duct in the epigastric furrow between the booklungs of a female

glabrous: hairless; smooth

granulate: rough and grainy

habitat: external environment

heart mark: marking on dorsal side of abdomen, above the heart

hirsute: hairy

infuscate: darkened with a fuscous or brownish tinge

integument: skin

kleptoparasitic spiders: small spiders living in webs of other larger spiders, stealing the food of the host

labium: mouthpart, lower lip

lateral: situated on the side

laterigrade: with legs directed to side, like those of a crab

lenticular: shaped like a lentil; biconvex

littoral: pertaining to a region lying along the shore of a sea or lake

leg formula: ranking of the relative lengths of a spider's legs (e.g. 1:2:4:3)

longitudinal: running lengthwise

macroseta: any large, erect or suberect setae with a visible base

medially: situated in the middle

median: middle

metatarsus (pl. metatarsi): sixth leg segment

monotypic: having only one type or representative, especially of a genus containing only one species

morphological: concerning form and structure

mottled: with streaks or blotches of different shades

moulting: shedding the outer layer of skin

mygalomorph: one of the suborders of spiders; a large spider of a group that includes the tarantulas, trapdoor spiders, and funnel-web spiders. Mygalomorphs have several primitive features, including fangs that stab downwards rather than toward one another.

neurotoxic: affecting the nervous system

nocturnal: active at night

obtuse: with blunt or rounded end

onychium: ventral extension of tip of tarsus that bears the claws

operculum (pl. opercula): structure that closes or covers an aperture

ovoid: more or less egg-shaped

palp: appendage resembling a leg; in males it contains the secondary copulatory organ

palpal organ: secondary mating organ at tip of palp of male

patella (pl. patellae): fourth leg segment

pedicel: a slender abdominal segment joining the rest of the abdomen to the thorax

piriform: pear-shaped

plumose: feathery

porrect: said of chelicerae when directed forwards

posterior: the back or behind

posterolaterally: situated toward the rear and sides

process: small structure

procryptic: having a pattern or coloration adapted for natural camouflage

procurved: bending forward

prolateral: toward the front

protuberance: bulge, knob or swelling that protrudes

proximal: closest to the midline of the body

punctate: studded with or denoting dots or tiny holes

rastellum: row of spines on chelicerae used for digging

recumbent: resting on the surface from which it arises

recurved: bending backward

reticulation: a pattern or arrangement of interlacing lines resembling a net

retrolateral: projecting from, or on, the side facing backwards; outward facing

rugose: having many wrinkles or creases; ridged or wrinkled

sclerite: a single sclerotised part of external, hardened tegument

sclerotised: pertaining to the process by which the cuticle of an arthropod is hardened by substances other than chitin

scopula: tuft of club-like hairs on leg

scutum (pl. scuta): sclerotised shield on abdomen in some spiders

septum: partition separating two areas/chambers

serrula: row or cluster of small teeth along anterior margin of endite, often only visible as a dark line

seta (pl. setae): hair

setiform: bristle-shaped

setose: bearing setae; bristly

sexual dimorphism: condition where male and female look completely different

sigillum (pl. sigilla): small indentation on sternum indicating muscle attachment

spicules: minute sharp-pointed spines, typically present in large numbers

spiniform: spine-like

spinnerets: external openings of silk glands situated posteriorly on the abdomen

spinules: short spines almost as thick as long

stabilimentum (pl. stabilimenta): conspicuous white silken band used as web decoration

sternum: shield that covers ventral part of cephalothorax

striae: lines, streaks or grooves

striation: a series of ridges or furrows

stridulation: sound produced by rubbing one part of the body against another

stridulatory organs: organs used to produce sound

synanthropic: pertaining to undomesticated species living closely alongside human beings; associated with human dwellings

tactile: used for feeling

tarsus (pl. tarsi): last leg segment

tegument: external cuticular skin

tergite: the dorsal plate or dorsal portion of the covering of an arthropod

terrestrial: living on land

testaceous: of or pertaining to shells; consisting of a hard shell, or having a hard shell

tibia (pl. tibiae): fifth leg segment

tibial spur: in male, spur on tibia used during mating

transverse: lying across or between

trichobothria: vibratory sense hair

trochanter (pl. trochanters): second leg segment

truncated: having the apex cut off and replaced by a plane, especially one parallel to the base

tubercle: small rounded hump

tubule: very small tube

type specimen: the specimen of a species on which a genus is based and with which the genus name remains associated during any taxonomic revision

undulating: having a wave-like appearance

variegated: having marks or patches of different colours

venter: belly or abdomen

ventral: pertaining to the ventrum (i.e. the lower surface)

Female *Runcinia flavida* with spider prey

INDEX TO SCIENTIFIC NAMES

INDEX TO FAMILY COMMON NAMES

PICTURE CREDITS

b = bottom, **l** = left,
m = middle, **r** = right,
t = top
PW = Peter Webb; ADS =
Ansie Dippenaar-Schoeman

Cover: Vida van der Walt
Title page: Andrea Sander
4: Bruce Blake
5: Rudi Steenkamp
6: Desiré Pelser
7 tr: Nicky Bay, **bl:** PW,
   br: Luke Kemp
8: Rudi Steenkamp
10 both: Allen Jones
11 all: Rudi Steenkamp
12 t: PW, **m:** Martie Rheeder,
   b: Rudi Steenkamp
13 t: Bruce Blake, **b:** Luke
   Kemp
14 bl: Tinus Odendaal,
   br: JonRichfield, CC BY-
   SA 3.0, via Wikimedia
   Commons
15 t: Jonathan Leeming,
   m: Cindy Els
16: PW
17 ml to r 1: PW, **2:** Cecile
   Roux, **3:** PW, **4 and 5:** Les
   Oates, **bl to r 1:** Rudi
   Steenkamp, **2:** Les Oates,
   3: PW
18: PW
19 both: PW
20 tr: Bernard DUPONT from
   FRANCE, CC BY-SA 2.0, via
   Wikimedia Commons, **bl**
   to r 1: Elsa van Niekerk,
   2: Robin Lyle, **3:** ADS
23 both: Rudi Steenkamp
24: Nicky Bay
25: Bruce Blake
26 bl: Allen Jones, **br:** Cecile
   Roux
28 tl to br 1 and 2: PW,
   3: Jeremy Muller, **4, 5,**
   6 and 7: PW, **8:** Jeremy
   Miller, **9 and 10:** PW
29 t to b 1: Charles Haddad,
   2: Stefan Neser,
   3: PW, **4:** Anka Eichhoff,
   5: Ruan Booysen,

6: Charles Haddad
30 t to b 1: Richard Harris,
   2: PW, **3 and 4:** Leon Lotz,
   5: PW, **6:** Norman Larsen,
   7: Johan van Zyl, **8:** PW
31 tl to br 1 and 2: PW,
   3: Wynand Uys, **4, 5, 6** and
   7: PW
32 both: PW
33 t: PW, **m:** Rudi
   Steenkamp, **b:** PW
34 t: Linda Wiese, **b:** PW
35 tl: Warren Schmidt,
   tr: Magne Flåten, CC
   BY-SA, via Wikimedia
   Commons
36 tl and tr: PW, **bl:** Claire
   Hamilton, **br:** Jeremy Miller
37 tl and tr: Charles
   Haddad, **b:** Nicolene
   Josling
38: Ruan Booysen
39 t: Andrea Sander, **b:** Nico
   Dippenaar
40 tl and tr: Desiré Pelser,
   b: Vida van der Walt
41 t and m: PW,
   b: A. Harmsworth
42 t: PW, **b:** Len de Beer
43 t: Allen Jones, **m:** PW,
   b: Cindy Els
44 t and m: PW, **b:** Johan
   van Zyl
45 both: PW
46 t: Jessie Blackshaw,
   m: PW, **b:** Esther van der
   Walt
47 m: Desiré Pelser, **b:** John
   Roff
48 tl and tr: Tinus Odendaal,
   bl: R. Tippett, **br:** R. Tippett
49 tr: PW, **ml to r 1:** Allen
   Jones, **2:** Hannes Mitchell,
   3 and br: PW
50 ml and mr: PW,
   b: Lucarelli, CC BY-SA 3.0,
   via Wikimedia Commons
51 tl: S. Adams, **tr:** Lucarelli,
   CC BY-SA 3.0, via
   Wikimedia Commons,
   m: John Pritchard, **b:** PW
52 tl: Peter Stephen, **tr:** Ian

   Riddell, **bl** and **br:** PW
53 m: Nicky Bay, **b:** Johan
   van Zyl
54 t all: Jarrod Todd,
   b: Ernst Klimsa
55 t: Nicky Bay,
   bl: C. Whitehouse, **br:** PW
56–57 all: PW
58 t: Nicky Bay, **m** and
   bl: PW, **br:** PW
59 t, m and **bl:** PW, **br:** Rudi
   Steenkamp
60 t: Allen Jones, **m:** Martie
   Rheeder, **b:** PW
61 both: PW
62 t: Hennie de Klerk, **m, bl**
   and **br:** PW
63 tl, tr, ml and **mr:** PW,
   bl: Les Oates, **br:** PW
64 t: Linda Wiese, **m** and
   b: PW
65 tl and tr: PW, **m:** Linda
   Wiese, **b:** PW
66 t: Linda Wiese, **m, bl** and
   br: PW
67 t: PW, **ml** and **mr:** Nicky
   Bay, **b:** PW
68 t: Charles Haddad, **m** and
   b: PW
69 t: Les Oates, **bl:** Paul
   van Rensburg, **br:** Tinus
   Odendaal
70 t: PW, **m:** Len de Beer,
   b: Hennie de Klerk
71 t: Steve Woodhall
   bl: Nicky Bay, **br:** Ian
   Riddell
72 tl, tr and **ml:** PW,
   mr: Nicky Bay, **bl** and
   br: PW
73 tl: Allen Jones, **tr** and
   b: PW
74 t: Ernst Klimsa, **bl:** PW,
   br: Johan van Zyl
75 t: Johan van Zyl,
   m: Andre Coetzer, **bl:** PW,
   br: Margaret Reid
76: PW
77 t: Jeremy Miller, **m**
   both: ADS, **b:** Vida van
   der Walt
78 t: Jan Bosselaers, **m:** PW,

b: Linda Wiese
79 both: Bruce Blake
80 t: Aart Louw, **ml:** PW, **mr:** Stefan Neser, **bl** and **br:** Andrea Sander
81 m: PW, **bl:** Norman Larsen, **br:** Heather and Allen Hodges
82 t: PW, **b:** Allen Jones
83–84 all: PW
85 t: Norman Larsen, **m:** Esther van der Westhuizen
86 t: Charles Haddad, **m** and **b:** PW
87 tl: Willie Steenkamp, **tr**, **m** and **b:** PW
88 t and **m:** Charles Haddad, **b:** Stefan Neser
89 t: JMK, CC BY-SA 3.0, via Wikimedia Commons, **ml** and **mr:** Norman Larsen, **b:** E. Pietersen
90 t: Bernard DUPONT from FRANCE, CC BY-SA 2.0, via Wikimedia Commons, **ml:** Philip Fouche, **mr:** Linda Wiese, **b:** Wynand Uys
91 t: T. Bird, **b:** PW
92 t: Linda Wiese, **ml** and **mr:** Rudi Steenkamp, **b:** PW
93: John Luyt
94 m: Linda Wiese, **b:** PW
95 t: Rudi Steenkamp, **b:** Nicky Bay
96: Ruan Booysen
97 t: Rudi Steenkamp, **bl:** R. Harris, **br:** PW
98 tl: Hannes Mitchell, **tr:** PW, **bl:** Nicolene Josling, **br:** Rudi Steenkamp
99 t: PW, **b:** Leon Lotz
100 m: PW, **b:** Leon Lotz
101: PW
102 both: PW
103 both: PW
104 t: Rudi Steenkamp **m:** Jeremy Miller, **b:** Norman Larsen
105: PW
106 t: Vida van der Walt,

b: Nicky Bay
107 t and **m:** PW, **b:** Linda Wiese
108 t: PW, **m:** Rudi Steenkamp, **b:** PW
109: Jan Bosselaers
110 t: Astri Leroy, **b:** PW
111 t and **m:** PW, **b:** Koos Geldenhuys
112 all: PW
113: PW
114 t: Hannes Mitchell, **m:** Andre Coetzer, **b:** PW
115 t: PW, **m:** Ernst Klimsa, **b:** Linda Wiese
116 t: John Richter, **m** and **b:** PW
117 t and **m:** PW, **b:** Nicolene Josling
118 tl: Rene Theron, **tr:** M. Potgieter, **m** and **b:** Johan van Zyl
119 both: PW
120 t: PW, **ml:** Dawn Cory Toussaint, **mr**, **bl** and **br:** PW
121 all: PW
122 t: PW, **b:** Linda Wiese
123–124 all: PW
125: ADS
126: Johan van Zyl
127 t: PW, **bl:** Hannes Mitchell, **br:** PW
128 tl, **tr** and **m:** PW, **b:** Vida van der Walt
129 t: PW, **bl** and **br:** Norman Larsen
130 all: PW
131 t: Les Oates, **ml** to **r 1:** Wulf Avni, **2** and **3:** PW, **bl** and **br:** Vida van der Walt
132: Linda Wiese
133 t: Ernst Klimsa, **m all:** Rudi Steenkamp, **bl** and **br:** Len de Beer
134–135 all: PW
136 t, ml and **mr:** PW, **b:** Les Oates
137 tl and **tr:** PW, **ml** and **mr:** Les Oates, **b both:** Rudi Steenkamp
138 all: PW

139 tl and **tr:** PW, **b both:** Rudi Steenkamp
140 t: Johan van Zyl, **b:** PW
141 all: PW
142 t: PW, **b:** Linda Wiese
143 tl and **tr:** Len de Beer, **b:** PW
144–145: PW
146 t: PW, **b:** Linda Wiese
147 t to **b 1:** Linda Wiese, **2:** PW, **3** and **4:** Johan van Zyl
148: Vida van der Walt
149 tl: Stefan Foord, **tr:** PW, **bl:** PW, **br:** Bruce Blake
150 tl: John Richter, **tr:** PW, **mr:** Martie Rheeder, **bl:** Vida van der Walt, **br:** Bruce Blake
151–153 all: PW
154 t and **m:** PW, **b:** Warren Schmidt
155 t: Linda Wiese, **m:** PW, **b:** Len de Beer
156 tl and **tr:** PW, **m:** Andrea Sander, **bl** and **br:** PW
157: Craig Main
158 t to **b 1:** PW, **2:** Johan van Zyl, **3:** Les Oates, **4:** PW
159 t to **b 1:** PW, **2:** Johan van Zyl, **3:** PW, **4:** Linda Wiese
160: PW
161 t and **m:** PW, **b:** Linda Wiese
162 m: PW, **b:** Esther van der Westhuizen
163: PW
164 t: Nicolette Josling, **m:** Linda Wiese, **b:** PW
165: Wynand Uys
166 t: Johan van Zyl, **m:** PW, **b:** Stefan Foord
167 t: Vida van der Walt, **b:** PW
168 all: PW
169 all: PW
170 t and **m:** PW, **b:** John Andersen
171 t: John Richter, **m:** Gerbus Muller, **b:** PW
172 t: PW, **m:** Barbara

Knoflach, **b:** PW
173–174 all: PW
175 t: Les Oates, **m:** Jarrod Todd, **b:** PW
176 t: Nicolette Josling, **ml, mr** and **b:** PW
177 t: PW, **m** and **b:** Vida van der Walt
178 t and **m:** PW, **b:** Les Oates
179 t: Allen Jones, **m** and **b:** PW
180 t: PW, **m:** Les Oates, **b:** Vida van der Walt
181–225 all: Vida van der Walt
226 m: Stefan Neser, **b:** PW
227 t: Jonathan Leeming, **b:** Hennie de Klerk
228 t to **b 1:** PW, **2:** Les Oates, **3:** PW, **4:** Benanta Smit
229 t: Linda Wiese, **m:** Johan van Zyl, **b:** Jan Bosselaers
230 tl and **tr:** PW, **m:** Esther van der Westhuizen, **b:** Norman Larsen
231 t: Linda Wiese, **ml** and **mr:** PW, **b:** Dia Herbert
232 t: T. Anandale, **bl:** A. Martin, **br:** Charles Haddad
233 tl and **tr:** Rudi Steenkamp, **m** and **b:** PW
234–236 all: PW
237 tl: PW, **tr:** Martie Rheeder, **bl** and **br:** PW
238 t: PW, **m:** Les Oates, **b:** Vida van der Walt
239 all: PW
240 tl and **tr:** PW, **m:** PW **b:** Len de Beer
241 t: PW, **m:** Rudi Steenkamp, **b:** PW
242–243 all: PW
244 tl and **tr:** PW, **m:** Rudi Steenkamp, **b:** PW
245 t to **b 1:** PW, **2:** Linda Wiese, **3 bl** and **br:** PW
246 t: Bruce Blake, **ml:** PW, **mr** and **b:** Martie Rheeder
247 t: PW, **m:** Vida van der

Walt, **b:** PW
248 t: Linda Wiese, **m:** Jonathan Whitaker, **b:** John Wilkinson
249 tl and **tr:** Ruan Booysen, **b:** Andrea Sander
250 t to **b 1:** Vida van der Walt, **2** and **3:** PW, **4:** Bruce Blake, **5:** PW
251 tl and **tr:** Bruce Blake, **bl** and **br:** Brain Ashby
252 t: A. Sharp, **m:** Bruce Blake, **b:** PW
253 all: PW
254 t: PW, **m:** Charles Haddad, **b:** Nicolette Josling
255 t and **m:** Vida van der Walt, **b:** PW
256 tl and **tr:** Vida van der Walt, **b:** Koos Geldenhuys
257 t: PW, **m:** Bruce Blake, **bl** and **br:** PW
258 tl: Nicky Bay, **tr, m** and **b:** PW
259 tl, tr and **m both:** PW, **b:** Linda Wiese
260 t: Wynand Uys, **m:** Lynette Rudman, **bl** and **br:** PW
261 t: PW, **m:** Nicky Bay, **bl** and **br:** PW
262 tl: PW, **tr** and **m:** Martie Rheeder, **bl** to **r 1:** PW, **2:** Martie Rheeder, **3:** PW
263 all: PW
264 t both and **ml:** PW, **mr:** Linda Wiese, **bl** and **br:** PW
265 t: PW, **m:** Vida van der Walt, **b:** PW
266 all: PW
267 t: Johan van Zyl, **b:** Rudi Steenkamp
268 t and **m:** Les Oates, **b:** PW
269: PW
270 ml and **mr:** PW, **bl:** John Richter, **br:** PW
271 t to **b 1:** Charles Haddad, **2:** Renata Kruyswijk, **3:** Rudi Steenkamp, **4:** Matt Benic,

5: PW, **6:** ADS, **7:** PW
272 t to **b 1:** Dawn Cory Toussaint, **2–5:** PW, **6:** Ruan Booysen, **7:** Renata Kruyswijk, **8:** PW, **9:** ADS
273 all: PW
274 t to **b 1:** PW, **2:** Allen Jones, **3–6:** PW, **7:** Jason Bond, **8:** Marshal Hedin, **9:** Charles Haddad, **10:** PW
275 all: PW
276 t to **b 1–6:** PW, **7–8:** Linda Wiese
277 ml and **mr:** Renata Kruyswijk, **b:** Norman Larsen
278 m: Rudi Steenkamp, **b:** Jeremy Miller
279: Matt Benic
280: Dawid Jacobs
281 both: PW
282: Wynand Uys
283: Rudi Steenkamp
284 t to **b 1:** Rudi Steenkamp, **2:** ADS, **3** and **4:** PW
285 t: Neville Cornberg, **m:** ADS
286: Dawn Cory Toussaint
287 t: Charles Haddad, **m** and **b:** PW
288 t: Rudi Steenkamp, **b:** Charles Haddad
289 t and **m:** Ruan Booysen, **b:** Charles Haddad
290 all: Charles Haddad
291 tl and **tr:** Charles Haddad, **m:** PW, **b:** Charles Haddad
292 t: Charles Haddad, **b:** Bruce Blake
293 t: Charles Haddad, **m** and **b:** PW
294 t: Charles Haddad, **b:** PW
295 tl: C. Willis, **tr, m** and **b:** Charles Haddad
296: Aart Louw
297 all: PW
298 m: Peter Hawkes, **b:** Len de Beer
299 tl and **tr:** M. Leroy,

m: Linda Wiese, b: Rudi Steenkamp
300 t to b 1–3 PW, 4: Rudi Steenkamp
301 m and bl to r 1: Don Horne, CC BY 4.0, via Wikimedia Commons, 2 and 3: Charles Haddad
302 t: Rudi Steenkamp, m: Charles Haddad
303–304 all: PW
305 both: Lynette Rudman
306 both: PW
307 t: Rudi Steenkamp, m: PW
308 tl and tr: PW, m and b: Les Oates
309 t to b 1: Leon Lotz, 2: Anka Eichhoff, 3: PW, 4: Linda Wiese
310 all: PW
311 tl and tr: Charles Haddad, m: PW, b: Linda Wiese
312–314 all: PW
315 t and ml: Ruan Booysen, mr and b: PW
316 t and m: PW, b: ADS
317 t to b 1 and 2: ADS, 3 and 4: PW
318–319 all: PW
320 all: PW
321–322 all: PW
323 t: PW, b: ADS
324 t: Jason Bond, m: PW, bl and br: S. Henriques
325 t: John Leroy, m: Les Oates, b: Ralie Loubser
326 t: PW, m: Charles Haddad, b: PW
327 t: Jonathan Leeming, m: Rudi Steenkamp, b: PW
328: Charles Haddad
329 t: ADS, m and b: PW
330: PW
331 all: PW, b: PW
332 t: PW, m: John Wilkinson, b: PW
333 tl, tr and m: PW, b: Warren Schmidt
334 t: Anne Rasa, m: PW, b: Rudi Steenkamp
335–336 all: PW

337 t: PW, m and b: Rudi Steenkamp
338 all: PW
339 t: PW, m: Carina Cilliers, b: PW
340 all: PW
341 t: PW, m: Ruan Booysen, b: PW
342–343 all: PW
344 both: Jason Bond
345 t: Desiré Pelser, m: Charles Haddad, b: Jason Bond
346 both: Marcel Hedin
345 both: Marcel Hedin
347 t: Vida van der Walt, m: PW, b: Rudi Steenkamp
348: Charles Haddad
349 t: Nicolette Josling, b: PW
350–352 all: PW
353 t: PW, m: John Wilkinson, b: PW
354–355 all: PW
356 t to b 1 and 2: PW, 3: Ruan Booysen, 4: PW
357: PW
358 all: PW
359 t: PW, m: John Wilkinson, b: PW
360 m: PW, b: ADS
361 t: Warren Schmidt, m: PW, b: Jarrod Todd
362 m: Jonathan Leeming, b: John Richter
363 t to b 1: PW, 2: Peter Hawkes, 3 and 4: Nicolette Josling, 5: Marcel Hedin
364 t: Charles Haddad, m: Rudi Steenkamp
365 t: John Leroy, b: PW
366 t: PW, m: Ernst Klimsa, b: PW
367 t: John Leroy, m: Luke Kemp, b: Elton le Roux
368 t to b 1: Esther van der Westhuizen, 2: John Leroy, 3 and 4: Luke Kemp
369 t: PW, b: John Leroy
370 m: PW, b: Charles Haddad
371 t and m: PW,

b: Charles Haddad
372 t: PW, b: Rudi Steenkamp
373: Linda Wiese
374 all: PW
375 t: Ferdie de Moor, m: PW, b: Wynand Uys
376 t: Desiré Pelser, m and b: Rudi Steenkamp
377 all: PW
378 t and m: PW, b: I. Riddell
379 t: Allen Jones, bl and br: Rudi Steenkamp
380 tl and tr: PW, m: Wilmar Matthee, b: PW
381 t to b 1: Hennie de Klerk, 2: Warren Schmidt, 3: Rudi Steenkamp, 4: Nicolette Josling, 5: PW
382 both: PW
383 all: Linda Wiese
386: Bruce Blake
400: Bruce Blake
Back cover l to r: Jarrod Todd, John Richter, Rudi Steenkamp

ACRONYMS

DD: Data Deficient; where there is a lack of information on both sexes or where only known from a very small area and more sampling is needed

LC: Least Concern; species with a wide distribution pattern and with no known threats

NT: Near Threatened

Asianopis sp. with cast-web